The Layman's BIBLE DICTIONARY

Edited by
George W. Knight
and Rayburn W. Ray

D0054573

BARBOUR
PUBLISHING, INC.
Uhrichsville, Ohio

A-B-C: That's how I characterized this volume. A is for accuracy. The authors, whom I know personally, have been painstaking in their research to ensure that the information in this dictionary is correct. B is for brevity. Each item is described in a few words, with Bible references added for further study. C is for comprehensiveness. I believe every item that one might reasonably expect to be in a layman's Bible dictionary is in this one. It is a handy reference to keep close by during times of Bible study. That's what I plan to do with my copy.

John Ishee, Ed.D. Minister, Presbyterian Church, U.S.A.
Chaplain, Cumberland Heights Treatment Center
Nashville, TN

It has been my privilege to examine the content of *The Layman's Bible Dictionary* edited by George W. Knight and Rayburn W. Ray. I am impressed by the clarity and completeness of the content. It is an excellent publication which will meet a need in Bible study by serious lay students of the Bible by its terse and accurate content which will contribute greatly in their understanding and appreciation of God's Word. Better understanding should contribute to better living.

James L. Sullivan, Nashville, TN
Former President of the Southern Baptist Convention and the Baptist World Alliance

I am impressed with this Bible dictionary for lay people. I am impressed that it is so comprehensive, and that it is so thoroughly and yet simply written. It is especially helpful in explaining almost all of the obscure terms in the King James Version. I predict that it will be useful to any lay person or beginning Bible student.

Dan Gentry Kent, Professor of Old Testament
Southwestern Baptist Theological Seminary, Fort Worth, TX

© MCMXCVIII by George W. Knight and Rayburn W. Ray

ISBN 1-58660-241-1

All rights reserved. No part of this publication may be reproduced or transmitted in any form or by any means without written permission of the publisher.

Published by Barbour Publishing, Inc., P.O. Box 719, Uhrichsville, Ohio 44683 http://www.barbourbooks.com

Cover photograph courtesy of the Israel Government Tourist Office, Midwest Region

Printed in the United States of America.

Introduction

Many Bible dictionaries are being published today. So why do we need another? The short answer is that many of these books are cumbersome, expensive, and too complicated for lay Bible students and other general, nonspecialist users. Our goal with *The Layman's Bible Dictionary* was to create a brand-new dictionary, written from scratch, that would be compact, authoritative, and easy to understand.

Most large (and expensive) one-volume Bible dictionaries take an exhaustive approach to the Scriptures, including 5,000 to 7,000 individual articles which treat every person, place, and thing mentioned or implied in the Bible.

By contrast, *The Layman's Bible Dictionary* contains about 2,500 articles, carefully selected because of their biblical significance. The articles have been written in a terse, no-nonsense style, including only the most vital and essential information. The result is a dictionary in a handy, convenient size that is easy to understand and use—even to carry to Bible study along with your Bible, if you desire.

Let us hasten to say that there is certainly a place for larger works which treat biblical subjects in great detail. But we have developed this book for use by busy lay Bible students who want to find the most important information about key biblical topics quickly and easily.

Although the articles in this book are short, we have included thousands of Scripture references to document the biblical subjects under discussion. These should help Bible students dig deeper in their study of God's Word. Copious cross-references to related subjects also serve this same practical purpose.

You will notice that the key words or subject headings in *The Layman's Bible Dictionary* are based on the text of the familiar King James Version. Many people and places in the KJV text are called by other names in other parts of the Bible. For example, Jethro—Moses' father-in-law—is also called Hobab and Reuel. The ancient kingdom of Babylonia is also referred to as Chaldea, Sheshach, and Shinar.

Throughout *The Layman's Bible Dictionary*, these variant KJV names are listed with the key words themselves and separated by slash marks—**JETHRO/HOBAB/REUEL; BABYLONIA/SHESHACH/SHINAR/CHALDEA**—and also cross-referenced at the appropriate place in the dictionary text. This should clear up some of the confusion about variant biblical names for serious students of the Scriptures.

Since our goal was to create a simple, uncluttered, fundamental reference tool for the layperson, we have not included pronunciation helps. An excellent resource that will aid in this area is *Pronouncing Bible Names* by W. Murray Severance, published by Broadman & Holman Publishers.

Another category of variant words and names comes into play if you are using a translation other than the KJV for your Bible study. We have made *The Layman's Bible Dictionary* helpful in this situation by cross-referencing it to two additional popular translations—the New International Version (NIV) and the New Revised Standard Version (NRSV).

Throughout the dictionary, you will also find these variants listed with the key words and cross-referenced at the appropriate places in the dictionary text. However, the NIV and NRSV variants appear in parentheses following the key word. For example, the KJV word *firmament* is translated as "expanse" by the NIV and as "dome" by the NRSV. Here's how the key word appears: **FIRMAMENT (EXPANSE, DOME).**

Our thanks to the many people who assisted us in this challenging project—especially our wives Dorothy Knight and Rose Ann Ray, who proofread and critiqued our work and provided valuable support and encouragement. Dr. Dan Gentry Kent, professor of Old Testament at Southwestern Baptist Theological Seminary, reviewed the manuscript for factual and theological accuracy and made valuable suggestions. Our thanks also to our publishers, Barbour Publishing, for their confidence in this work, and their help in shepherding the book through the production process. The Israel Department of Tourism also made a valuable contribution by providing photos of key biblical sites from their extensive collection.

We hope *The Layman's Bible Dictionary* will serve as a valuable source of information for all students who, like the citizens of Berea of the New Testament, are eager to learn more about the Bible, studying expectantly and "with all readiness of mind" (Acts 17:11).

George W. Knight
Rayburn W. Ray
Nashville, Tennessee

-A-

AARON. The first high priest of the Israelites (Exod. 28:1) and Moses' brother (Exod. 4:14). Designated by God as spokesman for Moses (Exod. 4:13–16), Aaron helped Moses lead the Hebrew slaves out of Egypt (Exod. 7:8–12). In the wilderness, he was consecrated by God as Israel's first high priest, and his sons inherited this position from their father (Num. 3:32). Like Moses, Aaron was not allowed to enter the Promised Land because of his act of unfaithfulness in the wilderness (Num. 20:6–12). His earthly priesthood is compared unfavorably to the eternal priesthood of Christ (Heb. 5:4; 7:11). See also *High Priest; Priest*.

AARONITES. Descendants of Aaron who were a part of the priestly tribe of Levi. A large force of Aaronites fought with David against King Saul (1 Chron. 12:27–28).

AB. The fifth month of the Jewish year, roughly equivalent to our modern August. This month is referred to, though not specifically by name, in Num. 33:38.

ABADDON/APOLLYON. A Hebrew word meaning "destruction," used to characterize the angel of the bottomless pit (Rev. 9:11; *apollyon:* Greek form).

ABANA RIVER. A river of Syria which flowed through the city of Damascus. It was mentioned by Naaman the leper as more favorable for bathing than the Jordan River (2 Kings 5:12). See also *Pharpar*.

ABARIM. A rugged mountain range east of the Jordan River in Moab from which Moses viewed the Promised Land before his death (Deut. 32:48–50).

ABBA. An Aramaic word meaning "father," used by Jesus while praying in Gethsemane (Mark 14:32, 36). It was also used by Paul to express the Christian's sonship with God the Father (Rom. 8:15).

ABDON. A minor judge of Israel who ruled for eight years (Judg. 12:13–15). See also *Judges of Israel*.

ABED-NEGO/AZARIAH. One of Daniel's three friends. Thrown into the fiery furnace by King Nebuchadnezzar of Babylonia (Dan. 3:13–27), he was later promoted by the king after his miraculous deliverance at the hand of God (Dan. 3:28–30). *Azariah:* Hebrew form (Dan. 1:7).

ABEL.

1. Second son of Adam and Eve (Gen. 4:2). Abel's animal sacrifice was pleasing to God (Gen. 4:4). Abel was then killed by his brother Cain in a jealous rage (Gen. 4:5, 8). Jesus regarded "righteous Abel" as the first martyr (Matt. 23:35). Abel's works were called "righteous" (1 John 3:12), and his sacrifices were commended as a testimony of faith (Heb. 11:4).

2. A fortified city in northern Israel where Sheba sought refuge during his rebellion against David. The citizens of Abel killed Sheba to end the siege by the king's army (2 Sam. 20:14–22).

ABIA. See *Abijah.*

ABIAH. A son of Samuel and corrupt judge of Israel. Abiah's dishonesty, along with that of his brother Joel, led the people to ask Samuel to appoint a king to rule the nation (1 Sam. 8:2–5). See also *Joel,* No. 2.

ABIATHAR. A high priest under David who remained faithful to the king during Absalom's rebellion (2 Sam. 15:24–35). He was later banished from the royal court by Solomon for supporting Adonijah as king (1 Kings 1:7–25; 2:22–35).

ABIB/NISAN. The first month of the Hebrew year, the time when barley opened (Exod. 13:4). Roughly equivalent to our modern April, this month was known as *Nisan* after the Babylonian Exile (Esther 3:7).

ABIGAIL. A wife of David and the mother of Chileab (2 Sam. 3:3). While married to Nabal, Abigail appeased David's anger after Nabal rejected David's servants (1 Sam. 25:14–35). She became David's wife after Nabal's death (1 Sam. 25:36–42). See also *Nabal.*

ABIHU. One of Aaron's four sons. Abihu and his brother Nadab offered "strange fire," or a forbidden sacrifice, to God—an act for which they were destroyed by fire from God (Lev. 10:1–7). See also *Nadab.*

ABIJAH/ABIJAM/ABIA. The son and successor of Rehoboam as king of Judah (reigned about 913–911 B.C.; 2 Chron. 11:20–22). *Abijam:* 1 Kings 14:31; *Abia:* Jesus' ancestry (Matt. 1:7).

ABILENE. A province of Syria governed by the tetrarch Lysanias during the ministry of John the Baptist (Luke 3:1–2). See also *Lysanias*.

ABIMELECH.

1. A Philistine king of Gerar in Abraham's time. He took Sarah, Abraham's wife, into his harem, then returned her to Abraham when he was informed in a dream that she was married (Gen. 20:1–8). After this incident, Abraham and Abimelech signed a treaty (Gen. 21:22–32).

2. A rebellious son of Gideon who killed all his brothers after his father's death in an attempt to become king over all Israel (Judg. 9:5–22). He was killed by his armorbearer after a woman dropped a stone on his head from a city wall (Judg. 9:50–54).

ABINADAB.

1. A man of Kirjath-jearim whose household kept the ark of the covenant for twenty years after it was returned by the Philistines (1 Sam. 7:1–2).

2. A son of King Saul killed at Gilboa, along with Jonathan (1 Chron. 10:1–6).

ABIRAM. A rebel against Moses in the wilderness who died in an earthquake because of his disobedience (Num. 16:1–33).

ABISHAG. A young woman who served as David's nurse in his old age (1 Kings 1:1–15). David's son Adonijah was killed by Solomon for desiring to marry her after David's death (1 Kings 2:13–25).

ABISHAI. The deputy commander of David's army (2 Sam. 10:9–10). Loyal to David in Absalom's rebellion (2 Sam. 16:9–12), he also saved David's life by killing a giant (2 Sam. 21:16–17).

ABISHALOM. See *Absalom*.

ABITAL. A wife of David and mother of his son Shephatiah, who was born at Hebron (2 Sam. 3:2–5).

ABLUTION. The ceremonial washing of a person's body or clothing to make them pure. Such washing was commanded in the O.T. law (Exod. 40:12–13). True cleansing is found only in the blood of Christ (Rev. 1:5). See also *Clean*.

ABNER. The commander-in-chief of Saul's army. He introduced David to King Saul (1 Sam. 17:55–58) and established Saul's son Ish-bosheth as king after Saul's death (2 Sam. 2:8–10). Later he shifted his loyalty to David and persuaded all the tribes to follow David's leadership (2 Sam. 3:16–21). Although killed by David's commander Joab, Abner was buried with honor at David's command (2 Sam. 3:27–39).

ABOMINATION. Something considered repulsive by the Hebrews. Examples of these despised practices are heathen idolatry (Deut. 7:25–26), blemished animal sacrifices (Deut. 17:1), sexual transgressions (Lev. 18), child sacrifice (Deut. 12:31), and the practice of witchcraft, magic, and spiritism (Deut. 18:9–12). Most of these despised practices were also regarded as an abomination to God (Lev. 18:26).

ABOMINATION OF DESOLATION. The action of Antiochus Epiphanes in sacrificing a pig in the Jewish temple about 165 B.C. This despised act of the Syrian ruler is considered fulfillment of Daniel's prophecy (Dan. 9:24–27; Matt. 24:15). See also *Antiochus IV Epiphanes; Maccabees*.

ABRAHAM/ABRAM. The father of the nation of Israel (Ps. 105:6, 9). A native of Ur in southern Babylonia, he married Sarah and went to Haran (Gen. 11:28–31). Later he obeyed God's call to leave Haran for a "land that I will shew thee" (Gen. 12:1–5). God made a covenant with Abraham to bless all nations of the world through him (Gen. 12:2–3). The land of Canaan was also promised to Abraham's descendants (Gen. 12:7; 13:14–18).

Although Abraham and Sarah were childless at an advanced age, God promised Abraham a son (Gen. 15:1–21; 17:21). At Sarah's urging, Abraham fathered Ishmael by Sarah's servant Hagar (Gen. 16:1–4, 15). God changed the name of Abraham and Sarah from *Abram* and *Sarai* (Gen. 17:5–16) and established circumcision as a covenant sign (Gen. 17:6–27). The covenant was to be fulfilled through Isaac rather than Ishmael (Gen. 17:20–21; Gal. 4:22–31). Isaac was born in the couple's old age (Gen. 21:1–5).

As a test of faith, God asked Abraham to sacrifice Isaac (Gen. 22:1–13). Then God Himself intervened to save Isaac and again promised to bless Abraham for his unwavering faith (Gen. 22:16–18). Abraham died at 175 years of age and was buried beside Sarah near Hebron (Gen. 25:7–10).

The sea wall of the ancient city of Accho, located on the coast of the Mediterranean Sea. *Courtesy Israel Ministry of Tourism*

Abraham remains a model of righteousness and faith for all believers (Gen. 26:24; Ps. 47:9; Isa. 41:8). An ancestor of Christ, he is viewed as a spiritual father of all who share a like faith in Christ (Matt. 1:1; 3:9; Rom. 11:1; Gal. 3:6–9). See also *Sarah*.

ABRAHAM'S BOSOM. A symbolic expression for the blissful state after death (Luke 16:22). The Jews believed they joined their forefathers, particularly "father Abraham," upon their death (Gen. 15:15).

ABSALOM/ABISHALOM. The vain, rebellious son of David (2 Sam. 3:3). He killed his brother Amnon for molesting their sister Tamar (2 Sam. 13:22–33). Absalom conspired against David and seized Jerusalem (2 Sam. 15:1–29). Massing an army against David (2 Sam. 17:24–26), he was killed by David's commander Joab after his hair was tangled in a tree (2 Sam. 18:9–18). David mourned grievously at Absalom's death (2 Sam. 18:19–33). *Abishalom:* 1 Kings 15:2–10. See also *David*.

ABSTINENCE. To refrain from eating or drinking harmful substances or participating in sinful acts. Priests and Nazarites abstained from strong drink (Lev. 10:9; Num. 6:1–4). Gentile Christians were advised to abstain from fornication and idolatry (Acts 15:20). All believers are counseled by Paul to refrain from any practices that might offend a weak brother (Rom. 14:21). See also *Moderation; Temperance*.

ABYSS/BOTTOMLESS PIT. A word translated literally as "bottomless pit" in the book of Revelation, indicating the place where Satan dwells (Rev. 9:1–2, 11).

ACACIA. See *Shittah*.

ACCAD (AKKAD). A fortified city built by Nimrod, a descendant of Noah (Gen. 10:8–10), in the land of Shinar—an ancient kingdom between the Tigris and Euphrates rivers. *Akkad:* NIV.

ACCHO/ACRE (ACCO). A coastal city near Mount Carmel in the territory of Asher (Judg. 1:31). This is the same city as N.T. *Ptolemais* (Acts 21:7). It is known today as *Acre*. *Acco:* NIV, NRSV.

ACCOUNTABILITY. The biblical principle that each person is answerable to God and responsible for his actions (Rom. 14:12). Accountability also involves the obligation to act with love toward fellow believers (Rom. 14:15–19).

ACELDAMA (AKELDAMA, HAKELDAMA). A field near Jerusalem purchased with the money which Judas was paid to betray Jesus. The name means "field of blood" (Acts 1:15–19). *Akeldama:* NIV; *Hakeldama:* NRSV.

ACHAIA. A province of Greece visited by the apostle Paul (Acts 18:12). Christians at Achaia contributed to their impoverished brethren at Jerusalem (Rom. 15:26). Paul commended the Christians at Achaia (2 Cor. 11:10).

ACHAICUS. A Christian from the city of Corinth who visited Paul (1 Cor. 16:17–18).

ACHAN/ACHAR. A warrior under Joshua who was stoned to death for withholding the spoils of war (Josh. 7:16–25). *Achar:* 1 Chron. 2:7.

ACHAZ. See *Ahaz*.

ACHISH. A Philistine king of the city of Gath who provided refuge to David when he fled from King Saul (1 Sam. 21:10–15; 27:5–7).

ACHMETHA (ECBATANA). The capital city of the empire of the Medes and later one of the capitals of the Persian Empire (Ezra 6:2). *Ecbatana:* NIV, NRSV.

ACHSHAPH. A royal Canaanite city captured by Joshua (Josh. 11:1; 12:7, 20).

ACRE. See *Accho.*

ACTS OF THE APOSTLES. The one book of history in the N.T. which traces the expansion and development of the early church from the ascension of Jesus to Paul's imprisonment in Rome—a period of about thirty-five years. Written by Luke as a companion or sequel to his Gospel and addressed to Theophilus (see Luke 1:3–4; Acts 1:1–2), Acts shows clearly how the Christian witness spread in accordance with the Great Commission of Jesus (see Acts 1:8): (1) in Jerusalem (1:1–8:3), (2) throughout Judea and Samaria (8:4–12:25), and (3) to the entire world (13:1–28:31). See also *Luke.*

ADAM. The first man. Created in God's image (Gen. 1:26–27), Adam was an upright and intelligent being (Gen. 2:19–20)—the first worker (Gen. 2:8, 15) and the first husband (Gen. 2:18–25). He received God's Law (Gen. 2:16–17) and knowingly sinned, along with Eve (Gen. 3:6). Their sin resulted in broken fellowship with the Creator (Gen. 3:8) and brought God's curse (Gen. 3:14–19) and eviction from Eden (Gen. 3:22–24). Adam fathered Cain and Abel (Gen. 4:1–2), Seth (Gen. 4:25), and other children (Gen. 5:3–4). He died at age 930 (Gen. 5:5).

As head of the human race, Adam introduced sin into the world. He represents the lost and dying condition of all unrepentant sinners (Rom. 5:12–19; 1 Cor. 15:22). But Christ, referred to in the N.T. as the "Second Adam," offers deliverance from the curse of sin and death (Rom. 5:14–19; 1 Cor. 15:22). See also *Eden, Garden of; Eve; Fall of Man.*

ADAMANT. A precious stone, possibly corundum (Ezek. 3:9; Zech. 7:12).

ADAR. The twelfth month of the Jewish year, roughly equivalent to parts of our modern February and March. Haman ordered the massacre of the Jews on the thirteenth day of this month (Esther 3:13).

ADDER. See *Asp.*

ADMAH. One of the five cities near the Dead Sea destroyed with Sodom and Gomorrah (Gen. 10:19; Deut. 29:23). See also *Cities of the Plain*.

ADONAI. The Hebrew name for God, translated "Lord" (Ezek. 11:8). See also *God; Lord*.

ADONIJAH. David's fourth son and rival of Solomon for the throne (2 Sam. 3:4; 1 Kings 1:5, 30). Adonijah was executed by Solomon (1 Kings 2:19–25).

ADONI-ZEDEC. One of five Amorite kings who joined forces to oppose Joshua's army at Gibeon. He was defeated and killed by Joshua (Josh. 10:1–26).

ADOPTION. The legal act of giving status of a family member. (Exod. 2:9–10; Esther 2:7). Paul spoke of adoption in symbolic, spiritual terms (Rom. 11:1–32; Gal. 4:4–7). Adoption as God's children is made possible by faith in Christ (Gal. 3:24–26). See also *Inheritance*.

ADORAIM. A city in southwest Judah rebuilt and fortified by King Rehoboam, son of Solomon (2 Chron. 11:5, 9). Now known as *Dura,* it is located five miles southwest of Hebron.

ADRAMMELECH. A pagan God worshiped by Assyrian colonists who settled in Samaria after the fall of the Northern Kingdom. Children were offered as sacrifices to this god (2 Kings 17:31).

ADRAMYTTIUM. An important seaport in the Roman province of Asia. Paul boarded a "ship of Adramyttium" to begin his voyage to Rome (Acts 27:2).

ADRIA/ADRIATIC SEA. A name for the central part of the Mediterranean Sea, south of modern Italy. Paul was shipwrecked here during his voyage to Rome (Acts 27:27). *Adriatic Sea:* NIV.

ADULLAM. A royal Canaanite city conquered by Joshua (Josh. 12:7, 15). In later years David sought refuge in a cave near here (1 Sam. 22:1–2).

ADULTERY. Sexual intercourse with a person other than one's husband or wife. Adultery is specifically prohibited by the seventh of the Ten Commandments (Exod. 20:14). Jesus expanded the concept to prohibit the cultivation of lust and desire which leads to adultery (Matt. 5:28). See also *Fornication*.

ADVENT OF CHRIST, THE FIRST. The birth of Jesus Christ in human form to the virgin Mary. His coming was foretold in the O.T. (Isa. 7:14; 9:6). Joseph was reassured by an angel that Mary's pregnancy was supernatural (Matt. 1:20–21). The angel Gabriel announced His coming birth to Mary (Luke 1:26–35).

Jesus was born to Mary in Bethlehem (Matt. 1:25; 2:1). His birth was revealed to shepherds (Luke 2:8–16). Wise men from the East brought gifts to the Christ child (Matt. 2:1–11). His birth was defined as a redemptive mission (Matt. 1:21–23; Luke 2:10–11). It nullified the O.T. ceremonial system (Heb. 9) and introduced the gospel age (Acts 3:20–26). See also *Incarnation of Christ; Virgin Birth*.

ADVERSARY. An active opponent; a term descriptive of Satan (1 Pet. 5:8). God's wisdom is promised to believers when they face the adversary (Luke 21:15). We are also promised that God's judgment will ultimately fall on His enemies (Heb. 10:27).

ADVERSITY. Difficult or unfavorable circumstances, perhaps caused by sin (Gen. 3:16–17) or disobedience toward God (Lev. 26:14–20). Adversity may also be used by God to test our faith (1 Pet. 1:5–8) or to chasten and correct (Heb. 12:5–11). See also *Suffering; Tribulation*.

ADVOCATE. One who pleads the cause of another (1 John 2:1). As the advocate, the Holy Spirit provides power for worldwide evangelism (Acts 1:8) and will abide with believers forever (John 14:16). See also *Comforter; Counsellor; Holy Spirit; Paraclete*.

AENEAS. A lame man healed by Peter at Lydda near Joppa. His conversion influenced many people to turn to Christ (Acts 9:32–35).

AENON. A place near Salim, exact location unknown, where John the Baptist baptized. It was probably near the Jordan River, "because there was much water there" (John 3:23).

AFFLICTION. Any condition which causes suffering or pain. Affliction may come as a result of God's judgment on sin (Rom. 2:9), or it may be an instrument of purification and perfection for believers (Rom. 5:3–5; 2 Thess. 1:4–7). See also *Anguish; Persecution; Suffering*.

AFRICA. See *Libya*.

AGABUS. A Christian prophet who warned Paul in Antioch of Syria of a worldwide famine (Acts 11:28). At Caesarea, Agabus used a symbolic demonstration to predict Paul's impending arrest (Acts 21:10–11).

AGAG.

1. A king of Amalek in Balaam's prophecy. Balaam predicted that Israel's king would be more powerful than Agag (Num. 24:7).

2. An Amalekite king spared by King Saul, in disobedience of God's command. Saul's disobedience led to his rejection as king of Israel by the Lord (1 Sam. 15:8–23). This may be the same king as Agag, No. 1.

AGAPE. A Greek word for selfless love, the type of love which characterizes God (John 15:13; 1 John 3:16). Agape is primarily an act of the will rather than the emotions (John 3:16; Rom. 5:8). Agape love for others is a badge of discipleship (John 13:34–35). This love is the greatest and most enduring of all Christian virtues (1 Cor. 13). See also *Love*.

AGAR. See *Hagar*.

AGATE. A precious stone in the breastplate of the high priest (Exod. 28:19), probably a distinct variety of quartz. See also *Chalcedony*.

AGORA. See *Marketplace*.

AGRIPPA. See *Herod*, No. 5 and 6.

AGUE. See *Burning Ague*.

AGUR. The author of Proverbs 30. Nothing else is known about Agur.

AHAB. The wicked king of Israel (reigned about 874–853 B.C.) and husband of Jezebel. Ahab was known as an aggressive builder (1 Kings 22:39). Influenced by Jezebel, he introduced Baal worship into Israel (1 Kings 16:31–33). His pagan practices were denounced by the prophet Elijah (1 Kings 17:1). Ahab waged war against King Ben-hadad of Syria (1 Kings 20:1–43) and was killed in a battle at Ramoth-gilead (1 Kings 22:34–38). See also *Jezebel*.

AHASUERUS. A king of Persia who married Esther and listened to her counsel regarding the Jewish people. He ordered his aide Haman executed—an act which saved the Jewish people from destruction (Esther

7:1–10). Most scholars agree that this Ahasuerus is the same person as King Xerxes I of Persian history (reigned 485–464 B.C.). See also *Esther; Haman.*

AHAVA/IVAH (IVVAH). A town in Babylonia where the Jewish exiles gathered after their deportation to this pagan nation. Ezra camped near a stream with this name before leading a group of exiles back to Jerusalem (Ezra 8:15–31). *Ivah:* 2 Kings 18:34; *Ivvah:* NIV, NRSV.

AHAZ/ACHAZ. A king of Judah (reigned about 742–727 B.C.) who practiced idolatry. Ahaz defended Jerusalem against Rezin of Syria and Pekah of Israel (2 Kings 16:5–6), but he was eventually defeated and many citizens of Judah were taken captive (2 Chron. 28:5–8). He foolishly paid tribute to the king of Assyria (2 Kings 16:7–9). *Achaz:* Jesus' ancestry (Matt. 1:9).

AHAZIAH.

1. A king of Israel (reigned about 853–852 B.C.) and son of Ahab. A Baal worshiper (1 Kings 22:51–53), he was seriously injured in a fall from the balcony of his palace. After consulting a pagan god for help, he died, in fulfillment of Elijah's prophecy (2 Kings 1:2–18).

2. A king of Judah (reigned about 841 B.C.). The son of Jehoram and Athaliah, he followed in their evil ways by practicing idol worship. He was eventually assassinated by Jehu (2 Kings 9:27–28). *Jehoahaz:* 2 Chron. 21:17; *Azariah:* 2 Chron. 22:6.

AHIHUD. A leader of the tribe of Asher, appointed by Moses to help divide the land of Canaan after its occupation by the Israelites (Num. 34:27).

AHIJAH. A prophet who revealed to Jeroboam the forthcoming split of Solomon's united kingdom (1 Kings 11:29–30). Later, Ahijah foretold the death of Jeroboam's son and the elimination of his line from the kingship (1 Kings 14:1–8). See also *Jeroboam,* No. 1.

AHIKAM. An officer in King Josiah's court who protected the prophet Jeremiah from the persecution of King Jehoiakim (Jer. 26:24).

AHIMAAZ. A son of Zadok the high priest (1 Chron. 6:8–9) who warned David of Absalom's plans for rebellion. Ahimaaz also reported Absalom's defeat and death to David (2 Sam. 18:19–30).

AHIMELECH. The high priest at Nob during the reign of Saul (1 Sam. 21:1). He befriended David during his flight from Saul (1 Sam. 21:2–9). Ahimelech was killed at Saul's command (1 Sam. 22:16–19).

AHINOAM. One of David's wives (1 Sam. 25:43) and the mother of his son Amnon (2 Sam. 3:2).

AHITHOPHEL. One of David's aides who joined Absalom's rebellion (2 Sam. 15:12, 31). He committed suicide when he realized Absalom's plot was doomed (2 Sam. 17:23).

AI/AIATH/AIJA/HAI. A royal Canaanite city which first defied Joshua and then later was defeated and destroyed by the invading Israelites (Josh. 7:2–5; 8:18–21). *Aiath:* Isa. 10:28; *Aija:* Neh. 11:31; *Hai:* Gen. 12:8.

AIJALON/AJALON. A city in the territory of Dan (1 Sam. 14:31) where Joshua battled the five Amorite kings, during which the sun stood still (Josh. 10:12–13). *Ajalon:* Josh. 19:42.

AIJELETH SHAHAR. A musical term in the title of Ps. 22, probably indicating the melody to be sung.

AIN. The sixteenth letter of the Hebrew alphabet, used as a heading over Ps. 119:121–128.

AJALON. See *Aijalon.*

AKELDAMA. See *Aceldama.*

AKKAD. See *Accad.*

ALABASTER. A soft stone, similar to gypsum, which was carved into vases, boxes, jars, etc. Jesus was anointed with perfume from an alabaster box (Mark 14:3).

ALAMOTH. A musical term in the title of Ps. 46, perhaps referring to a choir of women's voices (1 Chron. 15:20).

ALEPH. The first letter of the Hebrew alphabet, used as a heading over Ps. 119:1–8.

ALEXANDER.

1. An unfaithful disciple at Ephesus condemned by Paul (1 Tim. 1:19–20).

2. Alexander the Great or Alexander III of Macedonia, Greek ruler and world conqueror. Alexander took the throne in 336 B.C. and extended his empire from Greece around the Mediterranean Sea to Egypt and then to India. He died in Babylonia at age 33. Although he is not mentioned

by name in the Bible, Alexander is perhaps the "mighty king" of Dan. 11:3–4. (See also Dan. 7:6; 8:21.)

ALEXANDRIA. A city of Egypt founded by Alexander the Great which was a cultural center and capital city of Egypt in N.T. times. Citizens of Alexandria opposed Stephen (Acts 6:9). Apollos was a native of this city (Acts 18:24). Paul left Malta for Rome on a ship from Alexandria (Acts 28:11). Jewish scholars were commissioned in this city to translate the O.T. from Hebrew into Greek—the famed version of the Bible known as the Septuagint. Alexandria was well known for its extensive library, which drew scholars from throughout the ancient world. See also *Septuagint*.

ALGUM/ALMUG. A tree imported from Lebanon (2 Chron. 2:8). Its wood was used in Solomon's temple in Jerusalem. *Almug:* 1 Kings 10:11–12.

ALIEN. A foreigner or stranger from a country other than Israel. Regarded as Gentiles, aliens did not enjoy the rights of the citizens of Israel (Deut. 14:21; Job 19:15). See also *Foreigner*.

ALLEGORY. A story which communicates an important truth in symbolic fashion. Paul spoke of the births of Ishmael and Isaac in allegorical terms (Gal. 4:22–26).

ALLELUIA. The Greek form of the Hebrew word *Hallelujah,* meaning "praise ye the Lord" (Rev. 19:1–6).

ALLIANCE. A treaty between nations or individuals. Alliances with conquered Canaanite nations were forbidden (Deut. 7:2–5; Exod. 23:32). The prophets warned Israel against forming alliances that might replace their dependence on God (Jer. 2:18). Nevertheless, alliances between O.T. characters and foreigners were common. Examples are: (1) Abraham with Abimelech of Gerar (Gen. 21:22–34); (2) King Solomon with Hiram of Tyre (1 Kings 5:1–12); and (3) Solomon's many marriage alliances (1 Kings 3:1; 11:1–3). See also *League*.

ALMIGHTY. A title of God which indicates His absolute power and majesty. God used this term to identify Himself as He talked to Abraham (Gen. 17:1). Ezekiel portrayed God in this light in his vision of God's glory (Ezek. 1:24; 10:5).

"Almighty" is also used of Christ (Rev. 1:8). See also *Sovereignty of God*.

ALMOND. A small tree known for its early spring blossoms. Jeremiah visualized an almond branch as a sign of God's rapidly approaching judgment against the nation of Judah (Jer. 1:11–12). See also *Hazel*.

ALMS. Voluntary gifts to the needy. The Israelites were commanded to be generous to the poor (Deut. 15:11). Jesus cautioned His disciples not to give alms for show or the praise of others (Matt. 6:2–4). See also *Poor*.

ALMUG. See *Algum*.

ALOES. A spice for embalming the dead, used by Joseph of Arimathea on the body of Jesus (John 19:38–39).

ALPHA AND OMEGA. The first and last letters of the Greek alphabet. Symbolic of the eternity of Christ, this title is applied to God the Father and God the Son (Rev. 1:8; 21:6–7). The risen Christ described Himself in this fashion, indicating He is the Creator, Redeemer, and Final Judge of all mankind (Rev. 22:13).

ALTAR. A platform, table, or elevated structure on which sacrifices were placed as offerings. Altars were originally made of earth or rocks (Exod. 20:24–25), but they evolved into more sophisticated structures after the construction of the tabernacle (Lev. 9:24). Pagan Canaanite altars were often called "high places" because they were built on hills or high platforms (Num. 33:52). See also *High Place*.

ALTASCHITH. A word of uncertain meaning in the titles of Pss. 57, 58, 59, and 75.

AMALEK. The son of Eliphaz, grandson of Esau, and ancestor of the Edomites (Gen. 36:9–12).

AMALEKITES. A tribal enemy of the Israelites. Their animosity against the Hebrews apparently began during the years of wilderness wandering with an unprovoked attack (Exod. 17:8–16). Saul battled this tribe as well (1 Sam. 14:48), and they suffered a major defeat at the hands of David (1 Sam. 30:1–31).

AMARNA TABLETS. Ancient clay tablets found in Egypt which were written by various kings shortly after the Israelites invaded Canaan under Joshua.

These tablets provided new insights into the culture and political unrest of the period. See also *Clay; Nuzi Tablets.*

AMASA. David's nephew and commander of Absalom's rebel army (2 Sam. 19:13). Later forgiven by David and appointed to command his army, Amasa was killed by Joab (2 Sam. 20:9–12).

AMAZIAH. A king of Judah (reigned about 796–767 B.C.; 2 Kings 14:1–20). He assembled an army to attack Edom and embraced the false gods of Edom (2 Chron. 25:5–15). Amaziah was assassinated by his political enemies (2 Chron. 25:25–28).

AMBASSADOR. A messenger, spokesman, or representative of a ruler or king. Paul considered himself an ambassador for Christ (Eph. 6:20) and applied this term figuratively to all believers (2 Cor. 5:20).

AMBASSAGE (DELEGATION). A group of ambassadors, or messengers (Luke 14:32). *Delegation:* NIV, NRSV.

AMBER. A gem or precious stone known for its yellowish-orange brilliance. Ezekiel compared God's glory to amber (Ezek. 1:4, 27; 8:2).

AMEN. A solemn word used to express approval (Neh. 8:6), confirm an oath (Neh. 5:13), or close a prayer (1 Cor. 14:16). Jesus is called "the Amen," meaning He is true and reliable (Rev. 3:14).

AMETHYST. A violet-colored precious stone in the breastplate of the high priest (Exod. 28:19), also used in the foundation of New Jerusalem (Rev. 21:20).

AMMIEL. One of the twelve spies who scouted the land of Canaan, representing the tribe of Dan (Num. 13:12). See also *Spies.*

AMMONITES. A race or tribe descended from Ammon who became enemies of the Israelites during the Exodus (Deut. 23:3). Their chief pagan god was Chemosh (Judg. 11:24), and the Israelites often indulged in their idolatrous practices (Ezra 9:1). Tobiah, an Ammonite, tried to prevent Nehemiah from rebuilding the walls of Jerusalem (Neh. 2:10, 19).

AMNON. A son of David. Amnon assaulted his half sister Tamar—an act avenged with his death at the hand of her brother Absalom (2 Sam. 3:2; 13:1–29). See also *Tamar.*

AMON. An evil and idolatrous king of Judah who reigned for only two years, about 643–641 B.C. Assassinated by his own servants, he was succeeded by his son Josiah after his assassins were killed by the people of Judah (2 Kings 21:18–26). Amon is listed as an ancestor of Jesus (Matt. 1:10).

AMORITES. One of the tribal groups of Canaan defeated by the Israelites. Descendants of Ham through his son Canaan (Gen. 10:6), the Amorites were a formidable enemy, but Joshua broke their strength with victories over the armies of Sihon and Og (Josh. 12:1–6). Remnants of the Amorites were reduced to servitude under King Solomon (1 Kings 9:19–21). See also *Canaan,* No. 1.

AMOS. A herdsman from Tekoa in the Southern Kingdom (Judah) who prophesied against the Northern Kingdom (Israel) during the tenure of King Jeroboam II (Amos 1:1; 7:14–15). Known as the great "prophet of righteousness" of the O.T., he condemned the rich and indulgent for oppressing the poor (Amos 8:4–6) and foretold Israel's collapse and captivity by Assyria (Amos 7:17). A contemporary of Isaiah and Hosea, he regarded himself as a shepherd or herdsman who heeded God's call rather than a professional prophet (Amos 7:14–16).

AMOS, BOOK OF. A prophetic book of the Old Testament written by the prophet Amos about 760 B.C. to call the wayward people of the Northern Kingdom back to worship of the one true God. A short book of only nine chapters, Amos falls naturally into three major divisions: (1) Pronouncement of judgment on surrounding nations and Israel (1:3–2:16); (2) three sermons of judgment against the idolatry, corruption, and oppression of Israel (3:1–6:14); and (3) five visions of God's approaching judgment against the nation (7:1–9:10).

Perhaps the greatest contribution of the book is the concept that religion demands righteous behavior. True religion is not a matter of observing rituals and feast days, Amos declared. It consists of following God's commands and treating others with justice: "Let judgment run down as waters, and righteousness as a mighty stream" (Amos 5:24).

AMPHIPOLIS. A city in the province of Macedonia through which Paul and Silas passed during the second missionary journey (Acts 17:1).

AMPLIAS. A fellow believer at Rome greeted and commended by Paul in his epistle to the Roman Christians (Rom. 16:8).

AMRAPHEL. A king of Shinar, or ancient Babylonia, who invaded the land of Canaan in Abraham's time (Gen. 14:1, 9).

ANAK. The son of Arba and ancestor of a tribe of giants (Deut. 9:2), or men of renown.

ANAKIMS (ANAKIM, ANAKITES). A tribe of giants, descended from Anak, who inhabited Canaan and were greatly feared in Joshua's time (Num. 13:28, 33; Deut. 9:2). The term may also refer to prominent people, or men of renown. Joshua divided their forces and captured their major walled city, Hebron, or Kirjath-arba (Josh. 14:12–15). The remnants of the Anakims may have been absorbed into the Philistine people. *Anakim:* NRSV; *Anakites:* NIV. See also *Emims.*

ANAMMELECH. A false god worshiped at Samaria by foreigners who settled the land after the defeat of the Northern Kingdom by Assyria (2 Kings 17:24, 31).

ANANIAS.

1. An early believer at Jerusalem struck dead for lying and withholding money he had pledged to the church's common treasury (Acts 5:1–11). See also *Sapphira.*

2. A believer at Damascus who befriended Paul. Ananias obeyed God's command to seek out Paul in spite of his reputation as a persecutor of Christians. He ministered to Paul as a fellow believer (Acts 9:10–18).

ANATHEMA. The transliteration of a Greek word which means "accursed" or "separated." In 1 Cor. 16:22, anathema expresses the concept of excommunication, or a cutting off of the offending party from the church.

ANATHOTH. A village about three miles north of Jerusalem and the birthplace of the prophet Jeremiah (Jer. 1:1).

ANCHOR. A heavy weight used to hold a ship steady (Acts 27:29, 40).

ANCIENT OF DAYS (ANCIENT ONE). A title for God used by the prophet Daniel to show His ruling authority over the world empires of his day (Dan. 7:9–22). *Ancient One:* NRSV.

ANDREW. One of the twelve disciples of Jesus and brother of Simon Peter. A fisherman from Bethsaida (John 1:44) on the shore of the Sea of Galilee, Andrew was a follower of John the Baptist before he became a disciple of Jesus (John 1:35–40). He was known as one who introduced others to Jesus, including his brother Simon (John 1:41–42), the boy with the loaves and fish (John 6:5–9), and certain Greek citizens who came to talk with Jesus (John 12:20–22). See also *Twelve, The.*

ANDRONICUS. A fellow believer at Rome greeted and commended by Paul in his letter to the Roman Christians (Rom. 16:7).

ANGEL. A spiritual or heavenly being whom God sends as His special messenger or helper to human beings. Angels are not to be identified with God Himself, since He created them (Ps. 148:2, 5). They serve under His direction and obey His commands (Ps. 103:20). Special functions of angels are delivering God's message to human beings (Luke 1:13), protecting God's people (Dan. 3:28), relieving human hunger and thirst (Gen. 21:17–19), and praising the name of the Lord (Ps. 103:20–21).

Before the creation of the world, certain angels revolted against God and were cast out of heaven. The ringleader of this revolt was Satan (Rev. 12: 7–9). Another of these fallen angels is Abaddon or Apollyon, "the angel of the bottomless pit" (Rev. 9:11). See also *Angel of the Lord; Gabriel; Michael,* No. 2.

ANGEL OF THE LORD. A heavenly being sent by God to human beings as His personal agent or spokesman. This messenger appeared to Hagar in the wilderness (Gen. 16:7–12), to Moses (Exod. 3:2–3), and to Gideon (Judg. 6:11–12).

ANGER. A strong feeling of displeasure. God is sometimes pictured as slow to anger (Nah. 1:3). Jesus condemned anger that was not godly anger (Matt. 5:22). See also *Wrath.*

ANGUISH. Mental or emotional stress caused by physical pain (2 Sam. 1:9), conflict of soul (Job 7:11), or physical hardships (Exod. 6:9). See also *Affliction; Suffering.*

ANISE (DILL). A common plant of little value used for seasoning food and for medicinal purposes. Jesus condemned those who tithed this insignificant plant but overlooked more important matters, such as judgment, mercy, and faith (Matt. 23:23). *Dill:* NIV, NRSV.

ANNA. An aged prophetess who praised God at Jesus' presentation as an infant in the temple at Jerusalem (Luke 2:36–38).

ANNAS. A Jewish high priest who presided at the trial of Jesus. He questioned Jesus about His disciples and His doctrine. After interrogation, Annas sent Jesus bound to Caiphas (John 18:12–24). The apostles Peter and John also appeared before Annas (Acts 4:6–7).

ANNUNCIATION. The angel Gabriel's announcement to Mary that she had been chosen to give birth to the Son of God (Luke 1:26–38). See also *Mary,* No. 1.

ANOINTED ONE. See *Jesus Christ; Messiah.*

ANOINTING. The act of setting a person apart for a specific work or task. In O.T. times kings, priests, and prophets were anointed by having oil poured on their heads (Exod. 29:7). Anointing for healing was practiced in N.T. times with the application of oil (Mark 6:13). All Christians are anointed for service in God's kingdom (2 Cor. 1:21). See also *Oil.*

ANT. A small insect cited as an example of hard work (Prov. 6:6–8).

ANTEDILUVIANS. Persons who lived before the great flood. All except Noah were condemned for their wickedness (Gen. 6:5–8). See also *Flood, The.*

ANTHROPOMORPHISMS. Human attributes ascribed to God. For example, God is described as having an arm of deliverance (Exod. 6:6), eyes too pure to look upon evil (Hab. 1:13), and a nature that is provoked to anger and jealousy by idolatry (Ps. 78:58).

ANTICHRIST. The archenemy of Christ and all Christians who will be defeated in the end-time. Rooted in the prophecies of Daniel (Dan. 7:7–8), the Antichrist receives his authority and power from Satan (Rev. 13:4). He is lawless and deceitful (2 Thess. 2:3–12; 2 John 7). Characterized as a "beast," the Antichrist will appear before the return of Christ to wage war against Christ and His people

(Rev. 13:6–8). However, he will be defeated by Christ and cast into a lake of fire (Rev. 19:20; 20:10). See also *Dragon*.

ANTINOMIANISM. The concept that grace exempts a person from the moral law. According to Paul, this idea is based on an erroneous view of grace (Rom. 6:1–2). Inconsistent with life in the spirit, antinomianism may cause a weak brother to stumble (1 Cor. 8:9). Abuse of Christian liberty violates the spirit of brotherly love (Gal. 5:13–16).

ANTIOCH OF PISIDIA. A city of Pisidia, a district in Asia Minor. Paul preached in the synagogue in this city, where resistance to the gospel caused him to redirect his ministry to the Gentiles (Acts 13:14–51). Paul later recalled his persecution at Antioch (2 Tim. 3:11). See also *Pisidia*.

ANTIOCH OF SYRIA. A city in Syria and site of the first Gentile Christian church which sent Paul on his missionary journeys (Acts 13:1–4; 15:35–41). Believers were first called Christians in this city (Acts 11:26). The church at Antioch was troubled by Judaizers who insisted that Gentile believers be circumcised (Acts 15:1–4).

ANTIOCHUS IV EPIPHANES. The cruel ruler of the Seleucid dynasty in Syria (ruled about 175–164 B.C.) whose atrocities led the Jewish people to revolt. He is not mentioned by name in the Bible, but see *Abomination of Desolation; Maccabees*.

ANTIPAS. A Christian martyr of the church at Pergamos (Rev. 2:13).

ANTIPATRIS. A city between Jerusalem and Caesarea where Paul was lodged as a prisoner while being transported to Caesarea (Acts 23:31).

ANVIL. A block of iron on which metal was shaped by a blacksmith (Isa. 41:7).

APE. A type of monkey, perhaps a baboon or chimpanzee, imported into Judah by King Solomon (1 Kings 10:22).

APELLES. A fellow believer at Rome greeted and commended by Paul in his letter to the Roman Christians (Rom. 16:10).

APHEK. A town in Jezreel where Syria's defeat was

prophesied by the prophet Elisha (2 Kings 13:14–19).

APOCALYPSE. A Greek word translated "revelation" which refers to an unveiling of the hidden things known only to God (Gal. 1:12). The book of Revelation depicts the end of the present age and the coming of God's future kingdom through symbols, visions, and numbers. This imagery was probably used to hide the message in a time of persecution. Other examples of apocalyptic writing in the Bible are Dan. 7–12, Isa. 24–27, Ezek. 37–41, Zech. 9–12, Matt. 24, and Mark 13. See also *Revelation of John*.

APOCRYPHA. A group of books written about 150 B.C. to A.D. 70 and included in the Bibles of some religious groups. These books are generally not considered authoritative in the same sense as the universally recognized books of the Bible.

The books of the Apocrypha are Baruch; Bel and the Dragon; the Wisdom of Jesus, the Son of Sirach; the First and Second Books of Esdras; Additions to the Book of Esther; Epistle of Jeremiah; Judith; First and Second Maccabees; Prayer of Azariah and the Song of the Three Young Men; Prayer of Manasseh; Susanna; Tobit; and Wisdom of Solomon.

APOLLONIA. A town between Amphipolis and Thessalonica in the province of Macedonia. Paul and Silas passed through this city during the second missionary journey (Acts 17:1).

APOLLOS. A Jewish believer from Alexandria in Egypt who worked with the church at Ephesus after it was founded by Paul. Eloquent and learned, Apollos was a disciple of John the Baptist (Acts 18:24–25). Aquila and Priscilla instructed him in the true doctrines of the faith, and he became an effective church leader, preaching also in Achaia and Corinth with great success (1 Cor. 3:4–6, 22). Paul mentioned Apollos as one whom a faction of the Corinthian church favored (1 Cor. 1:12). See also *Aquila*.

APOLLYON. See *Abaddon*.

APOSTASY. A falling away from the truth or renunciation of one's faith in Christ (Heb. 3:12). Apostasy is caused by Satan (Luke 22:31–32) and influenced by false teachers (2 Tim. 4:3–4). Professed believers may fall away because of persecution (Matt. 13:21) or love of worldly things (2 Tim. 4:10). Apostasy will not occur if believers are grounded in the truth (Eph. 4:13–16) and depend on God's protective armor (Eph. 6:10–18).

APOSTLE. A person personally commissioned by Christ to represent Him (Matt. 10:1–4). The original twelve apostles or disciples were chosen by Jesus after He had prayed all night (Luke 6:12–16). Apostles are persons sent with a special message or commission (John 15:16). Jesus empowered His apostles to cast out evil spirits and to heal (Matt. 10:1). Paul regarded himself as an apostle because of his encounter with Christ on the Damascus Road and his personal call by Jesus to missionary work (1 Cor. 15:8–10). In Paul's letters, persons who saw the risen Christ and who were specially called by Him are regarded as apostles (1 Cor. 15:5–8). See also *Disciple; Twelve, The*.

APOTHECARY (PERFUMER). A person who made perfumes, which were used in worship ceremonies or to anoint the bodies of the dead (Exod. 30:25–35) *Perfumer:* NIV, NRSV.

APPII FORUM (FORUM OF APPIUS). A station on the Roman road known as the Appian Way about forty miles south of Rome. Paul's friends traveled here to meet him as he approached the Roman Empire's capital city (Acts 28:15). *Forum of Appius:* NIV, NRSV.

AQUILA. A Christian believer who, with his wife Priscilla, worked with Paul at Corinth (Acts 18:2) and continued Paul's work at Ephesus (Acts 18:24–26). They were also associated with the church at Rome (Rom. 16:3).

ARABAH. The valley on both sides of the Jordan River which stretches for about 240 miles from Mt. Hermon in the north to the Red Sea in the south (Josh. 18:18).

ARABIA. A hot, dry, and sparsely inhabited desert area southeast of Palestine about 1,400 miles long by 800 miles wide. The queen of Sheba came from Arabia, bringing gold and precious jewels to King Solomon (1 Kings 10:2–15).

ARAD. A Canaanite city south of Hebron captured by Joshua (Josh. 12:7, 14).

ARAM.

1. A son of Shem (Gen. 10:22–23).

2. Another word for the nation of Syria (Num. 23:7). See also *Syria*.

ARARAT, MOUNT. A mountainous region where Noah's ark landed (Gen. 8:4). The location of this mountain is uncertain. Several unsuccessful expeditions to find the ark on Mount Urartu in eastern Armenia (modern Turkey) have been undertaken. See also *Ark, Noah's*.

ARAUNAH/ORNAN. A Jebusite from whom David bought a threshing floor as a place to build an altar (2 Sam. 24:16–24). This plot of ground was the site on which Solomon's temple was built in Jerusalem in later years (2 Chron. 3:1). *Ornan:* 1 Chron. 21:15; 2 Chron. 3:1.

ARBA. The father of Anak and ancestor of a tribe of giants known as the Anakims or Anakim (Josh. 14:15). See also *Anakims*.

ARCHAEOLOGY OF THE BIBLE. The study of remains of past civilizations in an attempt to understand the life and times of biblical peoples. Archaeology involves scientific excavations, examination, and publication by museums and laboratories. Fragments of ancient writings as well as bones, metal, stone, and wood are studied. The focus area for N.T. archaeology largely coincides with the ancient Roman Empire. For the O.T. period, the focus of archaeology includes Palestine (Canaan), Syria, Egypt, the Mesopotamian Valley, and Persia (modern Iran).

Major methods of establishing dates for archaeological finds are (1) examination of the layers of soil in mounds or "tells" (stratigraphy), (2) the study of pottery materials and designs (typology), and (3) measurement of the radioactivity of an object's carbon content (radiocarbon dating).

Archaeology helps us understand the Bible better by revealing what life in biblical times was like, throwing light on obscure passages of Scripture, and helping us appreciate the historical setting of the Bible. For example, exploration of the city of Ur revealed that the home of Abraham was a thriving city of industry and idolatry in O.T. times. The Dead Sea Scrolls, the greatest manuscript discovery of modern times, includes a complete scroll of the book of Isaiah and fragments of most of the other O.T. books.

See also *Amarna Tablets; Dead Sea Scrolls; Nuzi Tablets; Ras Shamra Tablets*.

ARCHANGEL. A chief angel or perhaps a spiritual being next in rank above an angel. In the end-time Michael the archangel will contend with Satan (Jude 9) and proclaim the Lord's return (1 Thess. 4:16). See also *Angel; Michael,* No. 2.

ARCHELAUS. See *Herod,* No. 2.

ARCHER. A warrior skilled in shooting arrows with a bow (1 Sam. 31:3).

ARCHEVITES. Foreign colonists who settled in Samaria after the Northern Kingdom fell to Assyria (Ezra 4:9–16). See also *Samaritan*.

ARCHIPPUS. A fellow believer in the church at Colossae whom Paul encouraged (Col. 4:17).

ARCTURUS. A constellation of stars cited as evidence of God's sovereignty (Job 9:9).

AREOPAGUS. A council of Greek philosophers in Athens before whom Paul appeared to defend his claims about Jesus and His resurrection (Acts 17:19). The hill on which these philosophers met was apparently called Mars' Hill (Acts 17:22). See also *Athens*.

ARETAS. A ruler in northern Arabia whose deputy tried to capture Paul in Damascus after his conversion (2 Cor. 11:32).

ARGOB. A district of Bashan included in Solomon's kingdom. Argob contained sixty fortified cities (1 Kings 4:13).

ARIEL. A symbolic name for the city of Jerusalem, meaning "lion of God" (Isa. 29:1–2, 7). See also *Jerusalem*.

ARIMATHAEA (ARIMATHEA). A city in the Judean hills about five miles northwest of Jerusalem and home of the Joseph who buried the body of Jesus in his own tomb (John 19:38) *Arimathea:* NIV, NRSV. See also *Joseph,* No. 3.

ARISTARCHUS. A Christian who accompanied Paul on the third missionary journey (Acts 20:4). Later he traveled with Paul to Rome (Acts 27:2).

ARISTOBULUS. A fellow believer at Rome greeted and commended by Paul in his letter to the Roman Christians (Rom. 16:10).

ARK, NOAH'S. A large wooden ship in which Noah and his family and selected animals were delivered by God. The ark was necessary because God wished to preserve righteous Noah and his family while destroying the rest of mankind because of its wickedness. Noah built the ark according to God's directions (Gen. 6:14–16). Then he and his family entered the ark, along with a pair of all living creatures (Gen. 6:19–20). Rain fell for forty days (Gen. 7:17) and water covered the earth for 150 days (Gen. 7:24).

Finally, God sent a wind to restrain the water (Gen. 8:1–3) and the ark rested on a mountain in Ararat (Gen. 8:4). Noah and his passengers were delivered safely to dry land (Gen. 8:18, 19). Upon leaving the ark, Noah built an altar and offered sacrifices to God for their deliverance. God promised Noah that the earth would not be destroyed by water again (Gen. 8:20–22).

The ark is symbolic of baptism (1 Pet. 3:20–21) and God's preserving grace (Luke 17:26–27; Heb. 11:7). See also *Ararat, Mount; Noah*.

ARK OF THE COVENANT/ ARK OF THE TESTIMONY. A wooden chest containing two stone tablets on which the Ten Commandments were inscribed. The ark symbolized God's presence to the nation of Israel (Deut. 10:3–4). It was taken into battle by the Israelites (1 Sam. 4:4–5) and captured by the Philistines (1 Sam. 4:10–11). After its return to Israel (1 Sam. 6:1–15), the ark was later placed in the temple in Jerusalem (1 Kings 8:1–11). It was probably carried away by King Nebuchadnezzar of Babylonia along with other treasures after the fall of Jerusalem (2 Chron. 36:6, 18). *Ark of the Testimony:* Exod. 25:22.

ARM OF GOD. Phrase which symbolizes God's strength and power (Ps. 89:10, 13).

ARMAGEDDON. A Greek word for the valley between Mount Carmel and the city of Jezreel. This valley was the site of many battles in Bible times due to its strategic location on two major trade routes. Because of its bloody history, this region became a symbol of the final conflict between God and the forces of evil, and of God's ultimate victory (Rev. 16:16). See also *Megiddo*.

ARMENIA. A mountainous land north of Syria formerly known as Ararat (Isa. 37:38). See also *Ararat, Mount*.

ARMOR. Defensive covering used as protection during battle. The word is also symbolic of God's spiritual protection (Eph. 6:11).

ARMORBEARER. An aide or attendant who carried the armor and weapons of a military officer or warrior of high rank (Judg. 9:54).

ARNON. A swift river which runs through the mountains east of the Jordan River and into the Dead Sea (Josh. 12:1).

AROMATIC CANE. See *Calamus*.

ARPHAXAD. A son of Shem born after the great flood (Gen. 11:10–13).

ARROW. A projectile shot from a bow. This word is also used symbolically to denote a calamity inflicted by God (Job 6:4) or to signify something injurious, such as false testimony (Prov. 25:18).

ARTAXERXES I. The successor of Cyrus as king of Persia and the king in whose court Ezra and Nehemiah served (Ezra 7:1, 7). About 458 B.C. Artaxerxes authorized Ezra to lead a large group of Jews back to Jerusalem for resettlement (Ezra 7:1–28). About thirteen years later he allowed Nehemiah to return to rebuild the walls of Jerusalem (Neh. 2:1–10; 13:6). See also *Ezra; Nehemiah*.

ARTEMAS. A faithful coworker with Paul at Nicopolis (Titus 3:12).

ARTEMIS. See *Diana*.

ARTIFICER. A workman especially skilled in metalworking. Solomon hired craftsmen from Tyre with these skills to help build the temple in Jerusalem (2 Chron. 2:3, 7). See also *Smith*.

ASA. Third king of Judah (reigned about 911–869 B.C.) who led in a national religious revival. He destroyed the places of idol worship (2 Chron. 14:2–5) and fortified Judah to usher in a period of peace (2 Chron. 14:6–8). Reproved by Hanani the prophet for not relying on the Lord, he died from a foot disease (2 Chron.

16:7–14). Asa is listed as an ancestor of Jesus (Matt. 1:7).

ASAHEL. David's nephew and a captain in his army (1 Chron. 27:7). Asahel was killed by Abner, commander in Saul's army (2 Sam. 2:17–23).

ASAIAH. A Levite who helped David move the ark of the covenant to Jerusalem (1 Chron. 15:6, 11).

ASAPH. A Levite choir leader and writer of psalms mentioned in the titles of Pss. 50 and 73–83.

ASCENSION OF CHRIST. Jesus' return to His Father after His crucifixion and resurrection (Luke 24:50–51). Foretold in the O.T. (Ps. 68:18), the Ascension occurred forty days after the Resurrection (Acts 1:2–11). The event prompted great joy among early believers (Luke 24:52–53). Christ will return to earth as surely as He ascended to heaven (Acts 1:11).

ASCETICISM. Strict self-discipline and denial of bodily appetites. Asceticism was practiced by the Nazarites (Num. 6:1–21) and John the Baptist (Matt. 3:4). See also *Nazarite*.

ASENATH. The Egyptian wife of Joseph and mother of Manasseh and Ephraim (Gen. 46:20). The pharaoh of Egypt approved this union and probably arranged the marriage (Gen. 41:45). See also *Joseph,* No. 1.

ASHDOD. A major Philistine city (Josh. 13:3) and center of Dagon worship (1 Sam. 5:1–7). It was called *Azotus* in N.T. times (Acts 8:40). See also *Dagon; Philistines*.

ASHER/ASER. A son of Jacob by Zilpah (Gen. 30:12–13) and ancestor of one of the twelve tribes of Israel (Deut. 33:24). Asher's tribe settled in northern Canaan. *Aser:* Greek form (Luke 2:36). See also *Tribes of Israel*.

ASHES. Residue from burning. A symbol of mourning and repentance, ashes were also used for purification (Heb. 9:13).

ASHTAROTH/ASHTORETH. A pagan fertility goddess worshiped by the Philistines and also by the Israelites soon after the death of Joshua (Judg. 2:13). Her symbol was an evergreen tree, a pole, or a pillar near a pagan altar. *Ashtaroth, Ashtoreth:* plural forms (1 Sam. 7:4; 1 Kings 11:33).

ASHIMA. A false god worshiped by foreign colonists who settled in Samaria after the fall of the Northern Kingdom to Assyria (2 Kings 17:30).

ASHKELON/ASKELON. One of five major cities of the Philistines (Judg. 14:19) and a pagan center denounced by the prophet Amos (Amos 1:8). *Askelon:* Judg. 1:18. See also *Philistines*.

ASHKENAZ. A descendant of Noah through Japheth (Gen. 10:3).

ASIA. A Roman province in western Asia Minor which included the cities of Ephesus, Smyrna, and Pergamos—the first three cities mentioned in the book of Revelation (Rev. 1:11; 2:1–17). At first forbidden by a vision to enter Asia (Acts 16:6), Paul later did extensive evangelistic work in this province, and his message was well received (Acts 19:10).

ASKELON. See *Ashkelon*.

ASNAPPER (ASHURBANIPAL, OSNAPPAR). The last of the great kings of Assyria (reigned about 668–626 B.C.), called the "great and noble" (Ezra 4:10). Asnapper required King Manasseh of Judah to kiss his feet and pay tribute to him. This is probably the same king as the Ashurbanipal of Assyrian history. *Ashurbanipal:* NIV; *Osnappar:* NRSV. See also *Assyria*.

ASP. A deadly snake of the cobra variety which is symbolic of man's evil nature (Isa. 11:8). This is probably the same snake as the *adder* and *viper*.

ASS. A donkey; a common beast of burden in Bible times (Gen. 22:3). Jesus rode a young donkey rather than a prancing war horse into Jerusalem to symbolize His humble servanthood and the spiritual nature of His kingdom (Luke 19:30–38). See also *Foal*.

ASSEMBLY. A gathering or congregation of people for worship. God directed Moses to assemble the Israelites at the door of the tabernacle (Num. 10:2–3). The psalmist gathered with God's people for worship and praise (Ps. 111:1). Assembling for worship is enjoined for all Christians (Heb. 10:25). See also *Congregation*; *Church*.

ASSHUR. A son of Shem and ancestor of the Assyrians (Gen. 10:22). See also *Assyria*.

ASSOS. A seaport in Asia Minor through which Paul passed on the third missionary journey (Acts 20:13–14).

ASSUR. See *Assyria.*

ASSURANCE. Complete confidence in God's promises. Our spiritual security is based on our adoption as God's children (Eph. 1:4–5). Believers are secure in the grip of the Father and Son (John 10:28–30). Our love for one another as fellow believers also provides assurance of eternal life (1 John 3:14). Obedient Christians are assured of answered prayer (1 John 5:14–15) and victorious living (Rom. 8:18, 37).

ASSYRIA/ASSHUR/ASSUR. An ancient kingdom between the Tigris and Euphrates rivers which became the dominant power in the ancient world from about 900 to 700 B.C. The aggressive and warlike Assyrians were known for their cruelty in warfare, often cutting off their victims' hands or heads, and impaling them on stakes. For this cruelty and their pagan worship, they were soundly condemned by the O.T. prophets (Isa. 10:5; Ezek. 16:28; Hos. 8:9).

The region which developed into Assyria was originally settled by the hunter Nimrod, a descendant of Noah (Gen. 10:8–12). An early name for Assyria was *Asshur,* after a son of Shem who was connected with their early history (Gen. 10:11). King Sennacherib of Assyria invaded Judah (2 Kings 18:13) and exacted tribute from King Hezekiah (2 Kings 18:14–16). Later, about 722 B.C., King Shalmaneser overthrew the Northern Kingdom, enslaved many of its inhabitants, and resettled the region with foreigners (2 Kings 18:9–11). *Assur:* Ezra 4:2. See also *Asshur; Nineveh.*

ASTROLOGER. One who studied the stars in an attempt to foretell the future—a practice especially popular among the pagan Babylonians (Isa. 47:1, 13). See also *Wise Men.*

ASWAN. See *Sinim.*

ASYNCRITUS. A fellow believer at Rome greeted and commended by Paul in his letter to the Roman Christians (Rom. 16:14).

ATHALIAH. The daughter of Ahab and Jezebel who murdered all the royal heirs and claimed the throne (reigned as queen of Judah about 841–835 B.C.; 2 Kings 11).

ATHEISM. The denial of God's existence. This defiant attitude is illustrated by the Egyptian pharaoh's refusal to release the Hebrew slaves (Exod. 5:2). The psalmist declared that disbelief in God is a characteristic of the foolish (Ps. 14:1). God's clear revelation of His nature and His intent for man leaves unbelievers without excuse (Rom. 1:18–25). See also *Infidel; Unbelief*.

ATHENS. The capital city of ancient Greece where Paul debated with the philosophers about Christ and Christianity during the second missionary journey. Known as the center of Greek art, literature, and politics, Athens also struck Paul because of its idolatry, with shrines erected to numerous deities, including the "unknown god" (Acts 17:23). See also *Areopagus*.

ATONEMENT. Reconciliation of God and man through sacrifice (Rom. 5:11). In O.T. times such reconciliation was accomplished through animal sacrifices symbolic of the people's repentance. But true reconciliation is made possible by Christ's atoning death and resurrection (Rom. 5:1; Eph. 1:7). Man's justification in God's sight is made possible by repentance and faith (Eph. 2:8).

God's righteousness is imparted through Christ's sacrifice (2 Cor. 5:21). His atonement is the foundation for peace among men (Eph. 2:13–16). All who are redeemed through their acceptance by faith of the sacrifice of Christ are called as ministers of reconciliation (2 Cor. 5:18–21). See also *Atonement, Day of; Justification; Reconciliation*.

ATONEMENT, DAY OF. A Jewish holy day (Yom Kippur) on which atonement was made for all Israel (Lev. 16:29–30; 23:27). Preceded by special sabbaths (Lev. 23:24) and fasting, this event recognized man's inability to make atonement for himself (Heb. 10:1–10). On this day the Jewish high priest first made atonement for himself and then the sins of the people by sprinkling the blood of a sacrificial animal on the altar (Lev. 16:12–15) foreshadowing the once-for-all sacrifice of Christ. The scapegoat, representing the sins of the people, was released into the wilderness to symbolize pardon (Lev. 16:22–23). See also *Atonement; Scapegoat*.

The Parthenon, dedicated to the pagan goddess Athena, sits on the crest of the Acropolis in Athens.

Courtesy Rayburn W. Ray

ATTALIA. A seaport town of Pamphylia from which Paul sailed back to Antioch at the end of the first missionary journey (Acts 14:25–26).

AUGUSTUS. A title of honor, meaning "his reverence," bestowed upon the emperors of the Roman Empire (Luke 2:1). See also *Caesar; Roman Empire.*

AUL. See *Awl.*

AUTUMN RAIN. See *Former Rain.*

AVA. An Assyrian city whose citizens settled in Samaria after the Northern Kingdom fell to Assyria (2 Kings 17:24–31). This is perhaps the same place as Ahava. See also *Ahava; Samaritan.*

AVEN. See *On,* No. 2.

AVENGER OF BLOOD. The closest of kin to a slain person who was expected to kill the slayer. Cain feared the avenging relatives of his brother after he murdered Abel (Gen. 4:14). Six cities of refuge were established throughout Israel to provide a haven for those who had accidentally taken a human life (Num. 35:12). Jesus counseled against such vengeance, calling for love of one's enemies and unlimited forgiveness instead (Matt. 5:43–44). See also *Cities of Refuge; Manslayer*.

AWL/AUL. A tool used by carpenters and leather workers to punch holes. *Aul:* Exod. 21:6; Deut. 15:17.

AX. A tool for cutting wood (Deut. 19:5).

AZARIAH

1. Another name for Ahaziah, king of Judah. See *Ahaziah*, No. 2.

2. A prophet who encouraged King Asa of Judah to destroy all idols in the land (2 Chron. 15:1–8).

3. The Hebrew name of Abed-nego. See *Abed-nego*.

4. Another name for Uzziah, king of Judah. See *Uzziah*.

AZAZEL. See *Scapegoat*.

AZOTUS. See *Ashdod*.

AZZAH. See *Gaza*.

-B-

BAALAH. See *Kirjath-jearim*.

BAAL/BAALIM. The chief Canaanite god (Judg. 2:13), who, as the god of rain, was thought to provide fertility for crops and livestock. Baal worship was associated with immorality (Hos. 9:10) and child sacrifice (Jer. 19:5)—pagan rituals considered especially offensive to the one true God of the Israelites. During their history, the Hebrew people often committed idolatry by worshiping this god of their Canaanite neighbors. The prophet Elijah denounced the prophets of Baal, and the God of Israel won a decisive victory over this pagan god on Mt. Carmel (1 Kings 18:17–40). *Baalim:* plural form (1 Sam. 12:10).

BAALATH. A town built by Solomon (1 Kings 9:18) and apparently used as a storage city (2 Chron. 8:6).

BAAL-BERITH. A name under which the pagan Canaanite god Baal was worshiped at Shechem in the time of the judges (Judg. 9:4). See also *Baal*.

BAALIM. See *Baal.*

BAAL-PEOR. A local manifestation of the pagan Canaanite god Baal. Baal-peor was worshiped by the Moabites (Deut. 4:3). See also *Baal.*

BAAL-PERAZIM/PERAZIM. A place in central Palestine where David defeated the Philistines (2 Sam. 5:18–20). *Perazim:* Isa. 28:21.

BAAL-ZEBUB/BEELZEBUB. A name under which the pagan Canaanite god Baal was worshiped by the Philistines at Ekron (2 Kings 1:2). The N.T. form of this name was *Beelzebub,* used as a title for Satan, meaning "prince of devils" (Matt. 12:26–27).

BAASHA. A king of the Northern Kingdom (reigned about 909–886 B.C.) who gained the throne by killing King Jeroboam's heirs (1 Kings 15:16–30).

BABOON. See *Peacock.*

BABEL, TOWER OF. A tall structure known as a ziggurat built on the plain of Shinar in ancient Babylonia as a show of human pride and vanity. God confused the language of the builders so they could not communicate. After they abandoned the project, they were scattered abroad (Gen. 11:1–9). See also *Ziggurat.*

BABYLON. The capital city of the Babylonian Empire, built by Nimrod the hunter (Gen. 10:9–10). Site of the tower of Babel, Babylon was a magnificent city-state which attained its greatest power under Nebuchadnezzar (Dan. 4:1–3, 30). The Jewish people were taken to Babylonia as captives after the fall of Jerusalem in 587 B.C. (2 Chron. 36:5–21).

BABYLONIA/SHESHACH/SHINAR/CHALDEA. A powerful nation in Mesopotamia which carried the Jewish people into exile about 587 B.C. Also called *Sheshach* (Jer. 25:26), *Shinar* (Isa. 11:11), and the land of the *Chaldeans* (Ezek. 12:13), Babylonia reached the zenith of its power under Nebuchadnezzar (reigned about 605–560 B.C.). The nation was a center of idolatry dominated by worship of Merodach, the Babylonian god of war (Jer. 50:2). After holding the Jewish people captive for many years, the Babylonians were defeated by the Persians about 539 B.C., fulfilling the prophecies of Isaiah and Jeremiah

(Isa. 14:22; Jer. 50:9). See also *Mesopotamia; Sumer*.

BABYLONISH GARMENT. An expensive embroidered robe kept by Achan as part of the spoils of war after the battle of Jericho (Josh. 7:21).

BACKBITING. The act of reviling, slandering, or speaking spitefully of others—behavior considered unworthy of a Christian (2 Cor. 12:20).

BACKSLIDING. The act of turning from God after conversion. The causes of backsliding are spiritual blindness (2 Pet. 1:9); persecution (Matt. 13:20–21); or love of material things (1 Tim. 6:10). This sin separates the backslider from God's blessings (Isa. 59:2). But confession and repentance will bring God's forgiveness (1 John 1:9) and restoration (Ps. 51).

BADGER (GOATS' HAIR, HIDES OF SEA COWS). An animal whose skins were used as the covering for the tabernacle (Exod. 25:5). *Goats' hair:* NRSV; *Hides of sea cows:* NIV. See also *Coney*.

BAG. See *Scrip*.

BALAAM. A soothsayer or magician hired by the king of Moab to curse the Israelites to drive them out of his territory. Prevented from doing so by an angel, Balaam blessed the Israelites instead (Num. 22:4–24:25). See also *Balak*.

BALAK/BALAC. The king of Moab who hired Balaam the soothsayer to curse the Hebrews as they crossed his territory. His scheme failed when God forced Balaam to bless them instead (Num. 22–24). *Balac:* Greek form (Rev. 2:14). See also *Balaam*.

BALANCE, BALANCES (SCALES). An instrument with matched weights, used by merchants to weigh money or food in business transactions (Prov. 11:1). *Scales:* NIV.

BALM OF GILEAD. An aromatic gum or resin exported from Gilead in Arabia. It apparently was used as an incense and for medicinal purposes (Jer. 8:22).

BALSAM. See *Mulberry*.

BANNER. See *Standard*.

BANQUET. An elaborate and sumptuous meal, usually served on a special occasion. Esther exposed the plot of Haman to destroy the Jews during a banquet (Esther 7:1).

BAPTISM. An observance signifying a believer's cleansing from sin through Christ's atoning death. John the Baptist baptized converts to signify their repentance (Matt. 3:6–8). Jesus was baptized by John in the Jordan River to fulfill all righteousness and to set an example for us (Matt. 3:15). The Father's approval of Jesus' baptism was expressed by the descent of the Holy Spirit and a voice from heaven (Mark 1:10–11).

In the N.T. church, Gentiles who received the Holy Spirit were promptly baptized (Acts 10:44–48). Christian baptism memorializes the death, burial, and resurrection of Christ (Rom. 6:3–5). For the believer, baptism is a testimony of faith and a pledge to "walk in newness of life" with Jesus Christ (Rom. 6:4–14).

BARABBAS. A notorious prisoner, guilty of murder and insurrection, at the time when Jesus appeared before Pilate (John 18:40). Incited by Jewish leaders, the mob demanded that Barabbas be released instead of Jesus (Mark 15:9–11).

BARAK. A general under Deborah and judge of Israel. He and Deborah were victorious against the Canaanites (Judg. 4:1–24). See also *Deborah*.

BARBARIAN. A word meaning "uncivilized" and a title used by the Greeks to designate foreigners, or citizens of other nations besides Greece (Rom. 1:14).

BAR-JESUS/ELYMAS. A sorcerer and false prophet who opposed Paul and Silas at Paphos during the first missionary journey (Acts 13:6–12). Also called *Elymas*.

BAR-JONA. The surname of the apostle Peter, meaning "son of Jonah" (Matt. 16:17). See *Simon,* No. 1.

BARLEY. A grain similar to oats, used as food for livestock (1 Kings 4:28) and also ground into meal for bread by poor people (John 6:5, 13).

BARNABAS/JOSES. A Jewish Christian who befriended Paul after Paul's conversion, introduced the apostle to the Jerusalem church (Acts 9:27), and traveled with Paul during the first missionary journey (Acts 11:25–26). *Joses:* Acts 4:36.

BARREN. Unable to bear children. In the O.T., barrenness was seen as a sign of God's judgment (1 Sam. 1:5–7). See also *Children; Womb*.

BARRIER. See *Middle Wall of Partition*.

BARTHOLOMEW. One of the twelve apostles of Jesus (Mark 3:18). Some scholars believe he is the same person as *Nathanael* (John 1:45–49). According to tradition, Bartholomew became a missionary to Armenia and India and was flayed and crucified for his faith. See also *Twelve, The*.

BARTIMAEUS. A blind beggar healed by Jesus on the road to Jericho (Mark 10:46–52).

BARUCH. The friend and scribe of the prophet Jeremiah. Baruch faithfully recorded Jeremiah's messages warning of the impending defeat of the nation of Judah (Jer. 36:4–32). Like Jeremiah, he fled to Egypt after the fall of Jerusalem (Jer. 43:1–7). See also *Jeremiah*.

BARZILLAI. An aged friend of David who helped the king during his flight from Absalom (2 Sam. 17:27–29).

BASHAN. A fertile plain east of the Jordan River conquered by the Israelites (Num. 21:33) and allotted to the half-tribe of Manasseh (Josh. 13:29–30).

BASON (BASIN, BOWL). A container used in the home (2 Sam. 17:28) and as a ceremonial vessel in the temple or tabernacle (Exod. 24:6). *Basin:* NRSV; *Bowl:* NIV. See also *Bowl; Laver*.

BAT. A nocturnal flying mammal, considered unclean by the Hebrews (Lev. 11:19).

BATH. Standard Hebrew measure for liquids, equivalent to about six gallons (1 Kings 7:26).

BATHING. A washing of the body to make it ceremonially clean and pure (Lev. 15:5, 16). See also *Clean; Wash*.

BATH-SHEBA/BATH-SHUA. The wife of Uriah who committed adultery with David and became his wife (2 Sam. 11:6–27). Because of their sin, Bath-sheba's first child died. She later gave birth to four sons, including Solomon, who succeeded David as king. *Bath-shua*: 1 Chron. 3:5. See also *David; Solomon*.

BATTLEMENT (PARAPET). A railing around the roof of a house, required by law to prevent falls (Deut. 22:8) *Parapet:* NIV, NRSV.

BDELLIUM. A word which probably refers to a fragrant gum resin (Num. 11:7) as well as a precious stone (Gen. 2:12).

BEAR. A large animal similar to our brown bear which was common in Palestine in Bible times. David killed a bear to protect his father's sheep (1 Sam. 17:34–37).

BEARD. Trimmed and groomed facial hair—a mark of pride among Jewish men. To shave one's beard or pull out the hair was a gesture of anguish and grief (Jer. 48:37–38).

BEATITUDES. Pronouncements of blessing at the beginning of Jesus' Sermon on the Mount. God's special reward is promised to those who recognize their spiritual need (Matt. 5:3); those who mourn (5:4); those who are humble (5:5); obedient (5:6); merciful (5:7); pure in heart (5:8); those who practice peacemaking (5:9); and those who are persecuted for Jesus' sake (5:10–11). See also *Sermon on the Mount*.

BEAUTIFUL GATE. A gate which served as one of the main entrances into the temple area in Jerusalem in N.T. times (Acts 3:2).

BEDAN. A minor judge of Israel who served after Gideon and before Jephthah. His name is not recorded in the book of Judges (1 Sam. 12:11). See also *Judges of Israel*.

BEDCHAMBER (BEDROOM). The sleeping room in houses of Bible times (2 Sam. 4:7–11). *Bedroom:* NIV.

BEELIADA/ELIADA. A son of David, born at Jerusalem (1 Chron. 14:7). *Eliada:* 2 Sam. 5:16; 1 Chron. 3:8.

BEELZEBUB (BEELZEBUL). *Beelzebul:* NRSV; See *Baal-zebub*.

BEER.

1. A place in Moab where the Israelites camped during their wilderness wanderings (Num. 21:16–18). Possibly the same place as Beer Elim (Isa. 15:8).

2. A town in Judah where Jotham sought refuge from his brother Abimelech (Judg. 9:21).

BEER-SHEBA. The name of a well in southern Judah which

Abraham and Abimelech dug to seal their covenant of friendship (Gen. 21:31). The name was also applied to the surrounding wilderness (Gen. 21:14) and an important city which grew up around the well (Gen. 26:32–33; Judg. 20:1). See also *Well*.

BEGGAR. One who lives by handouts (Luke 16:3). The Israelites were commanded by God to care for the poor (Deut. 15:7–10). See also *Alms; Poor*.

BEGOTTEN. A word which describes Christ as the only and unique Son of His heavenly Father (John 3:16–18).

BEGUILE. To deceive, cheat, or defraud—actions characteristic of Satan. Eve was beguiled by the serpent in the Garden of Eden (Gen. 3:13).

BEHEADING. To cut off a person's head; a form of execution or capital punishment. John the Baptist was put to death in this manner (Matt. 14:10).

BEHEMOTH. A large beast mentioned by Job (Job 40:15–24), probably referring to the elephant or the hippopotamus.

BEKAH. A Hebrew weight equal to one-half shekel, or about one-quarter ounce (Exod. 38:26).

BELA. See *Zoar*.

BELIAL. A word for wickedness or wicked people (1 Kings 21:10). The word also means wickedness personified—a reference to Satan (2 Cor. 6:15). See also *Satan*.

BELIEVE. To accept or trust fully. Belief or trust in Christ is necessary for salvation (Acts 16:31) and essential to righteousness (Gal. 3:6). See also *Faith; Trust*.

BELIEVERS. A term for Christian converts (Acts 5:14). The believers at Pentecost enjoyed fellowship and shared property according to need (Acts 2:44–45). Paul encouraged Timothy to serve as an example for other believers (1 Tim. 4:12). See also *Brother*.

BELLOWS. A blacksmith's tool, used to force air onto a fire to make it hot enough to work metal (Jer. 6:29). See also *Smith*.

BELSHAZZAR. The son or grandson of Nebuchadnezzar and the last king of the Babylonian Empire (Dan. 5:1–2). Daniel interpreted a mysterious handwriting on the wall for Belshazzar as a prediction of doom for the Babylonians (Dan. 5:17). That night, Belshazzar was killed when the Persians captured Babylonia (Dan. 5:30–31). See also *Babylonia*.

BELT. See Girdle.

BELTESHAZZAR. See *Daniel,* No. 1.

BENAIAH. A loyal supporter of David and Solomon. A commander of David's bodyguard (2 Sam. 20:23), he later became commander-in-chief of Solomon's army (1 Kings 2:35).

BEN-AMMI. Lot's son by his youngest daughter. Born in a cave near Zoar (Gen. 19:30–38), he was the ancestor of the Ammonites. See also *Ammonites; Lot*.

BENEDICTION. A prayer for God's blessings upon His people. The benediction which priests were to use was spoken by God to Aaron through Moses (Num. 6:22–26). See also *Blessing*.

BENEVOLENCE. Generosity toward others. Paul commended generosity toward the needy (Gal. 2:10). Christian benevolence should be shown toward God's servants (Phil. 4:14–17) and even our enemies (Prov. 25:21).

BEN-HADAD. A general title for the kings of Damascus, Syria. Three separate Ben-hadads are mentioned in the Bible:

1. Ben-hadad I (reigned about 950 B.C.). In league with Asa, king of Judah, he invaded the Northern Kingdom (1 Kings 15:18–21).

2. Ben-hadad II (reigned about 900 B.C.). He waged war against King Ahab of Israel. This Ben-hadad is probably the unnamed "king of Syria" whose officer Naaman was healed of leprosy by the prophet Elisha (2 Kings 5:1–19).

3. Ben-hadad III (reigned about 750 B.C.). He was defeated by the Assyrian army, as the prophet Amos predicted (Amos 1:4).

BENJAMIN. The youngest of Jacob's twelve sons and ancestor of the tribe of Benjamin. His mother Rachel died at his birth (Gen. 35:16–20). Benjamin was greatly loved by his father Jacob (Gen. 42:2–4) and by his brother Joseph (Gen. 43:29–34). See also *Tribes of Israel*.

BEREA (BEROEA). A city in southern Macedonia visited by

Paul. The Bereans searched the Scriptures eagerly, and many became believers (Acts 17:10–15). *Beroea:* NRSV.

BERNICE. The sister of Herod Agrippa II, Roman governor of Palestine before whom Paul appeared. She was present when Paul made his defense (Acts 26:1–32).

BERODACH-BALADAN/ MERODACH-BALADAN. A king of Babylonia (reigned about 721–704 B.C.) who sent ambassadors to visit King Hezekiah of Judah. Hezekiah showed them his vast wealth—an act condemned by the prophet Isaiah (2 Kings 20:12–19). *Merodach-baladan:* Isa. 39:1. See also *Babylonia*.

BEROEA. See *Berea*.

BEROTHAI (BEROTHAH). A city of Syria taken by David (2 Sam. 8:8). *Berothah:* Ezek. 47:16.

BERYL (CHRYSOLITE). A precious stone, probably similar to emerald, used in the breastplate of the high priest (Exod. 28:20), and in the foundation of New Jerusalem (Rev. 21:20). *Chrysolite:* NIV. See also *Carbuncle; Chrysolite*.

BESEECH. To request or ask earnestly (Rom. 12:1).

BESIEGE. To surround with armed forces (Deut. 20:12). This battle tactic was used against walled cities of Bible times to starve the inhabitants into submission. See also *Fenced City; Wall*.

BESOR. A brook south of Ziklag crossed by David's army in pursuit of the Amalekites (1 Sam. 30:9–21).

BESTIALITY. Sex relations with an animal. The death penalty was imposed on those who were guilty of this offense (Exod. 22:19).

BETH. The second letter of the Hebrew alphabet, used as a heading over Ps. 119:9–16.

BETHABARA. A place on the Jordan River where John the Baptist baptized believers (John 1:28). Jesus was also apparently baptized at this place (John 1:29–34).

BETHANY. A village near the Mount of Olives outside Jerusalem (Mark 11:1) and home of Lazarus, Mary, and Martha—friends of Jesus (John 11:1). Jesus ascended to heaven from Bethany (Luke 24:50).

Modern Bethlehem, a village six miles south of Jerusalem, where Jesus was born. *Courtesy Israel Ministry of Tourism*

BETHEL/LUZ/EL-BETHEL. A city north of Jerusalem where Jacob had a life-changing vision of angels going up and down a staircase (Gen. 28:10–19). Before it was renamed by Jacob, Bethel was known by its Canaanite name, *Luz* (Gen. 28:19). *El-bethel:* Gen. 35:7.

BETHESDA (BETH-ZATHA). The name of a pool in Jerusalem believed to have miraculous healing powers. Jesus healed a lame man at this pool (John 5:2–8). *Beth-zatha:* NRSV. See also *Pool*.

BETH-HORON. Upper and Lower Beth-horon were twin towns in the territory of Ephraim which served as important military outposts in Bible times. They stood on the main pass through the mountains between the Mediterranean Sea and Jerusalem. Solomon fortified the cities to protect Jerusalem from invading armies (2 Chron. 8:5).

BETHLEHEM/ BETH-LEHEM-JUDAH/ EPHRATH/EPHRATAH. A town in southern Palestine near Jerusalem, also called *Beth-lehem-judah* (Judg. 19:18), where Jesus was born in fulfillment of prophecy (Mic. 5:2; Luke 2:4–7). It was called the

"City of David" because King David grew up there centuries before (1 Sam. 16:1–13). David's ancestor Ruth gleaned grain in the fields of Boaz nearby (Ruth 2:4–8). Bethlehem was known in O.T. times as *Ephrath* (Gen. 35:16–19) and *Ephratah* (Ruth 4:11). See also *City of David*.

BETH-MILLO. See *Millo*.

BETH-PEOR. A town of Moab east of the Jordan River in the territory where Moses was buried (Deut. 34:6).

BETHPHAGE. A village near Bethany and the Mount of Olives just outside Jerusalem mentioned in connection with Jesus' triumphant entry into the city (Matt. 21:1).

BETHSAIDA. A fishing village on the Sea of Galilee; the home of Andrew, Peter, and Philip—apostles of Jesus (John 1:44). Some scholars believe the Bethsaida where the 5,000 were fed (Luke 9:10–17) was a different city with the same name.

BETH-SHAN/BETH-SHEAN. A Philistine city where King Saul's corpse was displayed (1 Sam. 31:10–13). In later years, Solomon stationed troops in this city (1 Kings 4:12). *Beth-shean:* Josh. 17:11.

BETH-SHEMESH/IR-SHEMESH. A border town between the territories of Judah and Dan taken by the Philistines. Later the ark of the covenant was kept here (1 Sam. 6:10–7:2). *Ir-shemesh:* Josh. 19:41.

BETH-ZATHA. See *Bethesda*.

BETH-ZUR. A city in the mountains of Judah fortified by King Rehoboam as a defensive outpost along the road leading to Jerusalem (2 Chron. 11:7).

BETROTHAL. A marriage agreement, usually made by the groom with the parents of the bride. A betrothed woman was regarded as the lawful wife of her spouse. Joseph and Mary were betrothed before the birth of Jesus (Matt. 1:18–19; *espoused:* KJV). See also *Dowry; Marriage*.

BEULAH. A name for Israel after the Babylonian Exile when the nation would be in a fruitful relationship with God (Isa. 62:4).

BEZER. A fortified city in the territory of Reuben designated as one of the six cities of

Excavated ruins of the ancient city of Beth-shan.
Courtesy Israel Ministry of Tourism

refuge (Josh. 20:8). See also *Cities of Refuge*.

BIBLE. God's written record of His revelation which is accepted by Christians as uniquely inspired and authoritative for faith and practice. The Bible's O.T. books chronicle the expectation of a Messiah, while the N.T. books reveal the fulfillment of God's redemptive purpose through Jesus Christ and the church. The Bible was written under God's inspiration during a period of more than 1,000 years from the time of Moses through the first century A.D. The N.T. was completed within about sixty years of Jesus' resurrection. Much of the N.T., including the Gospels, was recorded by eyewitnesses of the events about which they wrote. The O.T. was written originally in Hebrew and Aramaic, while the N.T. was recorded in the Greek language.

All copies of the Scripture were written by hand until the invention of printing in the fifteenth century A.D. The original writings have been translated into hundreds of languages and dialects to make the Bible the world's best loved and most accessible book. The Geneva Bible, published in 1560, was the first complete English Bible translated from the original languages. The popular King James Version appeared in 1611, and numerous English versions and revisions have followed.

Although written by many people over a long period, the Bible has a remarkable unity, explained only by the inspiration and oversight of the Holy Spirit to bring God's redemptive message to mankind.

BIER. A portable frame for carrying a body to its burial place (2 Sam. 3:31).

BILDAD. One of the three friends who comforted the sorrowing Job (Job 2:11). His speeches expressed the conviction that all suffering is the direct result of sin (Job 8:1–22; 18:1–21; 25:1–6). See also *Job, Book of*.

BILHAH. Rachel's maid and a wife of Jacob. She bore two of Jacob's twelve sons, Dan and Naphtali (Gen. 30:1–8). See also *Jacob*.

BIRD OF PREY. See *Speckled Bird*.

BIRTHRIGHT. The inheritance rights of the firstborn son, who received a double portion of his father's assets (Deut. 21:17) plus the father's blessing and responsibility for family leadership. These inheritance rights could be taken away and conferred on another because of immoral acts or irresponsible behavior by the oldest son (Gen. 25:29–34). See also *Firstborn; Inheritance*.

BISHOP. An overseer, pastor, or elder who served as leader of a local church in N.T. times (Titus 1:5–8). See also *Elder; Pastor*.

BITHYNIA. A Roman province of Asia Minor which Paul was prevented from entering, through the intervention of the Holy Spirit (Acts 16:7). The gospel did enter this province later (1 Pet. 1:1).

BITTER HERBS. Herbs eaten by the Hebrew people during their celebration of the Passover to help them remember their bitter affliction during their enslavement in Egypt (Exod. 12:8). See also *Passover*.

BITTER WATER. A test or trial to which a woman was subjected when her husband suspected her of being unfaithful (Num. 5:11–31). See also *Water of Jealousy; Water of Separation*.

BITTERN (SCREECH OWL). A bird noted for its melancholy cries and thus symbolic of the loneliness and despair which follows God's judgment (Zeph. 2:14). *Screech owl:* NIV, NRSV. See also *Screech Owl*.

BITUMEN. See *Slime*.

BLACK VULTURE. See *Ospray*.

BLAINS (BOILS). Infectious boils on the skin; one of the plagues brought upon the Egyptians for their refusal to release the Hebrew slaves (Exod. 9:8–11). *Boils:* NIV, NRSV.

BLASPHEMY. The act of reviling, cursing, or showing contempt toward God. This was considered a capital offense by the Jewish people, punishable by death. Jesus was accused of blasphemy by the Jewish leaders. They considered Him only a man, while He claimed to be God's Son (Matt. 9:3).

BLASPHEMY AGAINST THE HOLY SPIRIT. A sin which consists of attributing Christ's miracles to the work of Satan (Matt. 12:31–32). Jesus declared such contempt for the work of God was an unforgivable sin (Mark 3:28–30). Paul regarded a person's bitter opposition to the gospel as a form of blasphemy against God (Rom. 2:24). See also *Unpardonable Sin*.

BLESSING. The act of invoking or declaring God's goodness and favor upon others, as Jacob did with his twelve sons (Gen. 49:1–28). God also blesses His people by giving life (Gen. 1:22) and forgiving our sins (Rom. 4:7–8). See also *Benediction*.

BLIND. Unable to see, in either a physical (Matt. 9:27) or spiritual (Eph. 4:18) sense. The Hebrews were enjoined to show compassion toward the blind (Deut. 27:18).

BLOOD. Life-sustaining fluid of the body. In the O.T., the blood of a sacrificial animal represented the essence of life and symbolized repentance and atonement for sin (Lev. 17:11). In the N.T., the phrase "the blood of Christ" refers to the sacrificial death of Jesus on the cross (Heb. 9:12–14). Jesus' sacrificial blood is the agent of redemption for believers (Heb. 9:12). Christ's shed blood is memorialized in the Lord's Supper (1 Cor. 10:16). Nothing perishable or material can save; only Christ's precious blood has the power to redeem (1 Pet. 1:18–19). See also *Atonement; Redeem*.

BOANERGES. A name, meaning "sons of thunder," given by Jesus to James and John, the sons of Zebedee (Mark 3:17). This was a reference to their fiery zeal. See also *James,* No. 1; *John the Apostle*.

BOAR. A male wild hog, noted for its vicious nature (Ps. 80:13).

BOASTING. To brag or to speak of one's accomplishments with pride and haughtiness (2 Chron. 25:19).

BOAZ/BOOZ. The husband of Ruth and an ancestor of Christ. Boaz granted Ruth the right to gather leftover grain in his fields (Ruth 2:8–9). He married Ruth, who gave birth to Obed, grandfather of David (Ruth 4:17). *Booz:* Jesus' ancestry (Matt. 1:5). See also *Ruth*.

BODY OF CHRIST. A symbolic expression for the church. Paul identified the church as Christ's body (Col. 1:24). The risen Christ dwells in His body and presides over the church (Eph. 1:19–23). Christ assigns spiritual gifts to His body to accomplish His work and bring believers to maturity (Eph. 4:7–13). Members of the body are to care for one another (1 Cor. 12:25–27). See also *Church*.

BODY, SPIRITUAL. The glorified or redeemed body of believers. Our hope of a glorified body is based on Christ's victory over the grave (Rom. 6:6). Believers will receive a glorified body, free of sin and death, at the return of Christ (1 Cor. 15:50–57). The redeemed body of a believer will be like that of Christ's glorified body (Phil. 3:21), immortal and incorruptible (1 Cor. 15:53–54). Christians need not fear death because we are provided a new spiritual body "eternal in the heavens" (2 Cor. 5:1–6).

BOILS. See *Blains*.

BOLDNESS. Courage and confidence. Boldness which honors God is aided by earnest prayer (Eph. 6:18–19).

BONDAGE. To be held against one's will by an oppressor. The Israelites were enslaved by the Egyptians for more than 400 years. Sin also holds a person in spiritual bondage (Rom. 8:15). See also *Slave*.

BONDSERVANT. A slave; a person who serves another against his will and without wages (1 Kings 9:21). See also *Slave*.

BONE. The skeletal framework of humans. The phrase "bone of my bones" uttered by Adam (Gen. 2:23) showed that he was united to woman in the closest possible relationship.

BOOK. Pieces of animal skin or papyrus written on and then bound together (Job 19:23). See also *Roll; Scroll*.

BOOK OF JASHER. A lost book which apparently described great events in the life of Israel (Josh. 10:13).

BOOK OF LIFE. God's record of the names of the saved (Mal. 3:16–18). This book will be used as the basis for God's final judgment (Rev. 20:12–15). Inclusion in the book of life by virtue of one's salvation by God's grace provides reason for joy (Luke 10:20) and hope of heaven (Rev. 21:27).

BOOK OF THE LAW. A term for the Law of Moses or the Pentateuch, the first five books of the O.T. After receiving and recording these instructions from God, Moses delivered the law to the priests for public reading (Deut. 31:9–11). In later years, the Book of the

Law became the basis for King Josiah's religious reforms (2 Kings 23:1–28).

BOOK OF THE WARS OF THE LORD. A lost book which may have celebrated Israel's victories in battle under Moses (Num. 21:14).

BOOTH. A temporary shelter made of tree branches. During the Feast of Tabernacles, also called the Feast of Booths, the Israelites lived in such shelters as a reminder of their harsh life in the wilderness after their deliverance from Egyptian slavery (Neh. 8:13–18).

BOOTHS, FEAST OF. See *Tabernacles, Feast of.*

BOOTY. Anything of value taken in war, including livestock, slaves, gold and silver, clothing, and tools (Zeph. 1:13). See also *Spoil*.

BOOZ. See *Boaz*.

BORN AGAIN. See *New Birth*.

BOSOM. Another word for the human chest, or breast, used symbolically to imply closeness or intimacy (Isa. 40:11). See also *Abraham's Bosom; Breast*.

BOTTLE (WINESKIN). A vessel made of animal skins (Josh. 9:4). Old wineskins became brittle and unable to hold new wine during the fermentation process. Thus, Jesus declared, "No man putteth new wine into old bottles; else the new wine will burst the bottles, and be spilled" (Luke 5:37). *Wineskin:* NIV, NRSV.

BOTTOMLESS PIT. See *Abyss*.

BOUNDARY MARKER, BOUNDARY STONE. See *Landmark*.

BOW. A weapon used in war and for hunting (Gen. 48:22). Soldiers of the tribe of Benjamin were especially skilled with the bow (1 Chron. 12:2).

BOWELS (INWARD PARTS). The internal digestive system of the human body. The bowels were considered the center of a person's feelings and emotions, expressive of compassion and tenderness (Job 30:27–28) *Inward parts:* NRSV.

BOWING. An act of reverence or submission, performed by kneeling on one knee and bending the head forward. Bowing is considered appropriate for prayer and worship (Ps.

95:6). Jesus knelt or bowed to pray in Gethsemane (Matt. 26:36–39). See also *Kneel*.

BOWL. A vessel for holding food or liquids. Bowls were made of wood, clay, or silver. Large bowls were used by priests in sacrificial rituals (Zech. 9:15). See also *Bason*.

BOX TREE (CYPRESS, PINE). An evergreen which produces a wood ideal for carving. Boxwood was used in the temple in Jerusalem (Isa. 60:13) *Cypress:* NIV; *Pine:* NRSV.

BOZRAH. The ancient capital city of Edom. Isaiah spoke of this city in figurative terms to describe the Messiah's victory over the pagan nations (Isa. 63:1). See also *Edom,* No. 2.

BRACELET. A piece of jewelry worn on the wrist (Isa. 3:19). The bracelet of King Saul (2 Sam. 1:10) was probably a military armband.

BRAMBLE (THORNBUSH). A bush of thistles. In Jotham's parable, the bramble bush, representing Abimelech, ruled over the trees of the forest, in spite of its lowly position (Judg. 9:7–15). *Thornbush:* NIV. See also *Brier*.

BRASEN SEA (BRONZE SEA). A large brass basin in the temple court which held water for purification rituals (2 Kings 25:13). *Bronze sea:* NIV, NRSV. See also *Molten Sea*.

BRASS. An alloy of copper with some other metal, perhaps zinc or tin (Num. 21:9). The word is also used as a symbol of stubbornness, insensibility, and rebellion toward God (Isa. 48:4).

BRASS SERPENT (BRONZE SNAKE). A serpent cast from metal and raised up by Moses in the wilderness on a pole as an instrument of healing for those who had been bitten by poisonous snakes (Num. 21:9). Jesus referred to this incident to illustrate the healing from sin made possible by His crucifixion (John 3:14). *Bronze snake:* NIV. See also *Fiery Serpents*.

BREAD. A word often used for food in general. True bread was made from flour or meal and baked in loaves. Jesus described Himself as the Bread of Life (John 6:35). See also *Corn; Wheat*.

BREAD OF THE PRESENCE. See *Shewbread*.

BREAST. The chest of the human body. To strike or beat

one's chest was to signify extreme sorrow (Luke 23:48).

BREASTPLATE (BREASTPIECE). The vestment worn by the Jewish high priest, containing twelve precious stones and engraved with the names of the tribes of Israel (Exod. 28:15–30) *Breastpiece:* NIV. Paul spoke figuratively of the "breastplate of righteousness" for Christians (Eph. 6:14).

BREASTS. See *Paps*.

BREATH. The air which a person inhales to sustain life. Job recognized this process as God's gift to His creatures (Job 12:10).

BREATH OF GOD. A symbolic phrase used to portray God as the source of life (Job 33:4). His breath demonstrates His power and creative ability (2 Sam. 22:14–16). In the N.T., God "breathed" the Holy Spirit upon His disciples (John 20:22).

BREECHES (UNDERGARMENTS). Trousers, or perhaps an undergarment, worn by priests (Exod. 28:42). *Undergarments:* NIV, NRSV.

BRIBERY. The act of giving gifts or favors inappropriately to influence others—a practice condemned often in the Bible (Amos 5:12).

BRICK. A building block made of clay, which was mixed with straw, then baked in the sun or placed in a kiln for curing. The Israelites made bricks during their enslavement in Egypt (Exod. 1:14). See also *Tile*.

BRICK-KILN. An oven or furnace for curing bricks (2 Sam. 12:31). See also *Furnace*.

BRIDE. A newly married woman. In the N.T., the Church is spoken of figuratively as the bride of Christ (Eph. 5:25–33). See also *Church*.

BRIDEGROOM. A newly married man. The N.T. speaks figuratively of Christ as the Bridegroom (John 3:29) and of the Church as His bride (Eph. 5:25–33).

BRIER. A shrub or plant with thorns and thistles. The word is often used figuratively to describe man's sinful nature (Mic. 7:4).

BRIGANDINE (COAT OF MAIL). Flexible body armor, probably worn by kings and commanders (1 Sam. 17:38; Jer. 46:4). *Coat of mail:* NRSV.

BRIMSTONE (BURNING SULFUR). A bright yellow mineral which burns easily and emits a strong odor. The cities of Sodom and Gomorrah were destroyed with burning brimstone (Gen. 19:24–25). *Burning sulfur:* NIV.

BRONZE SEA. See *Brasen Sea*.

BRONZE SNAKE. See *Brass Serpent*.

BROOM. See *Juniper*.

BROTHER. A male sibling. The word is also used figuratively for all Christian believers (Matt. 23:8). Christians are counseled not to offend a weak brother (Rom. 14:10–13). See also *Believers*.

BROTHERS OF CHRIST. The four earthly brothers, or half brothers of Jesus—James, Joses (Joseph), Simon, and Juda (Jude)—who were born by natural conception to Joseph and Mary after the virgin birth of Christ (Mark 6:3). James was leader of the church in Jerusalem (Acts 15:13–21) and likely the author of the epistle of James (Jas. 1:1). Jude wrote the N.T. epistle which bears his name (Jude 1).

BUCKLER (SHIELD). A small piece of protective armor worn on the arm by warriors (Song of Sol. 4:4). *Shield:* NIV. See also *Shield*.

BUKKI. A leader of the tribe of Dan, appointed by Moses to help divide the land of Canaan after its occupation by the Israelites (Num. 34:22).

BUL. The eighth month of the Hebrew year, roughly equivalent to parts of our October and November (1 Kings 6:38).

BULL. A general term for the male of the ox or cattle species (Job 21:10).

BULLOCK. A young bull used in animal sacrifices (Num. 15:24).

BULRUSH (PAPYRUS). A reedlike plant which grew in marshy areas of the Nile River and was used for making papyrus, an ancient writing material. The infant Moses was placed in a basket made of this plant (Exod. 2:3). *Papyrus:* NIV, NRSV. See also *Paper; Reed*.

BULWARK (RAMPARTS). A tower in a city's defensive wall which provided a better position for firing on the enemy below (Ps. 48:13). *Ramparts:* NIV, NRSV.

BURIAL. The ceremonial disposal of a body by placement in the ground or a tomb. In Bible times, burial usually took place as soon as possible because of the warm climate and because a body was considered ceremonially unclean (Deut. 21:23). Jesus' body was prepared for burial with aromatic oils and spices and wrapped in a linen cloth (John 19:39–40). See also *Funeral; Sepulchre*.

BURNING AGUE (FEVER). A severe fever, possibly a symptom of a serious illness, such as typhoid or malaria (Lev. 26:16). *Fever:* NIV, NRSV.

BURNING BUSH. The flaming shrub through which God spoke to Moses. As the bush burned, God expressed compassion for His captive people and called Moses to return to Egypt to deliver them from bondage (Exod. 3:9–10).

BURNING SULFUR. See *Brimstone*.

BURNT OFFERING. A meat sacrifice consisting of an unblemished animal, which was totally consumed by fire, except for the hide (Lev. 7:8). Burnt sacrifices were made to atone for sin and to restore the broken relationship between man and God (Num. 6:10–11).

BUSHEL. A dry measure of about one peck (Matt. 5:15).

BUSYBODY (MEDDLER, MISCHIEF MAKER). A gossip and troublemaker. This type of behavior is inappropriate for believers (1 Pet. 4:15). *Meddler:* NIV; *Mischief maker:* NRSV. See also *Gossip*.

BUTLER. See *Cupbearer*.

BUZZARD. See *Vulture*.

BYWORD. A degrading saying or remark, usually delivered in taunting fashion (1 Kings 9:7).

-C-

CAB (KAB). The smallest unit of measure for dry material, equal to about three pints (2 Kings 6:25). *Kab:* NRSV.

CAESAR. A formal title for several emperors of the Roman Empire. Four separate Caesars are mentioned in the N.T.:

1. Caesar Augustus (reigned about 27 B.C. to A.D. 14), who issued the taxation or census

Remains of an aqueduct, or water channel, built by the Romans at Caesarea near the Mediterranean Sea.
Courtesy Israel Ministry of Tourism

decree which required Joseph to go to Bethlehem, where Jesus was born (Luke 2:1).

2. Caesar Tiberius (reigned about A.D. 14–37), whose administration paralleled the public ministry of Jesus. Tiberius was known for his strict discipline of subject nations and his intolerance of potential rivals (John 19:12).

3. Caesar Claudius (reigned about A.D. 41–54), who sought to reduce strife throughout his empire. One of his tactics was to expel all the Jewish people living in Rome (Acts 18:2).

4. Caesar Nero (reigned about A.D. 54–68), the first emperor under whom the Christians were persecuted. As a Roman citizen, Paul appealed to him (Acts 25:8–12).

CAESAREA. A Roman coastal city founded about 10 B.C. and named for the Roman emperor Caesar Augustus. As the political capital of Palestine during N.T. times, it was the city of residence for Roman rulers of the district, including Agrippa II, before whom Paul appeared (Acts 26:28–32).

CAESAREA PHILIPPI. A city at the foot of Mt. Hermon in northern Palestine where Peter confessed Jesus as the Messiah (Matt. 16:13–28). Named for the Roman tetrarch Philip who rebuilt the city, it was called Caesarea Philippi to distinguish it from the city of Caesarea on the Mediterranean coast in central Palestine.

CAESAR'S HOUSEHOLD. A group of converts probably associated with the palace of the emperor in Rome. Paul sent greetings from this group to the church at Philippi (Phil. 4:22).

CAIAPHAS. The Jewish high priest who presided at the trial of Jesus and advised that He be put to death (Matt. 26:65–66; John 18:12–14). After Jesus' resurrection, the apostles John and Peter also appeared before Caiaphas (Acts 4:6).

CAIN. The oldest son of Adam and Eve who murdered his brother Abel. Exiled by God, he built a city which he named for his son (Gen. 4:1–17).

CAINAN. See *Kenan*.

CALAH. An ancient city of Assyria built by Nimrod (Gen. 10:8–12).

CALAMUS (FRAGRANT CANE, AROMATIC CANE). A reedlike plant known for its sweet fragrance (Song of Sol. 4:14). It was used in anointing oil (Exod. 30:23). *Fragrant cane:* NIV; *Aromatic cane:* NRSV.

CALDRON. A large kettle used by priests for boiling meats for sacrificial purposes (2 Chron. 35:13). See also *Kettle*.

CALEB. One of the twelve spies who scouted Canaan. Along with Joshua, he recommended that Israel attack the Canaanites immediately (Num. 13:30). He lived to enter the land forty years later and was given the city of Hebron for his faithfulness (Josh. 14:6–14). See also *Spies*.

CALF. A young cow prized as a delicacy (Gen. 18:7) and often sacrificed as a burnt offering (Lev. 9:8). See also *Fatling*.

CALF, GOLDEN. An idol built and worshiped by the Israelites in the wilderness as they waited for Moses to come down from Mt. Sinai (Exod. 32:1–4). It was probably an image of Apis, a sacred bull worshiped by the Egyptians. In later years, King Jeroboam of Israel set up pagan golden

Modern Cana, the village where Jesus performed His first miracle.
Courtesy Israel Ministry of Tourism

calves at Dan and Bethel (1 Kings 12:26–33). See also *Idol*.

CALLING. The special summons to service which all Christians receive as part of their salvation experience (1 Cor. 7:20). See also *Vocation*.

CALNEH/CALNO. An ancient city built in southern Mesopotamia by Nimrod (Gen. 10:9–10). This may be the same city as Canneh (Ezek. 27:23). *Calno:* Isa. 10:9.

CALVARY (THE SKULL). A hill just outside the city walls of Jerusalem where Jesus was crucified (Luke 23:33). The word comes from a Latin word which means "skull," thus "place of the skull." The Aramaic form of this word is *Golgotha* (Mark 15:22). *The Skull:* NIV, NRSV. See also *Cross*.

CAMEL. A hardy, humpbacked animal ideally suited to the desert climate of Palestine and used as a riding animal and beast of burden (Gen. 24:64).

CAMP. A place where tent dwellers and nomads pitch their tents. The Israelites camped in many different places during their years of wandering in the wilderness

(Num. 33:1–49). See also *Wilderness Wanderings*.

CAMPHIRE (HENNA). A plant which produced a valuable red dye, used by women to adorn their lips and fingernails (Song of Sol. 1:14). *Henna:* NIV, NRSV.

CANA OF GALILEE. A village near Capernaum in the district of Galilee where Jesus performed His first miracle—the transformation of water into wine at a wedding feast (John 2:1–11).

CANAAN.

1. A son of Ham whose descendants founded several tribal peoples in and around Palestine (Gen. 10:1, 6, 15–18).

2. The region between the Red Sea and the Jordan River where Canaan's descendants settled and the territory which God promised to Abraham and his descendants (Gen. 15:3–7). *Chanaan:* Greek form (Acts 7:11). See also *Land of Promise*.

CANAANITES.

1. The original inhabitants of Canaan who settled the land before Abraham arrived about 2000 B.C. (Gen. 12:5–6). They were eventually forced out of the land by Israel at God's command because of their pagan religious practices. Intermarriage with Canaanites by the Israelites was distinctly prohibited by God (Deut. 7:3).

2. Members of a Jewish sect in N.T. times known for their fanatical opposition to the rule of Rome. Jesus' apostle Simon the Canaanite may have been a member of, or a sympathizer with, this sect (Matt. 10:4). They were also known as the *zelotes* or *zealots*.

CANDACE. A title of the queens of Ethiopia in N.T. times (Acts 8:27).

CANDLE (LAMP). A shallow clay bowl filled with oil and a burning wick, used for illumination (Matt. 5:15). *Lamp:* NIV, NRSV.

CANDLESTICK (LAMPSTAND). A stand which held several small oil-burning lamps (Mark 4:21). *Lampstand:* NIV, NRSV.

CANKER (GANGRENE). A disease which led to rapid deterioration of the flesh (2 Tim. 2:17). *Gangrene:* NIV, NRSV.

CANKERWORM (LOCUST). A locust or grasshopper in the caterpillar stage of its growth (Joel 1:4). *Locust:* NIV, NRSV. See also *Locust; Palmerworm*.

CAPERNAUM. A city on the northwestern shore of the Sea of Galilee which served as the headquarters for Jesus during His Galilean ministry (Matt. 9:1; Mark 2:1). Capernaum was the home of His disciples Matthew (Matt. 9:9), Simon Peter, Andrew, James, and John (Mark 1:21–29).

CAPH. The eleventh letter of the Hebrew alphabet, used as a heading over Ps. 119:81–88.

CAPHTOR. The original home of the Philistines, probably the island of Crete (Jer. 47:4). See also *Crete; Philistines*.

CAPITALS. See *Pommels*.

CAPPADOCIA. A Roman province of Asia Minor. Christians of Cappadocia were addressed by Peter (1 Pet. 1:1).

CAPTAIN. A title for a civil or military officer (Judg. 4:7). This is also a title for Christ (Heb. 2:10). *Author:* NIV; *Pioneer:* NRSV.

CAPTIVITY. The carrying away of the citizens of a country by a conquering nation. The nation of Israel (the Northern Kingdom) was carried into captivity by the Assyrians about 722 B.C. (2 Kings 15:29), while Judah (the Southern Kingdom) suffered the same fate at the hand of the Babylonians in 587 B.C. (2 Chron. 36:6–7). See also *Dispersion*.

CARBUNCLE (BERYL, EMERALD). A precious stone of deep red color in the breastplate of the high priest (Exod. 28:17). *Beryl:* NIV; *Emerald:* NRSV. See also *Emerald*.

CARCHEMISH/CHARCHEMISH. An ancient city near the Euphrates River in Mesopotamia (Jer. 46:2), where the Assyrian army was victorious over the Egyptians. *Charchemish*: 2 Chron. 35:20–24.

CARMEL, MOUNT. A prominent mountain in northern Palestine where the prophet Elijah demonstrated the power of God in a dramatic encounter with the priests of the pagan god Baal (1 Kings 18:17–39).

CARNAL (WORLDLY). To give in to the desires of the flesh. Following their natural desires led the Christians of Corinth into division and strife (1 Cor. 3:1–5). *Worldly:* NIV.

CARNELIAN. See *Sardine; Sardius*.

CARPUS. A friend to whom Paul entrusted his cloak (2 Tim. 4:13).

CARRION VULTURE. See *Gier Eagle*.

CART. A two-wheeled wagon, usually pulled by oxen (1 Sam. 6:7–8). See also *Wagon*.

CASLUHIM (CASLUHITES). An ancient people descended from Mizraim (the Hebrew word for Egypt), son of Ham (Gen. 10:14). *Casluhites:* NIV. See also *Egypt; Mizraim*.

CASSIA. The dried bark of a tree similar to the cinnamon which was prized for its pleasing fragrance. Cassia was used as an ingredient of holy oil (Exod. 30:24).

CASTAWAY. A word for "worthlessness" or "rejection." Paul used this word to express the idea of "disqualified" or "rejected" (1 Cor. 9:27).

CASTLE (BARRACKS). A fortress or defense tower. The "castle" into which Paul was taken was the quarters of the Roman soldiers at Jerusalem in the fortress of Antonia near the temple (Acts 21:34). *Barracks:* NIV, NRSV.

CASTOR AND POLLUX (TWIN BROTHERS). The twin sons of Zeus in Greek and Roman mythology who were considered special protectors of sailors. Paul's ship to Rome featured a carving of these two pagan gods (Acts 28:11). *Twin Brothers:* NRSV.

CATHOLIC EPISTLES. See *General Epistles*.

CAVE. A natural passageway or cavern within the earth. Caves were used as residences (Gen. 19:30) and burial places (Gen. 49:29). See also *Sepulchre*.

CEDAR. A cone-bearing evergreen tree which produces a reddish, fragrant wood. Lumber from the cedars of Lebanon was used in the temple in Jerusalem (1 Kings 5:1–10).

CEDRON. See *Kidron*.

CENCHREA (CENCHREAE). A harbor of Corinth through which Paul passed during the second missionary journey (Acts 18:18). This was the site of a church mentioned by Paul (Rom. 16:1), perhaps a branch of the church at Corinth. *Cenchreae:* NRSV.

CENSER. A small, portable container in which incense was burned (Num. 16:6–39). See also *Firepan; Incense*.

CENSUS. A count of the population of a country or region (2 Sam. 24:1–9; Luke 2:1–3).

CENTURION. A Roman military officer who commanded a force of one hundred soldiers (Acts 10:1, 22).

CEPHAS. See *Simon,* No. 1.

CHAFF. The leftover husks of threshed grain, separated when the grain is tossed into the air. The ungodly are compared to chaff (Ps. 1:4). See also *Winnowing*.

CHALCEDONY (AGATE). A precious stone cut from multicolored quartz and used in the foundation of the heavenly city, or New Jerusalem (Rev. 21:19). *Agate:* NRSV. See also *Agate*.

CHALDEA, CHALDEANS. See *Babylonia*.

CHALKSTONE. A soft and easily crushed rock, similar to limestone (Isa. 27:9).

CHAMBER. A word for a room or an enclosed place in a house or public building (2 Kings 23:12).

CHAMBERLAIN (EUNUCH). An officer in charge of the royal chambers or the king's lodgings and wardrobe, and perhaps his harem (Esther 2:3). *Eunuch:* NIV, NRSV. See also *Eunuch*.

CHAMELEON. See *Mole*.

CHAMOIS (MOUNTAIN SHEEP). A word which probably refers to a wild goat or a wild mountain sheep (Deut. 14:5). *Mountain sheep:* NIV, NRSV.

CHANAAN. See *Canaan*.

CHANCELLOR (COMMANDING OFFICER, ROYAL DEPUTY). A high official of the Persian kings whose exact duties are unknown (Ezra 4:8). *Commanding officer:* NIV; *Royal deputy:* NRSV.

CHARCHEMISH. See *Carchemish*.

CHARGER (PLATTER). A dish or shallow basin used in sacrificial ceremonies (Num. 7:13, 79). The head of John the Baptist was placed on a charger (Matt. 14:11). *Platter:* NIV, NRSV. See also *Platter*.

CHARIOT. A two-wheeled carriage drawn by horses. High government officials rode in chariots, and they were also used as instruments of war (Judg. 4:15).

CHARIOT CITIES. The cities where Solomon stored or headquartered his chariots and chariot forces (1 Kings 9:19).

CHARIOT OF FIRE. The fiery chariot with blazing horses which came between Elijah and Elisha as Elijah was taken into heaven by a whirlwind (2 Kings 2:11). See also *Elijah*.

CHARIOTS OF THE SUN. Chariots dedicated to the sun—a popular custom among the Persians, who worshiped this heavenly body. All chariots devoted to this practice among the Israelites were burned by King Josiah of Judah (2 Kings 23:11). See also *Sun*.

CHARITY. An old English word for "love" (1 Cor. 13). See *Love*.

CHARMERS. Magicians who claimed to be able to commune with the dead (Isa. 19:3). See also *Magic; Medium; Necromancer*.

CHARRAN. See *Haran*.

CHASTISEMENT (DISCIPLINE). Punishment or discipline inflicted by God for guiding and correcting His children (Heb. 12:8). *Discipline:* NIV, NRSV. See also *Discipline*.

CHASTITY. A term for inward cleanliness, generally referring to sexual purity (2 Cor. 11:2). See also *Clean*.

CHEBAR. A river or canal of Babylonia where Jewish captives settled during the Exile. Ezekiel's visions came to him at Chebar (Ezek. 1:3; 10:15, 20).

CHEDORLAOMER. A king of Elam who invaded Canaan in Abraham's time (Gen. 14:1–16).

CHEEK. To strike a person on the cheek was considered a grave insult (Job 16:10). Jesus taught believers to react to such acts with kindness (Luke 6:29).

CHEMOSH. The chief pagan god of the Moabites and Ammonites to which children were sacrificed (2 Kings 23:13; Judg. 11:24). See also *Human Sacrifice*.

CHERETHITES/CHERETHIM. A tribe of the Philistines in southwest Palestine (1 Sam. 30:14). *Cherethim:* Ezek. 25:16.

CHERITH. A brook where the prophet Elijah hid and where he was fed by ravens during a famine (1 Kings 17:3–5).

CHERUBIM. An order of angelic, winged creatures (Gen. 3:24). Their function was to praise God and glorify His name (Ezek. 10:18–20).

CHETH. The eighth letter of the Hebrew alphabet, used as a heading over Ps. 119:57–64.

CHIEF. Head of a tribe or family (Num. 3:24, 32). See also *Duke*.

CHIEF SEATS. Places of honor sought by the scribes and Pharisees. Jesus taught His followers that the highest honor is to serve others (Mark 12:31, 38–39).

CHILD SACRIFICE. See *Human Sacrifice*.

CHILDREN. Children were looked upon as blessings from God (Ps. 127:3), and childlessness was considered a curse (Deut. 7:14). The word is also used symbolically of those who belong to Christ (Rom. 8:17). See also *Parents*.

CHILEAB/DANIEL. A son of David; also called *Daniel* (2 Sam. 3:3; 1 Chron. 3:1).

CHILION. The son of Elimelech and Naomi and brother-in-law of Ruth (Ruth 1:2–5).

CHINNEROTH. See *Galilee, Sea of*.

CHIOS. An island in the Aegean Sea passed by Paul on his way to Jerusalem after the third missionary journey (Acts 20:15).

CHISLEU (KISLEV, CHISLEV). The ninth month of the Hebrew year, roughly equivalent to parts of our November and December (Neh. 1:1). *Kislev:* NIV; *Chislev:* NRSV.

CHITTIM. See *Cyprus*.

CHLOE. A Christian disciple at the place from which Paul sent his first epistle to the Corinthians—probably Philippi (1 Cor. 1:11).

CHORAZIN. A city north of the Sea of Galilee where Jesus did many mighty works. He pronounced a woe on this city because of its unbelief (Matt. 11:21).

CHOSEN LADY. See *Elect Lady*.

CHRIST. The Anointed One, the O.T. Hebrew Messiah. See *Jesus Christ*.

CHRISTIAN. A disciple or follower of Christ. The name apparently was first used of the believers in the church at Antioch (Acts 11:26). Other words which express the same idea are saint (Acts 9:13) and brethren (Acts 6:3). See also *Way, The*.

CHRONICLES, BOOKS OF FIRST AND SECOND. Two historical books of the O.T. which cover several centuries of history, beginning with a genealogy of Adam and his descendants (1 Chron. 1–9) and ending with the return of Jewish captives to their homeland about 538 B.C. following a period of exile among the Babylonians and Persians (2 Chron. 36).

Major events covered in the books include: (1) the death of King Saul (1 Chron. 10); (2) the reign of King David (1 Chron. 10–29); (3) the reign of King Solomon (2 Chron. 1–9); and (4) the reigns of selected kings of Judah after the division of the kingdom into two nations following Solomon's death (2 Chron. 10–36).

CHRYSOLYTE (CHRYSOLITE). A precious stone, possibly yellow topaz, used in the foundation of the heavenly city, or New Jerusalem (Rev. 21:20). *Chrysolite:* NIV, NRSV. See also *Beryl*.

CHRYSOPRASUS (CHRYSOPRASE). A precious stone, green in color and similar to agate, used in the foundation of the heavenly city, or New Jerusalem (Rev. 21:20). *Chrysoprase:* NIV, NRSV. See also *Beryl*.

CHURCH. A local body of believers assembled for Christian worship (Acts 15:4; 1 Cor. 1:2) as well as all the redeemed of the ages who belong to Christ (Gal. 1:13; Eph. 5:27). The word *church* is a translation of a Greek term which means "an assembly." Christ is head of His body the Church and His will is to be preeminent (Col. 1:18) by virtue of His redeeming work and lordship (Col. 1:14; 3:15–17). The Church's mission is to win the lost (Luke 4:18) and minister to others in the world. See also *Assembly; Congregation; People of God; Saint*.

CHUSHAN-RISHATHAIM (CUSHAN-RISHATHAIM). A king of Mesopotamia who oppressed the Israelites. He was defeated by the first judge, Othniel (Judg. 3:8–10). *Cushan-rishathaim:* NIV, NRSV.

CILICIA. A province of Asia Minor whose major city was Tarsus, Paul's hometown. Paul visited Cilicia after his conversion (Acts 9:30; Gal. 1:21).

CIRCUMCISION. The removal of the foreskin of the male sex organ, a ritual performed generally on the eighth day after birth (Exod. 12:44). This practice, probably initiated with Abraham (Gen. 17:9–14), signified the covenant between God and His people, the Hebrews. In the N.T., the word is often used symbolically for the casting off of sin or worldly desires (Col. 2:11).

CIRCUMSPECT. Prudent and holy. Paul charged the Ephesian Christians to live circumspectly (Eph. 5:15).

CISTERN. A large pit or hole in the ground which served as a water reservoir (2 Kings 18:31). Empty cisterns were sometimes used as dungeons or prisons (Gen. 37:24). See also *Pit; Prison.*

CITIES OF REFUGE. Six cities assigned to the Levites and set aside as sanctuaries for those who killed other persons by accident. These cities, scattered throughout Palestine, were Bezer, Golan, Hebron, Kedesh, Ramoth-gilead, and Shechem (Josh. 20:7–9). See also *Avenger of Blood; Manslayer.*

CITIES OF THE PLAIN. Five cities on the plain of Jordan destroyed in Abraham's time because of the great sin of their inhabitants. These cities were Admah, Bela or Zoar, Gomorrah, Sodom, and Zeboiim (Gen. 19:22–30).

CITRON WOOD. See *Thyine Wood.*

CITY. A population center where trade and commerce flourished. Many biblical cities were protected by a massive defensive wall. The first city mentioned in the Bible was built by Cain (Gen. 4:17). See also *Fenced City.*

CITY CLERK. See *Town clerk.*

CITY GATE. A massive wooden door in a city wall, often reinforced with brass or iron for greater strength. Goods were often bought and sold and legal matters were discussed just inside the gate (Ruth 4:11). Gates in the wall of Jerusalem mentioned by specific name in the Bible include the Beautiful Gate (Acts 3:10), Fish Gate (Neh. 3:3), Horse Gate (2 Chron. 23:15), and Water Gate (Neh. 3:26). See also *Fenced City*.

CITY OF DAVID. A title applied to Bethlehem and Jerusalem because of David's close association with these cities (Neh. 3:15; Luke 2:11). See also *Bethlehem; Jerusalem*.

CITY OF GOD. A name applied to the city of Jerusalem, religious capital of the nation of Israel (Ps. 46:4–5).

CLAUDA. A small island about fifty miles from Crete, where Paul's ship sought protection during a storm (Acts 27:16).

CLAUDIA. A Christian believer mentioned by Paul (2 Tim. 4:21).

CLAUDIUS. See *Caesar,* No. 3.

CLAUDIUS LYSIAS. A Roman military officer who rescued Paul from an angry mob at Jerusalem (Acts 21:30–35; 23:22–30).

CLAY. Fine soil used for making bricks and pottery (Jer. 18:1–6). While still moist, squares of clay were also written on, then baked to produce a hard, permanent tablet. See also *Nuzi Tablets; Ras Shamra Tablets*.

CLAY TABLET. See *Tile*.

CLEAN. A word used by the Hebrews to describe things that were ceremonially pure (Lev. 11). The word is also used symbolically to signify holiness or righteousness (Ps. 24:4). See also *Purification; Wash*.

CLEAVE. To hold firmly to or to remain faithful. Husbands are instructed to cleave to their wives (Matt. 19:5).

CLEMENT. A Christian believer at Philippi commended by Paul (Phil. 4:3).

CLEOPAS. A Christian believer to whom Christ appeared on the road to Emmaus after His resurrection (Luke 24:18).

CLEOPHAS (CLOPAS). The husband of Mary, one of the women who viewed the crucifixion of Jesus (John 19:25). *Clopas:* NIV, NRSV.

CLOKE/CLOAK. A one-piece, sleeveless garment, similar to a short robe, worn by both men and women in Bible times (Matt. 5:40). *Cloak:* NIV, NRSV. See also *Mantle*.

CLOTH. See *Handkerchief; Napkin*.

CLOUD. A mass of water vapor in the sky. Clouds are often associated with God's presence and protection (Exod. 16:10). At His second coming, Christ will come in "the clouds of heaven" (Matt. 24:30). See also *Pillar of Fire and Cloud*.

CLUB. See *Maul*.

CNIDUS. A harbor city in southern Asia Minor passed by Paul during his voyage to Rome (Acts 27:7).

COAT OF MAIL. See *Brigandine*.

COCK. A rooster. The crowing of the cock in Mark 13:35 refers to the third watch of the night, just before daybreak.

COCKATRICE (VIPER, ADDER). A poisonous snake (Isa. 11:8). *Viper:* NIV; *Adder:* NRSV.

COCKLE (WEED). A weed which grows in fields of grain (Job 31:40). *Weed:* NIV, NRSV.

COLOSSE (COLOSSAE). A city about 100 miles east of Ephesus and the site of a church to which Paul wrote one of his epistles (Col. 1:2). *Colossae:* NRSV. Whether Paul visited this city is uncertain.

COLOSSIANS, EPISTLE TO THE. A short epistle of the apostle Paul on the theme of Christ's glory and majesty and His work of redemption (chaps. 1–2). Paul also challenged the Christians at Colosse to put on the character of Christ and to express His love in their relationships with others (chaps. 3–4).

COLT. A young donkey. Christ rode a colt into Jerusalem (Matt. 21:1–7). See also *Ass*.

COMFORTER (COUNSELOR, ADVOCATE). A title for the Holy Spirit which means "to strengthen" or "to bolster" (John 14:16–26). *Counselor:* NIV; *Advocate:* NRSV. See also *Advocate; Helper; Holy Spirit; Paraclete*.

COMMANDMENT. An order imposed by a person of rank or authority (Neh. 11:23). Jesus described the statute to love God and man as the greatest commandment (John 13:34). See also *Statute*.

COMMANDING OFFICER. See *Chancellor*.

COMMANDMENTS, TEN. See *Ten Commandments*.

COMMISSION. A special assignment from a person of authority (Ezra 8:36). Jesus' Great Commission to all His followers is to make disciples of all people everywhere (Matt. 28:19–20).

COMPACT. See *League*.

COMPANION. See *Yokefellow*.

COMPASSION. An attitude of mercy and forgiveness. As the compassionate Savior (Matt. 15:32), Jesus expects His followers to show compassion toward others (Matt. 18:33). See also *Mercy*.

CONCEIT. Vanity or pride; to have an exaggerated opinion of oneself. Paul warned Christians against such behavior (Rom. 11:25). See also *Pride; Vanity*.

CONCUBINE. A female slave or mistress; a secondary or common-law wife. Concubines were common among the patriarchs of the O.T. (Gen. 35:22), but Jesus taught the concept of monogamy—marriage to one person only (Matt. 19:4–9). See also *Paramour*.

CONCUPISCENCE (EVIL DESIRES). Sinful desire or sexual lust. Paul warned Christians of the dangers of this sin (Col. 3:5). *Evil desires:* NIV, NRSV.

CONDEMNATION. To declare a sinner guilty and deserving of punishment (Rom. 5:18). Jesus' mission was not to condemn but to save (John 3:17–18).

CONDUIT. A pipe or aqueduct through which water was channeled. King Hezekiah of Judah cut a conduit through solid rock to pipe water into Jerusalem (2 Kings 20:20). See also *Hezekiah*.

CONEY (BADGER). A small, furry animal which lived among the rocky cliffs of Palestine, probably the rock badger (Prov. 30:26). *Badger:* NRSV.

CONFESS. To admit or acknowledge one's sin (Josh. 7:19) and to proclaim one's faith in a bold and forthright manner (Rom. 10:9–10).

CONGREGATION. A gathering of people for worship or religious instruction (Acts 13:43). See also *Assembly*.

CONIAH. See *Jehoiachin*.

CONSECRATION. To dedicate or set apart for God's exclusive use. Believers are encouraged to consecrate or sanctify themselves to God's service (2 Tim. 2:21). See also *Ordain; Sanctification*.

CONSOLATION. A word which expresses the idea of comfort combined with encouragement. Believers find consolation in Jesus Christ and His Holy Spirit (Rom. 15:5).

CONTENTION (DISAGREEMENT). Severe disagreement which leads to sharp divisions among people, including Christian believers (Acts 15:39). Christians are encouraged to pursue peace with others (Rom. 12:18–21). *Disagreement:* NIV, NRSV. See also *Discord; Strife*.

CONTENTMENT. Satisfaction; freedom from worry and anxiety. This state of mind was modeled for all believers by Paul (Phil. 4:11).

CONTRITE. A meek or humble attitude (Ps. 51:17). A contrite person also shows genuine grief or sorrow over his sin (2 Cor. 7:10). See also *Humility; Meekness; Repentance*.

CONVERSATION. A word for behavior or lifestyle. Paul urged Christians to live in accordance with the gospel of Christ (Phil. 1:27).

CONVERSION. See *New Birth*.

CONVERT. See *Proselyte*.

CONVICTION. An awareness of one's sin and guilt (John 8:9) which leads to confession and repentance. The Holy Spirit is the agent of conviction (Heb. 3:7). See also *Holy Spirit; Repentance*.

CONVOCATION. A sacred assembly of the people of Israel for worship in connection with observance of the Sabbath or one of their major religious festivals, such as Passover or Pentecost (Lev. 23:2–8). See also *Assembly*.

COOS. A small island in the Mediterranean Sea which Paul passed on his way to Jerusalem at the close of the third missionary journey (Acts 21:1).

COPPER. See *Brass.*

COR. The largest liquid measure used by the Hebrew people, possibly equivalent to fifty or more gallons (Ezek. 45:14).

CORAL. A precious substance formed in the sea from the bodies of tiny sea creatures (Ezek. 27:16). Coral was apparently used for making beads and other fine jewelry (Job 28:18). See also *Ruby.*

CORBAN. A Hebrew word meaning a sacred gift, or an offering devoted to God. Jesus condemned the Pharisees for encouraging people to make such gifts while neglecting to care for their own parents (Mark 7:11–13).

CORD. See *Line; Rope.*

CORE. See *Korah.*

CORIANDER. A plant whose seeds were used as a medicine and as a seasoning for food (Num. 11:7).

CORINTH. A major port city in Greece on the trade route between Rome and its eastern provinces where Paul lived for eighteen months, establishing a church (Acts 18:1–11). The city was known for its immorality, paganism, and corruption.

CORINTHIANS, FIRST AND SECOND EPISTLES TO THE. Two letters of the apostle Paul to the church at Corinth, written to believers who were struggling to move beyond their pagan background and lifestyle.

First Corinthians deals mainly with problems in the church, including divisions (chaps. 1–4), sexual immorality (chaps. 5–6), and abuses of the Lord's Supper and spiritual gifts (chaps. 11–12; 14).

The themes of Second Corinthians include Paul's view of ministry and reconciliation (chaps. 1–6), support of the impoverished Christians at Jerusalem (chaps. 8–9), and Paul's example of suffering and abuse and defense of his credentials as an apostle (chaps. 10–13).

CORMORANT (DESERT OWL, HAWK). A large bird cited by Isaiah as a symbol of desolation and destruction (Isa. 34:11). *Desert owl:* NIV; *Hawk:* NRSV. See also *Pelican.*

CORN (GRAIN). A generic term for several different grains, including wheat, barley, and millet (Matt. 12:1).

Grain: NIV, NRSV. See also *Wheat.*

CORNELIUS. A Roman soldier from Caesarea who sought out the apostle Peter at Joppa and became the first Gentile convert to Christianity (Acts 10:1–48). This event showed clearly that the church was meant for Gentiles as well as Jews (Acts 15:7–11).

CORNER STONE. A stone strategically placed to align two walls and tie the building together. This is also a title for Christ as the keystone of the church (Eph. 2:20). See also *Foundation.*

CORNET (HORN). A musical instrument similar to the horn or trumpet (Dan. 3:5–7). *Horn:* NIV, NRSV.

COULTER (PLOWSHARE). An agricultural instrument of metal, probably the tip of a plow (1 Sam. 13:21). *Plowshare:* NIV, NRSV. See also *Plowshare.*

COUNCIL/SANHEDRIN. The highest court of the Jewish nation in N.T. times, composed of seventy-one priests, scribes, and elders; and presided over by the high priest. The Council accused Jesus of blasphemy against God, but it didn't have the power to put Jesus to death. It brought Him before Pilate, the Roman procurator, for sentencing (Matt. 26:65–66; John 18:31; 19:12). The Council also brought charges against Peter and John and the other apostles (Acts 4:1–23; 5:17–41) and Paul (Acts 22–24). *Sanhedrin:* NIV.

COUNSELLOR (COUNSELOR). A person who gives wise counsel or imparts advice. Kings employed counselors (1 Chron. 27:33). This is also one of the messianic titles of Christ (Isa. 9:6). *Counselor:* NIV, NRSV. See also *Comforter; Holy Spirit; Paraclete.*

COUNTENANCE. A word for the face or the expression on a person's face (Dan. 5:6).

COURAGE. Fearlessness and bravery in the face of danger (Acts 28:15). Moses exhorted Joshua to have courage (Deut. 31:7–8).

COURIER. See *Post.*

COURT. An enclosed yard or patio attached to a house or public building. Both the tabernacle (Exod. 27:9) and the temple in Jerusalem had courts or courtyards (1 Kings 6:36).

COURT OF THE GENTILES. An outer court in the Jewish temple beyond which Gentile worshipers could not go. The splitting of the curtain between this court and the inner court at Jesus' death symbolized the Gentiles' equal access to God (Matt. 27:51; Eph. 2:11–14). See also *Gentile; Middle Wall of Partition.*

COUSIN. A general term denoting any degree of relationship among blood relatives—cousin, nephew, aunt, uncle, etc. (Luke 1:36).

COVENANT. An agreement between two people or groups, particularly that between God and His people which promised His blessings in return for their obedience and devotion (Gen. 15:1–21). Through His sacrificial death, Jesus became the mediator of a new covenant, bringing salvation and eternal life to all who trust in Him (Heb. 10:12–17). See also *Testament.*

COVERED COLONNADE. See *Portico.*

COVETOUSNESS. Greed, or a burning desire for what belongs to others. This sin is specifically prohibited by the Ten Commandments (Exod. 20:17), and Paul warned against its dangers (Col. 3:5). See also *Greed.*

COW. See *Kine.*

CREATION. The actions of God through which He brought man and the physical world into existence. God existed before the world, and He produced the universe from nothing (Gen. 1:1–2). As the sovereign, self-existing God, He also rules over His creation (Ps. 47:7–9). See also *Creature.*

CREATOR. A title for God which emphasizes that He is the maker of all things and the sovereign ruler of His creation (Isa. 40:28; John 1:1–3; Col. 1:15–16). See also *Almighty; Sovereignty of God.*

CREATURE (CREATION). Any being created by God, including man (Gen. 2:19). Through God's redemption, a believer becomes a new creature (2 Cor. 5:17). *Creation:* NIV, NRSV. See also *Creation.*

CREEPING THING. A phrase for winged insects and reptiles (Lev. 11:21).

CRESCENS. A disciple who left Paul and went to Galatia (2 Tim. 4:10).

A rocky hill in Jerusalem known as "Gordon's Calvary," the site where Jesus was crucified, according to one tradition.
Courtesy Israel Ministry of Tourism

CRETE. A large island in the Mediterranean Sea by which Paul sailed during his voyage to Rome (Acts 27:1–13). Titus apparently served as leader of a church on Crete (Titus 1:4–5). See also *Titus*.

CRIMINAL. See *Malefactor*.

CRIMSON. See *Scarlet*.

CRISPING PIN (PURSE, HANDBAG). A purse or bag for carrying money (Isa. 3:22). *Purse:* NIV; *Handbag:* NRSV. See also *Purse*.

CRISPUS. Chief ruler of the synagogue at Corinth who became a Christian believer (Acts 18:8) and was baptized by Paul (1 Cor. 1:14).

CROCUS. See *Rose*.

CROSS. A wooden stake with a cross beam on which Jesus was put to death by the Roman authorities—a common form of capital punishment in N.T. times. Attached to the cross with nails or leather thongs, the victim generally suffered for two or three days before dying from exposure, exhaustion, and the loss of body fluids. But Jesus died after only six hours on the cross (John 19:30–33). His sacrificial death freed believers from the power of sin (Rom. 6:6–11) and sealed their reconciliation to God (2 Cor. 5:19). See also *Atonement; Redeem; Savior*.

CROWD. See *Multitude*.

CROWN. An ornamental headdress worn by kings and queens as a symbol of power and authority (2 Kings 11:12). The word is also used symbolically for righteous behavior befitting a believer (2 Tim. 4:8) and God's gift of eternal life (Jas. 1:12). See also *Diadem*.

CRUCIBLE. See *Fining Pot*.

CRUCIFIXION. See *Cross*.

CRUSE (JUG). A small earthen jug or flask for holding liquids (1 Kings 17:14–15). *Jug:* NIV, NRSV. See also *Pitcher*.

CRYSTAL. A transparent, colorless rock, perhaps a form of quartz (Rev. 22:1).

CUBIT. The standard unit for measurement of length, equivalent to about eighteen inches (Gen. 6:15–16).

CUCKOW (SEA GULL). A bird considered unclean by the Hebrews, probably a type of sea bird (Lev. 11:16). *Sea gull:* NRSV.

CUCUMBER. A climbing vine which produced vegetables probably similar to our cucumbers (Num. 11:5).

CUMMIN. A plant which produced seeds used for medicines and for seasoning food (Isa. 28:25–27). Jesus criticized the Pharisees for their shallow legalism in tithing the seeds from this insignificant plant while ignoring more important matters, such as mercy and faith (Matt. 23:23).

CUP. A drinking utensil (Gen. 44:12). The cup is also symbolic of the blood of the new covenant established by Christ (Matt. 20:22; 1 Cor. 10:16).

CUPBEARER. A royal household servant who tasted wine before serving to make sure it had not been poisoned (Neh. 1:11). The butler imprisoned with Joseph was probably a cupbearer to the Egyptian pharaoh (Gen. 40:1–13).

CURSE. A call for evil or misfortune against another (Gen.

4:11). Jesus taught that Christians are to return kindness for such actions (Luke 6:28).

CURTAIN. See *Veil*.

CUSH. Ham's oldest son and a grandson of Noah (1 Chron. 1:8–10).

CUSHAN-RISHATHAIM. See *Chushan-rishathaim*.

CUSHI. A messenger sent by Joab to announce Absalom's death to King David (2 Sam. 18:21–32).

CUTH/CUTHAH. A city or district of Babylonia which provided colonists who settled the Northern Kingdom after it fell to the Assyrians (2 Kings 17:30). *Cuthah:* 2 Kings 17:24.

CYMBALS. Curved metal plates used as musical instruments (1 Cor. 13:1).

CYPRESS. See *Box Tree; Fir; Gopher Wood*.

CYPRUS/CHITTIM/KITTIM. A large island in the Mediterranean Sea about 125 miles off the coast of Palestine which Paul and Barnabas visited during the first missionary journey (Acts 13:4–5). Barnabas was a native of Cyprus (Acts 4:36). *Chittim:* Jer. 2:10; *Kittim:* Gen. 10:4.

CYRENE. A Greek city in North Africa and home of the Simon of Cyrene who carried the cross of Jesus (Matt. 27:32).

CYRENIUS (QUIRINIUS). The Roman governor of Syria at the time of Jesus' birth (Luke 2:1–4). *Quirinius:* NIV, NRSV.

CYRUS. The founding king of the Persian empire (reigned about 559–530 B.C.). After defeating the Babylonians, he allowed the Jewish captives to return to their homeland about 536 B.C. (2 Chron. 36:22–23; Ezra 1:1–4). See also *Persia*.

-D-

DAGON. The chief pagan god of the Philistines, which apparently had the head of a man and the tail of a fish. This idol fell before the ark of the covenant in the pagan temple at Ashdod (1 Sam. 5:1–5). See also *Philistines*.

DALETH. The fourth letter of the Hebrew alphabet, used as a heading over Ps. 119:25–32.

Excavated ruins of the ancient city of Dan in northern Israel.
Courtesy Israel Ministry of Tourism

DALMANUTHA. A place on the western shore of the Sea of Galilee visited by Jesus (Mark 8:10).

DALMATIA. A province on the eastern coast of the Adriatic Sea visited by Titus (2 Tim. 4:10).

DAMARIS. A woman of Athens converted under Paul's ministry (Acts 17:33–34).

DAMASCUS (SYRIA-DAMASCUS). The capital city of Syria, located north of Mt. Hermon in northern Palestine. Paul was traveling to Damascus to persecute Christians when he met the risen Lord in a life-transforming vision (Acts 9:1–8). Damascus is considered the oldest continually inhabited city in the world. *Syria-damascus:* 1 Chron. 18:6. See also *Syria*.

DAMNATION. Judgment and consignment to everlasting punishment; the fate of the wicked or those who reject Christ (Mark 16:16). See also *Hell; Judgment, Last; Perdition*.

DAMSEL. A word for a young woman (Mark 5:39–42).

DAN.

1. Jacob's fifth son and ancestor of one of the tribes

of Israel (Gen. 30:6; Num. 1:38–39). See also *Tribes of Israel*.

2. A village in the territory allotted to the tribe of Dan. It was located further north than any other city of Palestine during most of the O.T. era. The phrase "from Dan even to Beersheba" (Judg. 20:1) described the entire territory of the Hebrew nation from north to south. *Laish:* Isa. 10:30.

DANCE. Rhythmic body movements, usually to musical accompaniment, to express joy and gratitude to God (Exod. 15:20–21). King David danced when the ark of the covenant was recovered and brought to Jerusalem (2 Sam. 6:14–16).

DANIEL.

1. A prophet of the O.T. known for his faithfulness to the God of Israel among the pagan Babylonians and Persians. Refusing to worship King Darius, he was thrown into a den of lions but was miraculously delivered by the Lord (Dan. 6:1–24). *Belteshazzar:* Persian form (Dan. 1:7).

2. Another name for Chileab, a son of David (1 Chron. 3:1). See *Chileab*.

DANIEL, BOOK OF. An apocalyptic book of the O.T. known for its images of horns and beasts that are similar to those described in the Revelation to John in the N.T. The two major sections of Daniel are (1) the trials and tribulations suffered by Daniel and his three friends as captives of the Babylonians and Persians (chaps. 1–7) and (2) Daniel's visions and dreams about the future (chaps. 8–12). The prophet's famous "seventy weeks" prophecy has been interpreted as a period of 490 years (seventy weeks, representing seventy years, multiplied by seven) from Daniel's time until the coming of the Messiah (9:20–27). See also *Apocalypse*.

DARIC. See *Dram*.

DARIUS. A title for the kings of Persia. Four different kings with this title are mentioned in the O.T.:

1. Darius I or Darius the Great (reigned about 522–485 B.C.). Successor to Cyrus, he continued Cyrus's policy of restoring the Jewish people to their homeland (Ezra 6:1–12).

2. Darius II or Darius the Persian (Neh. 12:22), who reigned about 424–405 B.C

3. Darius III or Darius Codomannus (reigned about 336–330 B.C.). He is probably the "fourth" king of Persia

mentioned by the prophet Daniel (Dan. 11:2).

4. Darius the Mede, who made Daniel ruler over several provincial leaders (Dan. 6:1–2). Some scholars believe this is the same king as Darius II.

DARKNESS. The absence of light. Darkness ruled the world before God's creation of light (Gen. 1:2). Thus, darkness is symbolic of man's sin, rebellion, and ignorance (Job 24:13–17). See also *Light*.

DART (JAVELIN, SPEAR). A javelin or short spear. Absalom was killed by darts (2 Sam. 18:14). *Javelin:* NIV; *Spear:* NRSV. See also *Javelin; Spear*.

DATHAN. A leader of the rebellion against Moses in the wilderness. All the rebels were destroyed by an earthquake (Num. 16:1–35).

DAUGHTER. A word used for female offspring of parents as well as a distant female relative, such as a granddaughter or niece (Gen. 20:12; 24:48).

DAUGHTER OF ZION. A symbolic expression for the city of Jerusalem and its inhabitants (Ps. 9:14). See also *Jerusalem*.

DAVID. The popular king of Judah described by God as "a man after mine own heart" and an earthly ancestor of the promised Messiah, Jesus Christ (Luke 2:4–7). A descendant of the tribe of Judah (1 Chron. 28:4), he was a native of Bethlehem (1 Sam. 17:12). As a shepherd boy, he defeated the Philistine giant Goliath (1 Sam. 17:44–52). He served as King Saul's musician and armor bearer (1 Sam. 16:14–21) and was later anointed king after Saul's sin and disobedience (1 Sam. 16:11–13). Forced to flee from Saul's jealousy and wrath (1 Sam. 21:10), he was befriended by Saul's son Jonathan (1 Sam. 19:1–3). After he became king, he united the Hebrew tribes into one nation with Jerusalem as the capital city (2 Sam. 5:1–10) and defeated many enemy nations (2 Sam. 8:1–15).

In a moment of weakness, David committed adultery with Bath-sheba (2 Sam. 11:1–4), but he later repented (Ps. 32; Ps. 51). He was forgiven and restored, but the consequences of his sin remained (2 Sam. 12:13–14). He suffered family tragedies (2 Sam. 12:15–20; 18:31–33) and wrote many psalms (see Pss. 54, 59, 65). He was succeeded as king by his son Solomon (1 Kings 2:12). In

Camels graze at the En-gedi Oasis near the Dead Sea, where David hid from King Saul. *Courtesy Israel Ministry of Tourism*

the N.T., Jesus was often called the "son of David" (Matt. 1:1; Mark 10:48). See also *Absalom; Bethlehem; Jerusalem*.

DAVID, TOWER OF. Fortress built by David at an unknown location (Song of Sol. 4:4).

DAY. The twenty-four hour period during which the earth rotates on its own axis. The Hebrews measured their day from sunset to sunset (Exod. 12:18). The twelve hours of daylight began with the first hour at sunup (about 6:00 A.M.). Midday or noon was the sixth hour, and the twelfth hour ended at sundown, or about 6:00 P.M.

DAY OF THE LORD. A phrase usually interpreted as a period in the end-time when God will bring His purpose for man and the world to fulfillment. This will be a day of judgment for the rebellious and sinful (Jer. 46:10) and a time of deliverance for the godly (Joel 2:28–32). Any time—whether now or in the distant future—when the Lord acts, intervening in history for the purpose of deliverance and judgment, may also be described as the "day of the Lord" (Isa. 13:6). See also *Damnation; Judgment, Last; Punishment*.

The Dead Sea, also known as the Salt Sea, in southern Palestine.
Courtesy Israel Ministry of Tourism

DAY STAR/LUCIFER (MORNING STAR). A star which appears just before daybreak, signaling the beginning of a new day (2 Pet. 1:19). *Morning star:* NIV. The word for day star is also translated as *Lucifer* (Isa. 14:12), and used as a name for the king of Babylon. See also *Morning Star*.

DAY'S JOURNEY. The distance that could be traveled in one day by camel or horse, probably about twenty-five miles (Jon. 3:3–4).

DAYSMAN (UMPIRE). A word for a mediator, umpire, or judge between contending parties (Job 9:33). *Umpire:* NRSV.

DAYSPRING. A word for dawn or daybreak (Job 38:12).

DEACON. An officer or servant of the church. The first "deacons" were probably the seven men of Greek background who were appointed by the church at Jerusalem to coordinate the distribution of food to the needy (Acts 6:1–7). The strict qualifications for deacons (1 Tim. 3:8–13) show this was an important office in the early church. Phoebe, a female believer, is called a "deacon" in the NRSV translation of Rom. 16:1 (*Servant:* KJV).

DEAD SEA/SALT SEA/ EAST SEA. A body of water (about fifty miles long by ten miles wide) into which the Jordan River empties at the lowest point on earth in southern Palestine. Because of the hot, dry climate, the water evaporates, leaving a high concentration of salt and other minerals. *Salt Sea:* Josh. 3:16; *East Sea:* Joel 2:20.

DEAD SEA SCROLLS. A group of scrolls or ancient manuscripts discovered since 1947 in caves around the Dead Sea. Written between 250 B.C. and A.D. 68 and placed in clay jars, the scrolls were preserved by the dry climate of the area. Among the scrolls was a complete manuscript of the book of Isaiah, written in Hebrew. See also *Qumran, Khirbet.*

DEAF. Unable to hear. The word is also used symbolically of spiritual coldness or apathy (Isa. 42:18–19).

DEATH. The end of physical existence. Death is the price man pays for his sin and rebellion against God, but God provides salvation and eternal life for believers through the atoning death of Jesus Christ (Rom. 6:23). "Second death" is eternal separation from God—the fate of unbelievers (Rev. 20:6).

DEBASED. See *Reprobate.*

DEBAUCHERY. See *Lasciviousness.*

DEBIR

1. A king of Eglon and one of the five Amorite kings killed by Joshua's army (Josh. 10:3–26).

2. A Canaanite city captured by Joshua (Josh. 10:38–39). *Kirjath-sanna:* Josh. 15:49; *Kirjath-sepher:* Judg. 1:11.

DEBORAH. A prophetess and judge of Israel who, along with Barak, defeated the Canaanite forces of Sisera (Judg. 4:4–14). She celebrated the victory in a triumphant song (Judg. 5:1–3). See also *Sisera.*

DEBT. Borrowed property or money which must be repaid. The Hebrews were encouraged not to charge interest to their own countrymen (Lev. 25:35–38), but foreigners could be charged (Deut. 23:20). See also *Usury.*

DECALOGUE. See *Ten Commandments.*

DECAPOLIS. A Roman province or district with a large Greek population which was situated mostly on the eastern side of the Jordan River in northern Palestine (Matt. 4:25).

DECEIT. See *Guile.*

DECEIVER. One who misleads another. Deception is one of the evil tricks used by Satan (2 John 7). See also *Satan.*

DECISION, VALLEY OF. See *Jehoshaphat, Valley of.*

DECREE. A command or official order issued by a king. Mary and Joseph were affected by the decree of the Roman emperor Caesar Augustus (Luke 2:1). See also *Statute.*

DEDICATION, FEAST OF. An eight-day festival commemorating the Jewish victories which restored the temple during the era of the Maccabees about 160 B.C. Jesus attended one of these festivals in Jerusalem (John 10:22–23). This feast was also known as the *Feast of Lights* or *Hanukkah.*

DEER. A fleet-footed animal which could be eaten by the Hebrews (Deut. 14:5). See also *Hart; Hind.*

DEFILEMENT. Contamination; to make something impure by acts of sin and rebellion. The O.T. law emphasized ceremonial cleanliness (Num. 9:13; Lev. 15:24), but Jesus emphasized the need for ethical living and moral purity (Mark 7:1–23).

DEGREES, SONGS OF. A title used in fifteen psalms of the book of Psalms (Pss. 120–134). The Hebrew word for degrees means "goings up." These songs of ascent may have been pilgrim psalms, sung by worshipers as they were "going up" to the temple at Jerusalem.

DEHAVITES. An Assyrian tribe which settled in Samaria after the defeat of the Northern Kingdom by the Assyrians. In later years the Dehavites opposed the rebuilding of the Jewish temple at Jerusalem (Ezra 4:9–16). See also *Samaritan.*

DELEGATION. See *Ambassage.*

DELILAH. A woman, probably a Philistine, who cut off Samson's long hair—the source of his strength—so he could be captured by his Philistine enemies (Judg. 16:13–21). See also *Samson.*

DEMAS. A fellow believer who deserted Paul (2 Tim. 4:10) after having worked with him on earlier occasions (Philem. 24; Col. 4:14).

DEMETRIUS.

1. A silversmith at Ephesus who made replicas of the temple where the pagan goddess Diana was worshiped. When his livelihood was threatened by Paul's preaching, Demetrius incited a riot against the apostle (Acts 19:24–31). See also *Diana*.

2. A Christian believer commended by John (3 John 12).

DEMON. An evil spirit with destructive power who opposes God. In His healing ministry, Jesus cast demons out of several people (Matt. 12:22–24; Luke 8:27–39).

DEMON POSSESSION. Invasion and control of a person by evil spirits. In N.T. times, these demons often caused disease (Mark 9:25), mental anguish (Matt. 8:28), and antisocial behavior (Luke 8:27–39). Jesus cast demons out of several people—an act which showed His power over the demonic forces of Satan (Mark 1:25; 9:29).

DEN OF LIONS. A deep cavern where lions were kept by the Persian kings, probably for the sport of lion hunting. Daniel was thrown into one of these pits, but he was miraculously delivered by God's hand (Dan. 6:16–24). See also *Daniel*.

DENARIUS. See *Penny*.

DEPOSIT. See *Earnest*.

DEPRAVED. See *Reprobate*.

DEPUTY. A person empowered to act for another (1 Kings 22:47). See also *Proconsul*.

DERBE. A city or village of the province of Lycaonia visited by Paul and Barnabas during the first missionary journey (Acts 14:6–20).

DESERT. A dry, barren, wilderness place (Isa. 48:21; Luke 1:80). See also *Wilderness*.

DESERT OWL. See *Cormorant; Hawk; Pelican*.

DESIRE OF ALL NATIONS (DESIRED OF ALL NATIONS, TREASURE OF ALL NATIONS). A title for the coming Messiah which emphasizes His universal rule and power (Hag. 2:6–7) *Desired of* *all nations:* NIV; *Treasure of all nations:* NRSV.

DEUTERONOMY, BOOK OF. A book of the O.T. containing a series of speeches which Moses delivered to the Hebrew people as they prepared to enter and conquer the land of Canaan. This book repeats many of the laws of God revealed to Moses on Mt. Sinai about two generations earlier—thus its name *Deuteronomy,* which means "second law."

In these speeches (chaps. 1–33), Moses cautioned the people to remain faithful to God in the midst of the pagan Canaanite culture they were about to enter. The final chapter (34) recounts the death of Moses and the succession of Joshua as the leader of the Hebrew people. See also *Moses; Pentateuch.*

DEVIL. A title for Satan which emphasizes his work as a liar and deceiver (Luke 4:3). See also *Satan.*

DEW. Moisture which condenses on the earth during the night (Exod. 16:13–14; Judg. 6:37–40). The heavy dews of Palestine during the dry season from April to September provide moisture for the growing crops (Gen. 27:28).

DIADEM (CROWN). A headpiece decorated with precious stones and worn by a king (Isa. 28:5). *Crown:* NIV. See also *Crown.*

DIAL. An instrument which shows the hour of the day through its shadow cast by the sun (Isa. 38:8).

DIAMOND (EMERALD, MOONSTONE). A precious stone in the breastplate of the high priest (Exod. 28:18). *Emerald:* NIV; *Moonstone:* NRSV.

DIANA (ARTEMIS). The Roman name for the pagan goddess of hunting and virginity. Paul's preaching at Ephesus, a center of Diana worship, caused an uproar among craftsmen who earned their living by making images of Diana (Acts 19:24–35). *Artemis:* NIV, NRSV. See also *Demetrius,* No. 1; *Ephesus.*

DIBON. An Amorite town taken by Israel during the years of wilderness wandering (Num. 32:3).

DIDYMUS. See *Thomas.*

DILL. See *Anise.*

DINAH. The daughter of Jacob who was assaulted by Shechem (Gen. 34:1–24).

DINAITES. An Assyrian tribe which populated Samaria after the Northern Kingdom fell to the Assyrians (Ezra 4:9). See also *Samaritan*.

DIONYSIUS. A member of the Areopagus of Athens who believed Paul's testimony about Jesus the Messiah (Acts 17:34). See also *Areopagus*.

DIOTREPHES. A church leader condemned by the apostle John for his false teachings (3 John 9–10).

DISAGREEMENT. See *Contention*.

DISCERNING OF SPIRITS (DISTINGUISHING BETWEEN SPIRITS). A spiritual gift which enables certain believers to tell the difference between true and false teachers and teachings (1 Cor. 12:10). *Distinguishing between spirits:* NIV.

DISCIPLE. A person who follows and learns from another person or group, especially a believer who observes the teachings of Jesus (Acts 6:1–7). See also *Apostle*.

DISCIPLINARIAN. See *Schoolmaster*.

DISCIPLINE. To train or teach, as parents impart important truths to a child (Prov. 22:6). A disciplined person also controls his impulses, speech, and actions (1 Pet. 3:10). God disciplines His children through corrective actions (Heb. 12:6). See also *Chastisement*.

DISCORD. Disagreement produced by a contentious spirit (Prov. 6:14). Discord is a sign of worldliness among believers (1 Cor. 3:3). See also *Contention*.

DISGRACE. See *Shame*.

DISH. See *Platter*.

DISPERSION. A word which refers to the scattering of the Jewish people among other nations. Jeremiah predicted such a scattering (Jer. 25:34), and this happened when the Babylonians overran Judah in 587 B.C. and carried its leading citizens into exile. See also *Captivity*.

DISPUTATION. Argument or dissension. Paul cautioned believers against such behavior (Phil. 2:14).

DISTAFF. The staff around which flax or wool was wound for spinning (Prov. 31:19). See also *Spinning; Warp; Weaver.*

DISTINGUISHING BETWEEN SPIRITS. See *Discerning of Spirits.*

DIVIDING WALL. See *Middle Wall of Partition.*

DIVINATION. Foretelling the future or determining the unknown through performing acts of magic or reading signs (Jer. 14:14). This practice was condemned by God (Deut. 18:10). See also *Magic; Soothsayer.*

DIVINER. See *Soothsayer.*

DIVORCE. A breaking of the ties of marriage. The divine ideal is for permanence in marriage (Matt. 19:3–6), and divorce violates the oneness which God intended (Gen. 2:24; Matt. 19:5–6). Under the Mosaic Law, divorce was permitted in certain situations (Deut. 24:1–4), but this provision was greatly abused (Matt. 19:8). Christ regarded adultery as the only permissible reason for divorce (Matt. 5:31–32; 19:9; Mark 10:11; Luke 16:18), and He reprimanded the Jews for their insensitive divorce practices (Matt. 19:3–9). Unfaithfulness to God was regarded as spiritual adultery (Hos. 2:2). See also *Marriage.*

DIZAHAB. A place in the wilderness of Sinai where Moses gave one of his farewell addresses to the Hebrew people (Deut. 1:1).

DOCTORS (TEACHERS). Teachers of the Law of Moses who were held in high esteem by the Jewish people. At the age of twelve, Jesus discussed the law with some of these teachers in Jerusalem (Luke 2:46). *Teachers:* NIV, NRSV. See also *Lawyer.*

DOCTRINE. A system of religious beliefs which followers pass on to others. Paul impressed upon young Timothy the importance of sound doctrinal teachings (1 Tim. 4:6).

DOEG. An overseer of King Saul's herds who betrayed the high priest Ahimelech for assisting David and his soldiers (1 Sam. 22:9–10).

DOG. An unclean animal (Deut. 23:18) looked upon with contempt by the Jewish people. Gentiles were called "dogs" (Matt. 15:26). See also *Gentile.*

DOME. See *Firmament.*

DOMINION. Authority to govern or rule. After his creation by God, man was given dominion over God's creation (Gen. 1:26–28).

DOOR (GATE). An opening through which a house or public building is entered. Jesus spoke of Himself as the doorway to salvation and eternal life (John 10:7–10). *Gate:* NIV, NRSV. See also *Gate.*

DOORKEEPER. A person who stood guard at the entrance of a public building (Ps. 84:10). See also *Gate Keeper; Porter.*

DOR. A royal Canaanite city captured by Joshua (Josh. 12:23).

DORCAS. See *Tabitha.*

DOTHAN. A city west of the Jordan River near Mt. Gilboa. Dothan was the place where Joseph was sold into slavery by his brothers (Gen. 37:17–28).

DOVE. See *Pigeon; Turtledove.*

DOWRY. Compensation paid by the groom to the bride's family for loss of her services as a daughter (Gen. 24:47–58). See also *Betrothal; Marriage.*

DOXOLOGY. A brief hymn or declaration which proclaims God's power and glory (1 Chron. 29:11; Luke 2:14).

DRAGON. A mythical sea creature or winged lizard. The name is applied to Satan (Rev. 12:9) and the Antichrist (Rev. 12:3). See also *Antichrist.*

DRAM (DRACHMA, DARIC). A Persian coin of small value (Neh. 7:70). *Drachma:* NIV; *Daric:* NRSV.

DRAWER OF WATER (WATER CARRIER). A person who carried water from the spring or well back to the household—a menial chore assigned to women, children, or slaves (Josh. 9:27). *Water carrier:* NIV.

DREAMS AND VISIONS. Mediums of revelation often used by God to make His will known. Joseph distinguished himself in Egypt by interpreting dreams for the pharaoh and his officers (Gen. 40–41). Daniel interpreted King Nebuchadnnezzar's dream that he would fall from power (Dan. 4:18–27). Paul's missionary thrust into Europe began with his vision of a man from Macedonia appealing for help (Acts 16:9–10).

DREGS. Waste which settled to the bottom of the vat in the wine-making process (Ps. 75:8). The word is also used symbolically of God's wrath and judgment (Isa. 51:17). See also *Lees*.

DRINK OFFERING. An offering of fine wine, usually given in connection with another sacrifice, such as a burnt offering (Num. 29:11–18).

DROMEDARY (YOUNG CAMEL). A distinct species of camel with one hump and known for its swiftness (Jer. 2:23). *Young camel:* NRSV.

DROPSY. A disease which causes fluid buildup in the body. Jesus healed a man with this disease on the Sabbath (Luke 14:2).

DROSS. Impurities separated from ore or metal in the smelting process (Prov. 25:4). The word is used symbolically of God's judgment against the wicked (Ps. 119:119).

DROUGHT. Lack of rainfall for an extended time (Ps. 32:4). The prophet Jeremiah spoke symbolically of a spiritual drought throughout the land (Jer. 14:1–7). See also *Famine*.

DRUNKARD. See *Winebibber*.

DRUNKENNESS. A state of intoxication caused by consuming too much wine or strong drink. This vice is condemned in both the O.T. and the N.T. (Deut. 21:20; 1 Cor. 5:11).

DRUSILLA. The wife of Felix, Roman governor of Judea, who heard Paul's defense (Acts 24:24–25.)

DUKE (CHIEF). A leader or chief of a clan (Gen. 36:15–43). *Chief:* NIV. See also *Chief*.

DULCIMER (PIPES). A musical instrument used in Babylonia, probably similar to the bagpipe (Dan. 3:5–15). *Pipes:* NIV.

DUMB. Unable to speak, or the temporary loss of speech (Ezek. 33:22). The word is also used figuratively of submission (Isa. 53:7).

DUNG (RUBBISH). Excrement of humans or animals (2 Kings 9:37). Dried dung was used for fuel in Palestine (Ezek. 4:12–15). The word is also used figuratively to express worthlessness (Phil. 3:8). *Rubbish:* NIV, NRSV.

DUNGEON. An underground prison. Some of these were little more than cisterns with the water partially drained. Joseph and Jeremiah were imprisoned in dungeons (Gen. 39:20; 40:15; Jer. 37:7–16). See also *Cistern; Pit; Prison*.

DURA. A plain in Babylonia where the golden image of King Nebuchadnezzar of Babylonia was set up (Dan. 3:1). See also *Adoraim*.

DUST. Dried earth in powdered form. Sitting in the dust was a symbol of dejection and humiliation (Lam. 3:29). The word is also used symbolically of man's mortality (Gen. 3:19).

DWELLING. See *Pavilion*.

DYSENTERY. See *Flux*.

-E-

EAGLE. A large bird of prey, considered unclean by the Hebrews (Lev. 11:13). Many scholars believe the eagle of the Bible was actually the griffon vulture.

EAR. The ears of the unregenerate are called dull or unhearing (Matt. 13:15). The "ears of the Lord" (1 Sam. 8:21) signify that He hears prayers, in contrast to dumb idols (Ps. 115:6).

EARLY RAIN. See *Former Rain*.

EARRING. A piece of jewelry worn suspended from the earlobe (Gen. 35:4).

EARNEST (DEPOSIT, FIRST INSTALLMENT). A down payment given as a pledge toward full payment of the loan. The Holy Spirit is given as a pledge of the believer's inheritance of eternal life (2 Cor. 1:22). *Deposit:* NIV; *First installment:* NRSV.

EARTHQUAKE. A violent shaking of the earth (Ps. 77:18). These earth tremors are a token of God's wrath and judgment (Judg. 5:4).

EAST SEA. See *Dead Sea*.

EAST WIND. A violent, scorching desert wind, also known as the sirocco (Job 27:21). See also *Wind*.

EASTER. A word which refers to the Passover festival (Acts 12:4). Easter as a celebration of the resurrection of Jesus developed among Christians many years after the N.T. era.

EBAL. A rocky mountain in Samaria, or the territory of Ephraim, where Joshua built an altar after destroying the city of Ai (Josh. 8:30).

EBED-MELECH. An Ethiopian eunuch who rescued Jeremiah from a dungeon (Jer. 38:7–13).

EBENEZER. Site of Israel's defeat by the Philistines (1 Sam. 5:1). Years later, Samuel erected an altar on this site and called it Ebenezer, meaning "the stone of help," to commemorate Israel's victory over the Philistines (1 Sam. 7:10–12).

EBER. A great-grandson of Shem (Gen. 10:21–24) and ancestor of the Hebrew race (Gen. 11:16–26).

EBONY. A hard, durable wood used for decorative carvings and musical instruments (Ezek. 27:15).

ECBATANA. See *Achmetha*.

ECCLESIASTES, BOOK OF. A wisdom book of the O.T., probably written by King Solomon, which declares that life derives joy and meaning not from riches, fame, or work but from reverence for God and obedience to His commandments. One of the book's most memorable passages is the poem on the proper time for all of life's events: "A time to be born, and a time to die; . . . A time to weep, and a time to laugh; . . .a time to keep silence, and a time to speak" (see 3:1–9).

EDEN, GARDEN OF. The fruitful garden created specifically by the Lord as the home for Adam and Eve. The four rivers of Eden, including the Euphrates, suggest that it may have been located in Mesopotamia. Because of their sin and rebellion against God, Adam and Eve were expelled from the garden (Gen. 2:8–3:24). See also *Adam; Eve*.

EDIFICATION. The process by which believers grow in holiness, wisdom, and righteousness (1 Cor. 14:3). See also *Sanctification*.

EDOM.

1. The name given to Esau, Jacob's brother, after he traded away his birthright (Gen. 25:30). See also *Esau*.

2. The land where the descendants of Esau settled. It was in extreme southern Palestine in the barren territory below the Dead Sea. Mount Seir was located in this territory (Gen. 36:8). Edom was referred to by the Greeks and Romans as *Idumaea* (Mark 3:8).

EDOMITES. The descendants of Esau who were enemies of the Israelites. The king of Edom refused to allow the Hebrews to pass through his territory after the Exodus (Num. 20:14–21). In later years, David conquered the Edomites (2 Sam. 8:14). But they apparently existed with a distinct territory and culture for several centuries (see Ps. 137:7). See also *Edom; Esau.*

EDREI. A capital city of Bashan. King Og was defeated here by the Israelites (Num. 21:33–35).

EGLAH. One of David's wives (2 Sam. 3:2–5).

EGYPT. The ancient nation along the Nile River which held the Hebrew people in slavery for more than 400 years before their miraculous deliverance by the Lord at the hand of Moses. Egypt had flourished as a highly civilized culture for several centuries before the time of Abraham about 2000 B.C. Soon after entering Canaan in response to God's call, Abraham moved on to Egypt to escape a famine (Gen. 12:10). This same circumstance led Jacob and his family to settle in Egypt after his son Joseph became a high official of the Egyptian pharaoh (Gen. 45–46). Ham's son *Mizraim* apparently was the ancestor of the Egyptians (1 Chron. 1:8). See also *Mizraim; Nile River; Pharaoh.*

EHUD. The second judge of Israel, who killed Eglon, king of Moab (Judg. 3:15). See also *Judges of Israel.*

EKRON. One of the five chief Philistine cities. It was captured by Judah the judge and allotted to Dan (Judg. 1:18). See also *Philistines.*

ELAH.

1. A valley in Judah where David killed the Philistine giant Goliath (1 Sam. 17:2, 49).
2. A king of Israel (reigned about 886–885 B.C.) who was assassinated and succeeded by Zimri (1 Kings 16:6–10).

ELAM. A son of Shem and ancestor of the Elamites (Gen. 10:22).

ELAMITES. Descendants of Elam who lived in Mesopotamia in the area later populated by the Medes and Persians (Jer. 25:25). See also *Persia.*

EL-BETHEL. See *Bethel.*

ELDER.

1. In the O.T., an older member of a tribe or clan who was a leader and official representative of the clan (Num. 22:7).

2. In the N.T., a local church leader who served as a teacher and ministered to the sick (1 Tim. 5:17; Jas. 5:14–15). See also *Bishop; Pastor.*

ELEAZAR. A son of Aaron who succeeded his father as high priest (Num. 20:25–28), serving under Moses and Joshua. He helped divide the land of Canaan among the twelve tribes of Israel (Josh. 14:1).

ELECT LADY (CHOSEN LADY). The person, or perhaps a local church, to which the Second Epistle of John is addressed (2 John 1:1). *Chosen lady:* NIV.

ELECTION, DIVINE. The doctrine which deals with God's choice of persons who will be redeemed. Conflicts between God's electing grace and Christ's invitation that "whosoever will" may come to Him are not easily resolved. God's intentional will is for all to "come to repentance" and be saved (2 Pet. 3:9), but those who reject His Son will be lost (John 5:40). God's grace is unmerited (Rom. 9:11–16), but it will be lavished on those who are committed to His truth and His will for their lives (2 Thess. 2:13). The elect are characterized by Christlikeness (Rom. 8:29), holiness (Eph. 1:4), good works (Eph. 2:10), and eternal hope (1 Pet. 1:2–4). See also *Foreknowledge; Predestination.*

EL-ELOHE-ISRAEL. A name, meaning "God, the God of Israel," given by Jacob to the altar which he built at Shechem after he was reconciled to his brother Esau (Gen. 33:20).

ELEVATION OFFERING. See *Wave Offering.*

ELI. A high priest of Israel with whom the prophet Samuel lived during his boyhood years (1 Sam. 1–4). Eli's own two sons, Phinehas and Hophni, were unworthy of the priesthood (1 Sam. 2:12–25). They were killed in a battle with the Philistines. Eli died upon learning of their death (1 Sam. 4:1–18).

ELIADA. See *Beeliada.*

ELIAKIM.

1. A son of Hilkiah and overseer of the household of King Hezekiah of Judah. Eliakim was praised by the prophet Isaiah for his role in mediating peace with the invading

Assyrian army (2 Kings 18:18; Isa. 22:20–25).

2. Another name for *Jehoiakim*, a king of Judah. See *Jehoiakim*.

ELIAS. See *Elijah*.

ELIDAD. A leader of the tribe of Benjamin, appointed by Moses to help divide the land of Canaan after its occupation by the Israelites (Num. 34:21).

ELIHU. A friend who spoke to Job after Eliphaz, Bildad, and Zophar had failed to answer Job's questions satisfactorily (Job 32:2–6).

ELIJAH/ELIAS. A courageous prophet who opposed King Ahab and his successor, Ahaziah, because of their encouragement of Baal worship throughout the Northern Kingdom. Because of Ahab's wickedness, Elijah predicted a drought would afflict the land (1 Kings 17:1–24). He wiped out the prophets of Baal after a dramatic demonstration of God's power on Mt. Carmel (1 Kings 18:17–40). After selecting Elisha as his successor, Elijah was carried into heaven in a whirlwind (2 Kings 2:1–11). The coming of the Messiah was often associated in Jewish thought with Elijah's return. Some people even thought Jesus was Elijah (Luke 9:8). *Elias:* Greek form (Matt. 17:4). See also *Elisha*.

ELIM. The second encampment of the Israelites after they crossed the Red Sea (Exod. 15:27).

ELIMELECH. The husband of Naomi and the father-in-law of Ruth. He died in Moab, leaving his family destitute (Ruth 1:2–17).

ELIPHALET/ELPALET/ELIPHELET. A son of David, born in Jerusalem to Bathsheba (2 Sam. 5:16). *Elpalet:* 1 Chron. 14:5; *Eliphelet:* 1 Chron. 3:5–6.

ELIPHAZ.

1. A son of Esau (Gen. 36:2–4).

2. One of Job's friends or "comforters" (Job 2:11). In his speeches, Eliphaz defended the justice, purity, and holiness of God (Job 2:11; 4:1; 15:1; 22:1; 42:7–9).

ELISABETH (ELIZABETH). The mother of John the Baptist and a relative of Mary, earthly mother of Jesus. Elisabeth rejoiced with Mary over the coming birth of the Messiah (Luke 1:36–45). *Elizabeth:* NIV, NRSV. See also *Mary,* No. 1.

ELISHA/ELISEUS. The prophet selected and anointed by Elijah as his successor (1 Kings 19:16–21). He followed Elijah for several years and was present at his ascension into heaven when the mantle of leadership fell upon him (2 Kings 2:9–14). Elisha served as a counselor and advisor to four kings of the Northern Kingdom—Jehoram, Jehu, Jehoahaz, and Joash—across a period of about fifty years (850–800 B.C.). *Eliseus:* Greek form (Luke 4:27). See also *Elijah.*

ELISHAMA/ELISHUA. A son of David, born in Jerusalem (1 Chron. 3:1–6). *Elishua:* 2 Sam. 5:15.

ELISHEBA. The wife of Aaron and mother of Abihu, Eleazar, Nadab, and Ithamar (Exod. 6:23).

ELIZAPHAN. A leader of the tribe of Zebulun, appointed by Moses to help divide the land of Canaan after its occupation by the Israelites (Num. 34:25).

ELON. A minor judge of Israel, from the tribe of Zebulun (Judg. 12:11–12). See also *Judges of Israel.*

ELOTH. An Edomite seaport city on the Red Sea captured by David, then later turned into a station for trading ships by King Solomon (1 Kings 9:26).

ELPALET. See *Eliphalet.*

EL-PARAN. See *Paran.*

ELUL. The sixth month of the Hebrew year, roughly equivalent to our September (Neh. 6:15).

ELYMAS. See *Bar-jesus.*

EMBALM. To prepare a body for burial to protect it from decay. This art was practiced by the Egyptians. Joseph was embalmed for burial (Gen. 50:2–26).

EMBROIDERY. The art of fancy needlework (Exod. 28:39).

EMERALD. A precious stone of pure green color used in the high priest's breastplate (Exod. 28:18) and the foundation of New Jerusalem (Rev. 21:19). See also *Diamond.*

EMERODS (TUMORS, ULCERS). A strange disease, exact nature unknown, which struck the Philistines when they placed the stolen ark of the covenant next to their false god Dagon (Deut. 28:27). *Tumors:* NIV; *Ulcers:* NRSV.

EMIMS (EMITES, EMIM). A race of giants east of the Dead Sea (Gen. 14:5). They were closely related to another race of giants known as the *Anakims* (Deut. 2:10–11). *Emites:* NIV; *Emim:* NRSV. See also *Anakims*.

EMMANUEL/IMMANUEL. The name given to the Christ child, meaning "God with us" (Matt. 1:23). The birth of a Savior bearing this name was foretold by the prophet Isaiah (Isa. 7:14; *Immanuel*). As this symbolic name suggests, God Incarnate came in the person of Jesus Christ (1 John 4:2). See also *Jesus Christ; Messiah; Son of God; Son of Man*.

EMMAUS. A village near Jerusalem where Jesus revealed Himself to two of His followers shortly after His resurrection (Luke 24:13–33).

EMPTY. See *Void*.

ENCHANTER (MEDIUM, SOOTHSAYER). A person who used magical chants and rituals to drive away evil spirits (Jer. 27:9). *Medium:* NIV; *Soothsayer:* NRSV. See also *Medium; Soothsayer*.

EN-DOR. A city in the territory of Manasseh (Josh. 17:11). King Saul sought advice from a witch in this city (1 Sam. 28:1–10).

EN-GEDI. An oasis on the western shore of the Dead Sea where David hid from King Saul (1 Sam. 23:29–24:1).

ENGINES (MACHINES). A word which refers to the ingenuity of a machine or apparatus. The "engines" in 2 Chron. 26:15 (*Machines:* NIV, NRSV) were used to hurl objects from the walls of besieged cities upon the enemy below. See also *Fenced City; Siege; Wall*.

ENGRAVER. A craftsman who engraved metals or carved wood and stone (Exod. 35:35).

ENMITY. Deep animosity toward another (Gen. 3:15). This sin is characteristic of unredeemed persons (Rom. 1:29–30). See also *Hate*.

ENOCH.

1. The firstborn son of Cain and the name of a city built by Cain and named after Enoch (Gen. 4:17).

2. The father of Methuselah who was taken into God's presence without experiencing physical death (Gen. 5:18–24). *Henoch:* 1 Chron. 1:3.

ENOS (ENOSH). A son of Seth and a grandson of Adam (Gen. 5:6) who is listed in the N.T. ancestry of Jesus (Luke 3:38). *Enosh:* NIV.

ENSIGN (BANNER). A symbol on a long pole which identified an army or tribe (Num. 2:2). *Banner:* NIV. See also *Standard*.

ENVY. Resentment toward another person's good fortune (Prov. 27:4). Paul cautioned Christians against the dangers of this sin (Rom. 13:13). See also *Jealousy*.

EPAENETUS (EPENETUS). A fellow believer at Rome greeted and commended by Paul (Rom. 16:5). *Epenetus:* NIV.

EPAPHRAS. A leader of the Colossian church (Col. 1:7–8) whom Paul called his "fellow prisoner" in Rome (Philem. 23).

EPAPHRODITUS. A believer from Philippi who brought a gift to Paul while he was imprisoned in Rome (Phil. 4:18).

EPENETUS. See *Epaenetus*.

EPHAH. A dry measure equal to about one bushel (Exod. 16:36).

EPHESIANS, EPISTLE TO THE. A letter from the apostle Paul to the church at Ephesus on the theme of the risen Christ as Lord of creation and head of His body, the Church. The first three chapters of the epistle focus on the redemption made possible by the atoning death of Christ and His grace that is appropriated through faith—"not of works, lest any man should boast" (2:9). Chapters 4–6 call on the Ephesian Christians to model their lives after Christ's example and to remain faithful in turbulent times.

EPHESUS. The chief city of Asia Minor and a center of worship of the pagan goddess Diana where Paul spent two to three years, establishing a church (Acts 18:19–21; 19:1–10). Archaeologists have uncovered the remains of the temple of Diana and a Roman theater on this site. See also *Diana*.

EPHOD. A sleeveless linen garment, similar to a vest, worn by the high priest while officiating at the sacrificial altar (2 Sam. 6:14).

EPHPHATHA. An Aramaic word, meaning "be opened," spoken by Jesus to heal a deaf man (Mark 7:34).

Excavated ruins of an ancient market or shopping mall at Ephesus.
Courtesy Rayburn W. Ray

EPHRAIM.
1. The second son of Joseph who became the founder of one of the twelve tribes of Israel (Gen. 48:8–20). Joshua was a member of this tribe. See also *Tribes of Israel*.
2. A name often used symbolically for the nation of Israel (Hos. 11:12; 12:1).
3. A city in the wilderness to which Jesus and His disciples retreated (John 11:54).
4. A forest where the forces of Absalom were defeated by David's army (2 Sam. 18:6).

EPHRATAH, EPHRATH. See *Bethlehem*.

EPHRON. A Hittite who sold the cave of Machpelah to Abraham as a burial site (Gen. 23:8–20). See also *Machpelah*.

EPICUREANS. Followers of the Greek philosopher Epicurus, who believed the highest goal of life was the pursuit of pleasure, tempered by morality and cultural refinement. Epicureans were among the crowd addressed by Paul in the city of Athens (Acts 17:18). See also *Athens; Stoicks*.

EPISTLE. A type of correspondence best described as a "formal letter." Twenty-two of the twenty-seven N.T. books were written as epistles.

ERASTUS. A Christian believer, apparently from Ephesus, whom Paul sent into Macedonia (Acts 19:22).

ERECH. One of the cities of Nimrod's kingdom in the land of Shinar on the Euphrates River (Gen. 10:10).

ESAIAS. See *Isaiah.*

ESAR-HADDON. A son of Sennacherib who succeeded his father as king of Assyria (reigned about 681–669 B.C.; 2 Kings 19:37). Esar-haddon apparently was the king who resettled Samaria with foreigners after the fall of the Northern Kingdom (Ezra 4:1–2). See also *Samaritan.*

ESAU/EDOM. The oldest son of Isaac who sold his birthright to his twin brother Jacob for a bowl of stew (Gen. 25:26–34). Esau was the ancestor of the Edomites. *Edom:* Gen. 36:8. See also *Edom; Edomites.*

ESDRAELON. See *Jezreel,* No. 3.

ESEK. A well in the valley of Gerar which the servants of Isaac and Abimelech quarreled over (Gen. 26:20).

ESH-BAAL. See *Ish-bosheth.*

ESHCOL. A valley or brook near Hebron explored by the spies sent into Canaan (Deut. 1:24).

ESPOUSED. See *Betrothal.*

ESSENES. A religious group of N.T. times which practiced strict discipline, withdrawal from society, and communal living. Although they are not mentioned by name in the Bible, many scholars believe they are the group which preserved the Dead Sea Scrolls in caves at Qumran near the Dead Sea. See also *Dead Sea Scrolls; Qumran.*

ESTHER. A young Jewish woman who became queen under King Ahasuerus of Persia and used her influence to save her countrymen. Her Persian name was *Hadassah* (Esther 2:7). See also *Ahasuerus; Haman.*

ESTHER, BOOK OF. A historical book of the O.T. named for its major personality, Queen Esther of Persia, who saved her people, the Jews, from annihilation by the evil and scheming

Haman—a high official of the Persian king. The book shows clearly that God protects and sustains His people.

ETERNAL LIFE. Life without end, or everlasting existence. Eternal life was promised to believers at their conversion by Christ (John 11:25–26) and affirmed by the appearance of Moses and Elijah to Jesus and the three disciples (Matt. 17:2–9). Through His resurrection, Christ became the "firstfruits" of eternal life for all believers (1 Cor. 15:12–58). Life everlasting represents man's final victory over sin and death (Rev. 21:4).

ETHAN. See *Jeduthun*.

ETHANIM. The seventh month of the Hebrew year, corresponding roughly to our October (1 Kings 8:2).

ETHIOPIA. An ancient nation south of Egypt. Moses married an Ethiopian woman (Num. 12:1). Philip witnessed to a servant of the queen of Ethiopia (Acts 8:27).

EUBULUS. A Christian at Rome who sent greetings to Timothy (2 Tim. 4:21).

EUNICE. The mother of Timothy. She was commended for her great faith by the apostle Paul (2 Tim. 1:5). See also *Timothy*.

EUNUCH. Male household servant of a king. These servants were often emasculated to protect the king's harem (2 Kings 9:32). See also *Chamberlain*.

EUODIAS. A Christian woman at Philippi (Phil. 4:2).

EUPHRATES. A major river in the territory of the ancient Babylonians and Persians in Mesopotamia which is also mentioned as one of the rivers of the Garden of Eden (Gen. 2:14). See also *Tigris*.

EUROCLYDON (NORTHEASTER). A violent wind which struck Paul's ship bound for Rome (Acts 27:14). *Northeaster:* NIV, NRSV.

EUTYCHUS. A young man who went to sleep and fell from a window during Paul's sermon at Troas. He was restored by Paul (Acts 20:9–12).

EVANGELIST. A person who traveled from place to place, preaching the gospel. Philip was one of the zealous evangelists of the early churches (Acts 21:8).

EVE. The name given by Adam to his wife as the mother of the human race (Gen. 3:20). Fashioned from one of Adam's ribs, she was created to serve as his helpmate and companion (Gen. 2:18–23). Because of her sin and rebellion, Eve was to experience pain and sorrow, especially in connection with the birth of children (Gen. 3:16). See also *Adam; Fall of Man*.

EVERLASTING LIFE. See *Eternal Life*.

EVIL. A force which stands in opposition to God and righteousness. This evil force originates with Satan, the archenemy of good, truth, and honesty (Matt. 13:19). In the end-time, God will triumph over evil, and Satan will be thrown into a lake of fire (Rev. 20:10). See also *Iniquity; Sin; Wickedness*.

EVIL-MERODACH. A successor of Nebuchadnezzar II as king of Babylonia (reigned about 562–560 B.C.). He released King Jehoiachin of Judah from prison (2 Kings 25:27–30). See also *Babylonia*.

EVIL DESIRES. See *Concupiscence*.

EWE LAMB. A female sheep (Gen. 21:30).

EXHORTATION. A strong message of encouragement or warning (Heb. 12:5).

EXILE. See *Captivity*.

EXODUS, BOOK OF. A book of the O.T. which recounts the release of the Hebrew people from Egyptian enslavement and the early years of their history as a nation in the wilderness.

Important events covered in the book include: (1) God's call of Moses to lead the people out of slavery (chaps. 3–4); (2) the plagues upon the Egyptians (chaps. 7–12); (3) the release of the Israelites and the crossing of the Red Sea at God's hand (chap. 14); (4) God's miraculous provision for His people in the wilderness (16:1–17:7); (5) Moses' reception of the Ten Commandments and other parts of the law (chaps. 20–23); and (6) the building of the tabernacle for worship at God's command (chaps. 36–40). See also *Moses*.

EXPANSE. See *Firmament*.

EYE. An organ of sight (Matt. 6:22). The word is also used symbolically to portray sinful desire (1 John 2:16).

EZEKIAS. See *Hezekiah.*

EZEKIEL. A prophet of Judah who was carried into exile by the Babylonians and who prophesied faithfully to his countrymen for more than twenty years. He is the author of the book of Ezekiel in the O.T.

EZEKIEL, BOOK OF. A prophetic book of the O.T. addressed to the Jewish captives in Babylon about 585 B.C. and offering God's promise that His people would be restored to their homeland after their period of suffering and exile was over. This promise from God is exemplified by Ezekiel's vision of a valley of dry bones, "I. . .shall put my spirit in you, and ye shall live, and I shall place you in your own land" (37:13–14).

EZION-GEBER/EZION-GABER. A place on the coast of the Red Sea where the Israelites camped during their years of wandering in the wilderness (Num. 33:35). This settlement later became a town, serving as a harbor for Solomon's trading ships (2 Chron. 8:17). *Ezion-gaber:* Deut. 2:8.

EZRA. A scribe and priest who led an important reform movement among the Jewish people after the Babylonian Exile. He is the author of the book of Ezra. See also *Nehemiah.*

EZRA, BOOK OF. A historical book of the O.T. which describes events in Jerusalem after the Jewish captives began returning to their homeland about 500 B.C. following their period of exile in Babylonia and Persia. After the rebuilding of the temple (6:14–15), the people under Ezra's leadership committed themselves to God's law, put away foreign wives (Ezra 10:1–17), and confessed their sins and renewed the covenant (Neh. 9–10).

-F-

FABLE. A story in which inanimate things are personalized, as in Jotham's narrative of the trees and the bramble (Judg. 9:1–15).

FACE. The front part of the head. This word is often used symbolically of God's presence (Deut. 31:18).

FAIR HAVENS. A harbor on the southern side of the island of Crete where Paul stopped during his voyage to Rome (Acts 27:8).

FAITH. Belief and confidence in the testimony of another, particularly God's promise of salvation and eternal life for all who place their trust in Jesus Christ (John 5:24). A gift of God, faith is essential to salvation (Eph. 2:8). The word also refers to the teachings of Scripture, or the "faith which was once delivered unto the saints" (Jude 3). See also *Trust*.

FALL OF MAN. A phrase which refers to Adam and Eve's state of sorrow and misery which followed their sin and rebellion against God (Gen. 2–3). Their original sin has afflicted the human race ever since (Rom. 3:23)—a condition cured only by the atoning death of Christ (Rom. 5:6). See also *Adam; Eve; Man; Sin*.

FALLOW DEER. A distinct species of deer, common in Mesopotamia in Bible times, and a clean animal to the Hebrews (Deut. 14:4–5). See also *Deer*.

FALLOW GROUND (UNPLOWED GROUND). A field plowed and left idle for a short time before planting again (Jer. 4:3). *Unplowed ground:* NIV.

FALSE PROPHETS. Persons who deliver a false or misleading message under the pretense that it comes from God. Believers are warned to beware of false prophets (Matt. 24:11, 24; 2 Pet. 2:1).

FALSE WEIGHTS. Deceptive measurements used in weighing merchandise—a practice condemned by the Lord (Deut. 25:13–14).

FALSE WITNESS (FALSE TESTIMONY). A person who gives false testimony or tells lies about others in an attempt to undermine their credibility or slander their character. Such testimony is specifically prohibited by the Ten Commandments (Exod. 20:16). *False testimony:* NIV.

FAMILIAR SPIRIT. The spirit of a dead person which a sorcerer "calls up" in order to communicate with that person (Deut. 18:11). The spirit of Samuel was called up by a witch at En-dor (1 Sam. 28:3–20). Such sorcery was considered an abomination by God. See also *Sorcery; Witchcraft*.

FAMILY. A group of persons related to one another by blood kinship and the ties of marriage. The N.T. implies that all

Christians are related to one another in a spiritual sense, since we are all members of the "household of faith" (Gal. 6:10). See also *Kindred.*

FAMILY RECORDS. See *Register.*

FAMINE. A time, often an extended period, when food or water is in short supply because of lack of rain and the failure of crops (Gen. 12:10). See also *Drought.*

FAN (FORK). A wooden pitchfork for winnowing grain (Isa. 30:24). The grain was thrown into the wind to separate it from the straw (Matt. 3:12). The fan is also spoken of as a symbol of God's judgment (Jer. 15:7). *Fork:* NIV, NRSV. See also *Winnowing.*

FARMER. See *Husbandman.*

FARTHING (PENNY). A Roman coin of small value (Matt. 10:29). *Penny:* NIV, NRSV. See also *Penny.*

FASTING. The practice of giving up eating and drinking for a specified time, generally as part of a religious ritual in times of peril. Elijah and Jesus each fasted for forty days (1 Kings 19:8; Matt. 4:2).

FAT CALF. See *Fatling.*

FATHER. The male head of a household who was the undisputed authority in the family. This word was also used by Jesus as a title for God (Matt. 11:25).

FATHOM. A nautical measure, equal to about seven feet. The term is mentioned in the account of Paul's shipwreck (Acts 27:28).

FATLING (FAT CALF). A young animal fattened for slaughter (Matt. 22:4). *Fat calf:* NRSV. See also *Calf.*

FEAR. An emotion aroused by danger or risk to one's safety (1 Sam. 21:10). The word is also used for respect or reverence toward God (Deut. 10:20).

FEAST. A festival, or a major religious holiday which marked some great event in Jewish history. The Jews celebrated several major festivals.

FEAST OF BOOTHS. See *Tabernacles, Feast of.*

FEAST OF HARVEST. See *Pentecost.*

FEAST OF INGATHERING. See *Tabernacles, Feast of.*

FEAST OF LIGHTS. See *Dedication, Feast of.*

FEAST OF UNLEAVENED BREAD. See *Passover and Feast of Unleavened Bread.*

FEAST OF WEEKS. See *Pentecost.*

FEET. The removal of sandals and the washing of one's feet upon entering a house or a holy place was a token of respect, similar to our custom of taking off the hat (Exod. 3:5).

FELIX. The governor of Judea who heard Paul's defense at Caesarea (Acts 23:24; 24:10–27).

FELLOWSHIP. A mutual sharing or friendly association, particularly that between believers who have a common faith in Jesus Christ (1 Cor. 1:9).

FENCED CITY (FORTIFIED CITY). A city with a strong defensive wall (2 Sam. 20:6). *Fortified city:* NIV, NRSV. The wall was erected to provide protection against enemies in times of war. See also *City; Siege; Wall.*

FERRET (GECKO). A burrowing animal considered unclean by the Hebrews (Lev. 11:30). *Gecko:* NIV, NRSV.

FESTUS. Successor of Felix as Roman governor of Judea. Paul made his defense before Festus (Acts 24:27).

FETTERS (SHACKLES). Metal bands for binding the wrists or ankles of prisoners (2 Kings 25:7). *Shackles:* NIV. See also *Stocks.*

FEVER. See *Burning Ague.*

FIELD OF BLOOD. See *Aceldama.*

FIERY SERPENTS (VENOMOUS SNAKES, POISONOUS SERPENTS). Snakes which attacked the Israelites in the wilderness. Moses erected a brass serpent on a pole as an antidote for those who were bitten (Num. 21:6–9). *Venomous snakes:* NIV; *Poisonous serpents:* NRSV. See also *Brass Serpent.*

FIG. The pear-shaped fruit of the fig tree. The spies sent into Canaan brought back figs to show the bounty of the land (Deut. 8:8). Figs were pressed into cakes and also preserved by drying (1 Sam. 25:18). The fig tree was considered a symbol of prosperity (1 Kings 4:25).

FIGHTING MEN. See *Mighty Men.*

FILTH. See *Offscouring*.

FILTHY LUCRE. A phrase for money (1 Tim. 3:3), which is condemned as an unworthy motive for ministry (1 Pet. 5:2). See also *Money*.

FINER (SILVERSMITH, SMITH). A craftsman who refined or shaped precious metals (Prov. 25:4). *Silversmith:* NIV; *Smith:* NRSV. See also *Smith*.

FINGER.

1. A digit of the human hand. The word is also used symbolically of God's power (Exod. 8:19).

2. A measure of length, equal to about three-fourths of an inch (Jer. 52:21).

FINING POT (CRUCIBLE). A vessel for melting and purifying metal (Prov. 17:3). *Crucible:* NIV, NRSV.

FIR (PINE, CYPRESS). An evergreen tree which grew on Mount Lebanon. Its lumber was used in the construction of Solomon's temple in Jerusalem (1 Kings 6:15, 34). *Pine:* NIV; *Cypress:* NRSV.

FIRE. Burning material used for cooking and in religious ceremonies. Fire is often associated with the presence and power of God (Exod. 3:2) as well as the final punishment of the wicked (Matt. 13:49–50). See also *Pillar of Fire and Cloud*.

FIREPAN. A vessel in which incense was burned during worship ceremonies in the tabernacle (Exod. 27:3). See also *Censer*.

FIRKIN. A liquid measure equal to about five or six gallons (John 2:16).

FIRMAMENT (EXPANSE, DOME). A word for the heavens, or the limitless sky above the earth (Gen. 1:6–8). *Expanse:* NIV; *Dome:* NRSV.

FIRST DAY OF THE WEEK. Sunday, or the day of Christ's resurrection, which was adopted as the day of worship by the early church (Acts 20:7).

FIRST INSTALLMENT. See *Earnest*.

FIRSTBORN. First child born into a family (Gen. 49:3). The firstborn son received a double portion of his father's property as his birthright and assumed leadership of the family. See also *Birthright; Inheritance*.

FIRSTFRUITS. The first or best of crops and livestock.

According to Mosaic Law, these were to be presented as sacrifices and offerings to the Lord (Exod. 23:19).

FISH GATE. A gate in the wall of Jerusalem, probably so named because fish from the Mediterranean Sea were brought into the city through this gate (Neh. 3:3).

FISHER, FISHERMAN. One who makes his living by fishing. Several of Jesus' disciples were fishermen, and He promised to make them "fishers of men" (Matt. 4:19).

FITCH (SPELT). A plant which produces grain similar to oats or rye (Ezek. 4:9). *Spelt:* NIV, NRSV. See also *Rie*.

FLAG (RUSH). A coarse grass which grows in marshes or wetlands (Isa. 19:6). *Rush:* NIV, NRSV.

FLAGON.

1. A cake of dried grapes or raisins served as a delicacy or dessert (Song of Sol. 2:5).

2. A flask or leather bottle for holding liquids (Isa. 22:24). See also *Spoon; Vial*.

FLASK. See *Vial*.

FLAX. A plant grown in Egypt and Palestine for its fiber, which was woven into linen cloth (Exod. 9:31). See also *Linen*.

FLEA. A tiny insect which sucks the blood of animals or humans. David used this word as a symbol of insignificance (1 Sam. 24:14).

FLEECE. Wool which grows on a sheep. Gideon used a fleece to test God's call (Judg. 6:36–40). See also *Sheep; Wool*.

FLESH. A word for the human body in contrast to the spirit (Matt. 26:41). The word is also used for unredeemed human nature and carnal appetites or desires which can lead to sin (Gal. 5:16–17). See also *Carnal*.

FLESHHOOK (MEAT FORKS). Large pronged fork used to handle meat for sacrificial purposes (2 Chron. 4:16). *Meat forks:* NIV.

FLINT. A very hard stone, perhaps a variety of quartz (Deut. 8:15). The word is also used symbolically to denote firmness (Ezek. 3:9).

FLOCK. A group of sheep or birds (Gen. 4:4). The word is also used to designate a Christian congregation under a pastor's leadership (1 Pet. 5:2).

FLOGGING. See *Scourging*.

FLOOD, THE. The covering of the earth by water in Noah's time; the instrument of God's judgment against a wicked world. This great deluge came after forty days of continuous rainfall, but Noah and his family and the animals in the ark were saved by the hand of God (Gen. 6–8). See also *Noah; Ark, Noah's*.

FLOUR. Wheat or barley ground into a fine powder and used for baking bread. Flour was often offered as a sin offering (Lev. 5:11–13). See also *Bread; Wheat*.

FLUTE (PIPE). A musical instrument, played by blowing, similar to the modern flute (Dan. 3:5–15). *Pipe:* NRSV. Flute players were hired for funerals during N.T. times (Matt. 9:23–24). See also *Organ; Pipe*.

FLUX (DYSENTERY). KJV word for dysentery, a common disease in the Mediterranean world. Paul healed Publius of this ailment (Acts 28:8). *Dysentery:* NIV, NRSV.

FOAL. A colt, or young donkey. Jesus rode a colt on His triumphant entry into Jerusalem (Matt. 21:5), an event foretold in the O.T. (Zech. 9:9). See also *Ass*.

FODDER. See *Provender*.

FOOD. Plants and animals eaten for nourishment. Specific foods mentioned in the Bible include lentils (Gen. 25:34), honey, nuts, and spices (Gen. 43:11). The meats of certain animals were considered unclean and unfit for eating (Lev. 11; Deut. 14).

FOOL. An absurd person; one who reasons wrongly (Prov. 29:11).

FOOLISH. Actions which show a lack of wisdom or faulty and shallow reasoning (Prov. 26:11). Jesus described the five virgins who were unprepared for the wedding feast as foolish (Matt. 25:1–13).

FOOT. See *Feet*.

FOOTMAN. A member of the infantry or walking unit of an army (Jer. 12:5); a swift runner who served as a messenger for a king (1 Sam. 22:17). See also *Post*.

FOOTSTOOL. A low stool upon which the feet are rested. The word is also used symbolically to describe the fate of God's enemies (Ps. 110:1).

FOOT-WASHING. An expression of hospitality bestowed upon guests in Bible times. Foot-washing was generally performed by lowly domestic servants, but Jesus washed His disciples' feet to teach them a lesson in humble ministry (John 13:5–15).

FORBEARANCE (TOLERANCE). Restraint and tolerance. God, in His forbearance or patience, gives people opportunity for repentance (Rom. 2:4). *Tolerance:* NIV. See also *Longsuffering; Patience.*

FORD. A crossing through shallow water across a brook or river (Gen. 32:22).

FOREHEAD. The part of the human face above the eyes. God's people were instructed to learn the law so well that it would be as if it were written on their foreheads (Deut. 6:8). See also *Frontlet.*

FOREIGNER (TEMPORARY RESIDENT). A word for an outsider or stranger—a person who was not of the same ethnic stock as the Hebrews and who had no loyalty to Israel's God (Exod. 12:45). *Temporary resident:* NIV. See also *Alien; Sojourner.*

FOREKNOWLEDGE. God's knowledge of events before they happen and His ability to influence the future by actually causing such events (Isa. 41:4). See also *Election, Divine; Predestination.*

FORERUNNER. One who goes before and makes preparations for others to follow (Heb. 6:20). John the Baptist was a forerunner of Christ.

FORESAIL. See *Mainsail.*

FORESKIN. The fold of skin which covers the male sex organ. This foreskin is removed in the rite of circumcision (Gen. 17:11). See also *Circumcision.*

FORGIVENESS. To pardon or overlook the wrongful acts of another person; God's free pardon of the sin and rebellion of man. Our sin separates us from God, but He forgives us and reestablishes the broken relationship when we repent and turn to Him in faith (Acts 10:43). Just as God forgives believers, He expects us to practice forgiveness in our relationships with others (Matt. 5:43–48). See also *Pardon.*

FORK. See *Fan.*

FORMER RAIN (AUTUMN RAIN, EARLY RAIN). The first rain of the growing season, essential for the germination of seed and the growth of young plants (Joel 2:23). *Autumn rain:* NIV; *Early rain:* NRSV.

FORNICATION (SEXUAL IMMORALITY). Sexual relations between two persons who are not married to one another; any form of sexual immorality or unchastity. Paul cited fornication as a sin which believers should scrupulously avoid (1 Cor. 6:18). *Sexual immorality:* NIV. See also *Adultery; Chastity.*

FORT. A high wall or fortification built to provide protection against one's enemies in times of war (Isa. 25:12). See also *Fenced City; Wall.*

FORTIFIED CITY. See *Fenced City.*

FORTRESS. See *Misgab.*

FORTUNATUS. A Christian from the city of Corinth who visited Paul (1 Cor. 16:17).

FORUM OF APPIUS. See *Appii Forum.*

FOUNDATION. The strong base on which a building is erected. The apostle Paul described Christ as the sure foundation for believers (1 Cor. 3:11). See also *Corner Stone.*

FOUNTAIN. A source of fresh, flowing water; a spring (Deut. 8:7). The word is also used symbolically of God's blessings upon His people (Jer. 2:13).

FOUNTAIN GATE. A gate in the wall of Jerusalem, perhaps named for the fountain or pool of Siloam (Neh. 12:37).

FOWLER. A person who captures birds by nets, snares, or decoys (Hos. 9:8). The word is also used symbolically of temptations (Ps. 91:3). See also *Hunter.*

FOX. An animal of the dog family known for its cunning (Judg. 15:4). See also *Jackal.*

FRAGRANT CANE. See *Calamus.*

FRANKINCENSE (INCENSE). The yellowish gum of a tree, known for its pungent odor when burned as incense during sacrificial ceremonies (Neh. 13:9). Frankincense was one of the gifts presented to the infant Jesus by the Wise Men (Matt. 2:11). *Incense:* NIV. See also *Incense.*

FREEDMEN. See *Libertines.*

FREEWILL OFFERING. An offering given freely and willingly (Amos 4:5), in contrast to one made to atone for some misdeed (Num. 15:3).

FRIEND. An intimate acquaintance who is loved and esteemed. Abraham was called "the Friend of God" (Jas. 2:23).

FRINGE (TASSEL). An ornament worn on the edges of one's robe as a profession of piety and commitment to God (Deut. 22:12). *Tassel:* NIV, NRSV. See also *Hem.*

FROG. An amphibious animal sent by the Lord as the second plague upon Egypt (Exod. 8:2–14).

FRONTLET. A small leather case with passages of Scripture, worn upon the forehead as a literal obedience of Deut. 6:6–9. See also *Forehead; Phylactery.*

FRUITFULNESS. Productive; reproducing abundantly. Paul declared that believers should be fruitful in righteousness and goodness toward others (Col. 1:10).

FULLER (LAUNDERER). A laborer who treated or dyed clothes and also did ordinary laundry work (Mal. 3:2). *Launderer:* NIV.

FULLER'S FIELD (WASHERMAN'S FIELD). A place near the wall of Jerusalem where fullers worked and perhaps where they spread their laundry to dry (2 Kings 18:17). *Washerman's Field:* NIV.

FUNERAL. A ceremony honoring the dead before burial. These ceremonies were sometimes accompanied by sad music and the loud wailing of friends and professional mourners (Eccles. 12:5; Matt. 9:23). See also *Burial; Minstrel.*

FURLONG. A Greek measure of length, equal to about 650 feet or one-eighth of a mile (Luke 24:13).

FURNACE (SMOKING FIREPOT). An enclosed oven for baking (Gen. 15:17), (*smoking firepot:* NIV, NRSV), smelting (Gen. 19:28), or drying and firing bricks (Dan. 3:15–17). See also *Brick-kiln.*

-G-

GAASH, MOUNT. A mountain in the hill country of Ephraim where Joshua was buried (Josh. 24:30).

GABBATHA. See *Pavement, The.*

GABRIEL. An archangel who appeared to Daniel (Dan. 8:16), Zacharias (Luke 1:18–19), and the Virgin Mary (Luke 1:26–38). See also *Archangel.*

GAD. The seventh son of Jacob, born of Zilpah (Gen. 30:10–11), and ancestor of one of the twelve tribes of Israel. Known as a fierce, warlike people, the Gadites settled east of the Jordan River (Josh. 13:24–25). See also *Tribes of Israel.*

GADARA. A Greek city about six miles southeast of the Sea of Galilee. In N.T. times, Gadara was the capital city of the Roman province of Perea.

GADARENES/GERGESENES. People from the area of Gadara in Perea. Jesus healed a wild, demon-possessed man in this area (Mark 5:1–20). *Gergesenes:* Matt. 8:28.

GADDI. One of the twelve spies who scouted the land of Canaan, representing the tribe of Manasseh (Num. 13:11). See also *Spies.*

GADDIEL. One of the twelve spies who scouted the land of Canaan, representing the tribe of Zebulun (Num. 13:10). See also *Spies.*

GAIN. See *Lucre.*

GAIUS.

1. A Macedonian and companion of Paul (Acts 19:29).
2. A man of Derbe and companion of Paul (Acts 20:4).
3. A Corinthian baptized under Paul's ministry (1 Cor. 1:14).
4. The person to whom John addressed his third letter (3 John 1, 5).

GALATIA. A territory of central Asia Minor which contained several cities visited by Paul during the first missionary journey—Antioch of Pisidia, Derbe, Iconium, and Lystra (Acts 13–14)—all located in southern Galatia. Paul's letter to the Galatians (Gal. 1:1–2) was apparently addressed to churches in and around these cities.

GALATIANS, EPISTLE TO THE. A short epistle of the apostle Paul to the churches at Galatia on the themes of Christian liberty and justification by faith alone. The content of the epistle includes: (1) a defense of Paul's apostleship and the gospel (chaps. 1–2); (2) his argument that salvation comes by God's grace through faith, not through obeying the law (chaps. 3–4); and (3) the practical dimension of one's faith —living in obedience to God and in harmony with others (chaps. 5–6).

GALBANUM. A gum from a plant used to produce sacred incense, which was burned at the altar (Exod. 30:34).

GALE. See *Whirlwind.*

GALILEAN. A native of the province of Galilee. All of Jesus' disciples except Judas were Galileans. Peter was recognized as a Galilean because of his distinct accent (Mark 14:70).

GALILEE, (GALILEE OF THE GENTILES). A Roman province in northern Palestine during N.T. times and the area where Jesus spent most of His earthly ministry (Mark 3:7). Because of its far-north location, Galilee had a mixed population of Jews and Gentiles. The prophet Isaiah referred to it as "Galilee of the nations" (Isa. 9:1). *Galilee of the Gentiles:* NIV.

GALILEE, SEA OF/SEA OF CHINNEROTH/LAKE OF GENNESARET/SEA OF TIBERIAS. A freshwater lake about fourteen miles long and seven miles wide which took its name from the surrounding Roman province. Fed by the Jordan River, it provided the livelihood for many commercial fishermen, including several disciples of Jesus: James, John, Peter, and Andrew (Mark 1:16–20). Jesus calmed the waters of this lake after He and His disciples were caught in a boat in a sudden storm (Mark 4:35–41). *Sea of Chinneroth:* Josh. 12:3; *Lake of Gennesaret:* Luke 5:1; *Sea of Tiberias:* John 21:1.

GALL. A bitter, poisonous herb used to make a pain-killing substance. While on the cross, Jesus was offered a drink containing gall (Matt. 27:34).

GALLIO. The Roman provincial ruler of Achaia who refused to get involved in the dispute between Paul and the

The Church of the Beatitudes near the site where Jesus delivered His Sermon on the Mount in Galilee.
Courtesy Israel Ministry of Tourism

Jewish leaders in Corinth (Acts 18:12–17).

GALLOWS. A structure used for executing people by hanging. The wicked Haman was hanged on the gallows which he had prepared for Mordecai (Esther 5:14; 7:10). See also *Haman.*

GAMALIEL. A teacher of the law under whom Paul studied (Acts 22:3). As a member of the Jewish Sanhedrin, he advised against persecution of the apostles and the early church (Acts 5:33–39). See also *Council.*

GAME. See *Venison.*

GANGRENE. See *Canker.*

GARDEN. A fenced plot generally outside the walls of a city where fruit trees or vegetables were grown. The most famous garden in the Bible is the Garden of Eden (Gen. 2:8–10). See also *Orchard.*

GARLAND (WREATH). A ceremonial wreath woven from flowers or leaves and worn on the head (Acts 14:13). *Wreath:* NIV.

GARLICK (GARLIC). A vegetable or herb similar to the onion which was used to flavor food. The Hebrews longed for this vegetable after leaving Egypt (Num. 11:5). *Garlic:* NIV, NRSV.

GARRISON. A company of soldiers stationed in a fortified military post (1 Sam. 13:3–4)

GASHMU. An influential Samaritan leader who opposed the Jewish people while they were rebuilding Jerusalem's walls under Nehemiah after the Exile (Neh. 6:6).

GATE. An entrance, door, or opening, particularly the strong gate in the walls of a fortified city (Judg. 16:3). The word is also used symbolically of salvation (Matt. 7:13) and heaven (Rev. 21:25). See also *Door*.

GATE KEEPER. A person who guarded the gate in a walled city (1 Chron. 9:19). See also *Doorkeeper; Porter*.

GATH. Royal Philistine city captured by David (1 Chron. 18:1) and home of the giant Goliath. (1 Sam. 17:4). See also *Philistines*.

GATH-HEPHER/GITTAH-HEPHER. A city in the territory of Zebulun and home of the prophet Jonah (2 Kings 14:25). *Gittah-hepher:* Josh. 19:13.

GAZA/AZZAH. A Philistine city where Samson was killed when he destroyed the temple of their pagan god Dagon (Judg. 16:21–30). *Azzah:* Jer. 25:20. See also *Philistines*.

GAZELLE. See *Roe*.

GAZER. See *Gezer*.

GEBAL. An ancient seaport town of the Phoenicians near the city of Tyre (Ezek. 27:9).

GECKO. See *Ferret*.

GEDALIAH. A friend of the prophet Jeremiah (Jer. 39:14; 40:5–6). After the fall of Jerusalem to the Babylonians in 587 B.C., Gedaliah was made supervisor of the vinedressers left in the land (2 Kings 25:22–25).

GEDEON. See *Gideon*.

GEHAZI. A servant of the prophet Elisha who was struck with leprosy because of his dishonesty and greed (2 Kings 5).

GEHENNA. See *Hell; Hinnom, Valley of*.

Ancient olive trees in the Garden of Gethsemane, the site where Jesus was delivered to His enemies by Judas.

Courtesy Israel Ministry of Tourism

GENEALOGY. A record of the descendants of a person or family (1 Chron. 5:1–5). These records were important to the Jewish people because they documented inheritance rights and the right of succession as a clan leader, king, or high priest. See also *Register*.

GENERAL EPISTLES. The epistles of Hebrews; James; 1 and 2 Peter; 1, 2, and 3 John; and Jude—so named because they are addressed to broad, general problems rather than to local, specific issues. They are also referred to as *Catholic Epistles*.

GENERATION. A single step or stage in the line of descent from one's ancestors (Gen. 5:1; Matt. 24:34). The word is used in a more general sense to designate a period or age (Gen. 7:1).

GENESIS, BOOK OF. The first book of the O.T., often referred to as "the book of beginnings" because of its accounts of the world's creation and the early history of the Hebrew people.

Major events and subjects covered in the book include:

1. God's creation of the physical world and Adam and Eve's life in the Garden of Eden; Adam and Eve sinned and introduced sin to mankind (chaps. 1–3);

2. Adam's descendants and the great flood (chaps. 4–9);

3. the tower of Babel and the scattering of mankind (chap. 11); and

4. the life stories of the Hebrew patriarchs: Abraham and Isaac (chaps. 12–27), Jacob (chaps. 25–35), and Joseph (chaps. 37–50).

GENNESARET. See *Galilee, Sea of*.

GENTILE. A member of any ethnic group other than the Jewish race. The Jews looked down upon other races as barbarous and unclean (Jer. 9:26). Jesus, however, abolished this distinction through His atoning death and His acceptance of all people through repentance and faith (Gal. 3:28). See also *Heathen*.

GERAH. A coin of small value, equal to one-twentieth of a shekel (Lev. 27:25).

GERAR. An ancient city of southern Canaan, or Philistia, where Abraham was reprimanded by Abimelech for lying about his wife Sarah's identity (Gen. 20:1–18).

GERGESENES. See *Gadarenes*.

GERIZIM, MOUNT. A mountain in central Canaan where Joshua pronounced God's blessings for keeping God's laws when the Hebrew people entered the land (Deut. 11:29; 27:4–26). In later years, this mountain was considered a sacred worship place by the Samaritans (John 4:20–23). See also *Samaritan*.

GESHEM. An Arabian who opposed the rebuilding of Jerusalem's walls under Nehemiah after the Exile (Neh. 2:19; 6:2).

GETHSEMANE. A garden near the Mount of Olives outside Jerusalem where Jesus prayed in great agony of soul on the night before He was betrayed and arrested (Mark 14:32–46). The garden was probably a grove of olive trees, since Gethsemane means "oil press."

GEUEL. One of the twelve spies who scouted the land of Canaan, representing the tribe of Gad (Num. 13:15). See also *Spies*.

GEZER/GAZER. A Canaanite city captured by Joshua (Josh. 10:33) and assigned to the Levites (Josh. 21:21). In later years, Solomon turned Gezer into an important military center (1 Kings 9:15–19). *Gazer:* 2 Sam. 5:25; 1 Chron. 14:16.

GHOST (SPIRIT). An old English word for spirit (Matt. 27:50; 28:19). *Spirit:* NIV, NRSV.

GIANTS. People of unusually large size, such as the Philistine Goliath (2 Sam. 21:22). Races of giants mentioned in the Bible are the *Anakims* (Deut. 2:11), *Emims* (Deut. 2:10), *Rephaims* (Gen. 14:5), and *Zamzummins* (Deut. 2:20).

GIBBETHON. A Canaanite town captured by Joshua and assigned to the Levites (Josh. 21:23).

GIBEAH/GIBEATH. The native city of King Saul and capital of his kingdom (1 Sam. 14:16; 15:34). This was apparently the same city destroyed by the Israelites during the period of the judges (Judg. 20:20–40). *Gibeath:* Josh. 18:28.

GIBEON. A royal Canaanite city whose inhabitants surrendered to Joshua to avoid the fate of Jericho and Ai (Josh. 9:6–15).

GIBEONITES. Inhabitants of Gibeon who were made slaves following their surrender to Joshua (Josh. 9:21).

GIDEON/GEDEON/JERUBBAAL. The famous judge of Israel who delivered the Israelites from oppression by defeating the mighty Midianite army with a force of only 300 warriors. Gideon came from an obscure family of the tribe of Manasseh, but he trusted God at every step of his military campaign and thus was successful (see Judg. 6–8). He is listed in the N.T. as one of the heroes of the faith (Heb. 11:32; *Gedeon*). *Jerubbaal:* Judg. 6:25–32. See also *Midianites*.

GIER EAGLE (OSPREY, CARRION VULTURE). Bird of prey considered unclean by the Hebrews (Lev. 11:18). *Osprey:* NIV; *Carrion vulture:* NRSV. This is probably the same bird as the Egyptian vulture.

GIFTS, SPIRITUAL. See *Spiritual Gifts*.

GIHON.

1. One of the four rivers of the Garden of Eden, associated with Ethiopia (Gen. 2:13). Some scholars believe this was either the Nile or the Ganges.

2. A place near Jerusalem

where Solomon was anointed and proclaimed king (1 Kings 1:33).

GILBOA, MOUNT. A mountain range in the territory of Issachar where King Saul died after his defeat by the Philistines (1 Chron. 10:1–8).

GILEAD.

1. A fertile, flat tableland east of the Jordan River (Judg. 20:1), known in N.T. times as the region of Perea.
2. A mountain or hill overlooking the plain of Jezreel where Gideon divided his army for battle against the Midianites (Judg. 7:1–7).

GILEAD, BALM OF. See *Balm of Gilead.*

GILGAL. A site between the Jordan River and the city of Jericho where the Hebrew people erected memorial stones to commemorate God's faithfulness in leading them into the Promised Land (Josh. 4:19–20). Gilgal apparently served as Joshua's headquarters in his campaign against the Canaanites (Josh. 6:11–14; 10:1–43). In later years, Saul was crowned as Israel's first king at Gilgal (1 Sam. 11:15).

GIMEL. The third letter of the Hebrew alphabet, used as a heading over Ps. 119:17–24.

GIRDLE (BELT). A belt or sash made of cloth or leather and worn by men and women to hold their loose outer garments (2 Kings 1:8). *Belt:* NIV, NRSV.

GIRGASITES/ GIRGASHITES. Members of an ancient tribe, descendants of Canaan (Gen. 10:15–16), which inhabited part of the land of Canaan before the arrival of the Hebrew people. *Girgashites:* Deut. 7:1.

GITTAH-HEPHER. See *Gath-hepher.*

GITTITES. Inhabitants of the Philistine city of Gath (Josh. 13:3).

GITTITH. A musical instrument or tune associated with the city of Gath. The word is used in the titles of Pss. 8, 81, and 84.

GLASS. A clear liquid mineral used to make utensils, ornaments, and vases. The "sea of glass" in John's vision probably represented God's purity or holiness (Rev. 4:6).

GLEANING. The gathering of grain left behind by the reapers—a courtesy offered to the needy (Lev. 19:9–10). Ruth gleaned in the fields of Boaz (Ruth 2:2–23).

GLEDE (RED KITE). Bird of prey, probably the kite or hawk (Deut. 14:13). *Red kite:* NIV.

GLORY. Splendor, honor, or perfection. The "glory of the Lord" signifies the supreme perfection of His nature (Exod. 16:7). Jesus also partook of the glory of His Father (John 2:11). He shares His divine glory with all believers (John 17:5–6). See also *Transfiguration of Jesus*.

GLUTTONY. The act of eating or drinking to excess—a sin against which believers are warned (Prov. 23:1–8, 21).

GNASH. See *Tooth*.

GNAT. A small, stinging insect considered a great pest in the marshlands of Egypt and Palestine (Matt. 23:24). See also *Lice*.

GNOSTICISM. A heretical movement of N.T. times which taught that salvation came through superior knowledge. While gnosticism is not mentioned by name in the N.T., it was probably what Paul condemned when he declared that true knowledge comes from God and does not consist of idle speculation (Col. 2:8–23).

GOAD. A sharp, pointed stick or rod used in guiding oxen. Shamgar used a goad as a weapon against the Philistines (Judg. 3:31). See also *Ox*.

GOAT. A domesticated animal used for food (Gen. 27:9), clothing (Num. 31:20), and in religious sacrifices (Exod. 12:5). See also *Kid*.

GOAT DEMON. See *Satyr*.

GOB. A place on the plain of Gezer where the Hebrews fought the Philistines (2 Sam. 21:18–19).

GOD. The Creator and ruler of the universe (Isa. 40:28–31); the first person of the triune Godhead: God the Father, God the Son, God the Spirit (Matt. 28:19; 2 Cor. 13:14) who reveals Himself through the natural world, the Bible, and His Son Jesus Christ (Col. 1:19). God is infinite in being and character: omnipresent (Jer. 23:23–24), all-powerful (Rev. 19:6), perfect in holiness (Lev. 11:44), and infinite in mercy (Ps. 136), wisdom (Col. 2:2–3), and truth (Titus 1:2).

God is active in salvation history. He covenanted with Abraham to "make of thee a great nation" and to make the Hebrew people a blessing to the rest of the world (Gen. 12:1–4). He called Moses to deliver the Israelites from Egyptian bondage (Exod. 3:9–10). He promised a Savior to rule Israel (Isa. 9:6–7). This promise was fulfilled in Jesus Christ (Matt. 1:18–21), God's love gift of salvation to the world (John 3:16, 36).

God's Spirit convicts unbelievers of sin and coming judgment (John 16:8–11). Man can know God through faith in Christ (John 14:1, 6) and obedience to the Father's will (Matt. 7:21; Mark 3:35). God welcomes the worship and fellowship of His adopted children (John 4:23–24; Rom. 8:15–17). See also *I Am; Jehovah; Yahweh.*

GODDESS. A female deity or idol. Goddesses were prominent in the pagan cultures of Mesopotamia, Egypt, Canaan, Greece, and Rome. For example, Ashtaroth was the wife of Baal in Canaanite mythology (1 Kings 11:33; Ashtoreth: plural form). Diana (or Artemis) was worshiped in the great temple at Ephesus (Acts 19:24–28). See also *Ashtaroth; Diana.*

GODLINESS. Holy living and righteous behavior which issues from devotion to God. Godliness also leads to love for others (1 Thess. 4:7–9). See also *Righteousness.*

GOG, PRINCE OF MAGOG. The leader of a tribal people, enemies of the Israelites, who was condemned by the prophet Ezekiel (Ezek. 38:2; 39:1). In the book of Revelation, Gog and Magog represent the forces of evil which oppose God and His people (Rev. 20:8).

GOLAN. A city in the territory of Manasseh designated as one of the six cities of refuge (Deut. 4:43). See also *Cities of Refuge.*

GOLD. A precious mineral used to make coins, jewelry, and utensils. Used extensively in Solomon's temple (1 Kings 7:48–50), gold also symbolized the splendor of the heavenly city, or New Jerusalem (Rev. 21:18).

GOLD FILIGREE SETTINGS. See *Ouches.*

GOLGOTHA. See *Calvary.*

GOLIATH. A Philistine giant from the city of Gath who defied the entire army of King Saul. He was killed by David the shepherd boy with a single stone from his sling (1 Sam. 17:4–54).

GOMER. The unfaithful wife of the prophet Hosea. After her unfaithfulness, Gomer left Hosea and was sold into slavery, but the prophet restored her as his wife at God's command. His forgiveness of Gomer represented God's unconditional love for His wayward people (Hos. 1; 3). See also *Hosea*.

GOMORRAH/GOMORRHA. A city near the Dead Sea destroyed by God with earthquake and fire because of the sin and wickedness of its inhabitants (Gen. 19:23–29). The city was cited in later years as an example of God's punishment (Isa. 1:9) *Gomorrha:* Matt. 10:15. See also *Cities of the Plain; Sodom*.

GOODMAN (LANDOWNER). A word for the head of a household, head of the house, or "master of the house," as rendered by some translations (Matt. 20:11). *Landowner:* NIV, NRSV.

GOODNESS. Purity and righteousness; a fruit of the Spirit which should characterize followers of Christ (Gal. 5:22). True goodness comes from God, who is holy, righteous, merciful, and loving (Ps. 31:19; Rom. 15:14). See also *Grace; Love; Righteousness*.

GOPHER WOOD (CYPRESS). The wood used in building Noah's ark, probably cypress (Gen. 6:14). *Cypress:* NIV, NRSV.

GOSHEN.

1. An Egyptian district where the Israelites settled and lived during their years in Egypt (Gen. 45:10).
2. A region and city in southern Judah (Josh. 10:41).

GOSPEL. The "good news" that God has provided salvation for all people through the atoning death of His Son (Mark 1:1–15). The word is also used of the teachings of Jesus and the apostles (Col. 1:5).

GOSPELS, FOUR. The four books at the beginning of the N.T. which describe the life and ministry of Jesus: Matthew, Mark, Luke, and John. Each Gospel tells the story from a slightly different perspective, giving us a fuller picture of the

Savior than we would get from a single narrative. See also *Synoptic Gospels.*

GOSSIP. Idle talk, rumors, or fruitless tales. This type of speech is associated with the wicked and troublemakers (Prov. 16:28; 1 Tim. 5:13). See also *Busybody; Talebearer.*

GOURD. A poisonous plant which produces fruit similar to the common melon (2 Kings 4:39). Jonah sat under the shade of a gourd vine (Jon. 4:6–10).

GOVERNMENT. A system of power and authority through which stability and order are maintained in society. Governments have a vital function and should be supported by Christians, as long as they do not intrude into the role which belongs to God alone (Mark 12:13–17).

GOVERNOR (RULER). A general term for rulers or officials of differing rank or status (1 Kings 10:15). The chief in command of a Roman province was called a governor (Matt. 27:2; Acts 23:24). This title was applied to Christ (Matt. 2:6). *Ruler:* NIV, NRSV. See also *Lieutenant; Tirshatha.*

GOVERNOR'S HEADQUARTERS. See *Praetorium.*

GOZAN. A town, district, or river of Mesopotamia to which the people of the Northern Kingdom were deported after the fall of Samaria to the Assyrians (2 Kings 18:11).

GRACE. God's unmerited favor and love which leads Him to grant salvation to believers through the exercise of their faith in Jesus Christ (Titus 2:11; Acts 15:11). Salvation cannot be earned; it is a gift of God's grace (Eph. 2:8). See also *Mercy; Salvation.*

GRAIN. See *Corn; Wheat.*

GRAIN OFFERING. See *Oblation.*

GRAPE. A fruit used for food and wine-making. It was one of the most important agricultural crops of Palestine (Num. 13:23). See also *Wine.*

GRASS. A word for various types of common plants, such as that which livestock grazed. It is used symbolically of the brevity of life (Ps. 90:5–6). See also *Hay.*

GRASSHOPPER. An insect of the locust species which destroyed vegetation. Also eaten by the Hebrews (Lev. 11:22), the grasshopper was a symbol of insignificance (Isa. 40:22). See also *Locust*.

GRATITUDE. See *Thanksgiving*.

GRAVE. A burial place for the dead. In Bible times, bodies were buried in pits (Gen. 35:8), caves (Gen. 25:9), and sepulchres hewn in rocks (Matt. 27:60). See also *Cave; Sepulchre*.

GRAVEN IMAGE (IDOL). An image of a false god made from wood or stone and set up in a prominent place as an object of worship (Exod. 20:4). The prophets warned God's people against such idolatry (Isa. 44:9–10; Hos. 11:2). *Idol:* NIV, NRSV. See also *Idol*.

GRAVING TOOL. An instrument or tool used for carving or engraving. Aaron used this tool to shape the golden calf (Exod. 32:4).

GREAT LIZARD. See *Tortoise*.

GREAT OWL. A species of owl considered unclean by the Hebrews (Deut. 14:16).

GREAT SEA. See *Mediterranean Sea*.

GREAVES. Armor for the legs, covering the area from the knees to the ankles (1 Sam. 17:6).

GRECIAN JEWS, GRECIANS. See *Greeks*.

GREECE/JAVAN. An ancient world power which reached its greatest strength in the time between the testaments, about 400 B.C. to A.D. 1. The O.T. word for Greece was *Javan* (Gen. 10:2). See also *Athens*.

GREED. Excessive desire for material things. The Bible warns that this sin leads to disappointment and destruction (Luke 22:3–6; 1 Tim. 6:9). See also *Covetousness*.

GREEKS (GRECIAN JEWS, HELLENISTS). Natives of Greece or people of Greek heritage or descent. The N.T. often uses the word for people influenced by Greek traditions who were not Jews (John 12:20). The word *Grecians* is used of Greek-speaking Jews (Acts 6:1). *Grecian Jews:* NIV; *Hellenists:* NRSV.

GREYHOUND (STRUTTING ROOSTER). An animal cited as an example of gracefulness (Prov. 30:31). *Strutting rooster:* NIV, NRSV.

GRIDDLE. See *Pan*.

GROVE. A wooden pole which represented the Canaanite fertility goddess Ashtoreth (2 Kings 21:7).

GUARANTEE. See *Surety*.

GUARD. A soldier who provided personal protection for a ruler; a bodyguard (2 Chron. 12:11).

GUILE (DECEIT). Craftiness, cunning, or deception (Ps. 55:11). Nathanael was commended by Jesus as an Israelite without guile—a model of honesty and truthfulness (John 1:47). *Deceit:* NRSV.

GUILT. Remorse for sin and wrongdoing (Lev. 6:4). The guilt of sin is covered for believers by the sacrificial death of Christ (Rom. 5:1–2). See also *Conviction; Repentance*.

GUM RESIN. See *Stacte*.

GUTTER (WATERING TROUGH). A drinking trough for animals (Gen. 30:38). *Watering trough:* NIV.

-H-

HABAKKUK. A prophet of Judah who was probably a contemporary of Jeremiah; and author of the book which bears his name (Hab. 1:1; 3:1).

HABAKKUK, BOOK OF. A short prophetic book of the O.T. which questions the coming suffering and humiliation of God's people at the hands of the pagan Babylonians (1:1–4; 1:12–2:1). God's response makes it clear that He is using the Babylonians as an instrument of judgment against His wayward people (1:5–11; 2:2–20). The book closes with a psalm of praise to God for His mercy and salvation (chap. 3).

HABERGEON. An old English word for the priest's breastplate (Exod. 28:32; 39:23). See also *Breastplate*.

HABITATION. A place of residence (Num. 15:2; Acts 17:26).

HADAD. An Edomite prince or ruler who became an enemy of King Solomon (1 Kings 11:14–25).

HADADEZER/HADAREZER. A king of Zobah in Syria. He was defeated by David and

Joab (2 Sam. 8:3–13; 10:16–19). *Hadarezer:* 1 Chron. 18:10.

HADASSAH. See *Esther*.

HADES. See *Hell*.

HAGAR/AGAR. Sarah's Egyptian slave who became the mother of Ishmael by Abraham (Gen. 16). She was driven into the wilderness with her son because of conflict with Sarah, but God intervened to save them (Gen. 21:9–21). *Agar:* Gal. 4:24. See also *Ishmael*.

HAGGAI. A prophet after the Babylonian Exile; and author of the book which bears his name.

HAGGAI, BOOK OF. A short prophetic book of the O.T. written to encourage the Jewish captives who had returned to their homeland after three generations under the Babylonians and Persians. The people were encouraged to finish the task of rebuilding the temple in Jerusalem (1:1–2:9) and to remain faithful to God in difficult times (2:10–23).

HAGGITH. A wife of David and the mother of Adonijah (2 Sam. 3:4).

HAI. See *Ai*.

HAIL. Frozen rain (Job 38:22). The word is also used as a symbol of God's judgment (Rev. 8:7).

HAIR. Fibers on the human body, especially the head. They are used as a symbol of God's special care of believers (Matt. 10:30).

HAKELDAMA. See *Aceldama*.

HALAH. A region in Assyria where captives from the Northern Kingdom were carried (2 Kings 17:6).

HALF-SHEKEL TAX. A temple tax, also called the two-drachma tax (Exod. 30:13–14; Matt. 17:24–27). See also *Tribute*.

HALF-TRIBE OF MANASSEH. A phrase which refers to the two distinct settlements of the tribe of Manasseh—one in central Palestine and the other east of the Jordan River (Num. 32:33–34; Josh. 22:10). See also *Manasseh*.

HALLELUJAH. See *Alleluia*.

HALLOW. To set apart for holy use; to make holy (Exod. 20:11; Luke 11:2). See also *Consecration*.

HAM. The youngest son of Noah. Ham's four sons are thought to be the ancestors of the people of several nations: Canaan (Canaanites), Cush and Phut (Africa and Ethiopia), and Mizraim (Egypt). See Gen. 10:6.

HAMAN. An aide to King Ahasuerus of Persia who plotted to kill the Jewish leader Mordecai and all the Jews, only to be hanged himself on the gallows which he had built for Mordecai's execution (Esther 3:1–9:25). See also *Esther; Mordecai.*

HAMATH/HEMATH (LEBO-HAMATH). A Hittite city north of Damascus (Josh. 13:5). *Lebo-Hamath:* NIV, NRSV. *Hemath:* Amos 6:14.

HAMMER. A driving tool (Judg. 4:21). It is used as a symbol of the power of God's Word (Jer. 23:29).

HAMMOTH-DOR/ HAMMATH/HAMMON. A city of refuge in the territory of Naphtali (Josh. 21:32). This is probably the same city as *Hammon* (1 Chron. 6:76) and *Hammath* (Josh. 19:35).

HAMMURABI, CODE OF. An ancient and influential law code named for an early king of Babylonia. The code was discovered in 1901–02 by an archaeologist at Susa.

HANAMEEL (HANAMEL). A cousin of Jeremiah the prophet (Jer. 32:7). *Hanamel:* NIV, NRSV. Jeremiah bought a field from Hanameel during the siege of Jerusalem by the Babylonians to signify hope for the future for God's people (Jer. 32:8–12).

HANANI. Nehemiah's brother, who became governor of Jerusalem (Neh. 7:2). Hanani brought news of the suffering citizens of Jerusalem to Nehemiah in Persia (Neh. 1:2–3).

HANANIAH. See *Shadrach.*

HAND OF GOD. A symbolic expression for the power of God (Exod. 9:3) and the guidance which He provides for His people (Ps. 63:8).

HANDBAG. See *Crisping Pin.*

HANDBREADTH. A measure of length (about four inches) based on the width of the palm of one's hand (Exod. 25:25). It is also symbolic of the frailty and brevity of life (Ps. 39:5).

HANDKERCHIEF (CLOTH). A small cloth for wiping the

face or hands (Acts 19:12) and also a burial cloth placed over the face of corpses (John 20:7). *Cloth:* NIV, NRSV. See also *Napkin*.

HANDMAID (MAIDSERVANT). A female servant (Gen. 29:24). *Maidservant:* NIV. This word also signified humility, as in Ruth's conversation with Boaz (Ruth 2:13–14).

HANDS, LAYING ON OF. See *Laying on of Hands*.

HANGING. A form of capital punishment (2 Sam. 18:10). Haman, the enemy of the Jews, was hanged on the gallows which he had prepared for Mordecai (Esther 7:9–10). See also *Haman*.

HANNAH. The mother of Samuel the prophet. She prayed earnestly for Samuel to be born (1 Sam. 1:5–11), devoted him to God's service (1 Sam. 1:24–28), and offered a beautiful prayer of thanksgiving for God's blessings (1 Sam. 2:1–10). See also *Samuel*.

HANNIEL. A representative of the tribe of Manasseh, appointed by Moses to help divide the land of Canaan after its occupation by the Israelites (Num. 34:23).

HANUKKAH. See *Dedication, Feast of*.

HANUN. An Ammonite king defeated by David (2 Sam. 10:2–14).

HARA. A site in Assyria where some of the captives from the Northern Kingdom were settled after the fall of their nation (1 Chron. 5:26).

HARAN/CHARRAN. A city of Mesopotamia known as a center of pagan worship (2 Kings 19:12). Abraham lived in Haran for a time before he left at God's command to settle in Canaan (Gen. 12:4–5). *Charran:* Acts 7:2, 4.

HARDNESS OF HEART. A symbolic expression for rebellion or a stubborn and unyielding spirit, such as that exemplified by the pharaoh of Egypt in refusing to free the Hebrew slaves (Exod. 9:35).

HARE (RABBIT). A rabbit-like animal with long ears and legs (Deut. 14:7). Hares were considered unclean by the Israelites (Lev. 11:6). *Rabbit:* NIV.

HAREM. A group of women married to one man, especially a king. Esther was a member of the harem of King Ahasuerus of Persia (Esther 2:8–14).

HARLOT (PROSTITUTE). Harlotry was forbidden among God's people (Lev. 19:29). Engaging in prostitution was often compared to the spiritual adultery of God's people (Isa. 57:7–9; Rev. 17:1–18). *Prostitute:* NIV.

HAROD. A spring or well near the mountains of Gilboa by which Gideon and his army camped (Judg. 7:1).

HARP (LYRE). A stringed musical instrument frequently used in worship (2 Chron. 29:25). David calmed King Saul by playing his harp (1 Sam. 16:16, 23). *Lyre:* NRSV. See also *Psaltery*.

HARPIST. See *Minstrel*.

HARROW. An agricultural tool or implement, probably used to level a plowed field for planting (Job 39:10).

HART (DEER). A male deer. The word is used to illustrate spiritual thirst (Ps. 42:1) and conversion (Isa. 35:6). *Deer:* NIV, NRSV. See also *Deer*.

HARVEST. The gathering of mature crops (Lev. 23:10). This word is used to illustrate the ripe spiritual harvest (Matt. 9:37–38). See also *Reaper*.

HARVEST, FEAST OF. See *Pentecost*.

HATE. Extreme dislike or animosity toward another. Jesus enjoined believers not to hate their enemies but to return love for malice (Luke 6:27). See also *Enmity; Malice*.

HAUGHTINESS. An arrogant spirit. God's Word indicates that haughty persons will be humbled (Prov. 16:18; Isa. 2:11, 17). See also *Conceit; Pride*.

HAURAN. A fertile district east of the Jordan River near Mt. Hermon (Ezek. 47:16).

HAWK. A bird of prey considered unclean by the Israelites (Deut. 14:15). See also *Cormorant*.

HAY (GRASS). A word for grass, which was cut and fed to livestock while fresh and green (Isa. 15:6). *Grass:* NIV, NRSV. See also *Grass*.

HAZAEL. A leader who was anointed king of Syria at God's command by the prophet Elijah (1 Kings 19:15). He murdered Ben-hadad in order to take the throne (2 Kings 8:7–15). Hazael conducted military campaigns against both Judah (2 Kings 12:17–18) and Israel (2 Kings 10:32). See also *Syria*.

HAZEL (ALMOND). A tree from which Jacob cut a rod or switch (Gen. 30:37). *Almond:* NIV, NRSV. See also *Almond*.

HAZEROTH. A camping place for the Israelites in the wilderness (Num. 11:35) where Aaron and Miriam rebelled against Moses (Num. 12:1–2).

HAZOR. A royal Canaanite city destroyed by Joshua (Josh. 11:1–13). The rebuilt fortress city was later ravaged by Deborah and Barak during the period of the judges (Judg. 4:2–24). Hazor was ultimately destroyed by King Tiglath-pileser of Assyria (2 Kings 15:29).

HE. The fifth letter of the Hebrew alphabet, used as a heading over Ps. 119:33–40.

HEALING. The process of restoring a person to good health. Jesus' healing ministry showed His compassion and God's power over sickness and death (Mark 1:34). See also *Balm of Gilead; Medicine*.

HEART. To the Hebrews, the heart was the center of one's existence, including emotions (Gen. 42:28), wisdom or skill (Exod. 35:35), and even physical life (Deut. 6:5). A person acts and speaks from the heart, so he should guard it carefully (Matt. 15:18–19).

HEATH. A dense shrub or bush which grew in the desert regions of Palestine (Jer. 17:6).

HEATHEN (NATIONS, GENTILES). A word for ethnic groups besides the Jews (Ezek. 22:15). *Nations:* NIV, NRSV. It was also used for unbelievers, pagans, or Gentiles (Gal. 1:16). *Gentiles:* NIV, NRSV. See also *Gentile*.

HEAVE OFFERING. An offering which consisted of the firstfruits of the harvest (Num. 15:19–21) and a tenth of all tithes (Num. 18:21–28). It was presented to God before being given to the priests. This was also known as a *peace offering* (Josh. 22:23).

HEAVEN. A word for (1) the atmosphere or the sky (Ps. 146:6), (2) the place where God dwells (1 Kings 8:45), and (3) the future home of all believers (Col. 1:5), who will dwell with

God eternally (Isa. 65:17). See also *Heavenly City; Paradise*.

HEAVENLY CITY. The future city built by God as a dwelling-place for those who belong to Him (Heb. 11:10–16). It will be known as "New Jerusalem," the place where God dwells eternally among the redeemed (Rev. 21:2–10). See also *Heaven; Paradise*.

HEBREWS, EPISTLE TO THE. An epistle of the N.T., author unknown, written to a group of believers of Jewish background to show that Jesus had replaced the O.T. ceremonial law and sacrificial system. Hebrews declares that Jesus is superior to angels (1:1–2:18) and Moses (3:1–16) and that He is our great High Priest who offered Himself—rather than a sacrificial animal—as an atoning sacrifice for our sins (chaps. 4–10). The book closes with an appeal to believers to remember the great heroes of the faith (chap. 11) and to remain steadfast and true in their commitment to Christ (chaps. 12–13).

HEBRON/KIRJATH-ARBA. An ancient town in Canaan where Abraham lived and where Sarah died (Gen. 23:2–6). After the conquest of Canaan, it was designated one of the six cities of refuge. *Kirjath-arba:* Josh. 14:15. See also *Cities of Refuge*.

HEIFER. A young cow (Gen. 15:9). This word is sometimes used figuratively of contentment or complacency (Jer. 50:11).

HEIR. See *Inheritance*.

HELAM. The place where David won a decisive victory over the Syrians (2 Sam. 10:16–19).

HELI. Father of Joseph (husband of Mary) in the ancestry of Jesus (Luke 3:23).

HELL. The place of eternal torment reserved for unbelievers. *Sheol,* a Hebrew word rendered as "hell" in the O.T., corresponds to the Greek word *Hades,* which means "unseen underworld" or "place of the dead." In the N.T. both *Hades* and *Gehenna* are rendered as "hell." *Gehenna* is derived from the Valley of Hinnom, a site for heathen worship that became a dumping ground near Jerusalem where filth and dead animals were burned; hence hell's association with the final state of lost souls in a place of eternal fire (Mark

9:47–48). Hell is described as a "lake of fire" (Rev. 19:20), "everlasting destruction" (2 Thess. 1:9), and the "second death" (Rev. 20:14). See also *Damnation; Hinnom, Valley of; Lake of Fire*.

HELLENISTS. Greek-speaking Jews. See *Greeks*.

HELMET. An armored covering for the head to protect soldiers in combat. Paul spoke of the "helmet of salvation" which protected believers in spiritual warfare (Eph. 6:17).

HELPER. One who assists another. This word is used for the Holy Spirit's comfort and intercession on behalf of believers (Rom. 8:26). See also *Advocate; Comforter; Holy Spirit; Paraclete*.

HELP MEET (HELPER). A helper, companion, or mate. God created Eve as a helper for Adam (Gen. 2:18). *Helper:* NIV, NRSV.

HEM. A decorative border or fringe on a piece of clothing, worn to remind the Jews of God's commandments (Exod. 28:33–34). See also *Fringe*.

HEMAN. A talented musician under David and a grandson of Saul (1 Chron. 6:33; 15:16–17). Heman was regarded as a person of spiritual insight (1 Chron. 25:5).

HEMATH. See *Hamath*.

HEMLOCK (WORMWOOD). A bitter and poisonous plant (Amos 6:12). *Wormwood:* NRSV.

HENA. A city on the Euphrates River captured by the Assyrians (2 Kings 18:34).

HENNA. See *Camphire*.

HENOCH. See *Enoch,* No. 2.

HEPHZI-BAH. A symbolic name, meaning "my delight is in her," which would be used for Jerusalem after her restoration to God's grace and favor (Isa. 62:4).

HERALD. A person sent by a high government official to deliver a formal and public message or to announce good news (Dan. 3:4)

HERB. A plant used to promote healing or to season food (Gen. 1:29). The Israelites used bitter herbs in their bread at the first Passover (Exod. 12:8). See also *Mallows*.

HERD. A group of cattle, sheep, or oxen (1 Sam. 11:5). In O.T. times, a person's wealth was measured by the size of his herd (2 Sam. 12:1–3).

HERDMAN (SHEPHERD). A tender or keeper of livestock. The prophet Amos was a herdman and farmer (Amos 7:14). *Shepherd:* NIV. See also *Shepherd*.

HERESY. False teachings that deny essential doctrines of the Christian faith—a serious problem condemned by Paul (1 Cor. 11:19). See also *Doctrine; Gnosticism; Judaizers*.

HERMAS. A fellow believer at Rome greeted and commended by Paul (Rom. 16:14).

HERMES

1. A fellow believer at Rome greeted and commended by Paul (Rom. 16:14).

2. NIV, NRSV word for the pagan god Mercurius. See *Mercurius*.

HERMOGENES. A believer from the province of Asia who turned away from Paul (2 Tim. 1:15).

HERMON, MOUNT/SIRION/SHENIR/SENIR. The highest mountain in Syria, with an elevation of almost 10,000 feet (Josh. 12:1). It was also called *Sirion* and *Shenir* (Deut. 3:9) and *Senir* (Ezek. 27:5).

HEROD. The name of several Roman rulers in Palestine during N.T. times:

1. Herod the Great (ruled 37 to 4 B.C.), in power when Jesus was born, who ordered the slaughter of innocent children (Matt. 2:3–10). Herod reconstructed the temple at Jerusalem and completed other ambitious building projects.

2. Herod Archelaus (ruled 4 B.C. to A.D. 6), the son and successor of Herod the Great as Roman ruler in Judea soon after the birth of Jesus (Matt. 2:22).

3. Herod Antipas (ruled 4 B.C. to A.D. 39), who granted his wife's request that John the Baptist be executed. This was the Herod who returned Jesus for sentencing by Pilate (Luke 23:6–12).

4. Herod Philip (ruled 4 B.C. to A.D. 33), ruler in extreme northern Galilee at the time when Jesus began His public ministry (Luke 3:1, 19–20).

5. Herod Agrippa I (ruled A.D. 37–44), who persecuted the apostles and executed James, leader of the Jerusalem church (Acts 12:1–19).

6. Herod Agrippa II (ruled A.D. 50–100), before whom Paul

made his defense at Caesarea (Acts 25:13–26:32).

HERODIANS. An influential Jewish group that favored Greek customs and Roman law in New Testament times. The Herodians joined forces with the Pharisees against Jesus (Mark 3:6).

HERODIAS. The wife or queen of Herod Antipas, the Roman provincial ruler of Palestine, who had John the Baptist executed. Herodias was angry at John because of his criticism of her immorality and illicit marriage (Matt. 14:1–11).

HERODION. A believer at Rome greeted and commended by Paul, who called him "my kinsman." (Rom. 16:11).

HERON. An unclean bird which lived in the lakes and marshes of Palestine (Deut. 14:18).

HESHBON. An ancient Moabite city east of the Jordan River captured by the Amorite king Sihon (Num. 21:25–34).

HETH. A son of Canaan and ancestor of the Hittites. Abraham dealt with the sons of Heth in securing a burial place for Sarah (Gen. 23:3–20).

HEWER (WOODCUTTER, STONECUTTER). A woodcutter (Josh. 9:21). *Woodcutter:* NIV, or stonecutter (2 Kings 12:12). *Stonecutter:* NIV, NRSV.

HEZEKIAH/EZEKIAS. The godly king of Judah (ruled about 716–686 B.C.) who implemented religious reforms by abolishing idol worship, restoring and reopening the temple in Jerusalem, and leading in celebration of major religious festivals, such as the Passover (2 Kings 18:4; 2 Chron. 29:3–36). Preparing for a siege against Jerusalem by the Assyrians, Hezekiah cut a tunnel through solid rock to bring water from a spring outside the city wall into the city (2 Kings 20:20). *Ezekias:* Matt. 1:9.

HIDDEKEL. See *Tigris River*.

HIEL. A native of Bethel who rebuilt the city of Jericho in King Ahab's time (1 Kings 16:34). This was a fulfillment of Joshua's curse against the city (Josh. 6:26).

HIERAPOLIS. A city of the district of Phrygia in Asia Minor. This city was mentioned by Paul, implying that Christianity had been planted here (Col. 4:13).

HIGGAION. A musical term translated "meditation" in Ps. 9:16, perhaps signifying a soft, quiet sound.

HIGH PLACE. An elevated place where worship of false gods was conducted (2 Kings 12:3). These shrines of idolatry provoked God's wrath (Ps. 78:58). See also *Altar*.

HIGH PRIEST. The chief priest or head of the priesthood—an office filled by succession of the oldest son of each generation through the lineage of Aaron, Israel's first high priest (Exod. 28). Jesus is called our "great high priest" (Heb. 4:14) because He laid down His life as a living "sacrifice" on our behalf (Heb. 9:26). See also *Priest*.

HIGHWAY. The "highways" of the Bible were little more than paths or crude trails, and they generally connected large cities or major trading centers (Isa. 19:23). See also *Road*.

HILKIAH. A high priest during the reign of King Josiah of Judah who found the lost Book of the Law and used it to bring about religious reforms (2 Kings 22:8–23:4).

HILL. An elevated site. Pagan altars were often built on hills (1 Kings 14:23). See also *High Place*.

HILL COUNTRY (MOUNTAIN REGION). A region of low, rugged mountains in southern Lebanon and northern Judea (Josh. 13:6). *Mountain region:* NIV.

HIN. A unit of measure, equal to about one and one-half gallons (Exod. 29:40).

HIND (DEER). A female deer. The word is used symbolically to show spiritual resilience (Hab. 3:19; Ps. 18:33; *Deer:* NIV, NRSV. See also *Deer*.

HINNOM, VALLEY OF. A deep, narrow ravine southwest of Jerusalem where pagan worship involving child sacrifice was conducted (2 Chron. 28:3; Jer. 19:2–4). Some scholars believe this site in N. T. times became a garbage dump for the city of Jerusalem known as *Gehenna*—a word translated as "hell" (Matt. 5:22; Mark 9:43). See also *Hell*.

HIRAM/HURAM. The king of Tyre—or perhaps a son and his successor—who assisted David and Solomon with their building projects in Jerusalem by providing materials and skilled workmen (2 Sam. 5:11; 1 Kings 5:7–11). *Huram:* 2 Chron. 2:3–12. See also *Tyre*.

HIRELING (LABORER, HIRED HAND). A common laborer hired for a short time to do farm chores (Job 7:1–2). *Laborer:* NRSV. Unlike a hireling, Jesus as the Good Shepherd takes a personal interest in His sheep (John 10:12–13). *Hired hand:* NIV, NRSV. See also *Laborer*.

HISS. A sound made by forcing air between the tongue and the teeth to show scorn and contempt (Job 27:23; Isa. 5:25–26).

HITTITES. An ancient people who lived in Canaan apparently before Abraham's time, since he bought a burial cave from Ephron, who was probably a Hittite (Gen. 23:10–20). Hittites also served in David's army (2 Sam. 11:6, 15).

HIVITES. Descendants of Canaan (see Gen. 10:6) who lived in the Promised Land before and after the Hebrew people occupied their territory (Deut. 7:1). Some scholars believe these are the same people as the Horites. See also *Horites*.

HOBAB. See *Jethro*.

HOE. See *Mattock*.

HOHAM. An Amorite king defeated by Joshua near the cave at Makkedah (Josh. 10:1–27).

HOLINESS. Moral purity; to be set apart and sanctified for service to God. God is holy (Exod. 15:11), and He expects holiness of His people (Rom. 12:1). Since Jesus was the perfect example of holiness, He was called the "Holy One of God" (Mark 1:24). See also *Righteousness*.

HOLY GHOST. An old English phrase for Holy Spirit (Acts 5:3). See *Holy Spirit*.

HOLY OF HOLIES (HOLY PLACE). The sacred innermost sanctuary of the temple and tabernacle, containing the ark of the covenant and the mercy seat, which only the high priest could enter. Even he could go in only one day a year on the Day of Atonement, when he made a special sacrifice for the sins of the people (Heb. 9:2–3, 7). *Holy Place:* NRSV. See also *Ark of the Covenant; Atonement, Day of; Mercy Seat*.

HOLY PLACE. KJV phrase for the section of the tabernacle just outside the holy of holies (Exod. 28:29).

HOLY SPIRIT. The third person of the trinity. The O.T. contains glimpses and promises of the Holy Spirit (Gen. 1:2, 6:3; Zech. 4:6) and the Spirit rested on Jesus from His birth (Luke 1:35), but the full manifestation of the Spirit's power occurred at Pentecost after Jesus' resurrection and ascension to the Father (Acts 2:1–21). Jesus promised He would send the Holy Spirit as a comforter and advocate in His absence (John 14:16; 1 John 2:1). The Spirit would glorify the Son (John 15:16), empower believers (John 14:12–27), and convict unbelievers of sin and coming judgment (John 16:8–11). Another function of the Holy Spirit is to inspire the Scriptures, thus providing guidance and direction to believers. See also *Advocate; Comforter; Helper; Paraclete*.

HOMER. The standard unit of dry measure, equal to about six bushels (Ezek. 45:11).

HOMOSEXUALITY. The practice of sexual activity among persons of the same sex—a sin strictly forbidden by the O.T. law (Lev. 18:22). Paul also condemned this practice (Rom. 1:26–27; 1 Cor. 6:9).

HONESTY. Speaking the truth and acting fairly and without deceit in human relationships. This is a virtue which all believers should practice (2 Cor. 13:7).

HONEY. A sweet liquid substance produced naturally from bees and artificially from fruit. It was used to sweeten food (Exod. 16:31). The word is also used symbolically for abundance (Exod. 3:8, 17).

HONEYCOMB. The wax cells built by bees to hold their eggs and honey (1 Sam. 14:27).

HONOR. Respect and esteem toward God and other people. The Ten Commandments enjoin honor toward one's parents (Exod. 20:12). God and His Son Jesus Christ are worthy of our highest honor (John 5:23).

HOOK. A metal grasping tool. Different types of hooks mentioned in the Bible include fleshhooks (Exod. 27:3), fish hooks (Matt. 17:27), pruning hooks (Isa. 18:5), and the hooks which supported the tabernacle curtains.

HOOPOE. See *Lapwing*.

HOPE. A sure and steady faith in God's promises. The believer has hope in God's promise of salvation (1 Thess. 5:8), resurrection (Acts 26:6–7), and eternal life (1 Cor. 15:19–26). See also *Promise*.

HOPHNI. A sinful and immoral son of Eli the high priest who was not considered worthy of conducting priestly duties (1 Sam. 1:3; 2:22–25). Along with his evil brother Phinehas, he was killed by the Philistines (1 Sam. 4:1–11). See also *Phinehas,* No. 2.

HOPHRA. See *Pharaoh*.

HOR, MOUNT. A mountain in the territory of the Edomites where Moses' brother Aaron died and was buried (Num. 20:22–29). A different mountain with the same name was located in northern Palestine (see Num. 34:7–8).

HORAM. A king of Gezer defeated by Joshua's forces (Josh. 10:33).

HOREB, MOUNT. See *Sinai*.

HORITES/HORIMS. Inhabitants of Mt. Hermon who were driven out by Esau's descendants (Gen. 36:20). These may have been the same people as the Hivites of Joshua's time. *Horims:* Deut. 2:22. See also *Hivites*.

HORMAH. See *Zephath*.

HORN. A bonelike protrusion from an animal's head. The word is also used as a symbol of strength (Hab. 3:4; Rev. 13:1). See also *Cornet*.

HORNET. A wasplike insect with a painful sting, portrayed as a symbol of God's judgment against the enemies of His people (Exod. 23:28).

HORNS OF THE ALTAR. Projections at the four corners of an altar (Exod. 27:1–2). The blood of a sacrificial animal was sprinkled on these four projections (Exod. 29:12). See also *Altar*.

HORSE. An animal used for transportation (Gen. 47:17) as well as in warfare. God warned his people not to "multiply" horses for use in war (Deut. 17:16).

HORSE GATE. A gate in the old wall of Jerusalem, mentioned by Nehemiah as having been destroyed and then rebuilt under his supervision (Neh. 3:28).

HORSELEACH (LEECH). A parasite which attaches to humans and animals and sucks blood; probably a leech (Prov. 30:15). *Leech:* NIV, NRSV.

HOSANNA. A triumphal shout by the crowds as Jesus entered Jerusalem a few days before His crucifixion (Matt. 21: 9, 15). The expression means "save us now."

HOSEA/OSEE. A prophet who delivered God's message of judgment to the Northern Kingdom in the years shortly before this nation fell to the Assyrians in 722 B.C. Author of the book of Hosea, he is best known for his marriage to a prostitute in obedience of God's command (Hos. 1:2–9). *Osee:* Rom. 9:25.

HOSEA, BOOK OF. A prophetic book of the O.T. which compares the spiritual adultery or idolatry of God's people with the physical adultery of the prophet's wife, Gomer (1:2–5; 2:2–5). Just as Hosea redeemed her from slavery and restored her as his mate, God promised that He would eventually restore His people as His own after a period of punishment at the hand of their enemies (4:1–14:9). This book is one of the greatest treatises in the Bible on the nature of God, emphasizing His demand for righteousness and impending punishment as well as His steadfast love. See also *Gomer*.

HOSEN (TROUSERS). An old English word for "trousers," possibly referring to the tunic or inner garment worn during Bible times (Dan. 3:21). *Trousers:* NIV, NRSV.

HOSHEA.

1. The original name of Joshua (Deut. 32:44). See *Joshua*.

2. The last king of Israel (reigned about 730–722 B.C.) who paid tribute to King Shalmaneser of Assyria. After Hoshea rebelled, Israel was defeated, and Hoshea was taken to Assyrian as a captive (2 Kings 17:1–6).

HOSPITALITY. The gracious provision of food and lodging to strangers. Kindness toward travelers and strangers was encouraged in both O.T. and N.T. times (Lev. 19:33–34; 1 Pet. 4:9).

HOST. A hospitable person who entertained guests (Heb.

13:2) or a multitude or crowd of people (Gen. 2:1).

HOSTS, LORD OF (LORD ALMIGHTY). A title of God which emphasizes His sovereignty (Isa. 1:9; 10:23). *Lord Almighty:* NIV.

HOST OF HEAVEN. Heavenly beings created by God and associated with His rule of the universe. These beings ("a multitude of the heavenly host") praised God at the angels' announcement of the birth of Jesus (Luke 2:13).

HOUR. A twelfth part of the working day between sunrise and sunset—a unit which varied with the season and the duration of daylight (Matt. 20:1–12).

HOUSE (TENT). A building or residence for a family (1 Sam. 9:18). The word is also used of a clan or all the descendants of a family (1 Sam. 20:16) as well as the believer's final dwelling-place in heaven (2 Cor. 5:1). *Tent:* NIV, NRSV. See also *Tent.*

HOUSEHOLD. Members of a family who lived together in the same dwelling or a compound of dwellings, perhaps including several generations (2 Sam. 6:11). Believers are members of God's household (Eph. 2:19).

HOUSEHOLD IDOLS. Images of pagan gods kept in the house in the belief that they protected the family (Gen. 31:19–35). See also *Teraphim.*

HOUSEHOLDER (OWNER). The head of a household or owner of a house (Matt. 13:27). *Owner:* NIV.

HULDAH. The wife of Shallum and a prophetess who foretold the collapse of Jerusalem (2 Kings 22:14–20).

HUMAN SACRIFICE. The practice of sacrificing children to a pagan god (2 Kings 3:26–27). This was common among the pagan religions of Bible times, but the custom was specifically prohibited by God (Lev. 20:2–5; Deut. 18:10). See also *Hinnom, Valley of; Jephthah.*

HUMILITY. The opposite of arrogance and pride; an attitude which grows out of the recognition that all we are and everything we own are gifts from God (Rom. 12:3; 1 Pet. 5:5). See also *Meekness.*

HUNTER. A person who stalks and kills wild animals. Nimrod, a descendant of Noah, was a "mighty hunter" (Gen. 10:9). See also *Fowler*.

HUR. A man who helped Aaron hold up the arms of Moses to give the Israelites victory over the Amalekites (Exod. 24:14).

HURAM. See *Hiram*.

HUSBAND. The male partner in a marriage relationship. Husbands had total authority over their wives in Bible times, but Paul called on male believers to love their wives (Eph. 5:25).

HUSBANDMAN (FARMER). A farmer or tiller of the soil (Gen. 9:20). In N.T. times a husbandman, like a tenant farmer, often took a share of the crops as payment for his labor (2 Tim. 2:6). *Farmer:* NIV, NRSV.

HUSHAI. A friend and advisor of King David (2 Sam. 15:32–37). Hushai remained loyal to David during Absalom's revolt (2 Sam. 17:1–16).

HUSKS (PODS). The fruit of the carob tree, a type of locust. The prodigal son in Jesus' parable was reduced to eating this coarse and unappetizing food in order to survive (Luke 15:16). *Pods:* NIV, NRSV.

HYMENAEUS. An early Christian who denied the faith and was excommunicated by Paul (1 Tim. 1:19–20; 2 Tim. 2:16–17).

HYMN. A song of praise and thanksgiving to God (Eph. 5:19). Jesus and His disciples sang a hymn after they finished the last supper (Matt. 26:30).

HYPOCRITE. A person who pretends to be something he or she is not. Jesus called the Pharisees hypocrites because they did good deeds to gain the praise of others and pretended to be godly and righteous but were actually insensitive to God's truth (Matt. 23:13–29).

HYSSOP. A plant used in purification ceremonies (Exod. 12:22). It was also symbolic of spiritual cleansing (Ps. 51:7). Hyssop was used to relieve Jesus' thirst on the cross (John 19:29).

-I-

I AM. The name by which God revealed Himself to Moses at the burning bush. It shows His eternity, self-existence, and unsearchableness (Exod. 3:14). See also *God; Jehovah; Yahweh*.

IBEX. See *Pygarg*.

IBHAR. A son of David, born at Jerusalem after he became king (1 Chron. 3:6).

IBZAN. A judge of Israel for seven years. A native of Bethlehem, he had thirty sons and thirty daughters (Judg. 12:8–10). See also *Judges of Israel*.

I-CHABOD. The son of Phinehas and grandson of Eli. He was given this symbolic name, meaning "inglorious," by his dying mother when she learned the ark of the covenant had been captured and that Eli and Phinehas were dead (1 Sam. 4:19–22).

ICONIUM. An ancient city in Asia Minor near Lystra and Lycaonia. Paul and Barnabas introduced Christianity here on the first missionary journey (Acts 13:51; 14:1, 21–22). Paul apparently also visited Iconium on the second journey (Acts 16:1–7).

IDDO. A leader of the tribe of Manasseh who served as an aide or government official under David (1 Chron. 27:21).

IDLENESS. Inactivity or laziness. This behavior is condemned in Proverbs (Prov. 24:30–34) and by Paul (2 Thess. 3:10). See also *Sluggard*.

IDOL, IDOLATRY. The worship of false gods or something created rather than the Creator (Rom. 1:25). Idolatry was prohibited by the first two of the Ten Commandments (Exod. 20:3–4). Abraham migrated to Canaan to escape idol worship (Josh. 24:2–3). Prominent idols mentioned in the Bible are the golden calves of Aaron (Exod. 32:4) and King Jeroboam (2 Chron. 11:15) and the grain god of the Philistines known as Dagon (Judg. 16:23). Elijah helped overthrow Baal worship in Israel (1 Kings 18:17–40), and the prophet Isaiah described the folly of idolatry (Isa. 44:9–20). In the N.T., idolatry is anything that comes between the believer and God (Col. 3:5). See also *Graven Image*.

IDUMAEA. See *Edom,* No. 2.

IGAL. One of the twelve spies who scouted the land of Canaan, representing the tribe of Issachar (Num. 13:7). See also *Spies*.

IGNORANCE. Lack of knowledge or understanding. While sins of ignorance are less grievous than premeditated sins (Lev. 4:2–14; Num. 15:30–31), they are still destructive (Hos.

4:6) and require repentance (Acts 17:30–31). At Pentecost, Peter declared Christ was crucified out of ignorance—a sin which required repentance (Acts 3:17, 19).

ILLYRICUM. A district on the eastern coast of the Adriatic Sea. Paul mentioned Illyricum as the furthermost point to which he had traveled (Rom. 15:19).

IMAGE. An exact likeness or representation of some object of idolatrous worship. God warned Israel to destroy such pagan images (Exod. 34:13–17).

IMAGE OF GOD. Human beings were created to perfectly reflect God's image, marred that image by sinning, but have the potential to be molded back into that image (Rom. 8:28–30). Jesus is the image of the "invisible God" (Col. 1:15), and man expresses God's image when he is in right relation with his Creator and faithfully tends God's creation (Gen. 1:26–28). Man's unique attributes of human reason, will, and personality are further evidences of divine image.

IMMANUEL. See *Emmanuel*.

IMMORALITY. Behavior which violates established moral principles or laws. This word is used to condemn illicit sexual activity outside of marriage (Prov. 2:16; Rom. 1:26–27) and to describe Israel's worship of pagan gods (Ezek. 23:8, 17). See also *Adultery; Fornication*.

IMMORTALITY. See *Eternal Life*.

IMMUTABILITY. An attribute of God's nature which refers to His unchangeableness (Mal. 3:6). The unchangeable nature of Christ assures us that God's mercy is constant (Heb. 13:8). God, who cannot lie, offers an anchor of hope for all believers, who are the "heirs of promise" (Heb. 6:17–19). See also *God*.

IMPARTIALITY. Justness and fairness. God is impartial in His loving concern for all persons (2 Pet. 3:9) and in His command for repentance (Rom. 3:6). Peter learned that all persons who are cleansed by the Lord are brothers (Acts 10:15, 34–35).

IMPUTATION. To transfer something to another person. Adam's sin was imputed to all persons (Rom. 5:12). Our iniquity was laid on Jesus (Isa. 53:5–6), and He bore our sins (John 1:29). Jesus, the "second Adam," imputed grace and righteousness to all who put their trust in Him (Rom. 5:17–19).

INCARNATION OF CHRIST. The birth and existence of Christ in human form. This was foretold by the O.T. prophets (Isa. 7:14). When Jesus was born into the world, He was described as "the Word . . .made flesh" (John 1:14). Belief in the incarnation of Christ is a mark of the Christian (1 John 4:2–3). See also *Advent of Christ; Virgin Birth*.

INCENSE. Sweet perfume extracted from spices or gums and used in worship ceremonies. Incense was burned on the altar of incense in the tabernacle by the priest (Exod. 30:7–8). See also *Censer; Frankincense*.

INCEST. Sex relations with members of one's own family. Prohibited by the Levitical Law (Lev. 18:6–12), incest was considered such a serious offense that it was punishable by death (Lev. 20:11–17). Lot committed incest with his two daughters (Gen. 19:30–38) and Reuben with his father's concubine (Gen. 35:22).

INDIA. A region near the Indus River which served as the eastern limit of the Persian Empire (Esther 1:1; 8:9). Scholars believe this "India" covered essentially the same region as the modern nations of India and Pakistan.

INDIFFERENCE. Lack of interest and concern—behavior characteristic of unbelievers and backsliders (Rev. 3:15–16). Indifference breeds moral callousness (Matt. 27:3–4; Acts 18:12–16).

INFIDEL (UNBELIEVER). An unbeliever (1 Tim. 5:8). *Unbeliever:* NIV, NRSV. Infidelity is caused by an unregenerate heart (Rom. 2:5) and hatred of the light (John 3:20). An infidel will be punished by eternal separation from God (2 Thess. 1:8–9). See also *Atheism; Unbelief*.

INHERITANCE. A gift of property or rights passed from one generation to another. In ancient Israel, a father's possessions were passed on to his living sons, with the oldest receiving a double portion (Deut. 21:17). Reuben lost his inheritance because he committed incest with Bilhah (Gen. 35:22; 49:4). Esau traded his birthright as the oldest son to his brother Jacob for a bowl of soup (Gen. 25:29–34). Christians enjoy a spiritual birthright (Eph. 1:13–14). All the redeemed, including Gentiles, become God's adopted children with full inheritance rights (Gal. 4:5–7). See also *Adoption; Birthright; Firstborn*.

INIQUITY (WICKEDNESS). Sin, wickedness, or evil. Jesus taught that evil or iniquity originates in the heart, or from within (Matt. 23:28). Christ redeems believers from their iniquity, purifies them, and sets them apart for His service (Titus 2:14). *Wickedness:* NIV. See also *Wickedness*.

INK. Writing fluid. The earliest ink was probably a mixture of water, charcoal or soot, and gum. The scribe Baruch used ink to write Jeremiah's prophecies (Jer. 36:18). See also *Paper; Writing*.

INKHORN. A carrying case for pens and ink, probably made from the horn of an animal and carried on a belt (Ezek. 9:2–11).

INN. A shelter which provided lodging for travelers. Inns were often crude stopping places with no indoor accommodations. Jesus was born at a stable of an inn, which provided shelter for people and their animals (Luke 2:7).

INSANE. See *Mad*.

INSCRIPTION. See *Superscription*.

INSPECTION GATE. See *Miphkad*.

INSPIRATION. Divine influence. God's inspiration is the source of human understanding (Job 32:8). Scripture is inspired by God for our correction and instruction (2 Tim. 3:16). The Holy Spirit moved holy men to prophesy and record God's message (2 Pet. 1:20–21). God has communicated with man in various ways, including a voice (Rev. 1:10–11), dreams (Dan. 7:1), and visions (Ezek. 11:24–25).

INTELLIGENT. See *Prudent*.

INTERCESSION. Prayer offered on behalf of others. Christ made intercession for those who were crucifying Him (Luke 23:34) and for His disciples (John 17:9–26). Elders of the early church were instructed to pray for the sick (Jas. 5:14–16).

Paul prayed for Israel to be saved (Rom. 10:1) and for the Colossians to grow spiritually (Col. 1:9–12). Christ, our high priest, lives to make intercession for us (Heb. 7:25–26). The Holy Spirit helps us intercede for others (Rom. 8:26). See also *Petition; Prayer*.

INTERCESSOR. An advocate for others (Isa. 59:16). Abraham interceded for Sodom to be spared (Gen. 18:23–32). Paul encouraged intercession for all people (1 Tim. 2:1–2). Christ is the Christian's advocate or intercessor (Heb. 7:25–26).

INTEREST. See *Usury*.

INTERMARRIAGE. Marriage between members of different races or religions. Intermarriage of the Israelites with the idolatrous Canaanites was forbidden by God (Josh. 23:12–13). Paul counseled the Corinthian Christians not to marry unbelievers (2 Cor. 6:14–17). See also *Marriage*.

INTERMEDIATE STATE. Some believe this to be a condition of believers between death and the resurrection. Paul characterized this state as being "absent from the body" (2 Cor. 5:8) while awaiting the resurrection (1 Thess. 4:13–18) and anticipating a glorified body like that of Jesus (Phil. 3:20–21). This condition is also characterized as a sleeplike state (John 11:11) that is enjoyable (Ps. 17:15) and unchangeable (2 Cor. 5:1).

INWARD PARTS. See *Bowels*.

IRON

1. A fortified city in the territory of Naphtali (Josh. 19:38), also known as *Beth-shemesh* and *Yiron*.

2. An ancient metal first mentioned in Gen. 4:22. Iron was used to make weapons (Job 20:24) and tools (1 Kings 6:7).

IR-SHEMESH. See *Beth-shemesh*.

ISAAC. The son born to Abraham and Sarah in their old age (Gen. 21:1–3) and thus the person through whom God's Chosen People, the Israelites, were descended (Gen. 21:9–13). He married Rebekah (Gen. 24:57–67)—a union to which twin sons Jacob and Esau were born (Gen. 25:19–26). Isaac was considered a man of faith (Heb. 11:9, 20), a patriarch of Israel (Exod. 32:13), and an ancestor of Christ (Luke 3:34). See also *Rebekah*.

ISAIAH/ESAIAS. A major prophet of Judah whose career spanned forty years (about 740–701 B.C.). The son of Amoz, he was married to a "prophetess" (Isa. 8:3). Working in the capital city of Jerusalem, Isaiah was the confidant of King Uzziah (Azariah) and his successors (Isa. 1:1). He warned that the city and nation would be destroyed by Assyria, but a righteous remnant would be saved (Isa. 1:2–9; 11:11). He gave his two sons symbolic names to underscore his message (Isa. 8:1–4; 7:3–4). Isaiah encouraged King Hezekiah but foretold the king's death (2 Kings 20:1). He was the author of the book of Isaiah, which prophesied the coming of the Messiah (Isa. 7:14), His rejection (Isa. 53), and the conversion of the Gentiles (Isa. 61:10–11). *Esaias:* Greek form (Matt. 4:14).

ISAIAH, BOOK OF. A major prophetic book of the O.T. noted for its prediction of the coming Messiah (7:14; 9:7) and particularly its emphasis on the Messiah as God's "suffering servant" (42:1–9; 49:1–6; 50:4–9; 52:13–53:12). These messianic passages occur in the midst of the prophet's prediction that God would punish the nation of Judah because of its rebellion and idolatry (1:1–12:6). Other prophecies in the book are directed at the pagan nations surrounding Judah (13:1–23:18).

Many Bible students call Isaiah the "fifth Gospel" because it echoes the N.T. themes of salvation and redemption. Jesus began His public ministry by identifying with this book's promise of comfort and healing for God's people: "The Spirit of the Lord God is upon me; because the Lord hath anointed me to preach good tidings unto the meek; he hath sent me to bind up the brokenhearted, to proclaim liberty to the captives" (Isa. 61:1; see also Luke 4:18–19). See also *Messiah.*

ISCARIOT, JUDAS. The disciple who betrayed Jesus (John 13:2, 26; 18:1–8). The word *Iscariot* identifies Judas as a citizen of Kerioth, a city in southern Judah (Josh. 15:25), to distinguish him from Judas (or Jude), brother of James, who was also one of the Twelve (Luke 6:16). Judas Iscariot apparently served as the treasurer for Jesus and His disciples (John 13:29). After realizing the gravity of his act of betrayal, Judas committed suicide (Matt. 27:3–5). See also *Twelve, The.*

ISH-BOSHETH/ESH-BAAL. The youngest son of Saul

who became king of Israel for two years (2 Sam. 2:8–10). He was eventually defeated by David and assassinated in his bed (2 Sam. 4:8–12). *Eshbaal:* 1 Chron. 8:33.

ISHI. A symbolic name, meaning "my husband," to be given to God when the Israelites returned to Him (Hos. 2:16–17). Ishi was to be used instead of Baali because the name Baal was associated with a pagan god.

ISHMAEL. Abraham's son born to Sarah's Egyptian maid Hagar (Gen. 16:1–11). After conflicts with Sarah, Hagar fled with Ishmael into the desert, where she was assured by angels that Ishmael would have many descendants (Gen. 21:8–18). Tradition holds that the Arab peoples are descendants of Ishmael. See also *Hagar*.

ISHMAELITES. Descendants of Ishmael, Abraham's son by Hagar (Gen. 16:15). God promised to bless the Ishmaelites, although Ishmael was not Abraham's covenant son (Gen. 21:12–13). Ishmael had twelve sons, whose descendants lived as nomads in the deserts of northern Arabia. Most modern-day Arabs claim descent from Ishmael. See also *Arabia*.

ISH-TOB. See *Tob*.

ISRAEL.

1. Another name for Jacob. Jacob was renamed Israel by an angel at Penuel because of his influence with God and man (Gen. 32:28; 35:10). His name was extended to the nation of Israel (Exod. 3:16) and finally narrowed to designate the Northern Kingdom after the nation divided following Solomon's administration. See also *Jacob*.

2. The Northern Kingdom. This nation was formed in 931 B.C. when the ten northern tribes rebelled against the two southern tribes and established its own kingship under Rehoboam (1 Kings 12). Samaria was established as the capital city. After about two centuries, the Northern Kingdom was carried into captivity by Assyria in 722 B.C. and Samaria was populated by foreigners (2 Kings 17:23–24). See also *Samaritan*.

ISRAELITES. Descendants of Israel, or Jacob (Lev. 23:42–43), a nation which was designated by God as His special people. The Israelites were regarded as children of the covenant and heirs of the promises which God made to Abraham (Gen. 12:1–3; Rom. 9:4; 11:1). See also *Jews*.

ISSACHAR. Jacob's fifth son by Leah; father of one of the twelve tribes of Israel (Gen. 30:17–18). The tribe occupied fertile land bounded on the north by Zebulon and Naphtali, on the east by the Jordan River, and on the south and west by Manasseh. The judges Deborah and Barak are assumed to be Issacharites, since they came from this territory (see Judg. 4–5). See also *Tribes of Israel*.

ITALIAN BAND (ITALIAN COHORT, ITALIAN REGIMENT). A unit of the Roman army stationed in Caesarea. Cornelius, one of the first Gentile converts to Christianity, was attached to this unit (Acts 10:1). *Italian Regiment:* NIV; *Italian Cohort:* NRSV.

ITALY. The boot-shaped country between Greece and Spain which juts into the Mediterranean Sea (Acts 18:2). Its capital city, Rome, was the seat of the Roman Empire in N.T. times. Paul sailed to Rome as a prisoner (Acts 27:1–6; 28:14–16).

ITCH. See *Scall*.

ITHAMAR. The youngest son of Aaron who was consecrated as a priest (Exod. 6:23). He oversaw the tabernacle during the wilderness wanderings (Exod. 38:21).

ITHREAM. A son of David, born at Hebron (2 Sam. 3:5).

ITUREA. A small province in Palestine at the base of Mt. Hermon. This area was ruled by Herod Philip when John the Baptist began his ministry (Luke 3:1).

IVAH, IVVAH. See *Ahava*.

IVORY. Decorative trim from the tusks of elephants which was a symbol of luxury. King Ahab's house was known as the "ivory house" (1 Kings 22:39). See also *Ahab*.

IYYAR. See *Zif*.

-J-

JAAZER. See *Jazer*.

JABBOK. A small stream which enters the Jordan River about twenty miles north of the Dead Sea (Num. 21:24). Beside this stream, at a point later called Peniel, Jacob wrestled with an angel (Gen. 32:24–31).

JABESH-GILEAD. A city of Gilead about twenty miles south of the Sea of Galilee. King Saul defended this city against Nahash, king of the Ammonites (1 Sam. 11:1–11).

JABIN.

1. The Canaanite king of Hazor who was killed by Joshua at the Merom Brook (Josh. 11:1–14).

2. Another king of Hazor who was defeated by Deborah and Barak at the Kishon River (Judg. 4).

JACHIN (JAKIN) AND BOAZ. Two ornamental bronze pillars, constructed by Hiram of Tyre, which stood in front of Solomon's temple at Jerusalem (1 Kings 7:13–22). *Jakin:* NIV.

JACINTH. A precious stone, perhaps the same as sapphire, used in the foundation of the heavenly city, or New Jerusalem (Rev. 21:20). See also *Ligure*.

JACKAL. A wild dog, or a scavenger which ran in packs. The "foxes" which Samson used to destroy crops of the Philistines may have been jackals (Judg. 15:4). See also *Fox*.

JACOB. The son of Isaac and Rebekah and father of several sons who became the ancestors of the twelve tribes of Israel. Jacob was the twin brother of Esau, who was the firstborn son and thus entitled to the birthright of his father Isaac. But he bought Esau's birthright for a pot of stew (Gen. 25:23–34). With his mother Rebekah's help, he deceived his father and received his blessing as well (Gen. 27:6–29). While fleeing his brother's wrath, Jacob struggled with an angel and was given the name *Israel,* meaning "prince with God" (Gen. 32:22–30). His descendants were known as Israelites, or descendants of Israel.

In his later years, after the birth of many children to his wives Rachel and Leah and their handmaids, Jacob mourned his favorite son Joseph, whom he presumed dead. But his joy was restored when Joseph was discovered alive and well in Egypt. Jacob died in Egypt after moving there at Joseph's initiative to escape a famine in Canaan. He was returned to his homeland for burial (Gen. 37–50). See also *Israel; Israelites*.

JACOB'S WELL. The well dug by Jacob and the site where Jesus offered the Samaritan woman "living water" (John 4:1–26). Not mentioned in the O.T., the site today is associated with the ancient city of Shechem (Tell Balatah) near the highway from Jerusalem to Galilee.

JAEL. The wife of Heber the Kenite who killed Sisera, a commander of the forces of King Jabin of Hazor (Judg. 4:17–22). See also *Sisera*.

JAFFA. See *Joppa*.

JAH. See *Jehovah*.

JAIR. The eighth judge of Israel, a member of the tribe of Gilead, who led the nation for twenty-two years (Judg. 10:3–5). See also *Judges of Israel*.

JAIRUS. A ruler of the synagogue near Capernaum whose daughter was raised from the dead by Jesus (Mark 5:22–23).

JAKIN. See *Jachin*.

JAMBRES. Magician of the Egyptian pharaoh who opposed Moses. While he is not mentioned in the O.T., Jambres was cited by Paul as one who resisted God's truth (2 Tim. 3:8).

JAMES.

1. A son of Zebedee and a disciple of Jesus. He and his brother John were called "sons of thunder" by Jesus because of their fiery temperament (Mark 3:17).

2. A son of Alphaeus and a disciple of Jesus (Matt. 10:3).

3. The half brother of Jesus who became a leader in the church at Jerusalem (Acts 21:17–18; Gal. 1:19). He was probably the author of the epistle of James. See also *Brothers of Christ*.

JAMES, EPISTLE OF. A short N.T. epistle—written probably by James, the half brother of Jesus—known for its plain language and practical application of the gospel to the believer's daily life. According to James, the true test of Christianity is in the living and doing of its truth rather than in speaking, hearing, and even believing its doctrines (1:22–27). Authentic faith results in acts of ministry to others, or as James puts it, "Faith, if it hath not works, is dead" (2:17). Other emphases in James are equality of all people before God (2:1–10) and the power of the tongue (3:3–10).

JANNES. A magician of the Egyptian pharaoh who opposed Moses. While he is not mentioned in the O.T., Jannes was cited by Paul as one who resisted God's truth (2 Tim. 3:8).

JAPHETH. A son of Noah who was saved in the ark (Gen. 5:32). Japheth is considered the father of the Indo-European races (Gen. 9:19–27; 10:2–5).

JAPHIA.

1. The king of Lachish and one of the five Amorite kings killed by Joshua's army (Josh. 10:3–27).

2. A son of David, born at Jerusalem after he became king (2 Sam. 5:15).

JAPHO. See *Joppa*.

JAR. See *Cruse; Pitcher*.

JARMUTH. A royal Canaanite city captured by Joshua (Josh. 10:3–27). Centuries later, Jarmuth was resettled by the Israelites after the Exile (Neh. 11:29).

JASHER. See *Book of Jasher*.

JASHOBEAM. The chief of David's mighty men, or brave warriors, who helped him become king and kept his kingdom strong (1 Chron. 11:10–11). See also *Mighty Men*.

JASON. A citizen of Thessalonica who was persecuted because he provided lodging for Paul and Silas (Acts 17:5–9). This may be the same Jason whom Paul referred to as "my kinsman" (Rom. 16:21).

JASPER. A precious stone, probably a type of quartz, used in the breastplate of the high priest (Exod. 28:20) and in the foundation of the heavenly city, or New Jerusalem (Rev. 21:19).

JAVAN. A son of Japheth and grandson of Noah. Javan was the father of the Ionians, or Greeks (Gen. 10:2; Isa. 66:19). See also *Greece*.

JAVELIN (SPEAR). A short spear or dart. A javelin was used by King Saul (1 Sam. 19:9–10) and by the high priest Phinehas (Num. 25:7). *Spear:* NIV, NRSV. See also *Dart; Spear*.

JAZER/JAAZER. A fortified Amorite city east of the Jordan River (2 Sam. 24:5) noted for its fertile land (Num. 32:1) and occupied by the conquering Israelites (Josh. 13:24–25). *Jaazer:* Num. 21:32.

JEALOUSY. Ill feelings toward others because of their blessings or favored position. Jacob's sons were jealous of their brother Joseph because he was their father's favorite (Gen. 37:11). Christians are counseled not to participate in such behavior (Rom. 13:13). See also *Envy*.

JEBUS. See *Jerusalem*.

JEBUSITES. Tribal enemies of the Israelites who were descended from Canaan (Gen. 10:15–16). They controlled Jerusalem (known as Jebus at that time) before David conquered the city (2 Sam. 5:6–8) and turned it into his capital. Remnants of the Jebusites became bondservants during Solomon's reign (1 Kings 9:20–21). See also *Jerusalem*.

JECONIAH. See *Jehoiachin*.

JEDIDIAH. A name for Solomon, meaning "beloved of Jehovah," bestowed at birth by Nathan the prophet (2 Sam. 12:25). This name suggests that David's sin of adultery had been forgiven.

JEDUTHUN/ETHAN. A Levite musician and writer of psalms (1 Chron. 9:16) who led in praise services when the ark of the covenant was returned to Jerusalem (1 Chron. 16:41–42). *Ethan:* 1 Chron. 6:44.

JEHOAHAZ.

1. The son and successor of Jehu as king of Israel (reigned 814–798 B.C.; 2 Kings 10:35). A wicked king, he led Israel into sin and idolatry (2 Kings 13:2).

2. The son and successor of Josiah as king of Judah about 610 B.C. A sinful monarch, he reigned only three months before being deposed by Pharaoh Nechoh of Egypt (2 Kings 23:31–34). *Shallum:* 1 Chron. 3:15.

3. Another name for Ahaziah, king of Judah about 850 B.C. See *Ahaziah,* No. 2.

JEHOASH. See *Joash,* No. 1.

JEHOIACHIN/CONIAH/JECONIAH/JECHONIAS. The son and successor of Jehoiakim as king of Judah (reigned only three months, about 597 B.C.). Evil like his father, Jehoiachin was king when the nation was captured by Nebuchadnezzar and the people were deported to Babylonia (2 Kings 24:8–16). He was released after thirty-seven years in prison (Jer. 52:31–34). Jehoiachin is listed as an ancestor of Christ (Matt. 1:11–12). *Coniah:* Jer. 22:24; *Jeconiah:* 1 Chron. 3:16–17; *Jechonias:* Matt 1:11–12.

JEHOIADA.

1. A military leader at Hebron who apparently recruited 3,700 of his countrymen to serve in David's army (1 Chron. 12:27).

2. A high priest who protected young King Joash from Queen Athaliah until Joash was crowned king of Judah. Jehoiada also led out in reducing Baal worship (2 Kings 11:3–21). See also *Joash,* No. 1.

JEHOIAKIM/ELIAKIM. The son and successor of Josiah as king of Judah (reigned about 609–597 B.C). An evil ruler who exploited the people and led them into idolatry, Jehoiakim died while Jerusalem was under siege by the Babylonians (2 Chron. 36:6). The prophet Jeremiah foretold his defeat (Jer. 22:17–19). *Eliakim:* 2 Kings 23:34.

JEHORAM/JORAM.

1. The wicked king of Judah (reigned about 848–841 B.C.) who murdered his own brothers (2 Chron. 21:2–13) in order to succeed his father Jehoshaphat (1 Kings 22:50). Struck down by God, he died in disgrace, as predicted by the prophet Elijah, from a mysterious disease (2 Chron. 21:12–20). *Joram:* 2 Kings 8:21.

2. Ahab's son and successor as Israel's king (reigned about 852–841 B.C.; 2 Kings 1:17). He died in battle against the Syrians (2 Kings 8:28–29). *Joram:* 2 Kings 8:16.

JEHOSHABEATH/ JEHOSHEBA. The daughter of King Jehoram of Judah who hid her nephew Joash from Queen Athaliah's wrath until Joash was crowned king (2 Chron. 22:11–12). *Jehosheba:* 2 Kings 11:2.

JEHOSHAPHAT/ JOSAPHAT. The son and successor of Asa as king of Judah (reigned about 870–848 B.C.). A reformer like his father, Jehoshaphat attacked idolatry and sent teachers to help people learn about God (2 Chron. 17:6–9). He was rebuked by the prophet Jehu for forming an alliance with King Ahab of Israel (2 Chron. 19:1–3). *Josaphat:* Matt. 1:8.

JEHOSHAPHAT, VALLEY OF. A place where God will judge the nations in the end-time, according to the prophet Joel (Joel 3:2–14). This site is believed to be part of the Kidron Valley between Jerusalem and the Mount of Olives. The name may refer to a symbolic "valley of decision," where God will judge all nations.

JEHOSHEBA.
See *Jehoshabeath.*

JEHOSHUA. See *Joshua.*

JEHOVAH/JAH. A translation of *Yahweh,* a Hebrew word for God in the O.T. which indicated his eternity and self-existence. This word is based on a Hebrew verb meaning "to be"; thus the name "I Am" by which God revealed himself to Moses at the burning bush. Yahweh is rendered as "Lord" and printed in capital and small capital letters (LORD) in most English versions of the Bible, although some translations use *Yahweh* or *Jehovah. Jah* is an abbreviated form of the word (Ps. 68:4) See also *I Am; Lord; Yahweh.*

JEHOVAH-JIREH. A name for God meaning "the Lord will provide." It was used by Abraham to commemorate God's provision of a ram in place of Isaac as a sacrifice (Gen. 22:14).

JEHOVAH-NISSI. A name for God meaning "the Lord is my banner." Moses used this name to show God's victory over the Amalekites (Exod. 17:15–16).

JEHOVAH-SHALOM. The name of an altar built by Gideon, meaning "the Lord is peace" (Judg. 6:24).

JEHOVAH-SHAMMAH. The name of a city of the future envisioned by the prophet Ezekiel, indicating that "the Lord is there" (Ezek. 48:35).

JEHOVAH-TSIDKENNU. The name for the coming Messiah used by the prophet Jeremiah, meaning "the Lord our righteousness" (Jer. 23:6).

JEHU.

1. A violent and deceitful king of Israel (reigned about 841–814 B.C.) who gained the throne by killing King Ahab's descendants (2 Kings 9:2–10:36).

2. A prophet who delivered a message of doom to King Baasha of Israel (1 Kings 16:1– 2) and rebuked King Jehoshaphat of Judah for forming alliances with King Ahab (2 Chron. 19: 1–3).

JEMIMA. The first of Job's three daughters to be born after his recovery from suffering and affliction (Job 42:14).

JEPHTHAH/JEPHTHAE. A judge of Israel who delivered the nation from the Ammonites. After making a rash and foolish vow, Jepthah sacrificed his only child as an offering to God

(Judg. 11:1–39). *Jephthae:* Heb. 11:32. See also *Judges of Israel.*

JEREMIAH/JEREMIAS/ JEREMY. A major prophet of the O.T. who preached God's message of doom to the nation of Judah for about forty years during the reigns of the last five kings of the nation: Josiah, Jehoahaz, Jehoiakim, Jehoiachin, and Zedekiah (Jer. 1:2–3). Called to his prophetic ministry even before he was born (Jer. 1:4–10), he wept openly over the sins of Judah (Jer. 9:1) and declared that the nation would fall to a foreign enemy as punishment for its sin and idolatry (Jer. 16:1–13). After Judah was overrun by the Babylonians, Jeremiah remained in Jerusalem while most of his countrymen were deported to Babylonia. Eventually he was taken to Egypt, where he continued to preach to a remnant of Jewish people (Jer. 43:5–13). *Jeremy:* Matt. 2:17; 27:9; *Jeremias:* Greek form (Matt. 16:14)

JEREMIAH, BOOK OF. A major prophetic book of the O.T. noted for its stern warnings to the nation of Judah that it was destined to fall to the Babylonians unless the people repented and turned back to God. After being called and assured of God's guidance and presence (1:1–19), Jeremiah pronounced prophecies of doom against Judah (2:1–45:5) and then the surrounding pagan nations (46:1–51:64). The book closes with a description of the destruction of Jerusalem (52:1–23) and the deportation of the influential people of Judah to Babylonia (52:24–30).

The concept of a new covenant (Jer. 31) is unique to the book of Jeremiah. This new agreement between God and His people, based on grace and forgiveness, was needed because the old covenant of law had failed to keep the people on the path of righteousness and holiness. See also *Babylonia.*

JERICHO. A fortified Canaanite city near the Jordan River and the Dead Sea (Deut. 32:49) which was captured by Joshua when the Israelites entered the Promised Land (Josh. 6:1–22). In N.T. times, Jesus encountered Zacchaeus at Jericho (Luke 19:1–10), a city which had been built near the site of O.T. Jericho. It is regarded as one of the world's oldest cities, probably inhabited as early as 7000 B.C.

JEROBOAM.

1. Jeroboam I. The first king of Israel (reigned about 931

–910 B.C.) after the kingdom of Solomon split into two separate nations following the death of Solomon. An official in Solomon's administration, Jeroboam led the ten northern tribes to rebel against the two southern tribes when Rehoboam succeeded Solomon as king (1 Kings 12:17–20). He established idol worship in the cities of Bethel and Dan (1 Kings 12:26–30) and was ultimately defeated by King Abijah of Judah and struck down by the Lord (2 Chron. 13:19–20).

2. Jeroboam II. A wicked king of Israel (reigned about 782–753 B.C.) who succeeded his father Jehoash (2 Kings 14:23–29). He was denounced by the prophet Amos for his evil deeds and encouragement of idol worship (Amos 7:7–9).

JERUBBAAL/JERUBBESHETH. A name given to the judge Gideon by his father after he destroyed the altar of Baal at Ophrah (Judg. 6:32). It probably means "let Baal contend." Another name given to Gideon was *Jerubbesheth* (2 Sam. 11:21; *Jerubbaal:* NRSV), probably meaning "contender with the idol." See also *Gideon*.

JERUEL. A wilderness in southern Judah where the prophet Jahaziel predicted King Jehoshaphat of Judah would meet the Ammonite and Moabite armies (2 Chron. 20: 14–16).

JERUSALEM/JEBUS/SALEM. The religious and political capital of the Jewish people. Situated forty-eight miles from the Mediterranean Sea and eighteen miles west of the Jordan River, Jerusalem was known as *Salem* in Abraham's time (Gen. 14:18) and as *Jebus* when the people of Israel entered Canaan, or the Promised Land (Josh. 15:8). David captured the city from the Jebusites, renamed it, and turned it into his capital (2 Sam. 5:6–9). It was often called the "city of David" (2 Chron. 32:5). Solomon built the magnificent temple in Jerusalem as the center of worship for the Jewish people about 950 B.C. (1 Kings 5:5–8). The city fell to the Babylonians in 587 B.C., and its leading citizens were taken away as captives (Jer. 39:1–8).

After the Persians defeated the Babylonians, King Cyrus of Persia allowed Jewish exiles to return to their homeland and rebuild Jerusalem, including the temple and the city wall (Ezra 1:1–4; Neh. 12:27–47; Zech. 4). In N.T. times, Christ wept over the city because of its sin and spiritual indifference (Luke 19:41–42). He predicted

The Dome of the Rock, a Moslem mosque which sits on the site once occupied by Solomon's temple in Jerusalem.
Courtesy Israel Ministry of Tourism

its destruction (Luke 19:43–44), entered Jerusalem as a conquering spiritual leader (Matt. 21:9–10), and was crucified on a hill just outside the city wall (Luke 9:31). As Jesus predicted, Jerusalem was destroyed in A.D. 70 during a fierce battle between the Roman army and Jewish zealots.

The church was launched in Jerusalem, where it experienced spectacular growth (Acts 2). The apostle John described the future heavenly city as "New Jerusalem" (Rev. 21:1–3). See also *City of David; Jebusites; Zion*.

JERUSALEM COUNCIL. A conference held during the early days of the Christian movement to determine how Gentile believers would be received into the church. Participants representing the church at Antioch and the church in Jerusalem included Peter, Paul, Barnabas, and James. The issue was whether Gentile converts first had to identify with Judaism by being circumcised before they could be baptized and received as full members of the church (Acts 15:6). The council concluded that since Gentile and Jewish believers are saved by grace alone, circumcision was unnecessary (Acts 15:8–19). This solution averted a conflict that would have hampered missionary efforts and could have made Christianity a sect of Judaism. See also *Judaizers*.

JESHANAH GATE. See *Old Gate*.

JESHUA

1. A priest who returned to Jerusalem with Zerubbabel after the Babylonian Exile and helped rebuild the temple and reestablish worship (Ezra 2:2; 3:2–9).

2. Another name for Joshua (Neh. 8:17). See *Joshua*.

JESSE. The father of David and an ancestor of Christ. Jesse presented his eight sons to the prophet Samuel, who anointed David as the future king of Israel (1 Sam. 16:10–13). Jesse is mentioned in Scripture as the root or shoot that would produce the royal line of David (Isa. 11:1, 10; Rom. 15:12) and ultimately the Savior (Matt. 1:5–6).

JESUS CHRIST. The Son of God and Savior of the world. Jesus is the Greek form of the name *Joshua,* meaning "Savior." Christ means "the anointed one," identifying Him as the promised Messiah of O.T. prophecy (Gal. 4:4–5).

Jesus was born during the reign of Herod the Great as Roman ruler over Palestine, some time before 4 B.C., the date of Herod's death (Matt. 2:1). After a public ministry of perhaps three years, He was crucified about A.D. 30. He preexisted as the eternal Word of God (John 1:1, 18; 8:58) and participated in the creation of the world (John 1:3). His advent in human form, including His virgin birth in Bethlehem (Isa. 7:14; Mic. 5:2), was foretold in the O.T. (Ps. 2:7–8; Isa. 9:6–7). As the God-man, Jesus was incarnated to reveal God in an understandable way (Matt. 1:23; John 1:14–18) and "to make reconciliation for the sins of the people" (Heb. 2:17–18).

As a boy, Jesus grew physically and advanced in knowledge (Luke 2:51–52). Yet, He had a consciousness of His divine mission (Luke 2:49). He was baptized by John the Baptist to "fulfill all righteousness" and to identify with humanity (Matt. 3:15–17). In resisting Satan's temptations at the beginning of His public ministry, the sinless Savior refused to break dependence on the Father and to establish His kingdom in any fashion other than by suffering

A view of Bethlehem, the village where Jesus was born, from inside the bell tower of the Church of the Nativity.
Courtesy Israel Ministry of Tourism

(Matt. 4:7–10).

Jesus' public ministry was short and revolutionary (John 17:4). He came preaching and healing (Mark 1:38–42), teaching (Luke 6:6), and seeking the lost (Luke 19:10). After an early campaign in Judea in southern Palestine, He began a major campaign in the region of Galilee in northern Palestine with Capernaum as His home base. His hometown synagogue in Nazareth rejected Him, but the common people heard Him gladly (Luke 4:16–32). He proclaimed a spiritual kingdom which required repentance and faith rather than blind and ritualistic obedience to the law and the legalistic demands of the Pharisees (Matt. 6:10, 33; Luke 13:3). His later ministry was devoted to training His disciples and preparing them for His death and their witness to others in the Holy Spirit's power (Luke 24:46–49).

Jesus' actions such as denouncing the Pharisees (Matt. 23), healing on the Sabbath (Matt. 12:8–14), and cleansing the temple angered the religious leaders among the Jews and disturbed Roman officials (Matt. 21:23). His triumphal entry into Jerusalem on a donkey disappointed His followers who wanted an earthly king (Luke 24:19–21). After observing the Passover with His disciples and instituting the Lord's Supper, He was betrayed into enemy hands (Luke 22:15–21).

In His trial before Pilate, Jesus acknowledged His kingship but declared His kingdom "not of this world" (John 18:36–37). Nevertheless, He was charged with treason and crucified between two thieves (John 19:14–16; Luke 23:33). On the third day He arose from the grave, conquering sin and death for believers (Acts 13:30; 1 Cor. 15:57). Jesus ascended to the Father, where He "ever liveth to make intercession" (Heb. 7:25). He will return for righteous judgment (Acts 17:31), to raise the dead (1 Thess. 4:14–17), and to usher in the time when all must confess that "Jesus Christ is Lord" (Phil. 2:9–11; Rev. 11:15).

See also *Emmanuel; Messiah; Son of God; Son of Man.*

JETHRO/REUEL/HOBAB. The father-in-law of Moses who was a priest of Midian. Moses married his daughter Zipporah (Exod. 2:16–22; 4:18). Jethro visited Moses in the wilderness and advised him to select leaders to share the responsibility of dispensing justice and settling disputes among the Hebrews (Exod. 18:17–26). *Reuel:* Exod. 2:18; *Hobab:* Judg. 4:11.

JEWELS. Precious stones used as ornaments or jewelry. The breastplate of Aaron the high priest contained twelve jewels, symbolizing the twelve tribes of Israel (Exod. 25:7).

JEWS. A word for the Israelites which came into general use during the period after the Babylonian Exile. In the N.T., it designates Israelites as opposed to Gentiles. See also *Israelites*.

JEZEBEL. The scheming wife of King Ahab who promoted Baal worship in the nation of Israel. She led Ahab to erect pagan altars (1 Kings 16:32–33), killed several prophets of the Lord (1 Kings 18:4–13), and plotted the death of Elijah (1 Kings 19:1–2), who prophesied her death (1 Kings 21:23). King Jehu had her assassinated when he came into power, in fulfillment of Elijah's prophecy (2 Kings 9:7–37). See also *Ahab*.

JEZREEL.

1. A symbolic name given

by the prophet Hosea to his son to show that King Jehu and his family would be punished for murdering King Ahab's family. The name means "God scatters" or "God sows" (Hos. 1:3–5).

2. A fortified city where King Ahab's palace was located (1 Kings 21:1) and where his family was assassinated by Jehu's forces (2 Kings 10:1–10).

3. The name of a valley in O.T. times which separated Samaria from Galilee. Many major battles have occurred here. Some scholars believe the battle of Armageddon in which Satan will be overthrown will be fought in this valley (Rev. 16:16; 20:1–10). The Greek word for this valley is *Esdraelon*.

JOAB. The commander of King David's army during most of David's reign (1 Kings 11:14–17). He became commander because he was the first to launch an attack against the Jebusites in their fortified city known as Jebus (later called Jerusalem; see 1 Chron. 11:6). His military exploits included victories over the Edomites (2 Sam. 2:13–16) and the Ammonites (2 Sam. 10:6–14). Joab carried out David's plan to have Uriah the Hittite killed in battle (2 Sam. 11:14). Joab was murdered on orders from the king when Solomon succeeded David as ruler of Judah (1 Kings 2:5, 31–34).

JOANNA. A woman who was a faithful follower of Jesus (Luke 8:1–3). She prepared spices for His burial and proclaimed His resurrection (Luke 23:55–56; 24:1–10).

JOASH.

1. The eighth king of Judah (reigned about 798–782 B.C.) who succeeded his father Ahaziah (2 Kings 11:2) at age seven. He was hidden by his aunt from the wicked queen Athaliah to prevent his assassination (2 Kings 11:1–3). Jehoiada the priest served as his counselor (2 Kings 11:12, 17). Joash brought needed religious reforms to Judah (2 Kings 12:4–5), but he turned to idol worship after Jehoiada's death (2 Chron. 24:17–19). He was assassinated by his own officers (2 Chron. 24:24–25). *Jehoash:* 2 Kings 11:21.

2. The son and successor of Jehoahaz as king of Israel (reigned about 798–782 B.C.). He led the nation into sin through his idolatry (2 Kings 13:10–25).

JOATHAM. See *Jotham*.

JOB. A godly man of the O.T. whose faith sustained him

through fierce trials and sufferings. Afflicted by Satan with God's permission (Job 1:6–19), Job refused to blame or curse God for his misfortune (1:20–22; 2:10), although he did complain to God, lamenting the day he was born (3:1–3). He and his three friends had long discussions about his misfortunes and what they meant. Job eventually came to a greater understanding of God's ways of dealing with man (42:3–6), and God restored his family and possessions (42:10–15). He was praised by James in the N.T. for his patience and faith (Jas. 5:11).

JOB, BOOK OF. A wisdom book of the O.T. which addresses the issue of human suffering, particularly the question of why the righteous suffer. The book is written in the form of a poetic drama revolving around the discussion of this problem by Job and his three friends: Eliphaz, Bildad, and Zophar.

After Job lost his children and earthly possessions (1:1–2:13), his three friends arrived to "comfort" him and discuss the reason for Job's suffering (3:1–37:24). God assured Job that He is the sovereign, almighty God who doesn't have to defend His actions (38:1–41:34). Armed with a new understanding of God and His nature ("I have heard of thee by the hearing of the ear: but now mine eye seeth thee"; 42:5), Job was rewarded by the Lord with the restoration of his family and possessions (42:10–15). See also *Wisdom Literature*.

JOBAB. A member of a confederacy of Canaanite kings defeated by Joshua at the Merom Brook (Josh. 11:1–12).

JOCHEBED. The mother of Moses, Aaron, and Miriam (Exod. 6:20). She is listed as one of the heroes of the faith (Heb. 11:23).

JOD. The tenth letter of the Hebrew alphabet, used as a heading over Ps. 119:73–80. See *Jot*.

JOEL.

1. A prophet of Judah in the days of King Uzziah and author of the O.T. book which bears his name. He predicted the outpouring of God's Spirit at Pentecost (Joel 2:28–32; Acts 2:16–21), proclaimed salvation through Christ (Joel 2:32), sounded the note of God's universal judgment (Joel 3:1–16), and pictured the eternal age with blessings for God's people (3:17–21).

2. The son of Samuel and a corrupt judge of Israel. Joel's dishonesty, along with that of his brother Abiah, led the people to ask Samuel to appoint a king to rule the nation (1 Sam. 8:2–5).

JOEL, BOOK OF. A brief prophetic book of the O.T. which uses a devastating swarm of locusts (chap. 1) as an early warning sign of God's judgment in order to call His people to repentance. The prophet predicted the outpouring of God's spirit (2:28–32), an event which happened on the day of Pentecost (Acts 2:16–21); proclaimed salvation through Christ (2:32); and pictured the eternal age with blessings for God's people (3:17–21). See also *Pentecost*.

JOHANAN. A supporter of Gedaliah, governor of Judah (2 Kings 25:22–23), who took a remnant of the Jews to Egypt, in spite of the prophet Jeremiah's warning (Jer. 41:16–18; 43:4–6).

JOHN THE APOSTLE. A fisherman from Galilee, the son of Zebedee and brother of James, who became one of the twelve apostles of Jesus (Matt. 4:21–22). He was described as the disciple "whom Jesus loved" and a member of Christ's inner circle of disciples, which included his brother James and Simon Peter (Mark 5:37; 9:2; 14:33). John was ambitious for position and prestige in Christ's kingdom (Mark 10:35 –37), but he showed a willingness to die for Jesus (Mark 10:38–39). Associated with Peter in bold evangelism in Jerusalem after Jesus' ascension (Acts 4:13; 8:14–15), he left Jerusalem about A.D. 65 for Ephesus, where he wrote the fourth Gospel and the three epistles of John. He wrote the Revelation while exiled as a political prisoner on the island of Patmos (Rev. 1:9–11).

JOHN THE BAPTIST. The prophet of righteousness and preacher of repentance who prepared the way for Christ. John's birth, Nazarite lifestyle, and unique role as the Messiah's forerunner was revealed to his father Zechariah (Luke 1:13–17) and his mother Elizabeth, a cousin of Mary—the earthly mother of Jesus (Luke 1:5–9, 39–41). He preached repentance and baptized converts in the Jordan River (Matt. 3:1–6), reluctantly agreeing to baptize Jesus after proclaiming Him as the "Lamb of God" (Matt. 3:13–17; John 1:29).

John denounced the hypocrisy of the Pharisees and the immorality and adultery of

Herod Antipas, a Roman ruler in Palestine (Matt. 3:7–8; 14:4). He was executed by Herod at the request of his wife Herodias's dancing daughter (Matt. 14:3–12). John always magnified Jesus rather than himself (John 3:30), and Jesus commended him highly for his faithfulness (Luke 7:24–28).

JOHN, EPISTLES OF. Three short epistles of the N.T. written by John, one of the twelve disciples of Jesus. First John, the longest of the three, focuses on such themes as the incarnation of Christ (1:1–5), Christian discipleship (1:6–10), false teachings about Christ (2:1–8), and the meaning of love and fellowship (2:15–5:3). Second John calls on believers to abide in the commandments of God (vv. 1–10) and reject false teachers (vv. 7–13). Third John commends the believers Gaius (vv. 1–8) and Demetrius (v. 12), while condemning Diotrephes (vv. 9–11). The apostle John probably wrote these epistles from Ephesus about A.D. 95. See also *Elect Lady; Demetrius,* No. 2; *Gaius,* No. 4; *John the Apostle*.

JOHN, GOSPEL OF. One of the four Gospels of the N.T., written by the apostle John to show that "Jesus is the Christ, the Son of God" (20:31). John is unique among the Gospels in that it majors on the theological *meaning* of the events in Jesus' life rather than the events themselves. Many of the miracles of Jesus are interpreted as "signs" of His divine power and unique relationship to the Father (2:1–12; 5:2–16). The "I am" sayings of Jesus, in which He reveals selected attributes or characteristics of His divine nature, are also unique to the Gospel of John: The bread of life (6:35), light of the world (8:12), the door of the sheep (10:7), the good shepherd (10:11), the way, the truth, and the life (14:6), and the vine (15:5). See also *John the Apostle; Synoptic Gospels*.

JOKSHAN. A son born to Abraham and his concubine Keturah (Gen. 25:1–2; 1 Chron. 1:32).

JOKTAN. A son of Eber and descendant of Shem. He was an ancestor of several tribes in the Arabian desert (1 Chron. 1:19–27).

JONAH/JONAS. An O.T. prophet who was swallowed by a "great fish" while fleeing from God's call to preach to the pagan citizens of Nineveh in Assyria (Jon. 1:17). In predicting His death and resurrection, Jesus referred to Jonah's experience (Luke 11:30; *Jonas*). See also *Assyria; Nineveh*.

JONAH, BOOK OF. A short prophetic book of the O.T. which emphasizes God's universal love. Jonah, the "reluctant prophet" (1:1–2:10) finally preached to the citizens of Nineveh in Assyria, a pagan nation noted for its cruelty and opposition to Israel. To his surprise and disappointment, the pagans repented and turned to God (4:1–10). Through this experience, Jonah learned that God is concerned for all people, not merely the citizens of his native land (4:1–11). See also *Assyria*.

JONATHAN.

1. King Saul's oldest son (1 Sam. 14:49), who was a loyal friend of David, even while his father was trying to kill David (1 Sam. 20:17–42). David mourned Jonathan (2 Sam. 1:17–26) after he was killed by the Philistines (1 Sam. 31:2–8). See also *Mephibosheth*.

2. A supporter of David during Absalom's rebellion. Jonathan hid in a well to warn David of Absalom's plans (2 Sam. 17:17–21).

JOPPA/JAPHO/JAFFA. A coastal city on the Mediterranean Sea where Peter had his vision on full acceptance of the Gentiles (Acts 10:9–23). This area is known today as *Jaffa*, a part of the city of Tel Aviv. *Japho:* Josh. 19:46.

JORAM. See *Jehoram*.

JORDAN RIVER. The largest and most important river in Palestine. It runs the length of the country, from the Sea of Galilee in the north to the Dead Sea in the south. Jesus was baptized by John in the Jordan (Matt. 3:5–13).

JOSAPHAT. See *Jehoshaphat*.

JOSEPH.

1. The son of Jacob by Rachel who was sold to a band of traders by his jealous brothers. Enslaved and imprisoned in Egypt, Joseph became an important official under the pharaoh. He was eventually reunited with his father and brothers when they came to Egypt to buy grain. A model of faith and forgiveness, Joseph saw God at work in human events (Gen. 37–50; Heb. 11:22). He was called *Zaphnath-paaneah* by the Egyptian pharaoh (Gen. 41:45).

2. The husband of Mary, Jesus' mother. A descendant of King David (Matt. 1:20), he was

a carpenter (Matt. 13:55) and a righteous man (Matt. 1:19). Joseph took Mary as his wife after an angel explained Mary's condition (Matt. 1:19–25). He was with Mary when Jesus was born in Bethlehem (Luke 2:16). He took his family to Egypt to escape Herod's wrath, then returned later to Nazareth, where the young Jesus was obedient to His earthly parents (Matt. 2:13–23; Luke 2:51). Since Joseph does not appear later in the Gospels, it is likely that he died before Jesus' public ministry.

3. A devout man of Arimathaea (Luke 23:50–51) and secret disciple of Jesus (John 19:38) who prepared Jesus' body for burial and placed Him in his own tomb (Mark 15:43–46; Luke 23:53).

4. A half brother of Jesus. See *Brothers of Christ*.

JOSES.

1. A half brother of Jesus (Mark 6:3).

2. Another name for Barnabas. See *Barnabas*.

JOSHUA/OSHEA/HOSHEA/ JEHOSHUAH/JESHUA. Moses' successor who led the Israelites into the Promised Land and rallied the people to victory over the Canaanites. One of two spies who gave Moses a favorable report on Canaan (Num. 13:8), he was the Lord's choice as Moses' successor (Num. 27:18–20). After his conquest of Canaan (Josh. 10–12), Joshua divided the land among the twelve tribes (Josh. 13–19). Before his death, he led the people to renew their covenant with God (Josh. 24:15–27). *Oshea:* Num. 13:8; *Hoshea:* Deut. 32:44; *Jehoshuah:* 1 Chron. 7:27; *Jeshua:* Neh. 8:17.

JOSHUA, BOOK OF. A book of the O.T. that details the conquest and settlement of the land of Canaan by the Israelites under the leadership of Joshua. Major events covered by the book include: (1) Joshua's succession of Moses as leader of the people and their spiritual preparation for conquest (1:1–5:15); (2) battles against the Canaanites and allied tribes (6:1–13:7); (3) division of the land among the tribes of Israel (13:8–19:51); (4) the cities of refuge and Levitical cities (20:1–21:45); and (5) the farewell address and death of Joshua (23:1–24:33). See also *Cities of Refuge; Joshua; Levitical Cities*.

JOSIAH/JOSIAS. The son and successor of Amon as king of Judah (reigned 640–609 B.C.;

2 Kings 21:26). Crowned at age eight, he made a covenant to obey God (2 Kings 23:3) and led an important reform movement to reestablish God's law, repair the temple (2 Kings 22:3–9), and abolish idolatry (2 Kings 23:4–24). *Josias:* Jesus' ancestry (Matt. 1:10–11).

JOT. The English word for the jod (yod), the smallest letter in the Hebrew alphabet (Matt. 5:18), used figuratively by Jesus for a matter of minor importance. See *Jod*.

JOTHAM/JOATHAM. The son and successor of Azariah (Uzziah) as king of Judah (reigned about 750–732 B.C.). A contemporary of the prophets Isaiah, Hosea, and Micah (Isa. 1:1; Mic. 1:1), he was a good king but failed to destroy places of pagan worship (2 Kings 15:34–35). Jotham improved the temple, strengthened the city wall, and fortified buildings throughout Judah (2 Chron. 27:3–4). *Joatham:* Matt. 1:9.

JOY. Great delight or positive feelings. Joy attended Christ's birth (Luke 2:10) and resurrection (Matt. 28:8). A believer's spiritual joy is produced by the Holy Spirit (Luke 10:21; Phil. 4:4).

JUBAL. A son of Lamech, descendant of Cain, and a skilled musician regarded as the ancestor of those who play the harp and the flute (Gen. 4:21).

JUBILE (JUBILEE). A year of celebration devoted to liberty and justice and observed every fifty years by the Israelites. During this year, Israelites serving as indentured servants were released from their debts and set free. All properties given up because of indebtedness since the last jubilee were returned to the original owners. Cropland was allowed to go unplanted as a conservation measure (Lev. 25:8–55). *Jubilee:* NIV, NRSV.

JUDAH.

1. A son of Jacob and Leah and ancestor of the tribe of Judah (Gen. 29:35). Judah interceded for his brother Joseph to be sold rather than killed (Gen. 37:26–27). He offered himself as a ransom for his brother Benjamin before Joseph in Egypt (Gen. 43:8–9; 44:32–34). His father Jacob bestowed Reuben's birthright on Judah, declaring "the sceptre shall not depart from Judah" (Gen. 49:10). He is listed as an ancestor of Christ (Matt. 1:2–3) and called *Juda*

in Luke's ancestry (Luke 3:33). The tribe Judah is spelled *Juda* in the N.T. (Heb. 7:14). See also *Tribes of Israel*.

2. The Southern Kingdom, or nation of Judah. Founded after Solomon's death, the Southern Kingdom was composed largely of the tribes of Judah and Benjamin, while the rebellious ten northern tribes retained the name of Israel. Solomon's son Rehoboam was the first king of Judah, with the capital at Jerusalem (1 Kings 14:21). The nation drifted into paganism and idolatry under a succession of kings, turning a deaf ear to great prophets such as Isaiah and Jeremiah, who tried to bring them back to worship of the one true God. Judah was overrun and taken into exile by the Babylonians about 587 B.C. A remnant returned to rebuild Jerusalem about 530 B.C. (2 Chron. 36:20–23).

JUDAIZERS. An early Christian sect which advocated that Gentiles must be circumcised before they could become Christians (Acts 15:1). They were denounced by Paul, who insisted that believers are justified by faith alone (Acts 15:12; Gal. 6:15). The Judaizers were also opposed by Peter and James at the Jerusalem Council (Acts 15:8–19). See also *Circumcision; Jerusalem Council*.

JUDAS. See *Iscariot, Judas; Jude*.

JUDAS, BROTHER OF JAMES/LEBBAEUS/ THADDAEUS. One of the twelve disciples of Jesus, also called *Lebbaeus* (Matt. 10:3) and *Thaddaeus* (Mark 3:18). He was called "brother of James" to set him apart from the Judas who betrayed Jesus (Luke 6:16). See also *Twelve, The*.

JUDE/JUDAS. The half brother of Christ and author of the N.T. epistle which bears his name. He did not believe in Jesus in the beginning (John 7:5), but he apparently became a disciple after His resurrection (Acts 1:14). *Judas:* Matt. 13:55. See also *Brothers of Christ*.

JUDE, EPISTLE OF. A short N.T. letter written like a brief essay or tract and addressed to the problem of false teachings in the early church. Jude called on believers to root their faith in the true doctrine taught by the apostles (v. 17) as well as the love of Christ (v. 21).

JUDEA. A district in southern Palestine in N.T. times. The name was derived from "Jewish," a word describing Jewish exiles who returned to southern Palestine from the Babylonian Exile about 530 B.C. Judea was a Roman province annexed to Syria when Jesus was born (Matt. 2:1).

JUDGES, BOOK OF. A historical book of the O.T. which records the exploits of several different judges, or military deliverers, in Israel's history. The key to understanding Judges is the phrase, "The children of Israel again did evil in the sight of the Lord" (see 4:1), which occurs several times throughout the book. After each period of sin against God, He would send enemy oppressors in judgment. The Israelites would repent and pray for a deliverer, and God would answer their prayer. After their deliverance at the hand of a judge, the cycle of sin / oppression / repentance / deliverance would start all over again. See also *Judges of Israel*.

JUDGES OF ISRAEL. Popular military leaders or deliverers who led Israel between the time of Joshua's death and the beginning of the kingship (about 1380–1050 B.C.). Israel's judges served in times of disunity and spiritual decline among the twelve tribes (Judg. 17:6; 21:25) as well as times when all the tribes were oppressed by their enemies. While some judges were weak or wicked, noteworthy exploits include Deborah and Barak's defeat of the Canaanite king Jabin (4:4–24), Gideon's 300 warriors who subdued the Midianites (7:1–8:21), and Samson's massacre of the Philistines (15:14–16).

Judges of Israel

Othniel ....Judg. 3:9–10
Ehud ....Judg. 3:15–30
Shamgar ....Judg. 3:31
Deborah and
Barak ....Judg. 4:4–8
Gideon ....Judg. 6:11–40
Abimelech ......Judg. 9:1–54
Tola ....Judg. 10:1–2
Jair ....Judg. 10:3–5
Jephthah ....Judg. 12:1–7
Ibzan..............Judg. 12:8–10
Elon ....Judg. 12:11–12
Abdon ....Judg. 12:13–15
Samson.............Judg. 15:20
Eli ....1 Sam. 4:15–18
Samuel ....1 Sam. 7:15
Samuel's sons..1 Sam. 8:1–3
Bedan ....1 Sam. 12:11

JUDGMENT. Divine retribution against human activities. God's judgment is designed to punish evil (Exod. 20:5), to correct the misguided (2 Sam. 7:14–15), and to deter His people from wrongdoing (Luke 13:3–5). His judgment is an expression of His chastening love for the believer (Heb. 12:5–6). Jesus, God's resurrected Son, has authority to judge all mankind (John 5:27; Acts 17:31). Believers in Jesus will avoid condemnation and enter eternal life (John 3:16–17). See also *Punishment; Retribution.*

JUDGMENT, LAST. Final judgment of unbelievers of all ages. The final judgment is called a day of wrath for unbelievers (Rom. 2:5–8) but a day when believers will enter into eternal life (Rom. 2:7). The Lord will appear suddenly to gather His elect (Matt. 24:32, 42) and to separate unbelievers for judgment (Matt. 25:31–33). We should be prepared for this time (1 Thess. 5:1–9) and avoid self-deception regarding God's final judgment (Matt. 7:21–27). See also *Day of the Lord; Hell; Tribulation, Great.*

JUG. See *Cruse.*

JULIA. A female believer at Rome to whom the apostle Paul sent greetings (Rom. 16:15).

JULIUS. A Roman soldier who guarded Paul and other passengers during their trip to Rome (Acts 27).

JUNIA (JUNIAS). A fellow believer at Rome greeted and commended by Paul (Rom. 16:7). *Junias:* NIV.

JUNIPER (BROOM). A bush with dense twigs which was used for charcoal (Ps. 120:4). *Broom:* NIV, NRSV.

JUPITER (ZEUS). The chief god of Roman mythology and a name applied to Barnabas by the superstitious citizens of Lystra (Acts 14:12). The Greek name for this god was *Zeus* (NIV, NRSV).

JUSTICE. Fair and impartial treatment; righteousness. Justice is characteristic of God's nature (Deut. 32:4) and descriptive of Christ (Acts 3:14) and believers (Heb. 12:14). Just dealings with others by God's people was demanded by the O.T. prophets (Mic. 6:8; Amos 5:24). God's justice is fair and merciful (Acts 17:31).

JUSTIFICATION. The act or event when God both declares and makes a person just or right with him (Rom. 5:9). Justification is not accomplished by personal merit or good works (Gal. 2:16) but by God's grace through personal faith in Christ (Eph. 2:8–9). To be justified is to have peace with God and hope for eternity (Titus 3:5–7). See also *Atonement; Propitiation; Reconciliation*.

JUSTUS. A friend and believer at Corinth with whom the apostle Paul lodged (Acts 18:7).

-K-

KAB. See *Cab*.

KADESH/KADESH-BARNEA. A wilderness region between Canaan and Egypt which served as the southern boundary of the Promised Land (Num. 34:4). The Israelites camped in this area during the wilderness wandering years before they entered the Promised Land (Num. 32:8; 27:14). *Kadesh-barnea:* Josh. 14:7. See also *Wilderness Wanderings*.

KANAH. A stream between the territories of Ephraim and Manasseh (Josh. 16:8–9; 17:9), likely the same as present-day Wadi Kanah, which runs into the Mediterranean Sea north of Joppa.

KEDAR. A son of Ishmael, grandson of Abraham, and founder of an Arabic tribe which lived in the desert between Arabia and Babylonia (Gen. 25:12–13).

KEDESH.

1. One of the six cities of refuge, situated in the territory of Naphtali in northern Palestine (Josh. 20:1–7). This city is now called *Keder*. See also *Cities of Refuge*.

2. A Canaanite town captured by Joshua (Josh. 12:7, 22) and allotted to the tribe of Issachar (1 Chron. 6:72). *Kishion:* Josh. 19:20; *Kishon:* Josh. 21:28.

KEILAH. A fortified city of southern Judah near Hebron taken from the Philistines by David's army (1 Sam. 23:1–5).

KEMUEL. A leader of the tribe of Ephraim who helped Moses divide the land of Canaan after its occupation by the Israelites (Num. 34:24).

KENAN/CAINAN. A son of Enoch and grandson of Adam who lived in the days before the great flood (1 Chron. 1:1–2). *Cainan:* Gen. 5:9.

KENITES. A nomadic Midianite tribe associated with the Amalekites (Gen. 15:19). Friendly toward the Israelites, this tribe was likely absorbed into Judah (1 Sam. 27:10).

KENIZZITES. A Canaanite tribe whose land was promised to Abraham's descendants (Gen. 15:18–19).

KENOSIS. Relating to the dual nature of Christ—His divinity and humanity. Citing Phil. 2:7, advocates of this theory claim that God's Son laid aside or "emptied himself" of certain divine attributes when He became human. Most scholars reject the notion that Jesus stopped being God or that He gave up any divine attributes. Rather, the phrase refers to Christ's voluntary servanthood (John 17:5).

KERIOTH. A town in southern Judah (Josh. 15:25). This may have been the hometown of Judas Iscariot, Jesus' disciple and betrayer, since Iscariot means "man of Kerioth."

KETTLE. A vessel used for cooking and in worship rituals (1 Sam. 2:14). The Hebrew word for kettle is also translated as "basket," "caldron," or "pot" (Jer. 24:2; Job 41:20). See also *Caldron*.

KETURAH. The wife of Abraham after Sarah's death (Gen. 25:1). The six sons born to their union were ancestors of six Arabian tribes in Palestine or Arabia (1 Chron. 1:33).

KEY. A tool used to unlock a door. In Bible times, keys were long rods with metal pins (Judg. 3:25). The word is also used figuratively as a symbol of authority (Isa. 22:22; Rev. 1:18).

KID. A young goat. Kids were used as sacrificial offerings or butchered for special occasions (Luke 15:29). See also *Goat*.

KIDNEY. See *Reins*.

KIDRON/CEDRON. A valley or ravine with a wet-weather stream near Jerusalem. David crossed the Kidron Brook while fleeing from his son Absalom (2 Sam. 15:23–30). Idols from pagan cults were burned in this valley (1 Kings 15:13). Jesus probably crossed this valley on the night of His arrest (John 18:1; *Cedron*).

KINDNESS. Cordiality toward others. Believers are to be kind and forgiving, following the example of Jesus (Eph. 4:32).

KINDRED. Relatives, or members of one's immediate or extended family. The clan or tribe was the basic family unit in early Hebrew history. Family members considered it their duty to protect one another (Gen. 34). See also *Family*.

KINE (COW). An archaic word for cow or ox (Gen. 32:15). The prophet Amos used this word for the oppressive, indulgent leaders of Israel (Amos 4:1–3). *Cow:* NIV, NRSV.

KING. The monarch or supreme ruler of a nation. Beginning with the first king, Saul, who was anointed with God's authority (1 Sam. 10:1), Judah and Israel had a succession of kings across several centuries until both nations were overrun by foreign powers. The books of 1 and 2 Samuel, 1 and 2 Kings, and 1 and 2 Chronicles report on the reigns of many of these kings. A few were godly and kind rulers who honored God and followed His law, but most were evil and corrupt. They led God's people into sin and idolatry. The believer should remember that God is our eternal king, worthy of all honor (1 Tim. 1:17). Christ, our ultimate ruler, is Lord of Lords and King of Kings (John 18:37; Rev. 17:14).

KINGDOM OF GOD. The spiritual reign of God in the hearts of believers (Luke 17:20–21). Partially attained in this life for those who seek God's will, God's kingdom will be fully established in the world to come (John 18:36). Jesus preached the "gospel of the kingdom" (Mark 1:14) and taught His disciples to seek His kingdom (Matt. 6:33) and to pray for its arrival on earth (Matt. 6:10). Unrepentant sinners cannot inherit this kingdom (Eph. 5:5). It is reserved for those who repent (Matt. 3:2) and experience spiritual rebirth (John 3:3–5). Other phrases for this kingdom are "kingdom of heaven" (Matt. 4:17) and "kingdom of Christ" (Col. 1:13).

KINGS, BOOKS OF. Two historical books of the O.T. which cover a period of roughly four centuries in Jewish history—from about 970 to 587 B.C. First Kings records the reign of Solomon as successor to David (1 Kings 1:1– 11:43); the division of the kingdom into two separate nations, Judah and Israel (12:1–14:31); and the reigns of selected kings in both these nations until the time of Ahaziah of Israel (about 853–852 B.C.)

Second Kings continues the narrative of Ahaziah's reign (1: 1–18) and reports on the reigns of selected kings in both nations up until the time of the fall of the Northern Kingdom under Hoshea (reigned about 730–722 B.C.; chap. 17). Chapters 18 through 25 cover the final years of the surviving nation of Judah, until it fell to the Babylonians in 587 B.C. See also *King*.

KING'S DALE/SHAVEH. The ancient name for a valley east of Jerusalem where Abraham met the king of Sodom and Melchizedek (Gen. 14:17–18). Also called *Shaveh,* this is perhaps the same place as the Valley of Jehoshaphat (Joel 3:2). See *Jehoshaphat, Valley of.*

KING'S GARDEN. A royal garden in the city of Jerusalem (2 Kings 25:4).

KING'S HIGHWAY. An important road linking Damascus and Egypt which ran through Israel. While in the wilderness, the Israelites were denied passage on this road as they traveled toward Canaan (Num. 20:17–21).

KINSMAN-REDEEMER. A close relative who had first option to buy back or redeem personal freedom or property that had been forfeited by impoverished members of the clan (Lev. 25:48–49). Boaz, a near kinsman of Naomi, acted as a redeemer in his marriage to Ruth (Ruth 4). Jesus is our "elder brother" who redeems the believer (Heb. 2:11–17).

KIRIOTH/KERIOTH. A fortified city in Moab and possibly its capital in the eighth century B.C., since the prophet Amos predicted its destruction (Amos 2:2). *Kerioth:* Jer. 48:24, 41.

KIRJATH-ARBA. See *Hebron*.

KIRJATH-JEARIM/ BAALAH. A fortified city of the Gibeonites where the ark of the covenant was kept for twenty years before being taken to Jerusalem (1 Chron. 13–16). *Baalah:* Josh. 15:9.

KIRJATH-SANNA, KIRJATH-SEPHER. See *Debir,* No. 2.

KISHION/KISHON. See *Kedesh,* No. 2.

KISHON/KISON. A river in the valley of Jezreel in northern Palestine where Elijah killed the prophets of Baal (1 Kings 18:40). *Kison:* Ps. 83:9.

KISLEV. See *Chisleu*.

KISS. A sign of affection practiced by parents and children (Gen. 27:26). Jesus was betrayed by Judas with a kiss (Matt. 26:49).

KITE. A bird of prey belonging to the hawk family and regarded as unclean by the Israelites (Deut. 14:12–13).

KITTIM. See *Cyprus.*

KNEADINGTROUGH. A large bowl used to knead dough to prepare it for baking (Exod. 12:34).

KNEEL. A symbol of respect (Ps. 95:6) or subjection and surrender (2 Kings 1:13). Kneeling was also a customary stance in prayer, indicating reverence for God (Luke 22:41). See also *Bowing.*

KNIFE. A sharp-edged weapon or tool made of flint or bronze (Josh. 5:2).

KNOP. An old English word for the ornamental cap on a column. The word is also used for a decoration on the golden candlesticks in the tabernacle (Exod. 25:31–36).

KNOWLEDGE. A body of facts or information gained through study and experience. The prophets of the O.T. lamented the Israelites' lack of knowledge (Isa. 5:13). Paul indicated that knowledge of God is to be desired above all else (Phil. 3:8). The verb "to know" was often used in the O.T. for sexual intimacy (Gen. 4:1).

KOHATH. The second son of Levi (Gen. 46:8, 11) and founder of the Kohathites, priests who cared for the ark of the covenant and other accessories used in the tabernacle in the wilderness (Num. 3:30–31). Moses and Aaron were Kohathites (Exod. 6:18–20).

KOPH. The nineteenth letter of the Hebrew alphabet, used as a heading over Ps. 119:145–152.

KORAH/CORE. A grandson of Kohath who incited a rebellion against Moses and Aaron in the wilderness. Korah and his followers were swallowed by the earth as punishment for their sin (Num. 16:30–33). *Core:* Greek form (Jude 11).

-L-

LABAN. A brother of Jacob's mother Rebekah and father of Leah and Rachel, who were given in marriage to Jacob. Jacob visited Laban to escape the wrath of his brother Esau (Gen. 27:43). He worked seven years for Laban for the privilege of marrying Rachel, only to be tricked into marrying Leah instead. Then Jacob worked another seven years for Rachel (Gen. 29:18–36).

LABORER. An unskilled worker who performed such menial tasks as tilling the fields and gathering the crops in Bible times (Ruth 2:2; Ps. 90:10). See also *Hireling*.

LACHISH. An Amorite city in southern Judah captured by Joshua (Josh. 10:31–35) and later besieged by King Sennacherib of Assyria (2 Kings 18:13–14). Lachish was reoccupied by the Israelites after the Babylonian Exile (Neh. 11:30).

LAISH. See *Dan,* No. 2.

LAKE OF FIRE. The place of final punishment. Filled with burning brimstone (Rev. 19:20), this place is described as the "second death" (Rev. 20:14). Those consigned to the lake of fire include Satan (Rev. 20:10), persons not named in the Book of Life (Rev. 20:15), and unbelieving sinners (Rev. 21:8). See also *Hell*.

LAKE OF GENNESARET. See *Galilee, Sea of.*

LAMB. A young sheep, used for food (2 Sam. 12:4), clothing (Prov. 27:26), and religious sacrifices (Exod. 12:5, 7). A lamb also symbolized the sufferings of Christ (Isa. 53:7) and the reign of the Messiah (Isa. 11:6). See also *Sheep*.

LAMB OF GOD. A title of Christ which emphasizes the sacrificial nature of His life and His atoning death. This aspect of His ministry was foretold by the prophet Isaiah (Isa. 53:7). John the Baptist greeted Jesus with this title (John 1:29). As the Lamb of God, Jesus is worthy of eternal honor and praise (Rev. 5:12–13). See also *Atonement; Cross*.

LAME. Inability to walk, due to an injury (2 Sam. 4:4) or a birth defect (Acts 3:2). Persons with this disability were healed by Jesus (Matt. 11:5) and Peter (Acts 3:2–7).

LAMECH. A son of Methuselah and a man of faith who found "comfort" in the birth of his son Noah (Gen. 5:25–31). Lamech is listed in the ancestry of Jesus (Luke 3:36).

LAMED. The twelfth letter of the Hebrew alphabet, used as a heading over Ps. 119:89–96.

LAMENTATIONS OF JEREMIAH. A short O.T. book which expresses in poetic form the prophet Jeremiah's deep grief and anguish at the destruction of Jerusalem and the Jewish temple by the pagan Babylonians. Chapter 4 paints a bleak picture of life in Jerusalem during the extended siege against the city. See also *Babylonia; Jeremiah.*

LAMP. See *Candle.*

LAMPSTAND. See *Candlestick.*

LANCE. See *Spear.*

LAND OF PROMISE. Canaan, or the land inhabited by the Israelites. This land was promised by God to Abraham's descendants (Gen. 12:1–7). The promise was fulfilled centuries later when Joshua led the Israelites to take the land from the Canaanites (Josh. 10–12). See also *Canaan,* No. 2; *Palestine.*

LANDMARK (BOUNDARY STONE, MARKER). A marker, usually consisting of a pile of stones, which indicated property lines. Removal of a landmark was forbidden (Deut. 19:14). *Boundary stone:* NIV; *Marker:* NRSV.

LANDOWNER. See *Goodman.*

LANTERN. A torch covered with skin or transparent horn for outdoor use. On the night before His crucifixion, Jesus was arrested by armed men with lanterns (John 18:3). See also *Torch.*

LAODICEA. A major city in Asia Minor, located on the Lycus River. One of the seven churches addressed in the book of Revelation was located in Laodicea (1:11). This church was rebuked because of its complacency (Rev. 3:14–18).

LAPIDOTH (LAPPIDOTH). The husband of Deborah the prophetess (Judg. 4:4). *Lappidoth:* NIV, NRSV. See also *Deborah.*

LAPWING (HOOPOE). A small European bird, considered unclean by the Hebrews, which wintered in Palestine (Lev. 11:19; Deut. 14:12, 18). *Hoopoe:* NIV, NRSV.

LASCIVIOUSNESS (DEBAUCHERY, LICENTIOUSNESS). Unbridled lust, a sin characteristic of life apart from Christ (1 Pet. 4:3; *debauchery:* NIV; *licentiousness:* NRSV), which believers are warned to avoid. According to Paul, victory over lasciviousness requires repentance (2 Cor. 12:21) and living in the spirit of Christ (Gal. 5:22–25).

LASHARON. A Canaanite town near Tabor captured by Joshua (Josh. 12:1–18). This may be the same city as Lasha (Gen. 10:19).

LAST SUPPER. See *Lord's Supper.*

LATCHET (THONGS). A strap which fastened a sandal to the foot (Gen. 14:23). John the Baptist declared he was unworthy to untie the latchet of Christ's sandals (Mark 1:7). *Thongs:* NIV, NRSV. See also *Sandal.*

LATTER RAIN (SPRING RAIN). The rain which fell late in the growing season, allowing crops to reach full maturity before the harvest (Jer. 3:3). *Spring rain:* NIV, NRSV. See also *Former Rain; Rain.*

LATTICE. A screened opening or porch on a house to provide privacy and let in night breezes (Judg. 5:28; 2 Kings 1:2).

LAUNDERER. See *Fuller.*

LAVER (BASIN). A container placed near the altar outside the tabernacle where priests could wash their hands and feet before offering animal sacrifices (Exod. 30:18–21). *Basin:* NIV, NRSV. See also *Bason.*

LAW, LAW OF MOSES. The authoritative rule of conduct spelled out in the Ten Commandments and the Pentateuch—the books of Genesis, Exodus, Leviticus, Numbers, and Deuteronomy. This code was revealed to Moses by the Lord on Mt. Sinai (Deut. 5:1–2). While many of the regulations are ceremonial or procedural in nature, the moral law embodied in the Law of Moses is eternal and unchangeable (Rom. 7:7–12). It was fulfilled by the gospel and confirmed by Christ (Matt. 5:17–18). See also *Moses.*

LAWYER. An interpreter or teacher of the law in the synagogues and schools of N.T. times (Matt. 22:34–40), also called a *scribe* (Luke 11:53). See also *Scribe.*

LAYING ON OF HANDS. A ritual blessing or ordination for service. This ritual was used by the high priest on the Day of Atonement. By placing his hands on the scapegoat, he ritually transferred the sins of the people to the animal (Lev. 16:21). The patriarchs placed their hands on their descendants to confirm birthright or convey special blessings (Gen. 48:14, 18). The church at Antioch laid hands on Paul and Barnabas to confirm their calling as missionaries and to set them apart for this service (Acts 13:2–3).

LAZARUS. A brother of Mary and Martha whom Jesus raised from the dead. This event impressed the common people (John 11:41–45) but provoked the Jewish leaders to seek the death of both Jesus and Lazarus (John 11:47–57; 12:10–11).

LEAD. A heavy metal cast into weights (Zech. 5:8). It was also a useful agent for refining gold and silver (Num. 31:22–23). The word is used figuratively for the cleansing of Israel (Jer. 6:29).

LEAGUE (COMPACT, TREATY). An alliance of nations for fostering common interests and providing protection against enemies (2 Sam. 5:3). *Compact:* NIV (1 Kings 5:12). *Treaty:* NIV, NRSV. Leagues with the Canaanites and other pagan nations were prohibited (Exod. 23:31–33). See also *Alliance*.

LEAH. Laban's oldest daughter and Jacob's first wife (Gen. 29:19–27). She bore seven children (Gen. 29:32–35; 30:17–21) and remained loyal to Jacob when he had to flee from Laban (Gen. 31:17–20). See also *Jacob*.

LEANNOTH. A musical term of uncertain meaning in the title of Ps. 88.

LEARNED. See *Prudent*.

LEATHER. Treated animal skins used for clothing (Lev. 13:48), tent coverings (Exod. 26:14), sandals (Ezek. 16:10), and water and wine containers (Matt. 9:17). See also *Tanner*.

LEAVEN (YEAST). A fermentation agent used in making bread or wine (Hos. 7:4). Jesus used the term to warn against the teachings of the Pharisees and Sadducees (Matt. 16:11–12). *Yeast:* NIV, NRSV.

LEBANON. A rugged mountainous region in northern Palestine. Cedar and fir trees from Lebanon were used in the construction of the temple in Jerusalem under Solomon (1 Kings 5:6–10; 7:2).

LEBBAEUS. See *Judas, Brother of James*.

LEBO-HAMATH. See *Hamath.*

LEECH. See *Horseleach.*

LEEK. An onionlike plant. In the wilderness, the Israelites longed for this vegetable which they had enjoyed in Egypt (Num. 11:5).

LEES (DREGS). The waste which settled to the bottom of the container in the process of wine-making (Isa. 25:6). The term is used figuratively for indifference or laziness (Jer. 48:11; Zeph. 1:12). *Dregs:* NIV, NRSV. See also *Dregs.*

LEGION

1. A Roman military division, consisting of several thousand foot soldiers plus cavalrymen (John 18:3–12).

2. Any large number, such as angels available to Jesus (Matt. 26:53) or demons inhabiting a demoniac (Luke 8:30).

LEHI. A site in the hill country of Judah where Samson killed 1,000 Philistines with the jawbone of a donkey (Judg. 15:9–15).

LEMUEL. An unknown king mentioned in the book of Proverbs (Prov. 31:1). Some scholars identify Lemuel as Solomon.

LENTIL. A plant of the pea family used in Jacob's pottage, or stew. Esau sold his birthright to Jacob for a bowl of this stew (Gen. 25:29–34).

LEOPARD. A wild animal of the cat family noted for its speed and fierceness (Jer. 5:6). The reign of the Messiah is pictured as a time when leopards will lie down with goats (Isa. 11:6).

LEPROSY. A variety of dreaded skin diseases. The Mosaic Law required a leper to live in isolation from others and to cry "unclean" so people could avoid him (Lev. 13:45–46). Jesus healed ten lepers and sent them to the priest for verification and purification (Luke 17:11–15).

LETTER. See *Jot.*

LEVI.

1. The third son of Jacob and Leah (Gen. 29:34) and ancestor of the Levites (Exod. 2:1; Num. 1:49). His three sons were ancestors of the three major branches of the Levitical priesthood: Kohathites, Gershonites, and Merarites (Gen. 46:11). See also *Levites; Tribes of Israel.*

2. Another name for Matthew. See *Matthew*.

LEVIATHAN. A sea monster, believed by some scholars to be the crocodile (Job 41:1). The word is also used figuratively to describe one of Israel's enemies, probably Egypt (Isa. 27:1).

LEVIRATE MARRIAGE. The marriage of a man to the widow of a deceased relative if she had no male heir. The purpose of this law was to provide an heir and an estate for the deceased relative and to provide for widows (Deut. 25:5–10). The union of Boaz and Ruth was a Levirate marriage (see Ruth 3–4). See also *Widow*.

LEVITES. Members of one of the twelve tribes of Israel who were descendants of Levi, third son of Jacob and Leah (Gen. 29:34). The Levites were responsible for taking care of the tabernacle and assisting the priests in their ceremonial duties (Num. 3:5–10). Moses and Aaron were Levites of the family of Kohath, Levi's son. When Canaan was divided, the Levites were assigned forty-eight towns in various tribal territories rather than a specific part of the land (Josh. 21:1–8). See also *Levitical Cities*.

LEVITICAL CITIES. Forty-eight cities assigned to the tribe of Levi instead of one specific territory (Num. 35:2–7). This arrangement gave the priestly class access to the spiritual needs of the other tribes. Six of these cities were designated as cities of refuge to protect those who accidentally killed persons from avenging relatives (Josh. 20:1–6). See also *Cities of Refuge*.

LEVITICUS, BOOK OF. An O.T. book filled with instructions about sanctification of the priests, regulations for worship and ceremonial offerings, and personal purification and dietary laws. The theme of the book is holiness. Because God is a holy God, He demands a holy and separated people who are totally committed to Him. This holiness is obtained through rituals of acceptable sacrifice, the emphasis of the first part of the book (1:1–17:16); and rituals of sanctification, the theme of the book's second major section (18:1–27:34). These instructions in holiness and appropriate worship were revealed by the Lord to Moses during the Hebrews' wandering years in the wilderness of Sinai. See also *Clean; Sacrifice; Unclean Animals*.

LIAR. One who tells untruths. Satan is the father of lies (John 8:44), and liars are his agents (Acts 5:3). Lying is associated with idolatry and perversion of truth (Rom. 1:18, 25).

LIBERALITY. A generous spirit of helpfulness toward those in need. Ministering in such a spirit validates our faith (Gal. 6:10). Those who are generous will be treated with generosity (Luke 6:38).

LIBERTINES (FREEDMEN). Jews carried to Rome by Pompey as captives (63 B.C.) and later freed. Members of the Jerusalem synagogue who opposed Stephen were Libertines (Acts 6:9). *Freedmen:* NIV, NRSV.

LIBYA/PHUT/LUBIM. The Greek name for the continent of Africa west of Egypt (Acts 2:10). Persons from Libya were in Jerusalem on the day of Pentecost (Acts 2:10). The man who carried Jesus' cross was from Cyrene, Libya's chief city (Matt. 27:32). In the O.T., Libya was also called *Phut* (Ezek. 27:10) and *Lubim* (Nah. 3:9). See also *Phut*.

LICE (GNATS). Small biting insects, perhaps sand ticks, gnats, or mosquitoes. An invasion of lice was the third plague sent by God to persuade the pharaoh to allow the Israelites to leave Egypt (Exod. 8:16–18). *Gnats:* NIV, NRSV. See also *Gnat*.

LICENTIOUSNESS. See *Lasciviousness*.

LIE. See *Liar*.

LIEUTENANT (SATRAP). A military officer (Ezra 8:36). Also, a general title for the governor of a Persian province (Esther 3:12). *Satrap:* NIV, NRSV. See also *Satrap*.

LIFE, ETERNAL. See *Eternal Life*.

LIGHT. Illumination. God's first act of creation was to bring light into existence (Gen. 1:3–5). The word is used figuratively in the Bible to represent truth and goodness (Ps. 119:105), which dispel the darkness of ignorance and wickedness (Matt. 4:16; 5:15). See also *Darkness*.

LIGHTS, FEAST OF. See *Dedication, Feast of*.

LIGN ALOES. A tree from which perfume was made (Num. 24:6).

LIGURE (JACINTH). A precious stone in the breastplate of the high priest (Exod. 28:19). *Jacinth:* NIV, NRSV. See also *Jacinth*.

LILY. A general term for any flower resembling the lily (Song of Sol. 5:13; Matt. 6:28).

LIME. Powdered limestone, used for plaster and cement work (Isa. 33:12).

LINE (CORD). A method of measuring land with a cord (Josh. 2:18). *Cord:* NIV, NRSV. Amos told Amaziah the priest that the Lord's punishment would include division of his land by line (Amos 7:17). See also *Cord; Rope*.

LINEN. Cloth made from flax. The rich wore "fine linen" (1 Chron. 15:27), while the poor wore garments of unbleached flax. Linen was also used for curtains and veils in the tabernacle (Exod. 26:1). See also *Flax*.

LINTEL. A beam of wood over a door (Amos 9:1). In Egypt, the Hebrews were commanded to place blood from a sacrificial lamb over the lintels of their doors to avoid the angel of death (Exod. 12:22–23).

LINUS. A Christian at Rome whose greetings were sent by Paul to Timothy (2 Tim. 4:21).

LION. A large catlike animal which preyed upon sheep (1 Sam. 17:34–36). Those who offended the king of Persia were thrown into a den of lions (Dan. 6:7–28).

LIPS. A part of the human body associated with speaking. Moses described his poor speaking skills as "uncircumcised lips" (Exod. 6:12, 30). Covering of the lips was a gesture of shame or mourning (Mic. 3:7). See also *Mouth; Throat; Tongue*.

LIQUOR. A fermented beverage associated with both festive occasions (Luke 15:23, 32) and drunkenness (Rom. 13:13). Paul counseled that believers should be "filled with the spirit" rather than strong drink (Eph. 5:18).

LITTER. A portable chair on poles upon which people were carried. A covering provided protection from the sun and rain (Isa. 66:20).

LIZARD. A reptile regarded as unclean by the Mosaic Law (Lev. 11:30). Numerous species of lizards are found in Palestine.

LOAF. See *Bread.*

LO-AMMI. A symbolic name, meaning "not my people," given by Hosea to his second son to signify God's rejection of rebellious Israel (Hos. 1:8–9). See also *Hosea.*

LOAN. Borrowed money which had to be repaid with interest. To secure a loan, a debtor often pledged his children or himself (2 Kings 4:1; Amos 8:6). The Mosaic Law specified that loans to the poor were not to accrue interest (Exod. 22:25). See also *Debt; Usury.*

LOCUST. A migratory, plant-eating insect similar to the grasshopper. Swarms of locusts were sent as a plague upon the Egyptians to convince the pharaoh to free the Israelite people (Exod. 10:1–4). See also *Cankerworm; Grasshopper; Palmerworm.*

LOD/LYDDA. A town near Joppa built by Shemed, a descendant of Benjamin (1 Chron. 8:12). Peter healed a lame man here (Acts 9:32–35; *Lydda*).

LOFT (UPPER ROOM, UPPER CHAMBER). The small room or upper story built on the flat roof of a house (1 Kings 17–19). *Upper room:* NIV; *Upper chamber:* NRSV. See also *Upper Room.*

LOG. A unit of liquid measure, equal to about one-twelfth of a hin (Lev. 14:10). See also *Hin.*

LOGOS. A Greek term which means both "the Word" and "reason." Jesus came into the world as the Logos, or the Word of God incarnate—in human form (John 1:1–3; Col. 1:15–17). See also *Word of God.*

LOINS. The midsection of the human body, just below the stomach. The Jewish people wrapped their loose garments around their loins when working or traveling to give greater freedom of movement (2 Kings 4:29). The word is used figuratively by Peter to counsel readiness for Christ's return (1 Pet. 1:13).

LOIS. The grandmother of Timothy who was commended by Paul for her faith (2 Tim. 1:5). See also *Timothy.*

LONGSUFFERING (PATIENT). Forbearance or patience; an attribute of God's nature (Exod. 34:6). His longsuffering is intended to bring people to repentance (2 Pet.

3:9). *Patient:* NIV, NRSV. See also *Forbearance; Patience.*

LOOPS. Fasteners which joined the curtains of the tabernacle together in a continuous unit (Exod. 26:3–11).

LORD. A rendering of various Hebrew words which refer to the God of Israel, Jesus, and persons in authority such as kings. The word is also used as a translation of the divine name *Yahweh,* which the Hebrews did not pronounce out of reverence (Gen. 12:8; Exod. 3:15–16). See also *Jehovah; Yahweh.*

LORD ALMIGHTY. See *Hosts, Lord of.*

LORD'S DAY. Sunday, the first day of the week, and the Christian day of worship (Rev. 1:10). The Jewish day of rest and worship fell on Saturday, the last day of the week. But after Christ's resurrection on the first day, Christians adopted this as their normal day of worship (Acts 20:7). The Christian custom of Sunday worship was already well established when the Roman emperor Constantine instituted the day as a Christian holiday in A.D. 321.

LORD'S PRAYER. Jesus' model prayer which He taught to His disciples in response to their request, "Lord, teach us to pray" (Luke 11:1). The prayer teaches us to approach God reverently (Matt. 6:9–10), to ask Him to meet our physical needs, and to seek His forgiveness and protection (Matt. 6:11–13). See also *Prayer; Sermon on the Mount.*

LORD'S SUPPER. Jesus' final meal with His disciples which He observed as a Passover ritual to symbolize His approaching death (Luke 22:15–16). In this act, He established a memorial supper, symbolizing His broken body and shed blood (Matt. 26:26–28), which Christians are enjoined to observe until the Lord's return (1 Cor. 11:26). See also *Love Feast.*

LO-RUHAMAH. A symbolic name for the prophet Hosea's daughter, meaning "unloved." It expressed God's displeasure with rebellious Israel (Hos. 1:6).

LOT. Abraham's nephew. He accompanied Abraham to Canaan and traveled with him to Egypt to escape a famine (Gen. 12:5; 13:1). His uncle gave him first choice of Canaan's land on which to settle. He selected the fertile Jordan Valley (Gen. 13:10–11) and settled with his family near the pagan city of Sodom. Lot escaped the destruction of this city, but his wife looked back on their possessions and was turned into a pillar of salt (Gen. 19:16–26). Lot was an ancestor of the Moabites and the Ammonites, tribes which became bitter enemies of the Israelites in later centuries (Gen. 19:37–38). See also *Ammonites; Lot's Wife; Moabites*.

LOTAN. See *Moab,* No. 2.

LOTS, CASTING OF. Decision making by casting small stones out of a container, similar to our modern practice of "drawing straws" (Josh. 18:6). It was believed that God made His will known through this method (Prov. 16:33). Matthias was chosen as an apostle to succeed Judas by casting lots (Acts 1:26).

LOT'S WIFE. The wife of Abraham's nephew who was turned into a pillar of salt as she looked back on Sodom (Gen. 19:26). Jesus used her experience to warn of the dangers of delay and disobedience (Luke 17:32).

LOVE. Unselfish, benevolent concern for other persons (1 Cor. 13:4–7; *charity:* KJV). To love God supremely and others unselfishly are the two most important commands of Jesus (Matt. 22:37–40). Christ's sacrificial death was the supreme expression of love (John 13:1; 15:13). See also *Agape*.

LOVE FEAST. Meal observed by the early churches in connection with the Lord's Supper. The purpose of the meal was to promote Christian fellowship and brotherly love (Acts 2:42, 46; 1 Cor. 10:16–17). Paul condemned some of the Corinthian Christians for their sinful behavior and selfish indulgence at such love feasts (1 Cor. 11:20–22). See also *Lord's Supper*.

LOVER. See *Paramour*.

LOVINGKINDNESS. God's gentle and steadfast love and mercy which He extends freely to His people (Pss. 63:3; 69:16; 103:4–12). See also *Mercy*.

LUBIM. See *Libya*.

LUCAS. See *Luke*.

LUCIFER (MORNING STAR, DAY STAR). A name for the pompous king of Babylonia used by the prophet Isaiah

(14:12). *Morning Star:* NIV; *Day Star:* NRSV. Some scholars believe this passage describes the fall of Satan (see Luke 10:18). See also *Devil; Satan.*

LUCIUS. A Jewish Christian and kinsman of Paul who greeted believers at Rome (Rom. 16:21). He may be the same person as Lucius of Antioch (Acts 13:1).

LUCRE (GAIN). Material wealth, represented by money or goods (1 Sam. 8:3; Titus 1:7, 11). *Gain:* NIV, NRSV. See also *Filthy Lucre; Money.*

LUDIM (LUDITES, LUD). A people descended from Mizraim, a son of Ham (Gen. 10:13, 22). *Ludites:* NIV; *Lud:* NRSV.

LUKE/LUCAS. A Christian of Gentile descent, apparently a physician by vocation (Col. 4:14), who accompanied Paul on some of his missionary journeys (Acts 16:10; 20:5; 28:30). Luke wrote the Gospel which bears his name as well as the Book of Acts. Paul commended Luke for his loyalty and friendship (2 Tim. 4:11). *Lucas:* Philem. 24. See also *Acts of the Apostles.*

LUKE, GOSPEL OF. One of the four Gospels of the N.T., written by Luke—a physician of Gentile background—to portray Jesus as the Savior of all people, Gentiles as well as Jews. Luke shows that Jesus associated with all types of people, including sinners (5:30; 15:2), the poor and outcasts (6:20–23; 16:19–31), and the Samaritans (17:11–19). This theme of Christ as the universal Savior was continued in the Book of Acts, which Luke wrote as a sequel to his Gospel. Acts tells how the gospel eventually spread from Jerusalem, the center of Judaism, to Rome, the capital city and nerve center of the Roman Empire. See also *Luke; Acts of the Apostles; Roman Empire.*

LUKEWARM. Neither hot nor cold; a term for indifference or complacency. Members of the church at Laodicea were criticized for their tepid spirituality (Rev. 3:16).

LUST. Evil desire, usually associated with the sex drive. Unbridled lust leads to sin and produces death (Eph. 2:3; Jas. 1:14–15). Believers are warned to flee worldly lust (Titus 2:12) and "follow righteousness" (Gal. 5:16; 2 Tim. 2:22).

LUZ. See *Bethel.*

LYCAONIA. A Roman province in southern Asia Minor visited by Paul. Cities in this region where he preached included Derbe, Lystra, and Iconium (Acts 14:1–6).

LYCIA. A province of Asia Minor which juts into the Mediterranean Sea. Paul made stops in Patara (Acts 21:1) and Myra, Lycia's major cities.

LYDDA. See *Lod.*

LYDIA. A businesswoman of Thyatira, a dealer in purple cloth, who was apparently converted under Paul's ministry at Philippi. After her conversion, she invited Paul and his friends to spend time in her home (Acts 16:14–15). See also *Philippi.*

LYE. See *Nitre.*

LYRE. See *Harp; Psaltery; Sackbut; Viol.*

LYSANIAS. The governor of Abilene, a region in Syria, when Herod was ruler over Galilee and when John the Baptist began his ministry (Luke 3:1). See also *Abilene.*

LYSIAS, CLAUDIUS. See *Claudius Lysias.*

LYSTRA. A city in the province of Lycaonia in central Asia Minor. Paul preached and healed a lame man here and was stoned by unbelieving Jews (Acts 14:6–20).

-M-

MAACAH/MAACHAH. One of David's wives and the mother of Absalom (2 Sam. 3:3). *Maachah:* 1 Chron. 3:2.

MACCABEES. A family of Jewish patriots who headed a religious revolt against the Syrians in Palestine from 167 to 63 B.C. See also *Antiochus IV Epiphanes.*

MACEDONIA. A mountainous country north of Greece and the first European territory visited by the apostle Paul. He planted churches in the cities of Philippi and Thessalonica (see Acts 16, 17, 20). Paul was beckoned to visit this region through his famous "Macedonian call"—a vision of a man pleading, "Come over into Macedonia, and help us" (Acts 16:9).

MACHINES. See *Engines.*

MACHIR (MAKIR). The oldest son of Manasseh (Josh. 17:1), a grandson of Joseph (Gen. 50:23), and a military hero who became the ancestor of the Macherites (1 Chron. 7:17–18). The Macherites won significant victories over the Amorites during the conquest of Canaan (Num. 32:39). *Makir:* NIV.

MACHPELAH. A field with a cave which Abraham bought as a burial ground (Gen. 23:9–18). Buried here were Abraham and Sarah, Isaac and Rebekah, and Jacob and Leah (Gen. 25:9–10; 49:29–33).

MAD (INSANE). A term for insanity, but it may also refer to anger or confusion (1 Cor. 14:23). David pretended to be insane in order to escape from Achish (1 Sam. 21:13–15). *Insane:* NIV.

MADAI. A son of Japheth and ancestor of the Medes (Gen. 10:2). See also *Medes*.

MADIAN. See *Midian,* No. 2.

MAGDALA. A city of Galilee near Capernaum, and probably the home of Mary Magdalene (Matt. 27:56).

MAGDALENE. See *Mary,* No. 2.

MAGI. See *Wise Men*.

MAGIC. The practice of illusion and sleight of hand to bring benefits or to deceive. The Israelites were forbidden to consult magicians or sorcerers (Lev. 19:31). See also *Sorcery; Witchcraft*.

MAGISTRATE. Civil authority or ruler. Magistrates in Philippi beat and imprisoned Paul and Silas for healing a demented slave girl (Acts 16:18–23).

MAGNIFICAT. The poem or song of the Virgin Mary upon learning she would give birth to the Messiah (Luke 1:46–55). Mary praised God for remembering "the lowliness of his servant" (NRSV) and for keeping His promise to bless Abraham and his descendants. See also *Mary,* No. 1.

MAGOG. See *Gog, Prince of Magog*.

MAHALATH, MAHALATH LEANNOTH. A phrase in the titles of Pss. 53 and 88 which probably refers to a musical instrument or a tune to be used in worship.

MAHANAIM. The name which Jacob gave to a site near the Jabbok River where he was visited by angels while waiting for his brother Esau (Gen. 32:1–2). The name means "two armies" or "two camps," perhaps referring to the meeting of his and Esau's forces or to the camps of Jacob and God. A city by the same name was established later on this site (Josh. 21:38).

MAHER-SHALAL-HASH-BAZ. The symbolic name given by the prophet Isaiah to his second son, meaning "hasten the booty" (Isa. 8:1–4). It signified that Assyria would conquer Israel and Syria.

MAHLON. Ruth's first husband and the elder son of Naomi. He died about ten years after his marriage to Ruth (Ruth 1:5).

MAID. A young unmarried woman, often of the servant class (Ruth 2:8). The word may also refer to a virgin or a female slave.

MAIDSERVANT. A female servant or handmaid (Ruth 3:9). Sometimes the word refers to a female slave. See also *Handmaid; Servant*.

MAIL, COAT OF. See *Brigandine*.

MAINSAIL (FORESAIL). The dominant or principal sail of a ship (Acts 27:40). *Foresail:* NIV, NRSV.

MAJESTY. A term referring to the dignity, power, and authority of a king or other high official (1 Chron. 29:24–25).

MAJOR PROPHETS. A term for the prophetic books which appear first in the O.T.—Isaiah, Jeremiah, Ezekiel, and Daniel—because of the longer length of their books. See also *Minor Prophets*.

MAKIR. See *Machir*.

MAKKEDAH. A royal Canaanite town captured by Joshua (Josh. 10:10–26) and assigned to the tribe of Judah (Josh. 15:20, 41).

MAKTESH. A district near Jerusalem where merchants bought and sold. They were denounced by the prophet Zephaniah for their sinful practices (Zeph. 1:11).

MALACHI. An O.T. prophet and the author of the book which bears his name. His name means "my messenger" (Mal. 1:1). He lived after the Babylonian Exile and was probably a contemporary of the prophet Nehemiah.

MALACHI, BOOK OF. A short prophetic book of the O.T. written about 100 years after the Babylonian Exile and directed against shallow and meaningless worship practices. The prophet condemned the people of Israel for presenting defective animals as sacrifices (1:8) and withholding tithes and offerings (3:8–10). The book closes with a note of hope regarding the future Messiah (chap. 4).

MALCHI-SHUA/MELCHI-SHUA (MALKI-SHUA). A son of King Saul who was killed by the Philistines in the battle at Gilboa (1 Sam. 14:49). *Malki-shua:* NIV. *Melchi-shua:* 1 Sam. 31:2.

MALCHUS. A servant of the high priest whose ear was cut off by Peter. Jesus rebuked Peter and restored the severed ear (John 18:10–11).

MALE SLAVE. See *Manservant.*

MALEFACTOR (CRIMINAL). A rebel or criminal. Christ was crucified between two malefactors (Luke 23:32–33). *Criminals:* NIV, NRSV.

MALICE. A burning desire or intention to hurt others. Christians are urged to renounce malice (Eph. 4:31) and pray for those guilty of this sin (Matt. 5:44). See also *Hate.*

MALKI-SHUA. See *Malchi-shua.*

MALLOWS (HERB). A wild plant or shrub which thrived in the dry, salty regions near the Dead Sea. It was sometimes eaten by the poor (Job 30:3–4). *Herb:* NIV.

MALTA. See *Melita.*

MAMMON (MONEY, WEALTH). Material wealth or possessions. Christ warned that money or physical goods were false gods that should not be worshiped (Matt. 6:24). He urged believers to seek kingdom interests and promised that their material needs would be met (Matt. 6:33). *Money:* NIV; *Wealth:* NRSV. See also *Filthy Lucre; Money.*

MAMRE.

1. A town or district near Hebron where Abraham lived (Gen. 13:18; 18:1).

2. An Amorite chief and supporter of Abraham who gave his name to the plain where Abraham lived (Gen. 14:13).

MAN. The being created by God in His image and for His glory (Gen. 1:26–27; 9:6; Isa. 43:7). The crown of God's creation, man was given dominion over the natural world (Ps. 8:4–6). Man's sin has separated him from God (Rom. 3:23), but he may be redeemed by God's grace through faith in Christ (Rom. 3:22–24). See also *Fall of Man; Sin*.

MANAEN. A prophet and teacher in the church at Antioch. Along with others, he laid hands on Paul and Barnabas, endorsing their call to missionary service (Acts 13:1–3).

MANASSEH.

1. Joseph's firstborn son whose descendants became one of the tribes of Israel (Gen. 48:4–6) and occupied both sides of the Jordan River (Josh. 16:4–9). *Manasses:* Rev. 7:6. See also *Tribes of Israel*.

2. The son and successor of Hezekiah as king of Judah (reigned about 687–642 B.C.; 2 Kings 20:21). A wicked ruler who encouraged pagan worship throughout Judah, Manasseh was captured and taken to Babylonia (2 Chron. 33:10–11). He later repented and was allowed to return to Jerusalem (2 Chron. 33:12–13). He was succeeded as king by his son Amon (2 Chron. 33:20).

MANDRAKE. A plant with an aromatic fragrance (Song of Sol. 7:13). Its fruit was thought to generate fertility (Gen. 30:14–16).

MANEH (MINA). A Hebrew weight equal to fifty shekels, or about two pounds (Ezek. 45:12). *Mina:* NIV, NRSV.

MANGER. A feeding trough for livestock. The infant Jesus was laid in a manger after His birth (Luke 2:7–16).

MANNA. Food miraculously provided by the Lord for the Israelites in the wilderness (Num. 11:7–9). Called "bread from heaven," (Exod. 16:4) manna was provided daily except on the Sabbath for forty years. A different substance by this name drops from various trees, particularly the tamarisk, in the valleys near the Sinai wilderness. See also *Wilderness Wanderings*.

MANOAH. A member of the tribe of Dan and father of Samson (Judg. 13:1–25).

MANSERVANT (MALE SLAVE). A male domestic servant, often a slave (Exod. 21:32). *Male slave:* NIV, NRSV.

MANSLAYER (SLAYER). A person who accidentally killed another. This person could seek asylum from the avenging relatives of the victim in a city of refuge (Num. 35:6–12). *Slayer:* NRSV. See also *Avenger of Blood; Cities of Refuge*.

MANTLE (CLOAK). An outer garment, similar to a robe, made of coarse cloth or sheepskin. Elijah's mantle was placed on Elisha as a symbol of succession and blessing (1 Kings 19:19–21). *Cloak:* NIV. See also *Cloke*.

MARA. A name, meaning "bitter," which was assumed by Naomi because it expressed her sorrow at the death of her husband and sons (Ruth 1:3–21).

MARANATHA. An Aramaic phrase, meaning "come, O Lord," which expresses hope for the second coming of Jesus (1 Cor. 16:22). See also *Second Coming*.

MARBLE. Crystalline limestone noted for its beauty and durability as a building material. Marble was used in the building of the temple in Jerusalem (1 Chron. 29:2).

MARCUS. See *Mark*.

MARDUK. See *Merodach*.

MARESHAH. A town of Judah (Josh. 15:20, 44) built for defensive purposes by King Rehoboam (2 Chron. 11:5, 8). A battle between King Asa of Judah and King Zerah of Ethiopia was fought here (2 Chron. 14:9–10).

MARINER. A seaman or sailor. Paul reassured the mariners on his ship during a storm (Acts 27:31–36). See also *Ship*.

MARK, JOHN/MARCUS. A relative of Barnabas who accompanied Paul and Barnabas on the first missionary journey as far as Perga and then returned to Jerusalem (Acts 13:3–5). After Paul's refusal to allow Mark to go with them on the second journey, Barnabas and Paul went their separate ways (Acts 15:36–41). In later years, Paul spoke of Mark with warmth and affection (Col. 4:10–11). Most scholars believe Mark was the author of the Gospel of Mark, drawing perhaps upon the reflections of Peter, who worked closely with Mark (1 Pet. 5:13; *Marcus*).

MARK, GOSPEL OF. One of the four Gospels of the N.T. and probably the first to be written, according to most scholars. A short Gospel of only sixteen chapters, Mark portrays Jesus as a person of action. He uses the words *immediately* (1:12; 2:8) and *straightway* (8:10) to show that Jesus was on an important mission for God and had no time to waste. While Mark makes it clear that Jesus was the Son of God (15:39), he also emphasizes the humanity of Jesus more than the other Gospel writers, including incidents which reveal His disappointment (8:12), anger (11:15–17), sorrow (14:34), and fatigue (4:38). See also *Mark; Synoptic Gospels*.

MARKER. See *Landmark*.

MARKET, MARKETPLACE. A large open area in a city where trade, public trials, and discussions were conducted (Acts 16:19–20). Children often played in this area (Luke 7:32). The Greek word for marketplace is *agora*.

MARRIAGE. The union of a man and a woman in commitment to one another as husband and wife. First instituted by God in the Garden of Eden (Gen. 2:18), marriage was also confirmed by Christ (Matt. 19:5). Love for and submission to one's mate were enjoined by Paul (Eph. 5:22–29). The love of a husband and wife for one another is symbolic of Christ's love for the Church (Eph. 5:23–25). See also *Betrothal; Dowry*.

MARROW. Tissue in the cavities of the bones. This word is used to illustrate the piercing power of God's Word (Heb. 4:12).

MARS' HILL. See *Areopagus*.

MARTHA. The sister of Mary and Lazarus (John 11:1–2). Jesus rebuked Martha because of her unnecessary worry after she welcomed Him into her home (Luke 10:38–42). She grieved at the death of her brother Lazarus and sought Jesus' help (John 11:20–22).

MARTYRDOM. Death in defense of one's faith. A Christian who gives a faithful testimony of the power of Christ in his or her life may face such an end (Rev. 6:9). But the wicked will eventually give account for the blood of the martyrs (Luke 11:49–51).

MARY.

1. The earthly mother of Jesus (Matt. 1:16). A descendant of David from Bethle-

hem, Mary was engaged to Joseph (Luke 1:27). She was informed by an angel that she had been divinely chosen to give birth to the Messiah (Luke 1:28–33). She traveled with Joseph to Bethlehem (Luke 2:4–5) and gave birth to Jesus in fulfillment of prophecy (Isa. 7:14). She was forced to flee to Egypt with Joseph to escape Herod's slaughter of innocent children (Matt. 2:13–18). After she and Joseph returned to Nazareth, she gave birth to other children (Mark 6:3).

Mary visited Jerusalem during the Passover feast with Joseph and Jesus (Luke 2:41–46). She attended a marriage in Cana of Galilee, where Jesus worked His first miracle (John 2:3). She was present at the cross when Jesus commended her to John's care (John 19:25–27). Mary was also present with one of the praying groups in the upper room after the ascension of Jesus (Acts 1:14).

2. Mary Magdalene. The woman who served Jesus faithfully after being delivered from seven demons (Luke 8:1–2). She witnessed the crucifixion and visited the tomb of Jesus (Matt. 27:55–61). She told the apostles of Jesus about the empty tomb (John 20:1–2) and was one of the first to see the risen Lord (Mark 16:9).

3. The sister of Martha and Lazarus. She was an eager listener at Jesus' feet while Martha performed household duties (Luke 10:38–41). She anointed the feet of Jesus and wiped them with her hair (John 12:1–3). Jesus defended her contemplative temperament (Luke 10:42).

4. The mother of the disciple James. This Mary is probably one of the women who provided food for Jesus and His disciples (Luke 8:2–3). She was also among those who went to the tomb to anoint Jesus' body and discovered He had been raised from the dead (Mark 16:1–8).

5. The mother of John Mark (Acts 12:12). Her house may have been a meeting place for the early Christians of Jerusalem.

6. A fellow believer at Rome greeted and commended by Paul in his letter to the Roman Christians (Rom. 16:6).

MASCHIL. A Hebrew word which appears in the titles of thirteen psalms, apparently giving directions for the melody to be sung (Pss. 32, 42, 44–45, 52–55, 74, 78, 88–89, 142).

MASON. A bricklayer or stoneworker. Phoenician masons were used by Solomon to build the temple in Jerusalem (1 Kings 5:17–18).

MASSAH AND MERIBAH. A site in the wilderness where the Israelites rebelled against Moses and Aaron (Exod. 17:4–7). Their complaints provoked the wrath of the Lord (Deut. 6:16). See also *Wilderness Wanderings*.

MAST. The rigging or wooden frame which held the sails on a ship (Ezek. 27:5). The word was used figuratively to show the strength of Israel's enemies (Isa. 33:23). See also *Ship*.

MASTER (TEACHER). Word meaning "teacher" which was often applied to Christ (Matt. 22:16, 24). *Teacher:* NIV, NRSV. The word was also used in the O.T. as a term of respect for one's superiors (Gen. 24:48–49). See also *Teacher*.

MATHUSALA. See *Methuselah*.

MATTANIAH. See *Zedekiah*.

MATTHEW/LEVI. A tax collector who became a disciple of Jesus (Matt. 9:9) and writer of the Gospel which bears his name. He was also known as *Levi* (Mark 2:13–17; Luke 5:27–32). See also *Publican*.

MATTHEW, GOSPEL OF. One of the four Gospels of the N.T., written by a tax collector who became one of the twelve apostles of Jesus. This Gospel apparently was written to show the Jewish people that Jesus was the Messiah promised in the O.T., since many events in His life are interpreted as fulfillment of the Scriptures (1:22; 4:14; 12:17; 21:4; 27:35). In Matthew's genealogies, Jesus' ancestry through Joseph, His earthly father, is traced to two of the greatest personalities in Jewish history—Abraham (1:2) and David (1:6).

Matthew's Gospel also emphasizes the teaching ministry of Jesus, particularly His instructions to His disciples in the Sermon on the Mount (5:1–7:27). Another prominent theme of this Gospel is the kingdom of God or the kingdom of heaven (5:3; 6:33; 8:11; 12:28; 13:43–46; 19:23; 21:31; 25:34). See also *Beatitudes; Kingdom of God; Sermon on the Mount*.

MATTHIAS. The person who replaced Judas as an apostle. Matthias was chosen by the other apostles through the casting of lots (Acts 1:15–26).

Excavated ruins of a Roman theater at Caesarea beside the Mediterranean Sea. *Courtesy Israel Ministry of Tourism*

See also *Lots, Casting of; Twelve, The*.

MATTOCK (HOE). An agricultural tool, similar to a crude hoe, used to loosen the soil and remove roots (Isa. 7:25). *Hoe:* NIV, NRSV.

MATURITY. See *Perfection*.

MAUL (CLUB). A heavy club used as a weapon of war. The head was often studded with spikes (Prov. 25:18). *Club:* NIV, NRSV (Jer. 51:20).

MAW (STOMACH). The stomach of an animal that chews the cud. Considered a delicacy by the Hebrews, the maw, shoulders, and cheeks became the priests' portion of sacrificial animals (Deut. 18:3). *Stomach:* NRSV.

MAZZAROTH. A constellation of stars cited by Job as evidence of the power and sovereignty of God (Job 38:31–33).

MEAT FORK. See *Fleshhook*.

MEAT OFFERING. An offering of a sacrificial animal, made to atone for sin (1 Chron. 21:23).

MEDDLER. See *Busybody*.

MEDEBA. An old Moabite town taken by Israel from King Sihon (Num. 21:23–30) and assigned to the tribe of Reuben (Josh. 13:8–16).

MEDES, MEDIA. Descendants of Japheth (Gen. 10:2) and an ancient kingdom between the Tigris River and the Caspian Sea to which Sargon of Assyria brought Hebrew captives (2 Kings 17:6; 18:11).

MEDIATOR, CHRIST THE. A title of Christ which describes His work in reconciling us to God. His sacrificial death has made it possible for us to have peace with God and with each other (Eph. 2:13–16). As our Mediator, He has made a full and final sacrifice for our salvation (Heb. 7:27). See also *Atonement; Propitiation; Reconciliation*.

MEDICINE. A healing substance. In Bible times, medicine was made from herbs, fruits, and minerals. The Balm of Gilead was probably made from the gum of an evergreen tree (Jer. 8:22). See also *Balm of Gilead; Healing*.

MEDITATION. Contemplation of spiritual truths (Ps. 119:148) which produces understanding (Ps. 49:3) and spiritual satisfaction (Ps. 63:5–6). Meditation on God's commands encourages obedience (Josh. 1:8).

MEDITERRANEAN SEA/GREAT SEA. The sea on Israel's western border which was also called the *Great Sea* (Josh 9:1). Solomon used the Phoenicians to provide import/export services for Israel across this body of water (1 Kings 9:27). Paul often sailed the Mediterranean during his missionary journeys (Acts 9:30; 18:18; Acts 27).

MEDIUM. A communicator between humans and the spirit world. The Mosaic Law specified that professing mediums or wizards were to be stoned to death (Lev. 20:27). The prophet Isaiah warned against consulting the dead rather than listening to the Lord (Isa. 8:19–20; 19:3). See also *Enchanter; Familiar Spirit; Wizard*.

MEEKNESS. A kind, gentle, and humble spirit. The meek will find spiritual satisfaction (Ps. 22:26) and receive God's instruction (Ps. 25:9). Paul cited meekness as one of the fruits of the spirit (Gal. 5:22–23). Jesus declared that the meek will inherit the earth (Matt. 5:5). See also *Humility; Kindness*.

MEGIDDO/MEGIDDON. A fortified city west of the Jordan River in the plain of Jezreel associated with the great battle in the end-time. This city was the site of Barak's victory over Sisera (Judg. 4:14–16) and King Josiah's death in a battle with Pharaoh Necho of Egypt (2 Chron. 35:22–24). In this area the final battle between God and the forces of evil will occur (Zech. 12:11; Rev. 16:16). *Megiddon:* Zech. 12:11. See also *Armageddon.*

MELCHI-SHUA. See *Malchi-shua.*

MELCHIZEDEK/MELCHISEDEC. The mysterious king of Salem who received tithes from Abraham (Gen. 14:18–20) and who is depicted as a type of Christ because of his endless priesthood (Heb. 5:6–10; 7:15–17). The Messiah who is to come was also described as a priest "after the order of Melchizedek" (Ps. 110:4). *Melchisedec:* Heb. 7:11.

MELITA (MALTA). An island south of Sicily in the Mediterranean Sea where Paul was shipwrecked while sailing to Rome (Acts 28:1–8). *Malta:* NIV, NRSV.

MELON. A fruit, apparently grown in Egypt, for which the Israelites longed during their wilderness wanderings (Num. 11:5). Various melons are grown today in Palestine.

MEM. The thirteenth letter of the Hebrew alphabet, used as a heading over Ps. 119:97–104.

MEMPHIS. See *Noph.*

MENAHEM. A cruel and idolatrous king of Israel (ruled about 752–742 B.C.) who killed Shallum in order to assume the throne. He paid tribute to Tiglath-pileser III, king of Assyria, in order to maintain his power. He was succeeded by his son Pekahiah (2 Kings 15:16–22).

MEPHIBOSHETH/MERIB-BAAL. The crippled son of David's friend Jonathan and a grandson of King Saul. He was dropped by his nurse and crippled at age five when she received the news that Jonathan and Saul had been killed by the Philistines (2 Sam. 4:4). David sought out Mephibosheth, restored his family's land, and gave him a place at the king's table. *Merib-baal:* 1 Chron. 8:34. See also *Jonathan,* No. 1.

MERARI. The third son of Levi and ancestor of the Merarites (Gen. 46:11; Exod. 6:19).

MERCHANDISE. Items bought and sold in business transactions. Many traders in caravans passed through Israel on their way to and from Egypt (Gen. 37:25–28). Solomon established maritime trading agreements with the king of Tyre (1 Kings 9:26).

MERCURIUS (HERMES). The Roman name for the pagan god Mercury—the god of commerce—and the name applied to Paul by the people of Lystra (Acts 14:12). *Hermes:* NIV, NRSV.

MERCY (COMPASSION). Compassion for others. God's mercies are abundant (1 Pet. 1:3) and fresh every morning (Lam. 3:22–23). Paul described God as "the father of all mercies" (2 Cor. 1:3). *Compassion:* NIV. Jesus commended the Samaritan who showed mercy for a wounded traveler (Luke 10:36–37). See also *Compassion; Lovingkindness; Pity.*

MERCY SEAT (COVER). The gold lid which covered the ark of the covenant. It was called the "mercy seat" because God was believed to be present to hear and answer prayers (Exod. 25:21–22). *Cover:* NIV. On the Day of Atonement, the high priest sprinkled blood of the sin offerings on the mercy seat as a propitiation for the people's sins (Lev. 16:11–16). See also *Ark of the Covenant; Atonement.*

MERIBAH. See *Massah and Meribah.*

MERIB-BAAL. See *Mephibosheth.*

MERODACH (MARDUK). The pagan Babylonian god of war whose overthrow was predicted by the prophet Jeremiah (Jer. 50:2). *Marduk:* NIV.

MERODACH-BALADAN. See *Berodach-baladan.*

MESHA.

1. The oldest son of Caleb (1 Chron. 2:42).

2. A king of Moab who led an unsuccessful invasion of Judah (2 Chron. 20). He offered his oldest son as a sacrifice to the pagan god Chemosh (2 Kings 3:4, 26–27).

MESHACH/MISHAEL. The Babylonian name for Daniel's friend who was thrown into the fiery furnace for refusing to worship an idol (Dan. 1:7). He was saved through God's miraculous intervention. His Hebrew name was *Mishael* (Dan. 1:6). See also *Daniel*.

MESOPOTAMIA/ PADAN-ARAM. The territory between the Tigris and Euphrates rivers also known as *Padan-aram* (Gen. 25:20). Abraham and his family migrated from the city of Ur in this region (Gen. 11:31–32; Acts 7:2). The Babylonian Empire flourished in this general vicinity during O.T. times. Citizens of Mesopotamia were present in Jerusalem on the day of Pentecost (Acts 2:9). See also *Ur of the Chaldees*.

MESS. A portion of food served at a meal (2 Sam. 11:8). To receive a larger-than-usual mess or portion was considered an honor (Gen. 43:34).

MESSENGER. A person sent to deliver a special message. Jewish kings sent couriers to distant cities to proclaim laws and edicts (2 Chron. 36:22–23). John the Baptist was a messenger who prepared the people for the coming of Jesus (Matt. 11:10).

MESSIAH/MESSIAS (ANOINTED ONE). The title given by the Jewish people to a future leader whom they expected to restore their honor and glory after delivering them from their oppressors (Dan. 9:25–26). *Anointed one:* NIV. Jesus fulfilled their longing but in an unexpected way by becoming a spiritual Savior who delivered believers from sin (Rom. 6:1–9). *Messias:* Greek form: (John 1:41; 4:25). See also *Emmanuel; Jesus Christ; Son of God*.

METHUSELAH/MATHUSALA. A son of Enoch (Gen. 5:21) and the grandfather of Noah. Methuselah lived to the age of 969, the oldest recorded age in the Bible. *Mathusala:* Luke 3:37.

MICAH. A prophet of the O.T., a contemporary of Isaiah, whose ministry paralleled the reigns of kings Jotham, Ahaz, and Hezekiah from about 750 to 687 B.C. (Mic. 1:1). A stern prophet of judgment, he denounced the social injustices of his time (Mic. 2:1–3).

MICAH, BOOK OF. A short prophetic book of the O.T. known for its prediction that the Messiah would be born in Bethlehem (5:2). The prophet also condemned the rich for oppressing the poor (2:1–2; 6:7–13) and announced that God's judgment against the nations of Judah and Israel would be wrought by the conquering Assyrians (1, 3, 7:10–13).

MICAIAH. An O.T. prophet who predicted that King Ahab of Israel would be killed in a battle at Ramoth-gilead, in contrast to false prophets who assured the king he would be victorious (1 Kings 22:8–28). Micaiah was imprisoned for his stinging message, but his prediction was correct (1 Kings 22:29–39).

MICHAEL.

1. A son of Jehoshaphat, king of Judah. Michael was killed by his brother Jehoram, who became king (2 Chron. 21:2–4).

2. An archangel who was thought to serve as a prince and guardian over the nation of Israel (Dan.10:21; 12:1). See also *Archangel*.

MICHAL. A daughter of King Saul presented to David as a wife after David killed 200 Philistine warriors (1 Sam. 14:49; 18:25–27). She died without children (2 Sam. 6:21–23).

MICHMAS/MICHMASH (MICMASH). A town near Jerusalem occupied by Saul's army (1 Sam. 13:2–4) and the site of Jonathan's victory over the Philistines (1 Sam. 14:6–18). Some Jewish citizens returned to this city after the Babylonian Exile (Ezra 2:27). *Michmash:* Isa. 10:28; *Micmash:* NIV.

MICHTAM. A word in the titles of Ps. 16 and Pss. 56–60, perhaps designating a particular type of psalm.

MIDDLE WALL OF PARTITION (BARRIER, DIVIDING WALL). The curtain or barrier in the Jewish temple at Jerusalem which separated Jews and Gentiles. Christ's atonement removed this partition and brought reconciliation and peace to people of all races and nationalities (Eph. 2:14–18). *Barrier:* NIV; *Dividing wall:* NRSV. See also *Court of the Gentiles*.

MIDIAN/MADIAN.

1. A son of Abraham by Keturah and founder of the Midianites (Gen. 25:1–4; 1 Chron. 1:32–33).

2. A region in the Arabian desert east of the Jordan River, including Edom and the Sinai Peninsula, which was occupied by the Midianites (Exod. 2:15). *Madian:* Acts 7:29.

MIDIANITES. Nomadic traders who occupied the land of Midian. A band of Midianites probably bought Joseph and sold him as a slave in Egypt (Gen. 37:28). This tribe joined the Moabites in attacking Israel but failed (Num. 22). The Midianites were probably absorbed into the Moabites and the Arabs. See also *Gideon*.

MIDWIFE. A Hebrew woman who assisted other women in the process of childbirth. Many midwives refused the Egyptian pharaoh's orders to kill male children (Exod. 1:15–17).

MIGDOL. A place in northeastern Egypt where some citizens of Judah fled after their nation fell to the Babylonians about 587 B.C. (Jer. 44:1; 46:14).

MIGHTY MEN (FIGHTING MEN, WARRIORS). The brave and loyal warriors who risked their lives for David before and after he became king (2 Sam. 23:8–39). Joshua also had the support of courageous warriors known as "mighty men of valor" (Josh. 1:14; 10:7). *Fighting men:* NIV; *Warriors:* NRSV. See also *Jashobeam*.

MILCOM/MOLECH/ MOLOCH. The supreme god of the Ammonites (1 Kings 11:5). *Molech:* NIV. Solomon built a sanctuary for worship of this pagan god, but it was destroyed during King Josiah's reforms (2 Kings 23:12–13). *Molech:* Lev. 20:2. *Moloch:* Acts 7:43. See also *Ammonites*.

MILE. A Roman unit for measuring distance which equaled 1,000 paces, or 1,616 yards. Jesus used this term to teach His followers forgiveness and forbearance (Matt. 5:41).

MILETUS/MILETUM. A coastal city of Asia Minor about forty miles south of Ephesus. Paul met the leaders of the Ephesian church here and gave a moving farewell address (Acts 20:15–38). *Miletum:* 2 Tim. 4:20.

MILK. A liquid for drinking and cheese-making taken from cows, goats, sheep, and camels (Gen. 32:14–15). The word is also used figuratively to indicate abundance (Exod. 3:8) and the diet of immature Christians (1 Cor. 3:1–2).

MILL. A device for grinding grain into flour, consisting of two stones which pulverized the grain between them (Exod. 11:5; Matt. 24:41).

MILLENNIUM. A term for the period of 1,000 years described in Rev. 20:1–8. Opinions vary on how to interpret this period. Premillennialists expect a literal reign of 1,000 years by Christ on earth after His return. Postmillennialists believe that 1,000 years of peace will precede Christ's second coming, during which time much of the world will be converted. While believing in the Lord's return, amillennialists view Christ's millennial reign in a spiritual sense.

MILLET. A plant which produced small heads of grain, used for making bread (Ezek. 4:9).

MILLO.

1. A stronghold or fortress at Shechem whose occupants proclaimed Abimelech as their king (Judg. 9:6, 20). *Beth-millo:* NIV, NRSV.

2. A defensive fortress tower built by David near Jerusalem (2 Sam. 5:9) and improved by Solomon in anticipation of an Assyrian siege (1 Kings 9:15).

MINA. See *Maneh; Pound.*

MIND. The reasoning faculty of human beings. In the Bible, the word *heart* often means "mind" (see Ps. 19:14). Those who reject God have corrupt minds (Rom. 1:28), and the carnally minded are enemies of God (Rom. 8:6–7). Jesus urged His followers to love God with all their mind and heart (Matt. 22:37). Paul encouraged the Christians at Rome to have their minds renewed so they would know and follow the will of God (Rom. 12:2).

MINE. A place where metals were extracted from the earth. Iron and copper were mined in the area around the Dead Sea, especially during Solomon's reign (1 Kings 9:26–28).

MINISTER. A term for a person who serves others, often used interchangeably with the word *servant.* In addition to the religious meaning of the word, it is also applied to court attendants (1 Kings 10:5) and civil rulers (Rom. 13:4–6). All Christians are instructed to "preach the word" and perform duty as God's servants (2 Tim. 4:2–5). See also *Deacon; Pastor; Priest; Shepherd.*

MINISTRY. Service in the name of God. Such service demands a spirit of sacrificial service after the example of Christ (Matt. 20:26–28). All Christians are called to be ambassadors for Christ in the work of reconciliation (2 Cor. 5:18–20), to be fishers of men (Mark 1:17), and to perfect believers (Eph. 4:11–12).

MINOR PROPHETS. The twelve prophets of the O.T. whose books were placed last in the prophetic writings because of their shorter length—Hosea, Joel, Amos, Obadiah, Jonah, Micah, Nahum, Habakkuk, Zephaniah, Haggai, Zechariah, and Malachi. See also *Major Prophets*.

MINSTREL (HARPIST, MUSICIAN). A singer or musician (2 Kings 3:15; *Harpist:* NIV; *Musician:* NRSV), often employed at funerals or wakes, as in the case of the daughter of Jairus (Matt. 9:23).

MINT. A common, inexpensive herb used in medicine and for seasoning foods. Jesus mentioned mint as an object scrupulously tithed by the scribes and Pharisees (Matt. 23:23).

MIPHKAD (INSPECTION GATE, MUSTER GATE). A gate in the walls of Jerusalem or the temple rebuilt by Nehemiah (Neh. 3:31). *Inspection Gate:* NIV; *Muster Gate:* NRSV.

MIRACLE. God's intervention or suspension of the natural laws of the universe. Miracles are described in the N.T. as signs, wonders, mighty works, and powers. Most miracles in the Bible occurred during (1) the period of the Exodus (Exod. 7, 9, 10, 14); (2) Elijah's and Elisha's ministry (2 Kings 4:2–7); (3) the period of the Exile (Dan. 3:9–27); (4) the ministry of Jesus, when miracles attested to His divine power (Matt. 15:33–39); and (5) the ministry of the apostles, signifying their apostleship (Acts 3:6). Jesus worked miracles to relieve suffering (Matt. 8:14–17), to raise the dead (Matt. 9:23–25), to calm nature (Luke 8:22–25), or to give an object lesson (Mark 11:12–14). See also *Sign*.

MIRIAM. The sister of Aaron and Moses (1 Chron. 6:3). Miriam protected her baby brother Moses by arranging for their mother Jochebed to care for him (Exod. 2:4–10). She led a triumphant song of praise and thanksgiving to God after the Hebrews were delivered from the pursuing Egyptian army at the Red Sea (Exod. 15:2–21). She died and was buried in the wilderness at Kadesh (Num. 20:1). See also *Aaron; Jochebed; Moses*.

MISCHIEF MAKER. See *Busybody*.

MISGAB (STRONGHOLD, FORTRESS). An unknown site in Moab, perhaps a mountainous region or fortified outpost (Jer. 48:1). *Stronghold:* NIV; *Fortress:* NRSV.

MISHAEL. See *Meshach.*

MISHEAL (MISHAL). A city in the territory of Asher assigned to the Levites and designated as a city of refuge (Josh. 19:26). *Mishal:* NIV, NRSV. See also *Cities of Refuge.*

MISSIONS. The process of carrying out Jesus' Great Commission to disciple and teach all peoples. Even in the O.T., Abraham was called to be a blessing to all nations (Gen. 12:1–3), and Jonah was sent by the Lord to preach to the pagan citizens of Nineveh (Jon. 1:2). Missions is prompted by God's love (John 3:16) and mankind's lost condition (Rom. 3:9–31). Believers are equipped for this task by the Holy Spirit's presence (Acts 1:8), the Word of God (Rom. 10:14–15), and the power of prayer (Acts 13:1–4). Christ's followers are to evangelize all nations, baptize believers, and teach His commands (Matt. 28: 19–20). See also *Commission.*

MIST. A vapor or fog. The earth was watered by a mist before the first rainfall (Gen. 2:6). Mist and darkness are used figuratively to describe spiritual blindness (Acts 13:11).

MISTRESS. A woman with power or authority (Gen. 16:4–9). The Queen of Sheba (1 Kings 10:1–3) and Queen Jezebel (1 Kings 21:7–11) were women of authority.

MITE. The coin of smallest value in N.T. times, worth less than a penny. Jesus commended a poor widow's sacrificial gift of two mites (Mark 12:42).

MITRE (TURBAN). A headdress worn by the high priest (Lev. 8:9). *Turban:* NIV, NRSV. A gold plate inscribed with "holiness to the Lord" was attached to the mitre (Exod. 39:28–31).

MITYLENE. The principal city of the island of Lesbos in the Aegean Sea. Paul spent a night at Mitylene (Acts 20:13–15).

MIZPAH. A place where Jacob and his father-in-law Laban made a covenant and agreed to a friendly separation. They marked the site with a pile of stones (Gen. 31:44–53).

MIZRAIM

1. The second son of Ham and father of Ludim (Gen. 10:6–13). His descendants settled in Egypt (Gen. 45:20; 50:11).

2. The Hebrew name for Egypt (Gen. 50:11). See *Egypt*.

MNASON. A Christian from the island of Cyprus who accompanied Paul on his last visit to Jerusalem (Acts 21:16).

MOAB.

1. A son of Lot and an ancestor of the Moabites (Gen. 19:33–37).

2. The country of the Moabites, lying east of the Jordan River and the Dead Sea and south of the Arnon River (Deut. 1:5–7). Its earliest name was *Lotan* or *Lot,* since the inhabitants were descended from Lot (Gen. 19:37).

MOABITE STONE. A black memorial stone which confirms a significant event of the O.T.—the rebellion of King Mesha of Moab against King Ahaziah of Israel (2 Kings 3:4–27).

MOABITES. Pagan inhabitants of Moab, worshipers of Chemosh (Num. 21:29), and enemies of the Israelites. The strength of the Moabites varied across several centuries of Israel's history. The tribes of Reuben and Gad settled in northern Moab before the conquest of Canaan (Num. 32:1–37). Ehud won a significant victory over their forces during the period of the judges (Judg. 3:15–30). David also fought and conquered the Moabites (2 Sam. 8:2). Ruth was a native of Moab (Ruth 1:22).

MODERATION. Temperance and forbearance. Paul described moderation as a quality of gentleness to be practiced before others (Phil. 4:5). Christians are counseled to be moderate in all things (1 Cor. 9:25). See also *Temperance*.

MOLE (CHAMELEON). A KJV word which probably refers to a chameleon or lizard since no true moles are found in Palestine (Lev. 11:30). *Chameleon:* NIV, NRSV.

MOLECH, MOLOCH. See *Milcom*.

MOLTEN SEA. A large bronze vessel made by King Hiram of Tyre for ceremonial use by the priests in Solomon's temple at Jerusalem (1 Kings 7:23). See also *Brasen Sea*.

MONEY. A medium of exchange. In O.T. times before

the Babylonian Exile, money was a specific weight of precious metal, such as silver or gold. The coins of N.T. times were issued by the Romans or Greeks (Matt. 17:27; Mark 12:42). The earliest coins used in Palestine before the N.T. era were Persian in origin. See also *Filthy Lucre; Mammon.*

MONEYCHANGERS. Independent agents, much like cashiers, who converted money into "shekels of the sanctuary," which could be used in the temple at Jerusalem. These "bankers" provided worshipers with the required temple tax, the half-shekel (Exod. 30:13–15). Jesus denounced these moneychangers who were charging excess fees for their services. He overturned their tables and drove them out of the temple (Matt. 21:12).

MONOGAMY. The marriage of a man to one woman only—the pattern established by God in the Garden of Eden (Gen. 2: 18–24). Many of the O.T. patriarchs, such as Jacob, had more than one wife (Gen. 29:16–35). See also *Marriage; Polygamy.*

MONOTHEISM. The belief in one—and only one—supreme God, in contrast to polytheism, or the worship of several gods. The one true God is to be loved supremely and His commands taught to others (Deut. 6:4–7). God demands absolute loyalty, and He will not tolerate the worship of any other god by His people (Exod. 20:3–5). See also *Polytheism.*

MONTH. One of the twelve divisions of the year. The length of the Hebrew month was calculated from one new moon to the next (Num. 10:10; 28:11–14).

MOON. The heavenly body or satellite which revolves around the earth, referred to as the "lesser light" in the account of creation (Gen. 1:16). Each new moon marked the beginning of another Jewish month, and its arrival was celebrated with special sacrifices (Num. 28:11–15). The moon was worshiped under various names by pagan peoples, but God forbade this practice by the Hebrews (Deut. 4:19).

MOONSTONE. See *Diamond.*

MORDECAI. A Jewish exile in Persia who befriended Esther, helping her to become the king's favorite and assume the queenship (Esther 2:5–11). With Esther's help, Mordecai thwarted the plot of Haman to destroy the Jews (Esther 2:19–23). He was honored by the king and promoted (Esther 6:10–11; 8:1–2). See also *Ahasuerus; Esther; Haman.*

MOREH. A place near Shechem where Abraham built an altar after entering Canaan (Gen. 12:6–7).

MORESHETH-GATH. The birthplace of Micah the prophet in the lowland plain of Judah (Mic. 1:14).

MORIAH. The mountainous area in Jerusalem where Abraham was commanded by God to sacrifice his son Isaac (Gen. 22:1–13). After God provided a sacrifice other than Isaac, Abraham renamed the site Jehovah-jireh, meaning "the Lord will provide" (Gen. 22:14).

MORNING STAR. The planet Venus as it appears at dawn and a figurative title for Christ (Rev. 22:16). Christ is described as the morning star, which outshines the light of prophetic witness (2 Pet. 1:19). See also *Day Star.*

MORTALITY. The human condition which leads eventually to physical death. Mortality is the common lot of all human beings, but it serves as the entrance to eternal life for believers (2 Cor. 5:4–6). For the Christian, bodily resurrection and eternal life are as certain as physical death (1 Cor. 15:21–23). See also *Eternal Life.*

MORTAR. A mixture of lime and sand used to build the tower of Babel (Gen. 11:3). The Israelites in Egypt worked with bricks and mortar (Exod. 1:14). See also *Untempered Mortar.*

MOSERA/MOSEROTH. A place in the wilderness where the Israelites camped on their way to Canaan. Aaron died and was buried here (Deut. 10:6). *Moseroth:* Num. 33:30–31.

MOSES. The great lawgiver and prophet of Israel who led the Hebrew people out of Egypt. His life is best understood in three forty-year periods.

Forty years in Egypt. Moses was born into slavery and hidden by his mother to escape the pharaoh's order that all male Hebrew babies should be killed (Exod. 1:22; 2:1–10). Discovered and "adopted" by the pharaoh's daughter, he was raised and schooled as an Egyptian (Exod. 2:10). After killing an Egyptian who was abusing an Israelite slave, he became a fugitive in the desert (Exod. 2:14–15).

Forty years in Midian. Moses became a shepherd (Exod. 3:1), married Zipporah, the daughter of a priest, and she bore two sons, Gershom and Eliezer (Exod. 18:3–4). He reluctantly answered God's call to lead His people out of slavery (Exod. 3: 11–4:9), and returned to Egypt, where he enlisted his brother Aaron as his helper and spokesman (Exod. 4:27–31). After ten plagues sent by the Lord upon the Egyptians, the pharaoh finally released the Hebrews, who entered the wilderness area in the Sinai Peninsula under Moses' leadership.

Forty years in the wilderness. In the wilderness, Moses received the Ten Commandments (Exod. 20:1–24) and other parts of the Mosaic Law, exhorted the people to remain faithful to God, built the tabernacle at God's command (Exod. 36–40), and sent spies to investigate Canaan (Num. 13). He impatiently struck a rock for water at Kadesh (Num. 20: 1–13), a sin which led God to deny his entrance into the Promised Land. He died in Moab at Canaan's border at the age of 120 (Deut. 34:1–8). See also *Aaron; Law*.

MOST HIGH. A name for God signifying His majesty (Acts 7:48–49). The title was used by nonbelievers in both the O.T. (Num. 24:16) and the N.T. (Acts 16:17). See also *I Am; Jehovah; Yahweh*.

MOTE (SPECK). A small particle of anything. Jesus used this word to indicate the hypocrisy of those who found small flaws in others while ignoring major defects of their own (Matt. 7:3–5). *Speck:* NIV, NRSV.

MOTH. A destructive insect. Since wealthy Jews stored clothes which could be destroyed by moths, Jesus used the word to indicate the fleeting nature of earthly riches (Matt. 6:19–20).

MOTHER. A term for a female parent as well as a grandmother and other female relatives. Eve is regarded as the "mother of all living" (Gen. 3:20). Mothers are worthy of honor and obedience by those who desire long life (Exod. 20:12; Eph. 6:1–3). The prophets alluded to Israel as "mother" in denouncing the nation's shameful sins (Jer. 50:12–13; Ezek. 19).

MOUNT OF THE AMALEKITES. A mountain in Ephraim where Abdon, one of the judges of Israel, was buried (Judg. 12:15).

MOUNT OLIVET. See *Olives, Mount of.*

MOUNT PARAN. See *Paran, Mount.*

MOUNTAIN REGION. See *Hill Country.*

MOUNTAIN SHEEP. See *Chamois.*

MOURN. To express grief or sorrow. The usual mourning period was seven days, but this was extended to thirty days for Moses and Aaron (Num. 20:29). Jesus mourned at the death of his friend Lazarus (John 11:33–36). See also *Sackcloth; Sorrow.*

MOUSE. A rodent (1 Sam. 6:5). Many species of these destructive animals are found in Palestine. They were "unclean," according to Mosaic Law (Lev. 11:29; Isa. 66:17).

MOUTH. The mouth has potential for good or evil. It may be used for praise and prayer (Ps. 34:1; 1 Sam. 1:12) or as an instrument of idolatry (1 Kings 19:18) and lying (1 Kings 22:13, 22). See also *Lips; Throat; Tongue.*

MUFFLER (VEIL, SCARF). A veil, or a long scarf worn about the head or chest (Isa. 3:19). *Veil:* NIV; *Scarf:* NRSV.

MULBERRY (BALSAM). A common tree of Palestine, probably the aspen, baca, or balsam (2 Sam. 5:23). *Balsam:* NIV, NRSV See also *Sycamine.*

MULE. A beast of burden of the horse family used extensively by the Hebrews. A runaway mule carried Absalom to his death (2 Sam. 18:9–15).

MULTITUDE (CROWD). A crowd or a large group of people. Jesus was often followed by "great multitudes" eager for learning or healing (Matt. 4:24–25). He miraculously fed two multitudes of several thousand (Matt. 14:15–21). *Crowd:* NIV, NRSV. See also *Host.*

MURDER. The unlawful killing of a human being, an act which was prohibited by Mosaic Law (Exod. 20:13). The Israelites exacted the death penalty for willful murder (Exod. 21:12; Lev. 24:17) but provided cities of refuge for persons guilty of manslaughter, or accidental killing (Num. 35:11). Jesus warned of intense anger that could lead to murder (Matt. 5:20–25). See also *Avenger of Blood; Manslayer*.

MURRAIN. A mysterious disease and the fifth plague which God brought against the Egyptians, attacking their animals (Exod. 9:1–6). It may have been anthrax.

MUSIC. Vocal and instrumental music was prominent in temple choirs (2 Sam. 6:5). Musical instruments were invented by Jubal, son of Lamech (Gen. 4:21). The Hebrews used cymbals, harps, organs, pipes, psalteries, and trumpets in their worship (1 Chron. 15: 16–22).

MUSICIAN. See *Minstrel*.

MUSTARD SEED. The tiny, almost microscopic seed from a common herb of Palestine. Jesus used this small seed to illustrate the power of faith in the believer's life (Luke 17:6). See also *Faith*.

MUSTER GATE. See *Miphkad*.

MUTH-LABBEN. A musical term in the title of Ps. 9, perhaps referring to the tune for the psalm.

MYRA. A town in the province of Lycia in Asia Minor where Paul changed ships during his voyage to Rome (Acts 27:5–6).

MYRRH (RESIN). An aromatic gum resin found chiefly in Arabia (Gen. 37:25). *Resin:* NRSV. It was one of the gifts presented to the infant Jesus (Matt. 2:11). Myrrh was used in incense perfume, anointing oil, embalming fluid, and medicine (Exod. 30:23; John 19:39).

MYRTLE. A common evergreen shrub of Palestine. Its branches were used at the Feast of Tabernacles (Neh. 8:15). A myrtle tree in the desert was symbolic of God's provision for His people (Isa. 41:19; 55:13).

MYSIA. A province in northwestern Asia Minor through which Paul and Silas passed on the second missionary journey (Acts 16:7–10).

MYSTERY (SECRET). Something unknown except through divine revelation (Rom. 16:25–26). The gospel is called a mystery (Eph. 3:8–9). Jesus taught in parables to reveal the mysteries of God's kingdom to His disciples (Luke 8:10). *Secret:* NIV, NRSV. Paul reveals that Christ within us inspires our hope to share in His glory (1 Cor. 15:51; Col. 1:26–27).

-N-

NAAMAN. A captain in the Syrian army who was healed of leprosy by the prophet Elisha. At first Naaman was reluctant to bathe in the Jordan River for healing, as commanded by Elisha. But he finally obeyed, received healing, and praised the God of Israel (2 Kings 5:1–15). Naaman was mentioned by Jesus (Luke 4:27).

NABAL. A wealthy herdsman who refused to provide food for the desperate David and his army in the wilderness. His wife Abigail secretly offered hospitality, and Nabal died ten days later (1 Sam. 25). See also *Abigail*.

NABOTH. An Israelite who was framed and killed by Jezebel so Ahab could take possession of his vineyard. God pronounced judgment against them for this despicable act (1 Kings 21:1–23).

NACHOR. See *Nahor*.

NADAB

1. The oldest son of Aaron who was destroyed, along with his brother Abihu, for offering "strange fire" to God (Lev. 10:1–2). See also *Abihu*.

2. A king of Israel (reigned about 910–909 B.C.), the son of Jeroboam I. Nadab was assassinated by Baasha, who succeeded him (1 Kings 15:25–31).

NAHASH. A king of Ammon who befriended David. David tried to return the favor to his son Hanun but was rejected (2 Sam. 10:1–4).

NAHBI. One of the twelve spies who scouted the land of Canaan, representing the tribe of Naphtali (Num. 13:14). See also *Spies*.

NAHOR/NACHOR. The grandfather of Abraham and father of Terah (Gen. 11:22–25). *Nachor:* Luke 3:34.

NAHUM. A prophet of Judah from Elkosh who prophesied against Nineveh before 612 B.C., probably during the reign of King Hezekiah (Nah. 1:1, 8, 13); author of the book of Nahum.

NAHUM, BOOK OF. A short prophetic book of the O.T. that predicted the downfall of the pagan nation of Assyria (3: 7–19) because of the atrocities which it committed against God's people. The prophet portrays God as the sovereign Lord of history who has the final word in the conflict between good and evil (1:1–15). See also *Assyria*.

NAIN. A village south of Nazareth near the Sea of Galilee where Jesus raised a widow's son from the dead (Luke 7:11–17).

NAIOTH. A place in Ramah where David fled from King Saul and where Samuel lived and conducted his school for prophets (1 Sam. 19:18–20).

NAME. The word or title by which someone or something is known. Adam gave names to the animals (Gen. 2:20). Persons and places in the Bible often bore symbolic names, such as the children of the prophets Isaiah (Isa. 8:3) and Hosea (Hos. 1:4).

NAOMI. The mother-in-law of Ruth. After marrying Elimelech, Naomi moved to Moab to escape a famine. Her husband and two sons died, leaving Naomi and her two daughters-in-law alone. She returned to Bethlehem with Ruth and helped arrange Ruth's marriage to Boaz (see Ruth 1–4).

NAPHTALI.

1. A son of Jacob by Bilhah, Rachel's maid (Gen. 30:1, 8). He received Jacob's blessing (Gen. 49:21–28), and his descendants became one of the twelve tribes of Israel.

2. The tribe consisting of Naphtali's descendants (Num. 1:42), who were assigned the fertile, mountainous territory in northern Palestine, including the cities of Hazor, Kedesh, and Ramah (Josh. 19:36–38; 20:7). Isaiah prophesied that Naphtali in "Galilee of the nations" would see a great light (Isa. 9:1–7). This was fulfilled in Jesus' Galilean ministry (Matt. 4:12–16). See also *Tribes of Israel*.

NAPHTUHIM (NAPTUHITES). The inhabitants of central Egypt who were descendants of Mizraim, son of Ham (Gen. 10:13). *Naptuhites:* NIV (1 Chron. 1:11).

NAPKIN (CLOTH). A handkerchief or small piece of cloth (Luke 19:20) used for wiping perspiration and other purposes (Acts 19:12). A similar cloth was used for binding the face and head of the dead for burial (John 11:44; 20:7). *Cloth:* NIV, NRSV. See also *Handkerchief*.

NARCISSUS. A Christian in Rome whose household was greeted by Paul (Rom. 16:11).

NARD. See *Spikenard.*

NATHAN.

1. A son of David by Bath-sheba, born after David became king (1 Chron. 3:5). A brother of Solomon (2 Sam. 5:14), he is listed as an ancestor of Jesus (Luke 3:31).

2. The brave prophet who used an allegory to rebuke King David for his sin with Bath-sheba and his plot to kill Bath-sheba's husband Uriah (2 Sam. 12:1–15). Nathan also assisted David when Adonijah attempted to seize the throne (1 Kings 1:8–45) and wrote histories of David's and Solomon's administrations (1 Chron. 29: 29; 2 Chron. 9:29).

NATHANAEL. See *Bartholomew.*

NATION. A word used in various ways in the Bible: (1) to describe all the inhabitants of a country or the country itself (Deut. 4:34); (2) to refer to natives of the same stock (Acts 26:4); (3) to denote the father or head of a tribe or clan; and (4) to refer to heathens or Gentiles (Isa. 9:1).

NATIONS. See *Heathen.*

NATURE. A word which refers to the physical universe as well as the essence or disposition of man. God created the natural world and gave man dominion over it (Gen. 1:1, 26–31). Adam and Eve's disobedience in the garden introduced sin and corrupted nature (Gen. 3:12–19). The natural world is intended to draw mankind to the Creator (Ps. 8; Rom. 1:20), but man's carnal nature has worshiped the creature instead of the Creator (Rom. 1:25). Fallen man's faith in Christ appropriates God's divine nature (2 Pet. 1:3–4).

NAVE (RIM). The hub or rim of a wheel into which spokes were fitted (1 Kings 7:33). *Rim:* NIV, NRSV.

NAVEL. The umbilical connection of a newborn child with its mother. Ezekiel compared Jerusalem's unfaithfulness and neglect with an untended newborn child whose navel cord had not been cut (Ezek. 16:1–4).

NAZARENE (NAZOREAN). A native or inhabitant of the city of Nazareth. Since this was His hometown, Jesus was referred to as a "Nazarene" (Matt. 2:23). *Nazorean:* NRSV (Mark 1:23–24).

NAZARETH. An obscure town in Galilee which was the boyhood home of Jesus (Mark 1:24). Mary, Joseph, and Jesus returned to Nazareth after their flight into Egypt (Matt. 2:20–23). The town was located in the district of Galilee beside the plain of Esdraelon, fifteen miles southeast of Mt. Carmel. Jesus was rejected by the townspeople of Nazareth at the beginning of His public ministry (Luke 4:16–30).

NAZARITE (NAZIRITE). A man or woman especially consecrated to God according to the law of the Nazarites (Num. 6:2). *Nazirite:* NIV, NRSV. Voluntarily or because of a devout parent's promise, a Nazarite assumed strict religious vows, including abstaining from strong drink and not cutting his hair. The vow might be for life or a fixed period. Samson (Judg. 13:4–7), Samuel (1 Sam. 1:11, 28), and John the Baptist (Luke 1:15) were Nazarites. See also *Asceticism*.

NEAPOLIS. A seaport at Philippi where Paul landed on the second missionary journey (Acts 16:11).

NEBO.

1. The highest point of Mount Pisgah in Moab near Jericho where Moses died after viewing the Promised Land and where he was buried (Deut. 32:49; 34:5–6). See also *Pisgah, Mount*.

2. The Babylonian god of science and knowledge. Mount Nebo was possibly a center of Nebo worship. Isaiah declared the vanity of such idols (Isa. 46:1).

NEBUCHADNEZZAR/ NEBUCHADREZZAR. The king of Babylonia (reigned about 605–561 B.C.) who captured Jerusalem and carried Judah into exile about 587 B.C. (see Dan. 1–4). The only strong Babylonian king, he was the son of Nabopolassar, founder of the empire. After a revolt by King Zedekiah of Judah, Nebuchadnezzar destroyed Jerusalem, burned the temple, and carried the nation's leading citizens into exile (2 Kings 25: 1–26). *Nebuchadrezzar:* Jer. 51:34. See also *Babylonia*.

NEBUZAR-ADAN. An officer in Nebuchadnezzar's army during the Babylonian siege of Jerusalem (2 Kings 25:8–20). He looked after the prophet Jeremiah, who remained in

Jerusalem after the siege (Jer. 39:11–14; 40:1–5).

NECHO. See *Pharaoh*.

NECK. A word used figuratively for stubbornness ("stiff-necked," Deut. 9:6). It was also used to express the coming siege of Judah by Assyria (Isa. 8:8) and to represent the burden which circumcision would place on Gentile Christians (Acts 15:10).

NECKLACE. An ornament or jewelry worn around the neck. The pharaoh placed a gold chain around Joseph's neck, symbolizing his appointment as governor of Egypt (Gen. 41:41–43)

NECROMANCER. One who communicated with the dead in an effort to foretell the future (1 Sam. 28:7–20). This practice was forbidden by Mosaic Law (Deut. 18:11). See also *Familiar Spirit; Medium; Wizard*.

NEEDLE. A tool for sewing. Jesus compared the difficulty of the wealthy reaching heaven with putting a camel through the eye of a needle (Matt. 19:24).

NEEDLEWORK. Embroidery or delicate sewing. Embroidered robes and curtains were used in the tabernacle (Exod. 28:39; 36:37).

NEEDY. See *Poor*.

NEGEV. See *South Country*.

NEGINAH/NEGINOTH. Phrases in the titles of several psalms which may refer to stringed instruments (Pss. 4, 6, 54, 55, 61, 67, 76).

NEHEMIAH. The governor of Jerusalem (445–433 B.C.) who helped rebuild the city wall after the Babylonian Exile; author of the book of Nehemiah. The son of Hachaliah, he was cupbearer to King Artaxerxes of Persia (Neh. 1:11; 2:1). He received permission from the king to return to Jerusalem to assist the returned exiles in their rebuilding efforts (Neh. 2:3–6). In addition to rallying the people to rebuild the city wall, he led a religious reform with the assistance of Ezra the priest (Neh. 8:1–13; 12:36). See also *Ezra*.

NEHEMIAH, BOOK OF. A historical book of the O.T. which records the rebuilding of Jerusalem's defensive wall after the Babylonian Exile under the leadership of Nehemiah (1:1–7:73). The book also recounts the religious reforms undertaken by Nehemiah and Ezra. They led the people to renew the covenant and recommit themselves to God's law (8:1–13:31). See also *Ezra*.

NEHILOTH. A musical term in the title of Ps. 5, probably denoting a wind instrument such as the flute.

NEHUSHTAN. A bronze serpent worshiped by the Israelites in the wilderness (2 Kings 18:4).

NEIGHBOR. A fellow human being. Paul declared that Christians should love and speak truth to their neighbors (Rom. 13:9–10; Eph. 4:25). The Pharisees confined the meaning of "neighbor" to people of their own nation, but Jesus' parable of the Good Samaritan indicates all people are neighbors and should help each other (Luke 10:25–37).

NEPHEG. A son of David, born in Jerusalem after David became king (2 Sam. 5:13–15).

NEPHEW. A term for a grandson (Judg. 12:14) or other male relative (Job 18:19). Lot, however, was a true nephew of Abraham (Gen. 11:27).

NEREUS. A Christian at Rome to whom the apostle Paul sent greetings (Rom. 16:15).

NERGAL. A Babylonian god of war which was worshiped by the men of Cuth (2 Kings 17:30). Images of Nergal were placed throughout Israel by King Shalmaneser of Assyria (2 Kings 17:24, 30).

NERGAL-SHAREZER. A Babylonian prince of King Nebuchadnezzar's court during the capture of Jerusalem (Jer. 39:1–3). He helped release Jeremiah from prison (Jer. 39:13–14).

NERO. The fifth emperor of Rome (reigned A.D. 54–68) who severely persecuted Christians. Although he is not named in the Bible, he is probably the emperor under whom Paul and Peter were martyred. Secular history confirms that Nero placed blame for Rome's great fire (A.D. 64) on the Christians and had many put to death during his administration. See also *Roman Empire*.

NEST. The dwellingplace of birds. The loftiness of the eagle's nest demonstrated the foolishness of man's pride (Jer. 49:16; Obad. 4).

NET. A meshed fabric used to capture birds or fish. The word is also used figuratively for entrapment of the innocent and for winning others to Christ (Matt. 4:18).

NETHANEEL (NETHANEL). A priest who helped transport the ark of the covenant to Jerusalem (1 Chron. 15:24). *Nethanel:* NIV, NRSV.

NETHER, NETHERMOST. The lower or lowest part. The children of Israel assembled on the nether part of Mt. Sinai to receive a message from God (Exod. 19:17).

NETHINIM (TEMPLE SERVANTS). Persons assigned to do menial work as assistants to the priests in temple service. Many of the Nethinim were slaves or captives of war assigned to the Levites (Ezra 8:17–20). *Temple servants:* NIV, NRSV.

NETTLE. A shrub with prickly briars (Prov. 24:31), possibly a variety of acanthus which grew near the Mediterranean Sea (Isa. 34:13).

NETWORK. The brass grate or grid on the altar of burnt offering in the tabernacle (Exod. 27:4).

NEW BIRTH. A state of regeneration or resurrection from spiritual death (Rom. 6:4–8). The Holy Spirit brings regeneration (John 3:5–8) and produces a changed person. This comes about by God's grace through faith in Christ rather than through one's own efforts or good works (Eph. 2:8–9). Regeneration helps the believer overcome the world and lead a victorious life (1 John 5:4–5). The new birth is required before a person can enter the kingdom of God (John 3:3–7). See also *Regeneration; Salvation*.

NEW COVENANT. God's final covenant with His people through which His grace is expressed to all believers. Prophesied by the prophet Jeremiah (Jer. 31:31–34), the new covenant was symbolized by Jesus at the Passover meal with His disciples. He called the cup the "new covenant in my blood" (Luke 22:20, NIV, NRSV). Christ, mediator of a new and better covenant, assures our eternal inheritance (Heb. 8:6; 9:11–15). See also *Covenant; Jeremiah, Book of; Testament*.

NEW JERUSALEM. See *Jerusalem*.

NEW MOON. See *Month; Moon.*

NEW TESTAMENT. The second major division of the Bible, composed of twenty-seven books, also known as the "new covenant" to magnify the coming of the Messiah and His redemptive ministry of grace (Jer. 31:31–34; Heb. 9:15). The complete N.T. in its current form was formally adopted by the Synod of Carthage in A.D. 397.

NIBHAZ. An idol of the Avites, a displaced Assyrian tribe that settled in Samaria (2 Kings 17:31). The name means "barker"; this pagan god was in the form of a dog-headed man.

NICANOR. One of the seven men chosen as "deacons" in the church at Jerusalem (Acts 6:1–5).

NICODEMUS. An influential Pharisee who talked with Jesus about the new birth. Impressed by Jesus' miracles, he came to Jesus at night. Jesus impressed upon him the necessity of being born of the Spirit (John 3:1–7). Later, Nicodemus cautioned the Jewish officials not to prejudge Jesus (John 7:50–51). He helped prepare Jesus' body for burial (John 19:39).

NICOLAITANES (NICOLAITANS). An early Christian sect whose origin is unknown. Their idolatrous practices were abhorrent to God, being compared to those of Balaam (Rev. 2:14). The church at Ephesus was commended for not tolerating the Nicolaitanes (Rev. 2:6), while the church at Pergamos was rebuked for its openness to their teachings (Rev. 2:15). *Nicolaitans:* NIV, NRSV.

NICOLAS (NICOLAUS). A person of Greek background who was one of the seven men chosen as "deacons" in the church at Jerusalem (Acts 6:1–5). *Nicolaus:* NRSV.

NICOPOLIS. A city, probably in northern Greece, where Paul spent the winter (Titus 3:12).

NIGER. See *Simeon,* No. 3.

NIGHT. The period of the day when darkness prevails. The Creator established night along with the daylight hours (Gen. 1:5). The word is used figuratively to denote death (John 9:4) or sin (1 Thess. 5:5).

NIGHT HAWK (SCREECH OWL). An unclean bird, probably an owl or other night creature (Lev. 11:13–16; Deut. 14:15). *Screech owl:* NIV.

NILE RIVER. The great river of Egypt which begins in Africa and runs for more than 4,000 miles across Africa and Egypt, emptying finally into the Mediterranean Sea. In Bible times, Egypt's fertility depended on the annual overflow of the Nile (Isa. 23:10). God's judgment on Egypt was often depicted as a drying up of the Nile (Zech. 10:11). The baby Moses was hidden in the tall grass at the edge of the river (Exod. 2:3). See also *Egypt*.

NIMROD. Ham's grandson and son of Cush. A skilled hunter and warrior, he became a powerful king and empire builder in Babylonia, or Shinar (Gen. 10:8–12; 1 Chron. 1:8–10).

NINEVEH/NINEVE. The capital of Assyria on the Tigris River where the prophet Jonah preached God's message of judgment. Founded by Asshur, a son of Shem, Nineveh reached the height of wealth and splendor during Jonah's time (Jon. 3:3). It was taken by the Medes about 750 B.C. and destroyed by the Medes and Babylonia about 606 B.C. *Nineve:* Luke 11:32. See also *Assyria*.

NISAN. See *Abib*.

NISROCH. An Assyrian god with a temple at Nineveh where King Sennacherib was killed about 698 B.C. It was believed to have a human body with an eagle's head (2 Kings 19:36–37).

NITRE (SODA, LYE). A mineral used as a cleaning agent; probably lye or sodium carbonate (Jer. 2:22). *Soda:* NIV; *Lye:* NRSV.

NO (THEBES). A thriving Egyptian city on both sides of the Nile River which served as the capital of upper Egypt (Nah. 3:8). No was destroyed in 81 B.C., as predicted by Jeremiah (Jer. 46:25). *Thebes:* NIV, NRSV.

NOADIAH. A prophetess who tried to frighten Nehemiah and hinder his efforts to rebuild the wall of Jerusalem (Neh. 6:14).

NOAH/NOE. The person chosen by the Lord to preserve life on earth by building an ark to escape the great flood. Noah was the son of Lamech and the father of Shem, Ham, and Japheth. He "found grace in the eyes of the Lord" (Gen. 6:8) and was described in the N.T. as a preacher of righteousness (2 Pet. 2:5). After building the ark, he entered with his family and selected animals (Gen. 7:1–24). Upon leaving the ark after the flood ended, he built an altar for worship (Gen. 8:18–22). God covenanted with Noah not to destroy the earth with water again (Gen. 9:1–19). After pronouncing blessings and curses on his sons, he died at the age of 950 (Gen. 9:29). *Noe:* Greek form (Luke 17:26). See also *Ark, Noah's*.

NOB. A Levitical city near Jerusalem (Isa. 10:32) where David fled to escape King Saul's wrath (1 Sam. 21:1–6). Saul ordered the slaughter of eighty-five priests here in retaliation for their kindness to David (1 Sam. 22:13–19).

NOBLEMAN (ROYAL OFFICIAL). A person of high rank or privileged position. A nobleman sought Jesus to heal his son who was seriously ill (John 4:46–54). *Royal official:* NIV, NRSV.

NOD. An unknown region east of Eden where Cain lived after murdering his brother Abel (Gen. 4:16–17). It may have been China, according to some scholars.

NOE. See *Noah*.

NOGAH. A son of David, born in Jerusalem after David became king (1 Chron. 3:7; 14:6).

NOMADS. Tent dwellers or herdsman who moved from one grazing ground to another with their flocks (Gen. 13:5–7). The children of Israel led a nomadic life in the wilderness for forty years (Num. 14:2). See also *Wilderness Wanderings*.

NOOSE. See *Snare*.

NOPH (MEMPHIS). An ancient royal city of the Egyptians (Jer. 46:19), *Memphis:* NIV, NRSV. Noph flourished about 3000 to 2200 B.C. on the west bank of the Nile River about thirteen miles south of modern Cairo. Many of the royal pyramids and the famous Spinx are located near the site of this ancient city.

NORTHEASTER. See *Euroclydon*.

NOSE JEWELS. Jeweled rings worn in the nose as ornaments (2 Kings 19:28).

NOSE, NOSTRILS. God created man and breathed life into his nostrils (Gen. 2:7). The word is figurative of God's power in parting the Red Sea for the Israelites (Exod. 15:8).

NOVICE (RECENT CONVERT). An inexperienced or recent Christian convert. Paul instructed Timothy that a novice in the faith lacked the maturity to serve as a pastor or bishop (1 Tim. 3:1, 6). *Recent convert:* NIV, NRSV.

NUMBERS, BOOK OF. An O.T. book which focuses on the Israelites in the wilderness of Sinai—a period of more than forty years between their departure from Egypt and their occupation of Canaan. The book describes the "numbering" of the people in two separate censuses (1–54; 26:1–51), their failure to trust God and fear of the Canaanites (chap. 13), their numerous rebellions and complaints in the wilderness (15:1–25:18), and their final preparation for entering the Land of Promise (26:1–36:13). See also *Wilderness Wanderings.*

NUN.

1. The father of Joshua and an Ephraimite servant of Moses who helped lead the Israelites across the Jordan River into the Promised Land (Josh. 1:1–2).

2. The fourteenth letter of the Hebrew alphabet, used as a heading over Ps. 119:105–112.

NURSE. A woman servant who breast-fed an infant or helped rear the child. Deborah, Rebecca's nurse, accompanied the family to Canaan (Gen. 24:59; 35:8).

NUZI TABLETS. Clay tablets of archaeological significance discovered during the 1920s on the site of the ancient city of Nuzi in present-day Iraq. These tablets describe life in ancient Mesopotamia from about the time of Abraham (2200 B.C.), listing goods produced, items traded, and other details of everyday life. The city of Nuzi is not mentioned in the Bible. See also *Clay; Ras Shamra Tablets.*

NYMPHAS (NYMPHA). A Christian of Laodicea to whom Paul sent greetings (Col. 4:15). *Nympha:* NIV, NRSV.

-O-

OAK. Several species of oak grew in Palestine. This word was often used to describe any strong tree or grove of trees (Gen. 35:8). Oak was used for carving idols (Isa. 44:9–15).

OAR. A paddle for pulling a ship through the water. Even large sailing vessels used oars when there was not enough wind to fill the sails (Isa. 33:21–23).

OATH. A solemn promise, often used to appeal to God to attest that a statement was true or to affirm a covenant (2 Sam. 21:7). The taking of an oath was accompanied by raising the hand or placing the hand under the thigh (Gen. 24:2–3). Jesus warned against careless oaths (Matt. 5:34–36).

OBADIAH.

1. A prophet of Judah and author of the O.T. book which bears his name (Obad. 1). He probably lived after the destruction of Jerusalem in 587 B.C. Nothing more is known about him.

2. A godly servant of King Ahab who hid 100 prophets in a cave so they could escape Jezebel's wrath (1 Kings 18: 3–16).

OBADIAH, BOOK OF. A prophetic book of only twenty-one verses—the shortest book in the O.T.—that pronounces judgment against the Edomites, the descendants of Esau (vv. 1, 6), because of their mistreatment of God's people, the Israelites (vv. 10–14). See also *Edomites; Esau*.

OBED-EDOM. A Philistine from the city of Gath. The ark of the covenant was left at his house for three months before its removal to Jerusalem (1 Chron. 13:13–14).

OBEY. To submit to authority. Children are commanded to obey their parents (Exod. 20:12; Eph. 6:1–3). Jesus was obedient to Joseph and Mary (Luke 2:51). Jesus was perfectly obedient to the Father, and He requires obedience of His followers (Heb. 5:8–9).

OBLATION (GRAIN OFFERING). An offering sanctified to God, consisting usually of meat, meal, firstfruits of the harvest, or land (Lev. 2:4). *Grain offering:* NIV, NRSV.

OBSERVER OF TIMES. A person who was thought to be able to foretell the future through reading signs (Deut. 18:10–14). See also *Omen; Witchcraft*.

ODED. A prophet of Samaria who urged kindness toward captives from Judah. His intervention led to the release of captives who were taken to Jericho (2 Chron. 28:9–15).

OFFENSE. A charge or accusation against another. Reconcilia-

The hill known as the Mount of Olives in Jerusalem, with the Church of All Nations in the foreground.
Courtesy Israel Ministry of Tourism

tion with an offended brother should take priority over making an offering (Matt. 5:24).

OFFERING. Something given to God as a confession, consecration, expiation, or thanksgiving, generally as a part of worship. Because of his sinfulness and frailty, man recognizes he cannot covenant with God without obedience and faith. Jesus offered Himself as a full and final sacrifice for sin (Heb. 7:25, 27). See also *Sacrifice*.

OFFSCOURING (SCUM, FILTH). Refuse; something vile or despised (Lam. 3:45). *Scum:* NIV; *Filth:* NRSV. Paul indicated that faithful Christians may be regarded as "scum of the earth" by the world (1 Cor. 4:13).

OFFSPRING. Children or descendants (Job 5:25). The risen Lord declared He was the "offspring of David" (Rev. 22:16). All people are regarded as offspring of the Creator (Acts 17:28–29). See also *Posterity; Seed*.

OG. An Amorite king of Bashan who was defeated by

the Israelites at Edrei (Num. 21:33). His territory was assigned to the tribe of Manasseh (Deut. 3:1–13).

OIL. A liquid extracted from olives which was burned in lamps (Matt. 25:3) and used for anointing (Ps. 23:5), food preparation (1 Kings 17:12), and medicine (Luke 10:34). Olive groves were numerous throughout Palestine. See also *Anointing; Olive.*

OIL TREE (OLIVE). The olive tree or the oleaster shrub (Isa. 41:19). *Olive:* NIV, NRSV. The oleaster shrub resembled the wild olive, with its yellow flowers and olivelike fruit.

OINTMENT (PERFUME). A salve or perfumed oil made of olive oil and spices and used in anointing ceremonies. Jesus was anointed by devoted followers (Mark 14:3). *Perfume:* NIV (John 12:3). See also *Perfume.*

OLD GATE (JESHANAH GATE). A gate in the walls of Jerusalem rebuilt by Nehemiah (Neh. 3:6; 12:39). *Jeshanah Gate:* NIV.

OLD TESTAMENT. The first major section of the Bible, containing thirty-nine books, also known as the "old covenant" because it points to the coming of the new covenant in Jesus Christ. The O.T. begins with God's creation of the world, contains the books of the law and wisdom, and ends with prophecies which point to the Messiah's coming (Isa. 53; Jer. 31:31–34).

OLIVE. The fruit of the olive tree which was used for food and olive oil. The branch of an olive tree was a symbol of peace (Gen. 8:11). See also *Oil.*

OLIVES, MOUNT OF/ MOUNT OLIVET. A hill in eastern Jerusalem where Jesus was betrayed by Judas on the night before His crucifixion (Matt. 26:30, 47). The branches of olive trees from the Mount of Olives were used to make booths for the Feast of Tabernacles (Neh. 8:15). *Mount Olivet:* Acts 1:12.

OLYMPAS. A Christian in Rome greeted by the apostle Paul (Rom. 16:15).

OMEGA. See *Alpha and Omega.*

OMEN. A sign used to predict future events. Witchcraft and divination were forbidden by the Mosaic Law (Deut. 18:10). The Lord frustrates the efforts of fortune-tellers and astrologers (Isa. 44:25). See also *Observer of Times; Witchcraft.*

OMER. A dry measure of two to three quarts (Exod. 16:16).

OMNIPOTENCE. The unlimited and infinite power which belongs to God. This characteristic of God's nature is expressed by His names *almighty* (Gen. 17:1) and *omnipotent* (Rev. 19:6). God controls nature (Amos 4:13) and the destiny of nations (Amos 1:1–2:16). God's omnipotence is also expressed by the Holy Spirit's power to convict and save (Rom. 15:19). See also *God; Sovereignty of God.*

OMNIPRESENCE. The universal presence of God. No person can hide from God (Jer. 23:23–24). Christ is present with the multitudes or with two or three believers (Matt. 18:20). God's Spirit is our companion in all circumstances (John 14:3, 18). See also *God.*

OMNISCIENCE. The infinite knowledge of God. The all-wise and all-knowing God requires no counselor (Isa. 40:14). Christ is the key who opens all the hidden treasures of God's wisdom and knowledge (Col. 2:2–3). God's Spirit reveals the "deep things of God" to those who are spiritually receptive (1 Cor. 2:10–14). See also *God.*

OMRI. The king of Israel who built Samaria as the capital city of the Northern Kingdom (reigned about 885–874 B.C.; 1 Kings 16:23–28). He was a wicked king who led the nation into idolatry (1 Kings 16:26). Omri was the father of the wicked king Ahab, who succeeded him (1 Kings 16:29), and grandfather of the ruthless queen Athaliah of Judah (2 Kings 11:1–3). See also *Samaria.*

ON.

1. A Reubenite leader who joined Korah and others in the rebellion against Moses and Aaron in the wilderness (Num. 16:1–14).

2. A city of lower Egypt noted for its learning and its prominence as a center of sun worship. Joseph's wife Asenath was from this city (Gen. 41:45). *Aven:* Amos 1:5.

ONAN. The second son of Judah who was killed because of his failure to consummate a marriage union with Tamar, wife of his slain brother (Gen. 38:8–10).

ONESIMUS. A slave of Philemon who was converted under Paul. Onesimus escaped and fled to Rome, where he came under Paul's influence. After his conversion, he returned to his master Philemon with an epistle from Paul, who appealed for Onesimus to be treated with mercy (Col. 4:9; Philem. 10). See also *Philemon*.

ONESIPHORUS. A Christian from Ephesus who befriended Paul when he was a prisoner in Rome. Paul commended him for his service (2 Tim. 1:16–18; 4:19).

ONION. A popular vegetable in Egypt and Palestine (Num. 11:5).

ONYCHA. An ingredient in sacred incense which Moses was instructed to prepare (Exod. 30:34). It may have come from the mollusk shell. See also *Incense*.

ONYX. A precious stone in the breastplate of the high priest (Exod. 28:20). David collected onyx to decorate the temple in Jerusalem (1 Chron. 29:2). See also *Sardonyx*.

OPHEL. The southern side of ancient Jerusalem's eastern hill, perhaps a tower or other fortification. The Nethinim lived here after the Babylonian Exile (Neh. 3:26–27).

OPHIR.

1. A son of Joktan and great-grandson of Eber (Gen. 10:26–29).

2. The territory, probably in Arabia, populated by Ophir's descendants (Gen. 10:29–30). A famous gold-producing region, Ophir was visited by the ships of Solomon and the Phoenicians (1 Kings 9:26–28).

OPHRAH. Gideon's hometown in Manasseh where an angel assured him of the Lord's guidance and protection (Judg. 6:11–14).

OPPRESSOR. One who defrauds and mistreats others. The Egyptians oppressed the Hebrews by making them slaves (Exod. 3:9). See also *Taskmasters*.

ORACLE. A revelation or wise saying given to a person for his guidance (Rom. 3:2). Ministers are charged to preach God's message (1 Pet. 4:11).

ORCHARD. A garden planted with trees (Eccles. 2:5), particularly fruit-bearing trees (Song of Sol. 4:13). See also *Garden*.

ORDAIN. To set a person apart for special service. Matthias was ordained to replace Judas as an apostle (Acts 14:23). Christ ordained His disciples to bear enduring fruit (John 15:16). Christ was ordained to be a merciful high priest and judge of the living and the dead (Heb. 5:1). See also *Consecration*.

ORDINANCES. Baptism and the Lord's Supper, rituals or procedures intended to commemorate the great events of redemption. The Lord's Supper memorializes the shed blood and broken body of Christ (1 Cor. 11:23–26). Baptism symbolizes the death, burial, and resurrection of Jesus and the believer's victory over sin and death (Rom. 6:3–6). See also *Baptism; Lord's Supper*.

OREB. A Midianite priest killed by Gideon and the Ephraimites (Judg. 7:25). His name was given to the rock east of Jordan where he died (Isa. 10:26).

ORGAN (FLUTE, PIPE). A wind instrument made of reeds of various lengths and played by blowing across their open ends (Gen. 4:21). *Flute:* NIV *Pipe:* NRSV. See also *Pipe*.

ORION. A constellation of stars cited as evidence of God's power (Job 9:9).

ORNAMENTS. Items of jewelry, such as rings on the fingers, ears, and nose (Isa. 3:18–23). Bracelets and earrings were presented to Rebekah by Abraham's servant (Gen. 24:22).

ORNAN. See *Araunah*.

ORONTES. The major river of Syria. The important cities of Kadesh, Riblah (2 Kings 23:33–35), and Hamath (1 Kings 8:65) were situated on the Orontes.

ORPAH. A Moabite woman who married Chilion, son of Naomi and Elimelech. She returned to her own people after the death of her husband (Ruth 1:4–15).

ORPHANS. Children whose parents have died. Kindness toward orphans was commanded by the Mosaic Law (Deut. 24:17). Visiting orphans and widows was considered a mark of true religion, or godliness (Jas. 1:27). Jesus promised believers would not be treated as orphans (John 14:18).

OSEE. See *Hosea*.

OSHEA. See *Joshua.*

OSNAPPER. See *Asnappar.*

OSPRAY (BLACK VULTURE). An unclean bird, perhaps similar to the eagle or hawk (Lev. 11:13). *Black vulture:* NIV. See also *Gier Eagle.*

OSSIFRAGE (VULTURE). An unclean bird, probably similar to the eagle, or perhaps the vulture (Deut. 14:12). *Vulture:* NIV, NRSV. See also *Vulture.*

OSTRICH. A large, flightless bird noted for its speed (Job 39:13–18) and its mournful cry (Mic. 1:8, NRSV). It was listed as "unclean" in the Mosaic Law (Lev. 11:16, NRSV).

OTHNIEL. The first judge of Israel who defeated the king of Mesopotamia (Judg. 3:9–11). See also *Judges of Israel.*

OUCHES (GOLD FILIGREE SETTINGS). Sockets or mountings in which precious stones were set in the ephod of the high priest (Exod. 28:11–14). *Gold filigree settings:* NIV, NRSV.

OUTCASTS. Dispossessed people. This word was used by the prophets to describe the Jews scattered among foreign nations (Isa. 11:12; Jer. 30:17). Jesus had compassion on lepers who were social outcasts (Luke 17:11–19). See also *Remnant.*

OVEN. A large earthenware container filled with hot coals and ashes. Utensils with food were placed over the opening for cooking (Hos. 7:7).

OVERSEER. An elder, bishop, presbyter, or supervisor in charge of a congregation (Acts 20:28).

OWL. A bird of prey with large eyes and strong claws which hunts at night (Ps. 102:6). It was considered unclean by the Israelites (Lev. 11:11–17).

OWNER. See *Householder.*

OX. An animal of the cow family used for plowing (Deut. 22:10), for threshing grain (Deut. 25:4), and as a beast of burden (1 Chron. 12:40). Oxen also supplied milk and meat and were used as sacrifices (Lev. 17:3–4). See also *Bull; Bullock.*

OX GOAD. A spike used to drive oxen. Shamgar, judge and deliverer of Israel, killed six hundred Philistines with an ox goad (Judg. 3:31; 5:6).

OZIAS. See *Uzziah.*

-P-

PACE (STEP). A measure of length, based on the step of a man (2 Sam. 6:13). *Step:* NIV.

PADAN-ARAM
See *Mesopotamia*.

PADDLE. A spadelike tool at the butt end of a spear for digging a hole in the ground to cover waste (Deut. 23:13).

PAINT. A cosmetic cover. Hebrew women painted around their eyes, but the practice was condemned (Jer. 4:30). Paint was also used to color walls and adorn pagan temples (Ezek. 23:14).

PALACE. A residence for a king or other high official. Solomon's palace on Mount Zion near the temple featured an ivory throne (1 Kings 7:1–12; 10:18). Jesus was tried in the hall of Herod's palace by Pilate (Mark 15:16) and in the palace of Caiaphas the high priest (Matt. 26:56–57).

PALESTINE/PALESTINA. The territory of the Canaanites which became known as the land of the people of Israel. The name *Palestine* referred originally to the territory of the Philistines, especially the coastal plain south of Mt. Carmel. The name was extended during the Christian era to include all of the Holy Land, including both sides of the Jordan River and the Dead Sea region south to Egypt. After the Canaanites were displaced, the country was called the land of Israel (1 Sam. 13:19) and the "land of promise" (Heb. 11:9). Three great world religions—Judaism, Christianity, and Islam—originated here. *Palestina:* Exod. 15:14. See also *Canaan,* No. 2; *Land of Promise*.

PALM. A tropical tree (Exod. 15:27), so named because its leaf resembles a human hand. Most biblical references are to the date palm, which grows sixty to eighty feet tall.

PALMERWORM (LOCUST). A caterpillar or a distinct species of locust which ate vegetation (Joel 1:4). This insect or worm was sent as a plague upon rebellious Israel (Amos 4:9–10). *Locust:* NIV, NRSV. See also *Locust*.

PALSY. A disease which caused paralysis and possible loss of feeling (Acts 8:7). Although it was regarded as incurable, Jesus healed many people with palsy (Matt. 4:24).

PALTI. One of the twelve spies who scouted the land of Canaan, representing the tribe of Benjamin (Num. 13:9). See also *Spies*.

PALTIEL. A leader of the tribe of Issachar, appointed by Moses to help divide the land of Canaan after its occupation by the Israelites (Num. 34:26).

PAMPHYLIA. A coastal region in southern Asia Minor visited by Paul (Acts 13:13; 14:24). Perga was its capital and Attalia its main seaport (Acts 14:25). Residents of Pamphylia were present in Jerusalem on the day of Pentecost (Acts 2:10).

PAN (GRIDDLE). A utensil or cooking container (Lev. 6:21). *Griddle:* NIV, NRSV.

PANTHEISM. A doctrine which teaches that God and His universe are identical, or that physical things are merely attributes of an all-encompassing God. Jews and Christians reject this doctrine because God created the universe separate and apart from Himself (Gen 1:1). He exists apart from, in addition to, and above the world (see Ps. 8). See also *Creation*.

PAPER. Papyrus, or an ancient writing material made from reeds which grew on the banks of the Nile River in Egypt (2 John 12). See also *Bulrush; Ink; Reed; Writing*.

PAPHOS. A city on the island of Cyprus where Paul blinded Elymas the magician. This led to the conversion of the Roman governor, Sergius Paulus (Acts 13:6–13).

PAPS (BREASTS). An archaic old English word for "breasts" (Luke 11:27). *Breasts:* NRSV.

PAPYRUS. See *Bulrush*.

PARABLE. A short story drawn from daily life which is used to convey an important truth; a favorite teaching device used by Jesus (Matt. 13:3). In the O.T., Nathan told a parable to convict King David of his sin of adultery (2 Sam. 12:1–7). Jesus used parables to present truth to His receptive hearers and to conceal the lesson from those who were critical or unreceptive (Matt. 13:10–16, 35). Drawn from daily life, His parables revealed lessons about salvation, the kingdom, and the future life (Luke 15).

PARACLETE (COUNSELOR, ADVOCATE). A Greek word for the Holy Spirit which

expresses the idea of a helper called to one's side. It is translated as "comforter" in the Gospels (John 14:16). *Counselor:* NIV; *Advocate:* NRSV. Also, as "advocate" in the epistle of John (1 John 2:1). See also *Advocate; Comforter; Helper; Holy Spirit.*

PARADISE. A word which describes the heavenly home of the redeemed (2 Cor. 12:4). Jesus used the term to comfort the repentant dying thief (Luke 23:43). See also *Heaven; Heavenly City.*

PARADOX. A contradictory statement which expresses a great truth; a favorite teaching device of Jesus. He declared that a person could find his life by losing it (Matt. 10:39) and that a person became great by serving others (Mark 10:43).

PARALYSIS. See *Palsy.*

PARALYTIC. A paralyzed person. Jesus honored the faith of a paralytic by offering forgiveness and healing (Matt. 9:1–7).

PARAMOUR (LOVER). A slave or concubine who provided sexual favors (Ezek. 23:20). *Lover:* NIV. See also *Concubine.*

PARAN/MOUNT PARAN/EL-PARAN. A mountainous wilderness region in the Sinai Peninsula, sometimes called *Mount Paran* (Hab. 3:3) and *El-Paran* (Gen. 14:6). The Israelites camped here during their years in the wilderness (Num. 10:12; 12:16).

PARAPET. See *Battlement.*

PARCHED CORN (ROASTED GRAIN, PARCHED GRAIN). Roasted grains of wheat, barley, or millet (1 Sam. 25:18). *Roasted grain:* NIV; *Parched grain:* NRSV.

PARCHMENT. Writing material made from the skin of sheep or goats. Paul asked Timothy to bring parchments to him in prison (2 Tim. 4:13).

PARDON. Forgiveness. God will pardon those who repent and turn to the Lord (Isa. 55:7). The loving father of Jesus' parable had compassion on his repentant son, extended pardon, and celebrated his return (Luke 15:18–24). God promised to pardon the iniquity of Judah and Israel that led to their captivity and exile (Jer. 33:8–9). See also *Forgiveness; Remission.*

PARENTS. People who bear and rear children. The duty of parents is to train (Deut. 4:9; 6:6–7) and correct (Deut. 21:18–21) their children. They should avoid favoritism (Gen. 25:28) and anger (Eph. 6:4). God promised to bless parents who bring up children in the nurture of the Lord (Prov. 22:6; Eph. 6:4). See also *Children*.

PARLOR. A room in a house for entertaining guests (1 Sam. 9:22), a secret chamber for retreat (1 Chron. 28:11), or a room on the roof for enjoying cool breezes (Judg. 3:20–25).

PARMENAS. One of the seven men of Greek background chosen as "deacons" in the church at Jerusalem (Acts 6:1–5).

PAROUSIA. A Greek word which refers to the second coming of Christ. See also *Second Coming*.

PARTHIANS. Inhabitants of Parthia, a country north of Media and Persia. Parthians were in Jerusalem on the day of Pentecost (Acts 2:1, 9).

PARTIALITY. To show favoritism or preference toward some people over others. God's wisdom is available to all and free of favoritism or hypocrisy (Jas. 3:17).

PARTITION. See *Middle Wall of Partition*.

PARTRIDGE. A wild bird in Palestine prized for its meat and eggs. Jeremiah likened ill-gotten wealth to a partridge sitting on eggs that will not hatch (Jer. 17:11).

PARVAIM. An unidentified place which provided gold for Solomon's temple (2 Chron. 3:6). Some scholars believe this was the same place as *Ophir* (1 Kings 9:28).

PASCHAL LAMB.
See *Passover*.

PASHUR. A priest who struck Jeremiah and had him imprisoned. Jeremiah predicted that Pashur and his household would die as captives in Babylonia (Jer. 20:3–6).

PASSOVER AND FEAST OF UNLEAVENED BREAD. A Jewish festival which commemorated the Exodus from Egypt (Josh. 5:10–12). The Passover celebrated how God "passed over" the Hebrew houses in Egypt that were sprinkled with blood while killing the firstborn of the

Egyptians on the eve of the Exodus (Exod. 12). The seven-day Feast of Unleavened Bread recalled the haste with which the slaves left Egypt (Exod. 12:33–34). Jesus observed the Passover with His disciples on the night He was betrayed (Luke 22:15). Paul declared that Christ is our Passover (1 Cor. 5:7). *Paschal lamb:* NRSV.

PASTOR. One who leads and instructs a congregation. Jeremiah predicted the coming of faithful pastors who would lead Israel back to God (Jer. 3:15). Pastors are called of God to perfect the saints and build up the body of Christ (Eph. 4:11–13). See also *Bishop: Elder; Minister; Shepherd.*

PASTORAL EPISTLES. The three letters of Paul—1 and 2 Timothy and Titus—which deal with pastoral concerns, or practical matters involving the operation and government of a local church.

PASTURE. Grazing lands for livestock. The word is also used figuratively for the protection of God's people under the Good Shepherd (Ps. 23:1–2; Ezek. 45:15).

PASTURE LANDS. See *Suburbs.*

PATARA. A port of Lycia in Asia Minor. Paul changed ships here on the way to Phoenicia (Acts 21:1–2).

PATH. A crude road. The word is also used figuratively for the route of one's life. The righteous are warned not to walk the paths of darkness (Prov. 2:13–15).

PATHROS (UPPER EGYPT). A name for upper Egypt where Egyptian civilization likely began. Jewish people lived here during the Babylonian Exile (Jer. 44:1, 15). *Upper Egypt:* NIV.

PATIENCE. Forbearance or restraint. God is the author of patience (Rom. 15:5), and Christ is its perfect model (2 Thess. 3:5). Believers are urged to labor with patience in the service of Christ (1 Thess. 5:14). See also *Forbearance; Longsuffering; Steadfastness.*

PATMOS. A desolate island in the Aegean Sea, used as a prison by the Romans, where the apostle John was exiled and where he wrote the book of Revelation. Christ revealed Himself to John and told him to send messages to the seven churches of Asia Minor (Rev. 1:9–19). See also *John the Apostle.*

PATRIARCH. Head of a tribe or clan in O.T. times who ruled by authority passed down from father to oldest son. Abraham, Isaac, and Jacob, along with the sons of Jacob and David, are notable examples of patriarchal rule (Acts 2:29; 7:8–9).

PATROBAS. A fellow believer at Rome greeted and commended by Paul (Rom. 16:14).

PAUL THE APOSTLE. The great apostle to the Gentiles; defender and advocate of the Christian faith in its early years through his thirteen N.T. letters. A complex personality, Paul demonstrated both toughness and tenderness in his devotion to Christ. His teachings are both profound and practical (Phil. 3:7–10). His Hebrew name as a Jew of Benjamite ancestry was *Saul,* but his Roman name was Paul (Acts 13:9). A Roman citizen born at Tarsus in Cilicia (Acts 22:3), he was a tentmaker by trade—a vocation by which he often supported himself as a minister to the churches which he established (Acts 18:3).

A strict Pharisee and member of the Jewish Sanhedrin, Paul opposed Christianity in its early years in Jerusalem. He consented to the death of Stephen, the first martyr of the church (Acts 7:58; 8:1). He was on his way to persecute Christians at Damascus when he was converted to Christianity in his famous "Damascus road" experience (Acts 9:1–19). From that point on, Paul was zealous for the cause of Christ.

Under the sponsorship of the church at Antioch in Syria, Paul undertook three great missionary journeys to the Roman world, extending westward through Cyprus and Asia Minor into Europe (Acts 16:9–10). His traveling companions on these tours included Barnabas, John Mark, Timothy, Silas, Titus, and Luke. Along with his successes in making disciples, healing, and planting churches, he suffered a "thorn in the flesh" (2 Cor. 12:7), was frequently arrested, was stoned, and imprisoned (Acts 16:22–23).

Falsely accused by his enemies, he appealed to the Roman emperor for justice (Acts 25:10–12). After an arduous voyage by ship, he spent two years in Rome under house arrest. While guarded by Roman soldiers, he received friends and preached the gospel (Acts 28:30–31; Phil. 1:12–14). Four of his epistles—Ephesians, Colossians, Philippians, and Philemon—were written from Rome. Most scholars believe he was beheaded in Rome about

A.D. 67 during Nero's reign (Phil. 2:17; 2 Tim. 4:6–8).

PAULUS, SERGIUS. The Roman proconsul of Cyprus who was converted under Paul's ministry (Acts 13:4–12). See also *Cyprus; Paphos*.

PAVEMENT, THE/ GABBATHA. An area in Pilate's courtroom paved with stone where Jesus was judged, sentenced to crucifixion, and turned over to the mob (John 19:13–16). Its Aramaic name was *Gabbatha*.

PAVILION (DWELLING, SHELTER). A tent or booth for kings or other members of the royal family. The word is also used figuratively for the dwellingplace of God (Ps. 27:5). *Dwelling:* NIV; *Shelter:* NRSV.

PE. The seventeenth letter of the Hebrew alphabet, used as a heading over Ps. 119:129–136.

PEACE. Harmony and accord brought about by cordial relationships. Peace has its source in God (Phil. 4:7) through Christ (John 14:27) and the Holy Spirit (Gal. 5:22). Christians are urged to pursue peace and to live peaceably with all people (2 Cor. 13:11; 2 Tim. 2:22).

PEACE OFFERING. See *Heave Offering; Wave Offering*.

PEACOCK (BABOON). An exotic animal imported by King Solomon, probably from Spain (2 Chron. 9:21). *Baboon:* NIV.

PEARL. Precious stone found in the shells of oysters. Jesus likened the kingdom of heaven to a merchant seeking valuable pearls (Matt. 13:45–46).

PEDAHEL. A leader of the tribe of Naphtali, appointed by Moses to help divide the land of Canaan after its occupation by the Israelites (Num. 34:28).

PEG. See *Pin*.

PEKAH. A king of Israel (reigned about 740–732 B.C.) who assassinated Pekahiah to gain the throne. He was killed by Hoshea in a conspiracy (2 Kings 15:23–31).

PEKAHIAH. An evil king of Israel (reigned about 742–740 B.C.) who was murdered and succeeded by Pekah, one of his military officers (2 Kings 15:23–26).

PELEG/PHALEC. A descendant of Shem (Gen. 10:25, 32). *Phalec:* Luke 3:35.

PELETHITES. A unit or division of David's soldiers who remained loyal to him during the rebellions of Absalom and Sheba (2 Sam. 15:14–18; 20:7).

PELICAN (DESERT OWL). A large bird, considered unclean by the Israelites (Lev. 11:13, 18), which was cited as a symbol of loneliness and desolation (Ps. 102:6–7). *Desert owl:* NIV. This may be the same bird as the *cormorant* (Isa. 34:11). See also *Cormorant*.

PEN. A word for various writing instruments, including those which wrote on scrolls (Jer. 8:8), skin or parchment, and stones (Job 19:24). See also *Ink; Writing*.

PENKNIFE (SCRIBE'S KNIFE). A small knife used for sharpening the writing pen, or reed pen (Jer. 36:23). *Scribe's knife:* NIV.

PENCE. See *Penny*.

PENIEL/PENUEL. A place east of the Jordan River near the Jabbok River where Jacob wrestled with an angel (Gen. 32:24–32). *Penuel:* Judg. 8:8. See also *Jacob*.

PENITENCE. See *Repentance*.

PENNY/PENCE (DENARIUS). A silver coin of small value (Matt. 20:2–13). *Denarius:* NIV. It varied in value, but it generally equaled the daily wage of an unskilled worker. *Pence:* plural form (Luke 10:35). See also *Farthing*.

PENTATEUCH. The Greek name for the first five books of the O.T.: Genesis, Exodus, Leviticus, Numbers, and Deuteronomy. It was called the Torah or the Law of Moses by the Hebrews (Ezra 7:6). Jesus recognized the value of the law and came to fulfill its spiritual requirements (Matt. 5: 17–18; 12:5). See also *Law*.

PENTECOST/FEAST OF WEEKS/FEAST OF HARVEST. An annual Jewish feast or holy period, commemorating the end of the harvest, which fell on the fiftieth day after the Passover. This was the holiday being observed in Jerusalem when the Holy Spirit came in power upon the early Christian believers (Acts 2). This feast was also known as the *Feast of Weeks* and the *Feast of Harvest* (Exod. 34:22).

PENUEL. See *Peniel*.

PEOPLE OF GOD. A phrase for the nation of Israel as well as the people of the new covenant, or the Church. The Israelites were called by God as His special people (Deut. 8:6–9), but all whose hearts have been "circumcised" are also His people (Rom. 2: 28–29). Peter declared that believing Gentiles were also part of God's "chosen generation" (1 Pet. 2:9–10). God's people include every kindred, tongue, and nation (Rev. 5:9; 7:9). See also *Church; Congregation; Saint.*

PEOR. A mountain of Moab across the Jordan River from Jericho. From Peor, Balak and Balaam observed the camp of the Israelites with the intention to curse them (Num. 23:28; 24:1–2).

PERAZIM. See *Baal-perazim.*

PERDITION. The state of the damned, or those who have rejected Christ. Jesus called Judas the "son of perdition" because of his betrayal of Christ (John 17:12). Perdition is the final destiny of the ungodly (2 Pet. 3:7) as well as the final abode of the Antichrist (Rev. 17:8–11). See also *Damnation; Hell; Judgment, Last.*

PEREA. A word used by some translations of the Bible for the territory east of the Jordan River across from Judea and Samaria. Jews often traveled from Galilee to Judea by Perea to avoid going through the territory of the despised Samaritans (Matt. 4:15; 19:1). This region is called the land "beyond Jordan" in the KJV.

PEREZ. See *Pharez.*

PEREZ-UZZAH. A name given by David to the site where Uzza was struck down for touching the ark (2 Sam. 6:6–8).

PERFECTION (MATURITY). A state of completion or fulfillment. Believers are urged to advance to mature teachings and "perfection" or fulfillment in good works (Heb. 6:1). *Maturity:* NIV. While disclaiming perfection, Paul urged believers to keep striving for perfection by being like Christ (Phil. 3:12–15).

PERFUME. A sweet-smelling fragrance, usually an extract of spices used in ointments, incense, and oils (Prov. 27:9). See also *Oil; Ointment.*

PERFUMER. See *Apothecary.*

PERGA. The capital of Pamphylia and a city visited by Paul.

John Mark left Paul and Barnabas at Perga (Acts 13:13–14), and Paul preached here on the return to Antioch after the first missionary journey (Acts 14:25).

PERGAMOS (PERGAMUM). A city where one of the seven churches of Asia Minor addressed by John in Revelation was located. The church was rebuked for its toleration of sexual immorality and false teachings. The phrase "where Satan's seat is" is probably a reference to a pagan temple in the city (Rev. 2:12–17). *Pergamum:* NIV, NRSV.

PERIZZITES. Descendants of Perez who were subdued by Joshua's forces. Natives of the hill country, they were associated with the Canaanites (Josh. 3:10).

PERSECUTION. Oppression in matters of conscience or religious practice, or punishment because of one's convictions. Believers who are not well grounded in the faith cannot endure persecution (Matt. 13:21). Jesus declared that those who are persecuted because of their commitment to Him will inherit the kingdom of God (Matt. 5:10–12). See also *Affliction; Suffering; Tribulation*.

PERSEVERANCE. Persistence, or the ability to endure through difficult circumstances. Paul counseled steadfastness in the Lord's work because labor for Him is never in vain (1 Cor. 15:58). Endurance of God's chastening or discipline is a mark of God's sonship (Heb. 12:7–8). See also *Patience; Steadfastness*.

PERSIA. A great empire whose territory covered what is now western Asia and parts of Europe and Africa, reaching the height of its greatness around 486 B.C. under Cyrus. The Persians conquered Babylonia in 539 B.C. and allowed the Israelites to return to their native land (2 Chron. 36:20–23). The Persian king Artaxerxes allowed Nehemiah to return to Jerusalem to rebuild the city wall (Neh. 2:1–8). The Persians were defeated by the Greek military conqueror Alexander the Great in 330 B.C. (Ezek. 38:5). See also *Elam; Elamites*.

PERSIS. A fellow believer at Rome greeted and commended by Paul (Rom. 16:12).

PESTILENCE. A plague or widespread fatal disease (Hab. 3:5), usually coming as a result of God's judgment against sin

(Exod. 5:3; Ezek. 33:27). See also *Plague*.

PESTLE. A short, blunt tool used for grinding grain or crushing other material in a container known as a mortar (Prov. 27:22).

PETER. See *Simon,* No. 1.

PETER, EPISTLES OF. Two short N.T. epistles, probably from the apostle Peter, written to encourage Christians experiencing persecution and discouragement (1 Peter) and to warn them against false teachers (2 Peter). In response to scoffers who doubted the second coming of Christ—since He had not yet returned—Peter declared, "The Lord is not slack concerning his promise, as some men count slackness; but is longsuffering to us-ward, not willing that any should perish, but that all should come to repentance" (2 Pet. 3:9).

PETHOR. A town in northern Mesopotamia near the Euphrates River; home of Balaam, who was sent to curse the Israelites (Num. 22:5–7).

PETITION. An earnest request. King Ahasuerus granted Esther's petition to save her people (Esther 7:2–5). Believers are confident their petitions will be answered (1 John 5:14–15). See also *Intercession; Prayer*.

PETRA. An ancient city located south of the Dead Sea. Named for its rocky terrain, Petra was once the capital of Edom and later of Nabatea. Some scholars believe it was the same city as *Selah* (2 Kings 14:7).

PHALEC. See *Peleg*.

PHARAOH. The title of the king of Egypt. The pharaoh of Egypt, who is unnamed (Exod. 1:8–11), refused to release the Israelites from slavery until God killed the Egyptian firstborn throughout the land. The named pharaohs of the Bible are:

1. Shishak, who attacked Jerusalem and plundered the temple (1 Kings 14:25–26).
2. So, who made an alliance with King Hoshea of Israel (2 Kings 17:4).
3. Tirhakah, who aided King Hezekiah of Judah against Sennacherib of Assyria (2 Kings 19:9).
4. Nechoh, whose archers mortally wounded King Josiah of Judah at Megiddo (2 Kings 23:29). *Necho:* Jer. 46:2.
5. Hophra, whom God declared would fall to his enemies (Jer. 44:30).

PHAREZ/PEREZ/PHARES. One of Judah's twin sons by Tamar (Gen. 38:24–30) and founder of the family or clan of Pharzites (Num. 26:20–21). *Perez:* Neh. 11:4; *Phares:* Matt. 1:3.

PHARISEES. Members of a Jewish sect pledged to uphold the oldest traditions of Israel. In Jesus' time the Pharisees were the most powerful party —political or religious—among the Jews. Jesus exposed the hypocrisy of the Pharisees, who emphasized minute details of the law while neglecting more important issues such as justice, mercy, and love (Matt. 23:1–7). Pharisees in the N.T. who were known for their generosity and noble spirit were the apostle Paul, Nicodemus, Gamaliel, and Joseph of Arimathea. See also *Sadducees*.

PHARPAR. One of two rivers of Damascus mentioned by the Assyrian commander Naaman. He was offended when told by Elisha to bathe in the Jordan River rather than the rivers of Damascus (2 Kings 5:9–12). See also *Abana River*.

PHEBE (PHOEBE). A believer at Cenchrea near Corinth who was commended by Paul for her support of him and others (Rom. 16:1–2). *Phoebe:* NIV, NRSV.

PHENICE/PHENICIA (PHOENICIA). A Mediterranean coastal region, including the cities of Ptolemais, Tyre, and Sidon. The inhabitants of Phoenicia, descended from the Canaanites, became a seafaring and colonizing people. King Hiram of Tyre furnished cedar timber and craftsmen for the construction of Solomon's temple in Jerusalem (2 Sam. 5:11; 1 Kings 5:1–10). Jesus ministered in this region (Matt. 15:21), and Christians fled here to escape persecution after Stephen's death (Acts 11:19). *Phenicia:* Acts 21:2. *Phoenicia:* NIV, NRSV. See also *Hiram; Tyre*.

PHILADELPHIA. A city of Lycia in Asia Minor and site of one of the seven churches of Asia Minor addressed in the book of Revelation (Rev. 1:11). This church was commended for its faithfulness (Rev. 3:7–9).

PHILEMON. A Christian at Colossae to whom Paul wrote on behalf of Philemon's slave Onesimus (Philem. 1). See also *Onesimus*.

PHILEMON, EPISTLE TO. A short N.T. book written by

Paul to help a runaway slave Onesimus—a convert under Paul's ministry. Philemon, the owner of Onesimus and a fellow believer, was encouraged to welcome his slave back as a Christian brother (v. 16). Paul also hinted that Onesimus be given his freedom in the spirit of Christian love (v. 21).

PHILETUS. A teacher condemned by Paul for his false teachings about the resurrection (2 Tim. 2:17–18).

PHILIP.

1. One of the twelve apostles of Jesus. He responded to Jesus' invitation to discipleship and brought another disciple, Nathanael, to Jesus (John 1:43–51). He also brought a group of Greeks, or Gentiles, to see Jesus in Jerusalem (John 12:21). See also *Twelve, The.*

2. One of the seven men of Greek background chosen as "deacons" in the church at Jerusalem (Acts 6:5–6) and an evangelist in the early church. Philip preached extensively in Samaria and responded to God's call to the Gaza desert (Acts 8:25–27), where he led a eunuch to Christ and baptized him (Acts 8:32–38). He entertained Paul's group of missionaries (Acts 21:8–9) and was the father of four daughters who prophesied (Acts 21:9).

3. A Roman ruler in northern Palestine. See *Herod,* No. 4.

PHILIPPI. A city of Macedonia where Paul and Silas were imprisoned but miraculously rescued by God. This was the first city in Greece to receive the gospel, and Lydia became the first convert (Acts 16:12–34). While imprisoned in Rome, Paul wrote a letter to the Christians in the church at Philippi (Phil. 1:1). See also *Lydia.*

PHILIPPIANS, EPISTLE TO THE. A short N.T. epistle written by Paul to the church at Philippi—a group for whom the apostle expressed great appreciation, thanksgiving, and admiration (1:1–11). Paul appealed to these fellow believers to follow Christ's example of humility (chap. 2), to continue to grow toward maturity in Christian service (chap. 3), and to experience the peace and joy which Christ promises to all believers (chap. 4). Philippians has been called Paul's "epistle of joy" because of his exhortation, "Rejoice in the Lord alway: and again I say, rejoice" (4:4). See also *Kenosis; Philippi.*

PHILISTIA. A coastal region about forty miles long beside the Mediterranean Sea which served as the land of the Philistines in O.T. times (Gen. 21:32–34). The name *Palestine* was derived from *Philistia*. The chief cities of Philistia were Ashdod, Askelon, Ekron, Gath, and Gaza (Josh. 13:3). See also *Palestine*.

PHILISTINES/PHILISTIM. The people of Philistia who were enemies of the Israelites, especially during the days of Saul and David. After settling in Canaan, the Philistines often battled the Israelites (2 Sam. 5:17–25). Their chief pagan gods were Dagon (Judg.16:23) and Baalzebub (2 Kings 1:2–3). Their kingdom disappeared after the Babylonian Exile. *Philistim:* Gen. 10:14. See also *Caphtor*.

PHILOLOGUS. A Christian at Rome to whom Paul sent greetings (Rom. 16:15).

PHILOSOPHY. The study of truths regarding ultimate reality. The early Christians encountered Greek dualism and the teachings of the Stoics and Epicureans (Acts 17:18; Col. 2:8–10).

PHINEHAS.

1. Aaron's grandson who became Israel's high priest and chief of the Korahite branch of the Levites (1 Chron. 9:19–20). He killed Zimri and Cozbi at God's command for allowing Israel to be corrupted with idolatry (Num. 25:6–15).

2. A priest who corrupted his office by immorality and corrupt leadership (1 Sam. 2:22–24). Phinehas and his brother Hophni died in battle with the Philistines, as foretold by a prophet (1 Sam. 2:27, 34; 4:10–11). Phinehas's wife also died in childbirth (1 Sam. 4:19–20). See also *Hophni*.

PHLEGON. A fellow believer at Rome greeted and commended by Paul (Rom. 16:14).

PHOEBE. See *Phebe*.

PHOENICIA. See *Phenice*.

PHRYGIA. A region of central Asia Minor visited by Paul (Acts 16:6). Jews from Phrygia were in Jerusalem on the day of Pentecost (Acts 2:10).

PHUT/PUT. A son of Ham (Gen. 10:6). This reference may be to people related to the Egyptians, or possibly to the Libyans. *Put:* 1 Chron. 1:8. See also *Libya*.

PHYGELLUS (PHYGELUS). A believer condemned by Paul

because he deserted the apostle Paul in the Roman province of Asia (2 Tim. 1:15). *Phygelus:* NIV, NRSV.

PHYLACTERY. A verse of Scripture worn on the forehead or near the heart (Exod. 13:11–16; Deut. 6:4–9). Jesus denounced the conspicuous wearing of phylacteries (Matt. 23:5). See also *Forehead; Frontlet.*

PHYSICIAN. A healer or person who practiced medicine. Medical studies were prominent in Egypt (Gen. 50:2), with midwives and physicians practicing among the Israelites (2 Chron. 16:12). Luke was described as a "beloved physician" (Col. 4:14).

PIG. See *Swine.*

PIGEON. A bird used for sacrifices, particularly by the poor. The word is used interchangeably with *dove* in most Bible passages. Mary and Joseph offered bird sacrifices when Jesus was dedicated to God in the temple (Luke 2:24). See also *Turtledove.*

PILATE. The procurator or Roman governor of Judea (ruled about A.D. 26–36) who presided at Jesus' trial. An opportunist, Pilate was unwilling to condemn Jesus as a criminal (John 18:30, 38), so he sought to have him tried by Herod at the next judicial level (Luke 23:11). Then he proposed that Jesus be the prisoner customarily dismissed at Passover, but this move also failed (John 18:39–40). Finally he released Jesus to be crucified but tried to dodge responsibility for the decision (Matt. 27:24–25).

PILGRIMAGE. A stay in a foreign country (Exod. 6:4). The term is applied figuratively to the earthly life span (Heb. 11:13). See also *Alien; Foreigner.*

PILLAR OF FIRE AND CLOUD. Supernatural signs which guided the Israelites in the wilderness (Exod. 13:21). Given to protect the Hebrews, the signs represented God's presence with His people (Num. 14:13–14). These signs were repeated in the transfiguration of Christ (Matt. 17:5). See also *Cloud; Fire.*

PILLOW. A head rest for sleeping. The Hebrews used quilts, stones (Gen. 28:18), netting of goat's hair (1 Sam. 19:13), or a leather cushion (Mark 4:38).

PIN (PEG). A peg or stake. Copper or brass tent pins were used to hold the cords of the tabernacle (Exod. 27:19). *Peg:* NIV, NRSV. The Hebrew word for pin is also rendered as nail (Judg. 4:21).

PINE. See *Fir; Box Tree.*

PINNACLE. A wing of the temple, perhaps an elevated area over Solomon's porch. Satan tempted Jesus to impress the crowds with a spectacular leap from this high place (Matt. 4:5–7). *Highest point:* NIV.

PINT. See *Pound.*

PIPE (FLUTE). A musical instrument probably blown like a flute (Isa. 30:29). This may have been similar to the instrument called an organ in some passages. *Flute:* NIV, NRSV. See also *Flute; Organ.*

PIPES. See *Dulcimer.*

PISGAH, MOUNT. A mountain peak in Moab from which Moses viewed Canaan before his death (Deut. 34:1–6). Balaam built altars and offered sacrifices on this mountain. The highest point of Pisgah was called *Nebo*. See also *Nebo.*

PISHON. See *Pison.*

PISIDIA. A large mountainous district in Asia Minor visited by Paul, who preached in the city of Antioch (Acts 13:14–16, 44). See also *Antioch of Pisidia.*

PISON (PISHON). One of four rivers which flowed out of the Garden of Eden (Gen. 2:10–14). *Pishon:* NIV, NRSV.

PIT (CISTERN). A hole in the ground. This word may refer to a deep hole lightly covered to trap animals (Jer. 18:22) as well as to an empty cistern like that into which Joseph was cast (Gen. 37:24). *Cistern:* NIV. Sometimes Sheol is referred to as a pit (Num. 16:30). See also *Cistern; Prison.*

PITCH. A tarlike substance used on Noah's ark, probably asphalt or bitumen found in the Dead Sea area (Gen. 6:14). It was used like mortar and caulk. See also *Slime.*

PITCHER (JAR). An earthenware vessel used to carry water (Gen. 24:14). *Jar:* NIV, NRSV. The word is also used symbolically of the human life span (Eccles. 12:6). See also *Cruse.*

PITHOM. An Egyptian city built by Hebrew slaves (Exod. 1:11). It was located in Goshen east of the Nile River.

PITY. Compassion toward others. James described God as "very pitiful and of tender mercy" (Jas. 5:11). God showed pity on the pagan peoples of Nineveh (Jon. 4:10–11) as well as His people, the Israelites (Isa. 63:9). See also *Mercy*.

PLAGUE. A disastrous affliction or epidemic. Plagues were often interpreted as signs of God's judgment (Exod. 9:14). Ten plagues were sent upon the Egyptians for their failure to release the Hebrew slaves (Exod. 7–11). The children of Israel were plagued for their complaining in the wilderness (Num. 11:1, 31–33). See also *Pestilence*.

PLAIN. A meadow or rolling expanse of land (Judg. 11:33). Given a choice by Abraham, Lot chose the fertile plain near Sodom rather than Canaan's hill country (Gen. 13:10–12).

PLASTER. A thick paste used as a coating for walls and stones (Lev. 14:42).

PLATTER (DISH, PLATE). A dish or utensil for food. Jesus used the word figuratively to condemn the scribes and Pharisees for their hypocrisy (Matt. 23:25–26). *Dish:* NIV; *Plate:* NRSV. See also *Charger*.

PLEDGE. A vow or something given for security of a debt. Under the Mosaic Law, an outer garment pledged by a poor man had to be returned at sunset for his use as a bed covering (Exod. 22:26–27). A creditor was forbidden to enter his neighbor's house to take a pledged item (Deut. 24:10–11). See also *Surety*.

PLEIADES. A constellation of stars cited as evidence of God's sovereignty (Job 9:9). See also *Seven Stars*.

PLOWSHARE. A piece of iron at the end of a plow shaft, used to till the soil. The word is also used figuratively for a coming age of peace (Isa. 2:4). See also *Coulter*.

PLUMBLINE. A tool used by carpenters to determine precise uprightness of a wall. The word is also used figuratively of God's test for the uprightness of His people (Amos 7:7–9).

PLUNDER. See *Spoil*.

PODS. See *Husks*.

POETIC WRITINGS. The five books of the O.T. which are written almost entirely in poetic form—Job, Psalms, Proverbs, the Song of Solomon, and Lamentations—as well as those sections of other books which use this form. Sections of several of the prophetic books, for example, appear in poetry.

POETRY, HEBREW. Unique form of Hebrew writing which uses a repetition technique known as parallelism rather than rhyming or alliteration to express ideas. In parallelism, one line of poetry is advanced, contrasted, or repeated by the next line to convey thought. For example, "Have mercy upon me, O Lord; for I am weak: / O Lord, heal me; for my bones are vexed" (Ps. 6:2).

POISON. A deadly substance when swallowed or introduced into the bloodstream. Dipping the tips of arrows into poison is probably referred to in Job 6:4. The word is also used figuratively for destructive speech (Jas. 3:8). See also *Venom*.

POISONOUS SERPENTS. See *Fiery Serpents*.

POLE. A staff upon which a standard or banner was flown. God instructed Moses to place a "fiery serpent" upon a pole (Num. 21:8–9). See also *Brass Serpent*.

POLLUX. See *Castor and Pollux*.

POLYGAMY. A family system under which a man is allowed to have more than one wife at the same time. The O.T. patriarchs practiced polygamy (for example, Abraham; Gen. 16:1–4), but it was contrary to God's original plan (Gen. 2:24) and divine ideal of marriage (Matt. 19:5). See also *Monogamy*.

POLYTHEISM. The practice of worshiping many gods, in contrast to monotheism, which emphasized devotion to the one and only true God. The nations surrounding Israel worshiped multiple gods, a practice which led to immorality (Num. 25:1–9), prostitution (2 Kings 23:13–14), and child sacrifice (Jer. 7:29–34). The first two of the Ten Commandments make it clear that devotion to the one and only supreme God was not to be mixed with worship of any other false or pagan god (Exod. 20:3–5). See also *Monotheism*.

POMEGRANATE. A small tree which bore apple-shaped fruit that was popular in Palestine. The spies who explored Canaan discovered this tree (Deut 8:7–8).

POMMELS (CAPITALS). Round ornaments at the top of pillars or columns; an architectural feature used in

Solomon's temple at Jerusalem (2 Chron. 4:11–12). *Capitals:* NIV, NRSV.

PONTIUS PILATE. See *Pilate.*

PONTUS. A coastal region along the Black Sea in northern Asia Minor where Priscilla and Aquila settled (Acts 18:2; 1 Pet. 1:1).

POOL. A water reservoir which supplied water for cities (John 5:2). King Hezekiah of Judah built a pool with an aqueduct to pipe water into Jerusalem (2 Kings 20:20). See also *Bethesda; Siloam; Solomon, Pools of.*

POOR. Needy or impoverished people. The Hebrews were instructed by the Lord to show compassion on the poor (Luke 14:13–14). Gleanings of the harvest were left for the poor (Lev. 19:9–10; Ruth 2). Jesus showed compassion for widows and other poor persons (Mark 12:42–44). The early church appointed "deacons" to serve the neglected poor (Acts 6:1). See also *Alms; Beggar.*

POPLAR. A tree of the willow family. Jacob used poplar branches to produce speckled flocks (Gen. 30:37–39). See also *Willow.*

PORCH (PORTICO, VESTIBULE,). A veranda or covered deck around a building. Solomon's porch was along the east side of the temple in Jerusalem (1 Kings 6:3). *Portico:* NIV; *Vestibule:* NRSV. See also *Portico.*

PORCIUS FESTUS. See *Festus.*

PORK. The flesh of pigs, an unclean meat to the Jews (Lev. 11:7–8).

PORTER (GATEKEEPER, DOORKEEPER). A doorkeeper or watchman stationed at city gates (2 Sam. 18:26; *Gatekeeper:* NIV), and at private houses (Mark 13:34). *Doorkeeper*: NRSV. Porters were also assigned to guard duty in the temple at Jerusalem (1 Chron. 23:5). See also *Doorkeeper; Gatekeeper.*

PORTICO (COVERED COLONNADE). A porch. Jesus healed a paralytic lying on one of the porches of the Pool of Bethesda (John 5:2–8). *Covered colonnade:* NIV. See also *Porch.*

PORTION. See *Mess.*

POST (COURIER). A person who relayed messages for a

king or other high official. King Hezekiah used posts to order the Israelites to keep the Passover (2 Chron. 30:6–10). *Courier:* NIV, NRSV. See also *Footman*.

POSTERITY. One's children and grandchildren. The prophet Jehu told King Baasha of Israel that his sinful leadership would destroy him and his family (1 Kings 16:2–4). See also *Seed*.

POT. A kitchen vessel, usually made of clay (Isa. 29:16), but brass pots were used in the sanctuary (1 Kings 7:45).

POTENTATE (SOVEREIGN). A person of great power or authority. Jesus Christ will be recognized as the only true Potentate (1 Tim. 6:15). *Sovereign:* NRSV.

POTIPHAR. A high Egyptian officer who had Joseph imprisoned because his wife accused Joseph of trying to seduce her (Gen. 39:1–20).

POTI-PHERAH. An Egyptian priest of the city of On whose daughter Asenath married Joseph (Gen. 41:45).

POTSHERD. A fragment of pottery, often used by the poor for a drinking vessel or for carrying coals (Ps. 22:15). See also *Pottery*.

POTTAGE (STEW). A thick vegetable soup (Hag. 2:12); the price paid by Jacob for his brother Esau's birthright (Gen. 25:29–34). *Stew:* NIV, NRSV.

POTTER. A craftsman who made vessels from clay on a revolving wheel (Jer. 18:3). To Isaiah, the power of the potter over the clay was symbolic of the Creator's sovereignty (Isa. 45:9).

POTTER'S FIELD. A burial place for poor people outside Jerusalem. This field was bought with the betrayal silver returned by Judas to Jewish officials (Matt. 27:6–8).

POTTERY. Vessels made from clay. The broken piece of pottery cited by Jeremiah was a symbol of Judah's coming destruction (Jer. 19:1–11). See also *Potsherd*.

POUND (PINT, MINA). A dry measure of uncertain volume. Mary of Bethany anointed Jesus with a pound of costly ointment (John 12:3). *Pint:* NIV. This term was also used of money (Luke 19:13). *Mina:* NIV.

PRAETORIUM (GOVERNOR'S HEADQUARTERS). The Roman governor's official residence at Jerusalem. After being scourged by Pilate, Jesus was taken to Pilate's residence, where he was mocked by the soldiers (Mark 15:16). *Governor's headquarters:* NRSV.

PRAISE. Worship of God with honor and thanksgiving (Ps. 42:14). God is pleased and glorified with our praise (Ps. 50:23). Our praise of the Father is commanded in Jesus' model prayer (Matt. 6:9–13). See also *Thanksgiving*.

PRAYER. Communion with God. Elements of sincere prayer are adoration (Matt. 6:9–10), confession (1 John 1:9), supplication (1 Tim. 2:1–3), intercession (Jas. 5:15), and thanksgiving (Phil. 4:6). Jesus was a model for His followers in the practice of prayer. He arose early in the morning to pray (Mark 1:35), prayed all night before choosing the Twelve (Luke 6:12), prayed in Gethsemane on the night of His betrayal (Luke 22:44), and prayed on the cross for His enemies (Luke 23:34). He also gave His disciples a model prayer to follow in their communion with the Father (Matt. 6:9–13). See also *Intercession; Petition*.

PREACH. To proclaim the truths of the gospel. Paul's preaching was motivated by the lost condition of His hearers (Rom. 10:1–3). The prophets were anointed by God to preach good tidings of His deliverance (Isa. 61:1–2). Jesus urged His disciples to preach the gospel to everyone (Mark 16:15).

PRECEPT. A command or directive. Vain worship results when human precepts rather than God's commands are given priority (Matt. 15:9).

PREDESTINATION. God's plan for the eternal salvation of those who choose Him. God has ordained good for those who love Him and are called within His purpose (Rom. 8:28). Those called to salvation will be justified and will share God's glory (Rom. 8:30). Those chosen before the foundation of the world will be adopted by God, redeemed, and given an eternal inheritance (Eph. 1:4–11). See also *Election, Divine; Foreknowledge*.

PREPARATION DAY. The day before the Jewish Sabbath or the celebration of a religious festival (Matt. 27:62). Preparation for the Passover celebration involved cooking the Passover meal, baking unleavened bread, and choosing appropriate clothing for the occasion.

PRIDE. Arrogance, vanity, or conceit. This sin results in self-righteousness (Luke 18:11–12) and self-deception (Jer. 49:16). Paul, however, expressed justifiable pride in his fellowship with the Philippians (Phil. 1:3–6). See also *Conceit; Haughtiness; Vanity*.

PRIEST. A religious leader who made sacrificial offerings. The priesthood originated with Aaron, and his descendants were sanctified to the office (Exod. 29:9, 44). Jesus, our faultless high priest, paid for our sins once and for all by sacrificing Himself (Heb. 7:26–28). See also *High Priest*.

PRIESTHOOD OF BELIEVERS. The doctrine that each believer has direct access to God. This was symbolized by the torn veil in the temple at Jerusalem when Jesus died on the cross, providing access to the holy of holies for all believers (Matt. 27:50–51). Christ is the only authorized mediator between God and man (Eph. 3:11–12). Therefore, we can come boldly and directly to Him (Heb. 4:15–16). As priests of God, believers should minister to others in a spirit of love (Gal. 3:28).

PRIESTHOOD OF CHRIST. One of Christ's offices as the Son of God, emphasizing His offering of Himself on our behalf. Christ obtained eternal redemption for believers by making a perfect sacrifice "by his own blood" (Heb. 9:11–12).

PRINCE (RULER). A leader or ruler; a title for tribal officials (Exod. 2:14). *Ruler:* NIV, NRSV. Also a title for Jesus, who is called the "Prince of life" (Acts 3:15) and the "prince of the kings of earth" (Rev. 1:5). The word is also applied to Satan as the ruler of evil (John 12:31).

PRINCESS. The daughter of a king. King Solomon had princesses among his hundreds of wives (1 Kings 11:3). Athaliah, daughter of King Ahab, killed all the royal descendants and usurped Judah's throne (2 Kings 11:1–3).

PRINCIPALITY. A powerful class of angels and demons. Christ is "far above" all earthly or cosmic powers (Eph. 1:21; 3:10). Believers will share His victory over hostile principalities (Col. 2:10).

PRISCILLA, PRISCA. See *Aquila.*

PRISON. A place of confinement for prisoners, often consisting of little more than a crude dungeon, cistern, or hole in the ground, particularly in O.T. times (Jer. 52:11). Paul wrote several epistles from prison and regarded his confinement as an opportunity to advance the gospel (2 Cor. 6:3–5; Phil. 1:12–14). See also *Cistern; Pit.*

PRIVY. Something kept private or secret. Solomon said Shimei's heart was privy to the wickedness plotted against King David (1 Kings 2:44).

PROCHORUS. One of the seven men of Greek background chosen as "deacons" in the church at Jerusalem (Acts 6:5).

PROCLAMATION. A reading or announcement of an official decree. King Cyrus of Persia proclaimed that the Jewish prisoners could return to Jerusalem to rebuild the temple (Ezra 1:1–3).

PROCONSUL. An official of a Roman province, perhaps the second in command. Paul was brought before the proconsul Gallio at Corinth (Acts 18:12). See also *Deputy.*

PRODIGAL SON. The main character in Jesus' parable who spent his inheritance foolishly, fell into poverty, and finally returned to his father to ask forgiveness and reinstatement as a servant. His father, representing the love and forgiveness of God, welcomed him back as a son (Luke 15:11–32).

PROGNOSTICATOR. A fortune-teller, or one who foretold the future by consulting the stars. The Lord promised to judge Babylonia, in spite of the power of these astrologers (Isa. 47:12–14). See also *Astrologer.*

PROMISE. A pledge or guarantee, particularly of some blessing from God. Israel's history included significant promises from God: (1) Promise of a son to Abraham (Gen. 18:10); (2) the land of Canaan promised to Israel (Exod. 6:4); and (3) a Savior promised from the house of David (Isa. 7: 13–14; Matt. 1:20–23). See also *Hope.*

PROPHET. An inspired messenger called by God to declare His will (Ezra 5:2). Prophets were described as God's servants (Zech. 1:6), watchmen (Ezek. 3:17), and holy men

(2 Pet. 1:21). In the N.T. the prophets were cited as a noble example of patient suffering (Jas. 5:10). Another word for prophet is *seer*.

PROPHETESS. A female prophet or the wife of a prophet. Noted prophetesses include Miriam (Exod. 15:20), Deborah (Judg. 4:4), Huldah (2 Kings 22:14), and Anna (Luke 2:36). Four daughters of Philip were said to prophesy (Acts 21:8–9).

PROPITIATION. Atonement or expiation. Christ was appointed to be a propitiation for our sins through "faith in his blood" (Rom. 3:24–25). His sacrificial death is the supreme demonstration of love (1 John 4:10). See also *Atonement; Mediator, Christ the; Reconciliation.*

PROSELYTE (CONVERT). A Gentile who converted to Judaism. Some of these converts renounced their pagan lifestyle but refused to accept such Jewish practices as circumcision. Well-known proselytes of the Bible include Cornelius, Lydia, and Nicolas of Antioch (Acts 6:5). *Convert:* NIV.

PROSTITUTE. See *Harlot.*

PROVENDER (FODDER). Food for livestock, consisting of chopped straw mixed with barley, beans, or dates (Gen. 24:32). *Fodder:* NIV, NRSV.

PROVERBS, BOOK OF. A book of wisdom in the O.T. filled with short, pithy sayings on how to live with maturity and integrity under the watchful eye of God—the source of all wisdom. These wise sayings, written by Solomon as well as other sages of Israel, deal with such practical matters as strong drink (23:20–21), pride (16:18), work (6:6–11), family (22:6), friendship (17:17), anger (19:11), speech (15:1–4), sexual temptation (5:1–23), and honesty in business (11 1–4). See also *Solomon; Wisdom Literature.*

PROVIDENCE. Divine guidance of human events (Neh. 9:6). This doctrine affirms God's absolute lordship over His creation and the activities by which He preserves and governs. God is constantly working in accord with His purpose (Eph. 1:11). He sustains the moral universe by operating within spiritual principles (Gal. 6:7–9).

PROVINCE. A district or section of a nation, often the outlying area of an extended world power such as the Persian and the Roman empires (Esther 3:12). In the N.T. this word refers to districts conquered and controlled by the Romans (Acts 25:1).

PROVISION. A supply or ration of some substance, such as food. Solomon's court required a large provision of food (1 Kings 4:22–23).

PRUDENT (LEARNED, INTELLIGENT). To have discernment or understanding (Matt. 11:25). *Learned:* NIV; *Intelligent:* NRSV. The prudent person foresees evil (Prov. 22:3) and is crowned with knowledge (Prov. 14:18).

PRUNINGHOOK. A tool for cutting shrubs and vines. To beat pruninghooks into spears was a sign of war (Joel 3:10). To do the opposite was a sign of peace (Isa. 2:4).

PSALMS, BOOK OF. A poetic book of the O.T. filled with hymns of praise and prayers of thanksgiving to God as well as laments against one's enemies and misfortune. Its title is derived from a Greek word which implies that these psalms were to be sung to the accompaniment of a musical instrument. King David of Judah wrote many of these psalms (see 54, 59, 65). But many other unknown writers contributed to this book, which was probably compiled across many centuries of Jewish history. Generations of believers have found the psalms to be a rich source of devotional inspiration, with its emphasis on the goodness, stability, power, and faithfulness of God. See also *David; Poetic Writings; Poetry, Hebrew*.

PSALTERY (LYRE, HARP). A stringed musical instrument that was probably similar to the harp (1 Sam. 10:5). *Lyre:* NIV; *Harp:* NRSV. See also *Harp*.

PTOLEMAIS. See *Accho*.

PTOLEMY. The title of Greek kings who ruled throughout Egypt and Palestine from about 323 to 30 B.C. These kings are possibly referred to in Daniel's visions (see Dan. 11:5–30). Their kingdom eventually fell to the Romans.

PUBLICAN (TAX COLLECTOR). A Jewish citizen who purchased the right to collect taxes in a specific area of his country for the Roman government. Publicans were hated and looked upon as traitors by their fellow citizens (Matt. 5:46). Matthew (Matt. 9:9–11) and Zacchaeus (Luke 19:1–10)

An ibex—called a *pygarg* in the KJV—in the hills of En-gedi, a modern Israeli nature reserve near the Dead Sea.

Courtesy Israel Ministry of Tourism

were prominent publicans who followed Jesus. *Tax collector:* NIV, NRSV. See also *Matthew*.

PUBLIUS. A Roman official who entertained Paul on the island of Miletus after a shipwreck. Paul healed his father of a fever (Acts 28:7–8).

PUDENS. A believer at Rome who joined Paul in sending greetings to Timothy (2 Tim. 4:21).

PUL. See *Tiglath-pileser*.

PULSE (VEGETABLES). Food made of vegetables, such as peas or beans; the food eaten by Daniel and his friends instead of the king's provisions (Dan. 1:12–16). *Vegetables:* NIV, NRSV.

PUNISHMENT. A penalty for wrongdoing. Cain reacted to God's penalties for murdering Abel with "my punishment is greater than I can bear" (Gen. 4:13). Jesus urged forgiveness of offenders rather than the Mosaic tradition of "an eye for an eye" (Matt. 5:38–39). See also *Judgment; Retribution; Wrath*.

PURIFICATION. Ceremonial or spiritual cleansing. The

Mosaic Law prescribed purification rites for those ceremonially defiled by touching a corpse, by contact with bodily discharges, by childbirth, and by leprosy (see Lev. 14–15). The mother of Jesus offered turtledoves and pigeons as a sacrifice in her ceremonial cleansing (Luke 2:21–24). See also *Clean; Wash*.

PURIM, FEAST OF. A Jewish festival which celebrated the rescue of the Jews from Haman's oppression in Esther's time (Esther 9:21–32).

PURPLE. The color preferred by kings and other royal officials; a bright dye made from shellfish. Lydia was a businesswoman who sold purple cloth (Acts 16:14).

PURSE. A bag for carrying items (Luke 10:4), generally placed in the folds of the sash around the waist. The purse in Jesus' instructions to His disciples was probably a money bag (Mark 6:8). See also *Crisping Pin*.

PUT. See *Phut*.

PUTEOLI. A seaport city of Italy visited by Paul (Acts 28:13–14).

The caves of Qumran, where the ancient manuscripts known as the Dead Sea Scrolls were discovered.

Courtesy Israel Ministry of Tourism

PYGARG (IBEX). An animal of the deer family, perhaps the antelope or the addax. It was considered unclean by the Jews (Deut. 14:5). *Ibex:* NIV, NRSV.

-Q-

QUAILS. Small game birds provided miraculously by the Lord as food for the Israelites in the wilderness (Exod. 16:12–13).

QUARTUS. A Christian at Corinth from whom Paul sent greetings to the church at Rome (Rom. 16:23).

QUATERNION. A company of four soldiers who guarded prisoners during a night "watch" assignment consisting of three hours (Acts 12:4).

QUEEN. A woman who exercised royal power, or the wife or mother of a king. Esther exercised great power as the wife of King Ahasuerus of Persia (Esther 5:2). Solomon provided a seat at his right hand for his mother, Bathsheba (1 Kings 2:19).

QUEEN OF HEAVEN. A fertility goddess worshiped by the citizens of Jerusalem during the idolatrous days before the fall of the nation of Judah (Jer. 7:18; 44:17). This may have been the goddess Ashtaroth. See also *Ashtaroth*.

QUEEN OF SHEBA. See *Sabeans*.

QUICKEN. To preserve or give life. The psalmist praised God who will "quicken me again" (Ps. 71:20). The Father and Son have authority to raise the dead and give eternal life (John 5:21).

QUICKSANDS (SYRTIS). Sandbars and shifting sands off the African coast in the Mediterranean Sea which posed a hazard for ships (Acts 27:17). *Syrtis:* NRSV.

QUIRINIUS. See *Cyrenius*.

QUIVER. A sheath for arrows carried by foot soldiers or hung on the sides of chariots (Lam. 3:13). The word is also used figuratively for God's protection (Isa 49:2) and the blessing of children (Ps. 127:5).

QUMRAN, KHIRBET. A site near the Dead Sea where the Dead Sea Scrolls were discovered. See also *Dead Sea Scrolls; Essenes*.

-R-

RAAMSES. See *Rameses*.

RABBAH/RABBATH. The capital city of the Ammonites (Deut. 3:11–12) captured by David's army under Joab. The city's destruction was prophesied by Amos (Amos 1:14). *Rabbath:* Ezek 21:20.

RABBI/RABBONI (RABBOUNI). A title of great respect, meaning "master" or "teacher," used by Nicodemus in addressing Jesus (John 3:2). Its Aramaic form is *rabboni* (John 20:16). *Rabbouni:* NRSV.

RABBIT. See *Hare*.

RAB-SHAKEH. The chief cupbearer or aide for King Sennacherib of Assyria who demanded the surrender of Jerusalem from King Hezekiah (2 Kings 18:17; Isa. 36:13–22).

RACA. A term of insult, meaning "worthless" or "good for nothing," which was forbidden by Christ. Expressing such contempt for a fellow human being will lead to God's judgment and condemnation (Matt. 5:21–22).

RACE. This word in the N.T. refers to popular Grecian contests, such as races by foot, horseback, or chariot. It is also used figuratively of the Christian's call to pursue the goal of Christlikeness (Heb. 12:1).

RACHAB. See *Rahab*.

RACHEL/RAHEL. Jacob's favorite wife (Gen. 29:28–30) and the mother of his sons Joseph and Benjamin (Gen. 30:23–24; 35:16–18). She died giving birth to Benjamin and was buried near Bethlehem (Gen. 35:16–20). Jeremiah referred to Rachel weeping for her children carried into the Babylonian Exile (Jer. 31:15–17; *Rahel*). See also *Jacob*.

RAHAB/RACHAB. A harlot in Jericho who hid the spies sent by Joshua to scout the city (Josh. 2:1–6). Later she and her family were spared when Jericho fell to the invading Israelites (Josh. 6:22–25). In the N.T. Rahab was commended for her faith (Heb. 11:31). *Rachab:* Jesus' ancestry (Matt. 1:5).

RAHEL. See *Rachel*.

RAID. See *Road*.

RAIN. God's life-giving moisture from the sky was sometimes withheld because of the sin of His people (Deut. 11:17).

Excessive rain produced the great flood in Noah's time as an instrument of God's judgment (Gen. 7:4). See also *Former Rain; Latter Rain.*

RAINBOW. A colored arch in the clouds after the great flood, given by God as a promise that He would never again destroy the world with water (Gen. 9:9–17).

RAISINS. Dried grapes which were preserved in clusters (1 Sam. 25:18) and used in cakes known as flagons (Song of Sol. 2:5). See also *Flagon,* No. 1.

RAM.

1. A long beam used to batter down the gates of walled cities (Ezek. 4:2).

2. A male sheep used for food (Gen. 31:38) and favored as a sacrificial animal (Num. 15:6).

RAMA (RAMAH). A Benjamite city near Jerusalem and the probable site of Rachel's tomb (Matt. 2:18). *Ramah:* NIV, NRSV.

RAMAH. Another name for the town of Ramoth-gilead. See *Ramoth-gilead.*

RAMESES/RAAMSES. A fertile district of Egypt where Jacob and his descendants settled (Gen. 47:11). This name may have been given later to a royal treasure city built by the Hebrew slaves (Exod. 1:11; *Raamses*).

RAMOTH-GILEAD/RAMAH/RAMOTH. An ancient Amorite stronghold east of the Jordan River which became one of the six cities of refuge after its conquest by the Israelites (Deut. 4:43). *Ramah:* 2 Kings 8:29; *Ramoth:* 1 Kings 22:3. See also *Cities of Refuge.*

RAMPART. A low wall around a military trench or embankment, which served as the first line of defense for a walled city (Lam. 2:8; Nah. 3:8). See also *Bulwark.*

RAM'S HORN. The curved horn of a ram which was blown like a trumpet as a signal to worshipers and warriors (Josh. 6:4–13). See also *Trumpet.*

RANSOM. To redeem or buy by making a payment. Because of His atoning death, Christ is described as a "ransom for all" (1 Tim. 2:6).

RAPTURE, THE. A doctrine held by some which deals with the transformation of the redeemed into a glorified state at Christ's return (Phil. 3:

20–21). The dead in Christ will be raised at Christ's return and given an incorruptible body (1 Cor. 15:51–53). They will be caught up into the air, along with living saints, to meet the Lord (1 Thess. 4:16–17). See also *Second Coming*.

RAS SHAMRA TABLETS. Clay writing tablets discovered by archaeologists at the ancient city of Ugarit in Syria. Dating from the fifteenth century B.C., these tablets describe the pagan religions mentioned in the O.T., particularly Baalism. See also *Clay; Nuzi Tablets*.

RAVEN. A bird of prey considered unclean under Mosaic Law (Lev. 11:15). God used ravens to sustain the prophet Elijah (1 Kings 17:4–6).

RAZOR. A sharp instrument made of flint, bronze, or steel, and used for cutting hair (Ezek. 5:1).

REAPER. A person who harvested grain (Ruth 2:3, 14). The spiritual law of the harvest declares we reap what we sow (Gal. 6:7–8). See also *Harvest*.

REBA. A Midianite chief killed by Joshua's army in the plains of Moab (Josh. 13:21).

REBEKAH/REBECCA. The wife of Isaac and the mother of his twin sons Jacob and Esau. She encouraged her favorite son Jacob to obtain Esau's birthright by deceiving the aging Isaac. Then she encouraged Jacob to flee to her relatives in Mesopotamia to escape Esau's wrath (Gen. 27). *Rebecca:* Greek form (Rom. 9:10). See also *Isaac*.

REBUKE. See *Reproof*.

RECENT CONVERT. See *Novice*.

RECHAB. The father of Jehonadab and founder of the Rechabites, a tribe committed to abstain from wine and live in tents. Because of their faithfulness, the prophet Jeremiah promised they would not cease to exist (Jer. 35:8–19). The descendants of this tribe still live in Iraq and Yemen.

RECOMPENSE. To pay back in kind (Prov. 12:14). Believers are assured their courage and faith will be rewarded (Heb. 10:35–36). See also *Reward*.

RECONCILIATION. The process of bringing opposing parties or people together. Believers, who are justified by faith and reconciled to God by

A Bedouin camel rider on the shore of the Red Sea.
Courtesy Israel Ministry of Tourism

Christ's victory over sin and death (Rom. 5:1, 10), are to be ambassadors of reconciliation for others (2 Cor. 5:18–20). See also *Atonement; Mediator, Christ the; Propitiation.*

RECORD (TESTIMONY). A witness or testimony to one's faithfulness. Jesus told His enemies, "my record is true" (John 8:14). *Testimony:* NIV, NRSV. Paul defended his record of faithfulness to God (Acts 20:26–27). See also *Testimony; Witness.*

RECORDER. An aide to a king who kept official records and served as a counselor or advisor (2 Kings 18:18, 37).

RED DRAGON. A name for Satan. After being cast out of heaven, Satan turned his fury on God's people (Rev. 12:3–17). See also *Satan.*

RED HEIFER. An unblemished cow or ox that had never been yoked. It was used as a sacrifice in a sin offering (Num. 19:1–9).

RED KITE. See *Glede; Vulture.*

RED SEA. The sea between Egypt and Arabia which the Israelites crossed miraculously through God's intervention when fleeing from the Egyptian army (Exod. 14:16; 15:4, 22). This body of water is also called the Sea of Reeds because of its reed-filled marshes at the head of the Gulf of Suez.

REDEEM. To buy back property which had been forfeited because of indebtedness or to buy back a person who had been sold into slavery (Exod. 6:6). This idea describes perfectly the work of Christ, who "bought us back" from sin and death through His atonement on the cross as our Redeemer (Matt. 20:28). See also *Atonement; Lamb of God.*

REED. A tall grass, common in marshes and swamps, used to make paper, musical instruments, and writing pens. The word is also used figuratively for weakness and fragility (Matt. 11:7). See also *Bulrush; Paper.*

REFINER. A craftsman who removed impurities from precious metals by melting the ore (Jer. 6:29)—an apt description for God, who purifies His people through affliction and chastisement (Isa. 48:10). See also *Finer.*

REFUGE, CITIES OF. See *Cities of Refuge.*

REFUSE (RUBBISH). Waste or worthless matter (Amos 8:6). Paul declared his accomplishments were as garbage, compared to the riches of knowing Christ (Phil. 3:8). *Rubbish:* NIV, NRSV. See also *Dung*.

REGENERATION. New birth; spiritual change brought about by the Holy Spirit in those who trust in Christ (2 Cor. 5:17–21). See also *New Birth; Salvation*.

REGISTER (FAMILY RECORDS, GENEALOGICAL RECORDS). A tablet on which census records or genealogical lists were inscribed, with the names of the living on one side and the dead on the other (Ezra 2:62). *Family records:* NIV; *Genealogical records:* NRSV. See also *Genealogy*.

REHOB. A city near the source of the Jordan River scouted by the spies who investigated the land of Canaan (Num. 13:21).

REHOBOAM/ROBOAM. Son and successor of Solomon as king of Judah (reigned about 931–913 B.C.). He refused to implement the reform measures requested by northern leaders after Solomon's death—a foolish act which resulted in the split of the ten northern tribes into the Northern Kingdom (1 Kings 12:1–24). *Roboam:* Jesus' ancestry (Matt. 1:7).

REHOBOTH. The name of a well dug by Isaac in the valley of Gerar south of Beer-sheba (Gen. 26:17, 22).

REINS. KJV word for the *kidneys*, a vital body organ in humans and animals. The reins of an animal were considered a special ceremonial sacrifice (Lev. 3:4–5). In humans, the kidneys were regarded as the seat of conscience and affection (Prov. 23:16).

REJOICE. To be glad or to express one's joy. Joy may result from God's blessings (Exod. 18:9) or assurance of salvation (Acts 8:39). See also *Joy*.

REKEM. A Midianite king killed by the Israelites under Moses (Num. 31:8; Josh. 13:21).

REMISSION. God's forgiveness or pardon of our sins. This forgiveness is based on Christ's atoning death (Matt. 26:28) and our repentance (Mark 1:4) and faith in Christ (Acts 10:43). See also *Forgiveness; Pardon*.

REMNANT (SURVIVORS). A small group of God's people

who remained loyal to Him in the midst of widespread sin and idolatry. The prophet Isaiah declared that Israel would be punished for its unfaithfulness (Isa. 1:9). *Survivors:* NIV, NRSV. However, a righteous remnant of His people would be preserved (Isa. 10:20–22). God continues to work through His righteous remnant, the church (Rom. 11:5). See also *Outcasts*.

REMPHAN (REPHAN). A star god of the Babylonians worshiped secretly by the Israelites —an act for which they were taken into exile by the Babylonians (Acts 7:41–43). *Rephan:* NIV, NRSV.

REND (TEAR). To tear apart by force. Rending one's clothes was a sign of great sorrow or repentance (Esther 4:1). *Tear:* NIV, NRSV.

REPENTANCE. The act of turning from sin and changing one's orientation from rebellion against God to acceptance of God's will and lordship. A patient God commands all persons to repent (Acts 17:30). Christ came to call sinners to repentance (Luke 5:32), and He also counsels believers to forgive a brother who repents (Luke 17:3). See also *Contrite; Conviction; Penitence*.

REPHAIM (REPHAITES).

1. A race of giants in Palestine defeated by Chedorlaomer, a king of Elam, and allied kings (Gen. 14:5). *Rephaites:* NIV.

2. A fertile valley near Jerusalem where David defeated the Philistines (2 Sam. 5:18–22).

REPHAN. See *Remphan*.

REPHIDIM. A camping site of the Israelites between the wilderness of Sin and Mt. Sinai where Moses struck the rock and where Amalek was defeated (Exod. 17:1).

REPROACH. Shame, blame, or scorn. Jesus the Messiah suffered reproach for our sake (Isa. 53:3–6; Rom. 15:3).

REPROBATE (DEPRAVED, DEBASED). A person who is depraved, corrupt, or worthless—a term applied to those who reject God (Rom. 1:28). *Depraved:* NIV; *Debased:* NRSV.

REPROOF. A sharp rebuke for misconduct. John the Baptist reproved Herod for his incestuous marriage (Luke 3:19–20).

RESH. The twentieth letter of the Hebrew alphabet, used as a heading over Ps. 119:153–160.

RESIN. See *Myrrh*.

RESTITUTION. To make a fair settlement with a person for property lost or for wrong done. Restitution was strictly required by the Mosaic Law (Exod. 22:1). Zacchaeus promised to make fourfold restitution of what he had taken unlawfully as a tax collector (Luke 19:8).

RESURRECTION. A raising to life beyond physical death which leads to eternal life for believers. This truth was taught by Jesus (John 6:40, 44) and demonstrated by His miracles (Matt. 9:25) as well as His own resurrection (Acts 2:32). Paul taught that Christians will have a glorified body like that of Christ (Phil. 3:20–21) and that it will last through eternity (Rom. 2:7).

RESURRECTION OF CHRIST. The return of Jesus to physical life following His death. His resurrection was foretold in Psalms (Ps. 16: 10–11) and prophecy (Isa. 53: 10–12), announced by Christ Himself (Mark 9:9–10), and proclaimed by the apostles (Acts 2:32; 3:15). It validates our faith and witness (1 Cor. 15:14–15), assures believers of resurrection (1 Cor. 15:18–20), emphasizes our final victory over sin and death (1 Cor. 15:17, 26, 54, 57), and inspires faithfulness in Christian service (1 Cor. 15:58).

RETRIBUTION. A repayment for wrong done; God's wrath and punishment against man's rebellion and unbelief (Rom. 1:18). Only trust in Jesus and His atoning death can deliver us from God's retribution (1 Thess. 1:10). See also *Judgment, Last; Punishment; Tribulation, The Great*.

REUBEN. The oldest son of Jacob and Leah and founder of one of the twelve tribes of Israel (Gen. 29:32). He lost his birthright by committing adultery with his father's concubines (Gen. 35:22; 49:3–4). Reuben likely saved Joseph's life when his brothers proposed to kill him (Gen. 37:21–22). The tribe of Reuben settled east of the Jordan River, along with Gad and Manasseh (Num. 32:1–25). See also *Tribes of Israel*.

REUEL. See *Jethro*.

REVELATION. The uncovering or presentation of truth at God's initiative (2 Cor. 12: 1–7). Christ, the only begotten Son, reveals the Father (John 1:18). God's searching Spirit (1 Cor.

2:10) interprets the divine purpose through the prophets (1 Pet. 1:12) and the apostles (Gal. 1:16).

REVELATION OF JOHN. The last book of the N.T., which consists of a series of seven visions revealed directly by the Lord to the apostle John. Through symbols such as angels, horsemen, and plagues, these visions are considered by some to portray the end of the present age and the coming of God's kingdom.

The seven visions serve as a convenient outline of the book: (1) Christ encouraging His church against attacks (1:9–3:22); (2) Christ the Lamb with a sealed scroll (4:1–7:17); (3) seven angels blowing trumpets (8:1–11:19); (4) Satan and the beast persecuting the church (12:1–14:20); (5) seven bowls pouring out the wrath of Christ (15:1–16:21); (6) the judgment of Babylonia, or Rome (17:1–19:20); and (7) the final victory of God and His final judgment (19:11–21). The book ends on a triumphant note with God's promise of a new heaven and a new earth (21:1–22:21). See also *Apocalypse; John the Apostle; Seven Churches of Asia*.

REVENGE. Retaliation against another, or "getting even." Jesus rebuked His disciples for a vengeful spirit (Luke 9:54–56) and commanded forbearance (Matt. 5:38–44). He commanded us to love our enemies and show mercy toward others (Luke 6:35–38). The Bible declares that vengeance should be exacted only by God (Prov. 20:22; Heb. 10:30).

REVERENCE. A feeling of deep respect and awe which believers are to show toward God and the sanctuary devoted to worship (Lev. 19:30; Ps. 89:8). Reverence should also be shown to kings (1 Kings 1:31), parents (Heb. 12:9), and family members (Eph. 5:33).

REVILER (SLANDERER). A mocker. Revilers will not inherit God's kingdom (1 Cor. 6:10). *Slanderer:* NIV. Those reviled for Christ's sake will be blessed and rewarded (Matt. 5:11–12).

REWARD. A. return or payment for service. God rewards those who diligently seek Him (Heb. 11:6). See also *Recompense*.

REZIN. The last king of Syria who was killed in the conquest by Tiglath-pileser of Assyria (2 Kings 15:37; 16:5–9).

RHEGIUM. A port in southern Italy where Paul landed on his way to Rome (Acts 28:13).

RHODA. A servant girl in the home of Mary, mother of John Mark, who answered the door for Peter after his miraculous release from prison (Acts 12:13–16).

RHODES. A Greek island in the Aegean Sea which Paul's ship passed when sailing from Assos to Palestine (Acts 21:1). This was the site of the ancient lighthouse known as the Colossus of Rhodes, one of the seven wonders of the ancient world.

RICHES. Material goods and earthly treasures, which are portrayed as deceitful (Matt. 13:22), fleeting (Prov. 23:5), and uncertain (1 Tim. 6:17). Jesus urged believers to lay up spiritual treasures in heaven rather than earthly possessions (Matt. 6:19–20).

RICH ROBE. See *Stomacher*.

RIDDLE. A story with a hidden meaning. Samson posed a riddle to the Philistines (Judg. 14:12–19).

RIE (SPELT). A common Egyptian grain plant which thrived in poor soil under hot, dry conditions (Exod. 9:32). *Spelt:* NIV, NRSV. See also *Fitch*.

RIGHT HAND. A symbol of power and strength (Ps. 77:10). Jesus is exalted in power at God's right hand (Eph. 1:20). See also *Hand of God*.

RIGHTEOUSNESS. An attribute of God which signifies His holiness, sinlessness, and justice (Ps. 35:24). Through faith in Christ, God's righteousness is imputed or granted to believers (Titus 3:5). Christians are encouraged to pursue the interests of God's righteous kingdom (Matt. 6:33). See also *Godliness; Goodness*.

RIM. See *Nave*.

RIMMON. A Syrian god worshiped by Naaman the leper (2 Kings 5:18), possibly a god of the sun or rain.

RING. A circular band worn as an ornament on fingers, wrists, ankles, and in ears and nostrils. The pharaoh of Egypt presented a ring to Joseph as a symbol of authority as his aide or advisor (Gen. 41:42).

RIVER. A freshwater stream. The largest rivers mentioned in the Bible are the Abana (2 Kings 5:12), Euphrates (Gen.

2:14), Jordan (Matt. 3:6), Nile (Exod. 7:21), Pharpar (2 Kings 5:12), and Tigris, or Hiddekel (Gen. 2:14).

RIVER OF EGYPT (WADI OF EGYPT). A small stream flowing into the Mediterranean Sea which marked the old boundary between Egypt and Palestine (Num. 34:5). *Wadi of Egypt:* NIV, NRSV.

RIZPAH. The concubine of King Saul who was taken by Abner after Saul's death (2 Sam. 3:6–8). Her two sons were hanged by the Gibeonites during David's reign (2 Sam. 21:8–11).

ROAD (RAID). A path or trail for public travel, also called a highway or way (Mark 10:46). The word is also used as a figure of speech for a raid by robbers or invaders (1 Sam. 27:10). *Raid:* NRSV. See also *Highway*.

ROBBER. A person who steals from others. The traveler in Christ's parable of the Good Samaritan was beaten by robbers (Luke 10:30).

ROBE. A long outer garment similar to a tunic or mantle. The soldiers mocked Jesus at His crucifixion by dressing him in a purple robe (Matt. 27:28). See also *Mantle*.

ROBOAM. See *Rehoboam*.

ROCK. A stone. The word is used metaphorically for God to show His strength and stability (Ps. 18:31). Jesus changed Peter's name to "rock" or "rocklike" (Greek: *petras*) when He called him as His disciple (John 1:42).

ROCK BADGER. See *Coney*.

ROD (SHOOT). A staff or stick (Ps. 23:4). The word is used figuratively for a branch or offshoot of a tribe or family; for example, in reference to Christ (Isa. 11:1). *Shoot:* NIV, NRSV.

ROE/ROEBUCK (GAZELLE). A graceful deer noted for its swiftness (2 Sam. 2:18). *Gazelle:* NIV, NRSV. It was considered a clean animal by the Jews (Deut. 12:15, 22). *Roebuck:* 1 Kings 4:23. See also *Deer; Hart; Hind*.

ROLL (SCROLL). A strip of parchment that was written on, then rolled on a stick (Jer. 36:2). *Scroll:* NIV, NRSV. It was unrolled for reading, just as a modern reader turns the pages of a book. See also *Scroll*.

ROMAN EMPIRE. The powerful pagan empire that dominated the known world during N.T. times (Rom. 1:7). Founded on the Tiber River in 735 B.C. by Romulus, the nation was governed by kings until 509 B.C., when it became a republic. Rome extended her borders greatly during the republic period, eventually annexing Palestine and Syria in 63 B.C. Augustus Caesar became emperor of the far-reaching empire in 27 B.C. and was reigning at Jesus' birth (Luke 2:1–7). Jesus was crucified by Roman soldiers under sentence from Pilate, the Roman governor of Judea (Matt 27:24–26).

ROMANS, EPISTLE TO THE. An epistle of the N.T. on the themes of righteousness and salvation, written by the apostle Paul to the Christians at Rome. The most systematic and theological of all of Paul's epistles, Romans expresses his conviction that the gospel is the power of salvation to all who believe (1:16–17). Other themes discussed in the epistle include: (1) the truth that all people, both Jews and Gentiles, are unworthy of God's grace (1:18–3:20); (2) God's imputed righteousness, through which He justifies and sanctifies believers (3:21–8:39); (3) Israel in God's plan of redemption (9:1–11:36); and (4) the practical application of faith in the life of believers (12:1–15:13). See also *Righteousness; Salvation*.

ROME. The capital city of the Roman Empire (Rom. 1:7) and the place where Paul was imprisoned during his final days and where he likely died as a martyr (Phil. 1:12–13; 4:22; 2 Tim. 4:6–8). His epistle to the Romans was addressed to the Christians in this city (Rom. 1:1–7). In the N.T., Rome is figuratively portrayed as Babylon (1 Pet. 5:13).

ROOT. The life-sustaining part of a plant. The word is also used figuratively to describe Christ's humiliation (Isa. 53:2) and exaltation (Isa. 11:10) and the believer's foundation in Christ (Col. 2:7).

ROPE/CORD. A heavy cord. Ropes on the head or neck signified distress (1 Kings 20:31–32) and perhaps submission, since cords were used to bind prisoners. *Cord:* Judg. 15:13. See also *Line*.

ROSE (CROCUS). A flowering plant, perhaps the narcissus—a fragrant flower which grew in the plain of Sharon (Isa. 35:1). *Crocus:* NIV, NRSV.

Interior view of the ruins of the ancient stadium or outdoor theater known as the Colosseum of Rome.

Courtesy Rayburn W. Ray

ROYAL DEPUTY. See *Chancellor*.

ROYAL OFFICIAL. See *Nobleman*.

RUBBISH. See *Dung; Refuse*.

RUBY (CORAL). A precious stone, perhaps coral or pearl (Prov. 3:15; Lam. 4:7). *Coral:* NRSV. See also *Coral*.

RUDDY. Having a reddish or fair complexion, in contrast to the dark skin of most people of the Middle East (1 Sam. 16:12).

RUE. An herb with a strong odor and bitter taste. Jesus denounced the Pharisees who were careful to tithe this insignificant plant while neglecting more important matters (Luke 11:42).

RUFUS. A fellow believer at Rome greeted and commended by Paul (Rom. 16:13). He was perhaps the son of Simon of Cyrene, who carried the cross of Jesus (Mark 15:21).

RUHAMAH. A symbolic name for Israel, meaning "having obtained favor," given by Hosea to his daughter to show that

Israel would be forgiven after their repentance (Hos. 2:1).

RULER. See *Prince*.

RUSH. A plant which grew in marshes, perhaps the same as the bulrush (Job 8:11). See also *Bulrush; Flag*.

RUST. A substance which corrodes metal. Jesus used this word to warn against the instability and uncertainty of earthly treasures (Matt. 6:19–20).

RUTH. A Moabite woman who remained loyal to her Jewish mother-in-law Naomi after the death of their husbands. Ruth moved with Naomi to Bethlehem (Ruth 1:16–19), where she gleaned grain in the fields of Boaz. She eventually married Boaz and became an ancestor of David and Christ (Ruth 4:9–22). See also *Boaz; Naomi*.

RUTH, BOOK OF. A short book of the O.T. which reads almost like a short story on the power of love in dismal circumstances. Love bound Ruth and her mother-in-law Naomi together in spite of the death of their husbands (1:1–2:23). And Ruth found happiness and security again through her marriage to Boaz, a kinsman of Naomi's family (3:1–4:22). See also *Levirate Marriage*.

-S-

SABAOTH. A Hebrew word for "hosts." See *Hosts, Lord of*.

SABBATH. The Jewish day of worship and rest, established when God rested after the six days of creation (Gen. 2:1–3). The fourth of the Ten Commandments called for the Sabbath to be observed and "kept holy" (Exod. 20:8). The Pharisees placed restrictions on Sabbath observance that prohibited acts of mercy or necessity (Mark 2:23–24). But Jesus declared that "the sabbath was made for man and not man for the sabbath" (Mark 2:27–28). The O.T. Sabbath fell on the seventh day of the week, or our Saturday. Most Christian groups observe Sunday as the day of worship because of Christ's resurrection on the first day of the week (1 Cor. 16:2).

SABBATH DAY'S JOURNEY. The distance under law by which a person was permitted to travel on the Sabbath—2,000 paces outside the city wall, or about 3,000 feet (Exod. 16:29–30; Acts 1:12).

SABBATICAL YEAR. Every seventh year—or a Sabbath year—considered sacred to the Lord, when the land went uncultivated and debtors were released from their obligations (Lev. 25:20–21).

SABEANS. Natives or inhabitants of ancient Sheba in southwest Arabia, a country now known as Yemen. Job's livestock was stolen by Sabeans (Job 1:13–15). The wealthy queen of Sheba visited King Solomon (1 Kings 10).

SACKBUT (LYRE, TRIGON). A triangular-shaped stringed musical instrument similar to a harp (Dan. 3:5–10). *Lyre:* NIV; *Trigon:* NRSV.

SACKCLOTH. A coarse fabric made of goat's hair which was worn to express grief, sorrow, and repentance (Joel 1:8, 13). Jacob wore sackcloth in anguish when he thought his son Joseph was dead (Gen. 37:34). See also *Mourn*.

SACRAMENT. A ritual or religious act which serves as a channel of God's grace. While Roman Catholics and most orthodox churches observe seven sacraments, most Protestants admit only two—baptism and the Lord's Supper—and even these are called "ordinances" by most evangelical groups (see Matt. 3: 13–15).

SACRIFICE. An offering made to God or to false gods for the purpose of gaining favor or showing respect. In O.T. times, animals were sacrificed on the altar to atone for transgression against God and His law (Deut. 18:3). Christ offered Himself as the final and perfect sacrifice for our sins (Heb. 9:9–14). See also *Atonement; Burnt Offering; Redeem*.

SACRILEGE. See *Blasphemy*.

SADDUCEES. A priestly aristocratic party of N.T. times which—in contrast to the Pharisees—rejected the oral traditions of the Jewish faith and accepted only the original teachings of Moses as authoritative. They did not believe in a bodily resurrection (Matt. 22: 23) or angels and spirits (Acts 23:8). They often opposed Jesus and His teachings (Matt. 16:6, 12). See also *Pharisees*.

SAFFRON. A plant used in perfume, dyes, and medicines and for flavoring food and drinks (Song of Sol. 4:13–14).

SAINT. A N.T. word for a Christian believer set apart for God's service (Rom. 1:7; Heb. 6:10). In the O.T., the word refers to a pious Jew (Ps. 16:3). Spiritual blessings are reserved for the saints of God's kingdom (Col. 1:12). See also *Church; Congregation; People of God.*

SALAMIS. A town on the island of Cyprus where Paul and Barnabas preached during the first missionary journey (Acts 13:4–5).

SALEM. See *Jerusalem.*

SALIM. A place near Aenon west of the Jordan River where John the Baptist baptized (John 3:23).

SALMON. The father of Boaz, Ruth's husband, who is listed as an ancestor of Christ (Matt. 1:4–5).

SALOME. A woman who witnessed the Crucifixion and visited Jesus' tomb after His resurrection (Mark 15:40; 16:1). She may have been the mother of Jesus' disciples James and John.

SALT. A mineral used to season and preserve food. Jesus called His followers the "salt of the earth" but warned that compromise would diminish their witness (Matt. 5:13; Luke 14:34–35).

SALT, CITY OF. A city in the wilderness of Judah near the Dead Sea, or "Salt Sea" (Josh. 15:62).

SALT SEA. See *Dead Sea.*

SALT, VALLEY OF. A valley with heavy salt deposits near the Dead Sea where King David and King Amaziah were victorious in battle (2 Sam. 8:13; 2 Kings 14:7–8).

SALUTATION. An elaborate greeting, usually involving repeated bowing and embracing (Luke 15:20). Perhaps because of the urgency of their message, Jesus advised His disciples whom He sent out to "salute no man by the way" (Luke 10:4).

SALVATION. The total work of God in delivering us from sin and reconciling us to Himself. The apostle Peter declared that salvation is found in Christ alone (Acts 4:12). See also *New Birth; Regeneration.*

SAMARIA. The capital city of Israel, or the Northern Kingdom, and a name often applied to the surrounding region. The city was built by Omri, king of

Israel, about 900 B.C. It was destroyed about 722 B.C. when the Assyrians overran the Northern Kingdom (2 Kings 17:3–24). See also *Omri*.

SAMARITAN. An inhabitant of the district of Samaria between Judea and Galilee. These people were considered inferior by the Jews because of their mixed-blood ancestry going back to their intermarriage with foreign colonists placed here by the Assyrians (2 Kings 17:3–24). Jesus, however, associated with Samaritans (Luke 9:52; John 4:4–30) and even used a kindhearted Samaritan as an example of a good neighbor (Luke 10:29–37).

SAMECH. The fifteenth letter of the Hebrew alphabet, used as a heading over Ps. 119:113–120.

SAMGAR-NEBO. A prince of the family of Nebuchadnezzar of Babylonia who sat in the middle gate of Jerusalem while the city was being captured (Jer. 39:3).

SAMOS. An island of Greece off the coast of Lydia visited by the apostle Paul (Acts 20:15).

SAMOTHRACIA (SAMOTHRACE). An island in the Aegean Sea visited by Paul on his way to Macedonia (Acts 16:11). *Samothrace:* NIV, NRSV.

SAMSON. A judge of Israel set apart as a Nazarite before his birth. Samson had great physical strength, which he used effectively against the Philistines, as long as he was faithful to his vows. But his strength failed when he revealed his secret to Delilah, who cut his hair and turned him over to his enemies. Samson died, along with his captors, when he destroyed the pagan Philistine temple at Gaza (see Judg. 14–16). See also *Nazarite*.

SAMUEL/SHEMUEL. A prophet and the last judge of Israel who anointed the first two kings of Judah—Saul (1 Sam. 10:1) and David (1 Sam. 16: 1–13). Samuel was dedicated to God's service by his mother Hannah even before his birth (1 Sam. 1:11–22), and he grew up under the tutelage of Eli the priest to prepare for priestly service (1 Sam. 3:1–20). A popular leader, he was mourned by the entire nation at his death (1 Sam. 25:1). *Shemuel:* 1 Chron. 6:33. See also *Hannah*.

SAMUEL, BOOKS OF. Two historical books of the O.T. named for the prophet Samuel, who anointed Saul and David as the first two kings of Israel. Their anointing marked the transition of the nation from a loose confederacy of tribes to a united kingdom under the leadership of a king.

Major events covered by these books include: (1) Samuel's rule as the last judge of Israel (1 Sam. 1:1–7:17); (2) King Saul's reign (1 Sam. 8:1–15:9); (3) the rivalry between Saul and David (1 Sam. 15:10–31:13); and (4) the accession of David to the throne; his military triumphs, shortcomings, and troubles (2 Sam.). Some of the information about David's administration in 2 Samuel is repeated in the book of 1 Chronicles. See also *Chronicles, Books of; David; Samuel; Saul.*

SANBALLAT. An influential Samaritan who plotted to kill Nehemiah to stop his rebuilding projects and reform projects in Jerusalem (Neh. 4:7–8; 6:1–4). See also *Tobiah.*

SANCTIFICATION. The process of consecrating or setting something apart for holy purposes. In the O.T., priests, Levites, and each family's firstborn child were consecrated to the Lord. In the N.T., sanctification was regarded as a work of grace following conversion (Phil. 1:6). God calls all believers to holiness and sanctification (1 Thess. 4:3, 7). Those sanctified are committed to God's truth and serve as witnesses to His power and grace in the world (Rom. 6:11–13). See also *Consecration.*

SANCTUARY. A holy place (Lev. 4:6), a place of public worship (Ps. 73:17), or a place of refuge where a person is safe under God's protection (Ezek. 11:16).

SAND. Fine, granular soil, which is seldom found in Palestine except along the seashore. The word is used figuratively for countless numbers or multitudes (Gen. 32:12).

SANDALS. Footwear, consisting of leather or wood bound to the feet with straps. They were removed before entering a house or holy place (Josh. 5:15; Luke 15:22). See also *Latchet.*

SANHEDRIN. See *Council.*

SAPPHIRA. An early believer at Jerusalem who was struck dead for lying and withholding money she had pledged to the church's common treasury (Acts 5:1–11). See also *Ananias.*

SAPPHIRE. A light blue gem or precious stone used in the breastplate of the high priest (Exod. 28:18) and in the foundation of New Jerusalem (Rev. 21:19).

SARAH/SARA/SARAI. A wife of Abraham and the mother of Isaac (Gen. 11:29; Rom. 9:9), also called *Sarai*. Although she was barren for many years, Sarah received God's promise that she would be "a mother of nations" (Gen. 17:15–16), and she bore Isaac past the age of ninety (Gen. 17:17–21; 21:2–3). She is commended in the N.T. for her faith and obedience (Heb. 11:11; *Sara:* Greek form). See also *Abraham*.

SARDINE (CARNELIAN). A precious stone (Rev. 4:3). *Carnelian:* NIV, NRSV. Probably the same as the sardius. See *Sardius*.

SARDIS. The chief city of Lydia in Asia Minor and site of one of the seven churches of Asia Minor. This church was characterized as "dead" (Rev. 3:1–5).

SARDIUS (CARNELIAN). A precious stone of blood-red color used in the high priest's breastplate (Exod. 28:17) and in the foundation of New Jerusalem (Rev. 21:20). *Carnelian:* NIV; NRSV.

SARDONYX (ONYX). A precious stone which combines the qualities of sardius and onyx, thus its name *sardonyx*. It was used in the foundation of New Jerusalem (Rev. 21:20). *Onyx:* NRSV. See also *Onyx; Sardius*.

SAREPTA. See *Zarephath*.

SARGON. The king of Assyria (reigned about 722–705 B.C.) who completed the siege of Samaria and carried the Northern Kingdom into captivity (Isa. 20:1). See also *Assyria*.

SARON. See *Sharon*.

SATAN. An evil being who opposes God; the devil. In the Garden of Eden, Satan was represented as a serpent, who tempted Eve (Gen. 3:1–6). He falsely accused and harassed Job (Job 1:6–12). Jesus regarded Satan as a person (Matt. 4:1–10), whom He described as a murderer and the father of lies (John 8:44). While he is called "the prince of this world" (John 16:11), Satan is subject to God's greater power (1 John 4:4) and will be cast into the bottomless pit (Rev. 20:1–3). See also *Belial; Lucifer*.

SATRAP. NIV, NRSV word for the governor of a province in the ancient Persian Empire

(Dan. 6:1). *Prince:* KJV. See also *Governor; Lieutenant.*

SATYR (GOAT-DEMON). A Greek mythological figure which was an object of idolatrous worship (2 Chron. 11:15). The word also describes wild animals which would dance among the ruins of Babylon (Isa. 13:21). *Goat-demon:* NRSV.

SAUL.

1. The first king of Israel who displeased God by his disobedience and his insane jealousy against David. Anointed privately by Samuel (1 Sam. 10:1) and publicly proclaimed king at Gilgal (1 Sam. 11:15), he waged war against the Philistines during his administration (1 Sam. 17–18). He kept the spoils of war from at least one battle, assumed duties of the priestly office, and murdered Ahimelech and eighty-four other priests (1 Sam. 22:14–19)—acts which brought God's judgment. After his sons were killed, Saul committed suicide rather than be captured by the Philistines (1 Sam. 31:1–6).

2. The original name of Paul the Apostle. See *Paul.*

SAVIOR. A title for Christ which emphasizes His work of salvation (Matt. 1:20–21)—a ministry foretold by the prophet Isaiah (Isa. 61:1–3).

SAW. A tool with sharp teeth used in building the temple in Jerusalem and sometimes used to execute prisoners of war (2 Sam. 12:31).

SCAB. A sore on the skin; or a hardened, scaly spot left by a skin disease (Lev. 13:2, 6, 7–8).

SCABBARD. See *Sheath.*

SCALES. See *Balance, Balances.*

SCALL (ITCH). An inflammation of the scalp (Lev. 13: 30–37). *Itch:* NIV, NRSV.

SCAPEGOAT (AZAZEL). A goat, symbolically bearing the sins of the people, sent into the wilderness by the high priest on the Day of Atonement (Lev. 16:8–22). *Azazel:* NRSV. This goat is a symbol of Christ, our sin bearer (see Isa. 53:6).

SCARF. See *Muffler.*

SCARLET (CRIMSON). A red color highly prized as a symbol of wealth and position (2 Sam. 1:24). *Crimson:* NRSV. Its brilliance symbolized Israel's glaring sin against God (Isa. 1:18).

SCENTED WOOD. See *Thyine Wood*.

SCEPTER. A staff or baton carried by a king or other high official as an emblem of authority (Esther 4:11).

SCEVA. Jewish priest at Ephesus whose sons tried in vain to cast out evil spirits in imitation of Paul (Acts 19:11–16).

SCHIN. The twenty-first letter of the Hebrew alphabet, used as a heading over Ps. 119:161–168.

SCHOOLMASTER (DISCIPLINARIAN). A household servant who accompanied children to school but did not function as a teacher. Paul used the word to show the shortcomings of the law. It could make a person aware of sin, but it fell short of providing salvation (Gal. 3:24–25). *Disciplinarian:* NRSV.

SCORN. Contempt and ridicule (Ps. 1:1). Scorners were regarded as foolish and wicked (Prov. 1:22).

SCORPION. An eight-legged insect with a poisonous tail (Deut. 8:15). The word is also used symbolically of a whip for scourging (2 Chron. 10:11–14). See also *Scourging*.

SCOURGING (FLOGGING). A severe beating with a leather strap containing bits of sharp metal. This punishment was limited to forty lashes (Deut. 25:3). Jesus was scourged before His crucifixion (Matt. 27:26). *Flogged:* NIV, NRSV.

SCREECH OWL. A bird noted for its strange cries at night (Isa. 34:14). See also *Bittern; Night Hawk*.

SCRIBE (TEACHER OF THE LAW). A public secretary who specialized in copying the law, in the days when documents had to be laboriously reproduced by hand. Many scribes became interpreters and teachers, and in N.T. times they were committed to preserving the law. Their burdensome technicalities brought Jesus' condemnation (Matt. 5:20). *Teacher of the law:* NIV. See also *Lawyer*.

SCRIBE'S KNIFE. See *Penknife*.

SCRIP (BAG). A small bag or satchel (Matt. 10:10) used for carrying food or other provisions on a journey (Luke 9:3). *Bag:* NIV, NRSV.

SCRIPTURE. See *Bible*.

SCROLL. A piece of papyrus or leather written on and then rolled on a stick. It was unrolled for reading (Rev. 6:14). See also *Roll*.

SCUM. See *Offscouring*.

SCURVY. A skin disease, caused by extended exposure and an unbalanced diet, characterized by dry, scaly skin with bright spots (Lev. 21:20; 22:22).

SCYTHIANS. Members of the nomadic tribes north of the Black Sea and the Caspian Sea. Paul used the word as a general term for barbaric persons (Col. 3:11).

SEA. A large body of salt water. In the O.T., the word is used for any large expanse of water, including rivers and lakes (Gen. 1:10; Isa. 19:5).

SEA GULL. See *Cuckow*.

SEA MONSTER. A giant sea creature of unspecified identity, perhaps a whale or large fish (Lam. 4:3).

SEA OF CHINNEROTH. See *Galilee, Sea of*.

SEA OF GLASS. A clear, crystal sea or lake which appeared to John in a vision, indicating God's purity and holiness and the victory of His redeemed people (Rev. 4:6).

SEA OF THE PLAIN. See *Dead Sea*.

SEA OF TIBERIAS. See *Galilee, Sea of*.

SEAL. See *Signet*.

SEBA. A son of Cush and grandson of Ham (Gen. 10:6–7); the nation made up of Seba's descendants (Ps. 72:10; Isa. 43:3).

SEBAT (SHEBAT). The eleventh month of the Hebrew year (Zech. 1:7). *Shebat:* NIV, NRSV.

SECOND COMING. Christ's return to earth to punish the wicked and unbelieving and to receive glory from believers (2 Thess. 1:9–10). This event will happen suddenly and will be "revealed from heaven with his mighty angels" (2 Thess. 1:7). He will raise the dead (1 Thess 4:13–18), destroy death (1 Cor. 15:25–26), gather the redeemed (Matt. 24:31), judge the world (Matt. 25:32), and reward God's people (Matt. 16:27). Christians should be prepared for His coming (Matt. 24:42) and remain faithful in Christian service (1 Cor. 15:58). See also *Maranatha; Rapture*.

SECRET. See *Mystery*.

SECT. A religious movement in Judaism (Pharisees, Sadducees, Essenes) as well as a political party (Herodians, zealots). Early Christians were regarded as "the sect of the Nazarenes" (Acts 24:5). The word is also applied to early perversions of Christian truth (Gal. 5:20).

SECUNDUS. A Christian who accompanied Paul on his third missionary journey (Acts 20:4).

SEED (OFFSPRING). A person's descendants and thus the means of transmitting life from one generation to another (Gen. 21:12). *Offspring:* NIV, NRSV. Believers in Christ were said to be born of "incorruptible seed" (1 Pet. 1:23) and true heirs of the promise made by God to Abraham (Gal. 3:29). See also *Offspring; Posterity*.

SEER. See *Prophet*.

SEIR, MOUNT. See *Edom*, No. 2.

SEIRATH (SEIRAH). A place in Mt. Ephraim where the judge Ehud hid after assassinating Eglon, king of Moab (Judg. 3:26). *Seirah:* NIV, NRSV.

SELAH. See *Petra*.

SELAH. A musical term in Psalms, possibly calling for a pause or a sudden outburst of voices or instruments (Ps. 44:8).

SELEUCIA. A seaport in Syria from which Paul and Barnabas set sail on the first missionary journey (Acts 13:4).

SELF-CONTROL. See *Sober; Temperance*.

SELF-DENIAL. Voluntary limitation of one's desires, a requirement of Jesus for His followers (Matt. 16:24). Paul also urged Christians to make an offering of themselves to God (Rom. 12:1). Sacrifices for Christ's sake will be rewarded (Luke 18:29–30).

SEM. See *Shem*.

SENIR. See *Hermon, Mount*.

SENNACHERIB. The king of Assyria (reigned about 705–681 B.C.) who captured all fortified cities of Judah except Jerusalem and then demanded tribute from King Hezekiah (2 Kings 18:13–16). Sennacherib was eventually assassinated by his own sons as he worshiped a pagan god (2 Kings 19:37). See also *Assyria*.

SENSIBLE. See *Sober*.

SENTINEL. See *Watchman*.

SEPHARVAIM. A city whose residents, the Sepharvaites, were sent to colonize the Northern Kingdom after Samaria was captured by the Assyrians (2 Kings 17:24–31). See also *Samaritan*.

SEPTUAGINT. The translation of the O.T. from Hebrew into the Greek language about 250 to 150 B.C.—a work accomplished by Jewish scholars who were brought to Alexandria, Egypt, especially for this purpose.

SEPULCHRE (TOMB). A natural cave or a place carved out of rock where bodies were buried (Gen. 23:6–9). *Tomb:* NIV. Some sepulchres were whitened for easy visibility (Matt. 23:27), since contact with a body made a person ceremonially unclean (Num. 19:16). Jesus was buried in a sepulchre or tomb prepared by Joseph of Arimathea (Matt. 27:57–60). See also *Cave; Grave*.

SERAIAH.

1. David's secretary or recorder who served also in Solomon's administration (2 Sam. 8:17). Also called *Sheva* (2 Sam. 20:25), *Shisha* (1 Kings 4:3), and *Shavsha* (1 Chron. 18:16).

2. A prince of Judah who carried Jeremiah's prophecy of doom to the city of Babylon (Jer. 51:59–61).

SERAPHIM (SERAPHS). Six-winged creatures which sang God's praises and also purified Isaiah's lips in his vision in the temple (Isa. 6:1–7). *Seraphs:* NIV, NRSV.

SERGIUS. See *Paulus Sergius*.

SERMON ON THE MOUNT. Jesus' ethical teachings in Matt. 5–7, delivered to His followers on a hillside near Capernaum. Subjects covered include true happiness (5:2–12); Christian influence (5:14–16); relation of the law and Christian conduct (5:17–48); the practice of charity, prayer, and fasting (6:1–18); God and possessions (6:19–24); freedom from anxiety (6:25–34); judging others (7:1–6); the key to God's blessings (7:7–12); warnings about deception (7:13–23); and building life on a secure foundation (7:24–27). See also *Beatitudes*.

SERPENT. A snake. Satan in the form of a serpent tempted Adam and Eve to sin (Gen. 3: 1–5). Poisonous serpents were sent to punish the Israelites for complaining in the wilderness

(Num. 21:6). Moses' upraised serpent symbolized Jesus' future sacrificial death (John 3:14).

SERVANT. One who serves others; any person under the authority of another (Matt. 8:9). Isaiah depicted the coming Messiah as a Suffering Servant (Isa. 53:3–12). Jesus declared His mission was to serve and save (Matt. 20:28; Luke 22:27). See also *Maidservant; Manservant.*

SERVANT GIRL. See *Handmaid.*

SETH/SHETH. The third son of Adam and the father of Enoch (Gen. 4:25–26). *Sheth:* 1 Chron. 1:1.

SETHUR. One of the twelve spies who scouted the land of Canaan, representing the tribe of Asher (Num. 13:13). See also *Spies.*

SEVEN. A number often used symbolically because it was considered a round or perfect number. God's creation established an order of seven days (Gen. 2:2). Seven times or sevenfold suggested abundance (Matt. 18:21–22).

SEVEN CHURCHES OF ASIA. The seven churches in Asia Minor addressed by John in Revelation. The messages to these churches—located at Ephesus, Smyrna, Pergamos, Thyatira, Sardis, Philadelphia, and Laodicea (Rev. 1:11)—ranged from warnings and rebukes to commendations for their faithfulness (see Rev. 2–3).

SEVEN SAYINGS FROM THE CROSS. The seven separate utterances which Jesus made as He suffered on the cross: (1) "Father, forgive them" (Luke 23:34); (2) "To day shalt thou be with me in paradise" (Luke 23:43); (3) "Woman, behold thy son" (John 19:26); (4) "My God, my God, why hast thou forsaken me?" (Matt. 27:46); (5) "I thirst" (John 19:28); (6) "It is finished" (John 19:30); and (7) "Father, into thy hand I commend my spirit" (Luke 23:46).

SEVEN STARS (PLEIADES). A brilliant cluster of stars named for the seven daughters of Atlas and Pleione in Greek mythology (Amos 5:8). *Pleiades:* NIV, NRSV. See also *Pleiades.*

SEVENTH MONTH FESTIVAL. See *Trumpets, Feast of.*

SEVENTY WEEKS. See *Daniel, Book of.*

SEXUAL IMMORALITY. See *Fornication.*

SHACKLES. See *Fetters; Stocks.*

SHADRACH. The Babylonian name of Hananiah, one of Daniel's friends, who was cast into the fiery furnace but miraculously delivered at God's hand (Dan. 3:1–28). See also *Daniel.*

SHALLUM. See *Jehoahaz,* No. 2.

SHALMANESER. An Assyrian king (reigned about 730–720 B.C.) who defeated Israel, or the Northern Kingdom, and carried its leading citizens into captivity (2 Kings 17:3–6.) See also *Assyria.*

SHAME. Disgrace or disrepute which produces a feeling of guilt. It may be caused by idleness (Prov. 10:5), excessive pride (Prov. 11:2), or evil companions (Prov. 28:7).

SHAMGAR. A judge who delivered Israel from oppression by killing 600 Philistines with an ox goad (Judg. 3:31). See also *Judges of Israel.*

SHAMHUTH. A captain in David's army who commanded 24,000 warriors (1 Chron. 27:8).

SHAMMUA

1. One of the twelve spies who scouted the land of Canaan, representing the tribe of Reuben (Num. 13:4). See also *Spies.*

2. Another name for Shimea, David's son. See *Shimea.*

SHAPHAN. A scribe who helped King Josiah carry out his religious reforms by recording temple contributions and proclaiming the law (2 Kings 22:3–13).

SHAPHAT. One of the twelve spies who scouted the land of Canaan, representing the tribe of Simeon (Num. 13:5). See also *Spies.*

SHARON/SARON. A fertile coastal plain between Joppa and Mt. Carmel along the Mediterranean Sea (1 Chron. 27:29). *Saron:* Acts 9:35.

SHAVEH. See *King's Dale.*

SHAVSHA. See *Seraiah.*

SHEARING HOUSE. A place between Jezreel and Samaria where Jehu assassinated the family of King Ahaziah of Judah in order to become king (2 Kings 10:12–14).

SHEAR-JASHUB. A symbolic name, meaning "a remnant

shall return," given by Isaiah to his son to show God's promise to His people after their period of exile (Isa. 7:3–4).

SHEATH (SCABBARD). A carrying case for a dagger or sword (1 Sam. 17:51). *Scabbard:* NIV (John 18:11).

SHEBA. See *Sabeans.*

SHEBAT. See *Sebat.*

SHEBNA. A treasurer under King Hezekiah who made a sepulchre for himself. Isaiah predicted Shebna would die in exile (Isa. 22:15–19).

SHECHEM.

1. A tribal prince who was killed by Simeon and Levi for seducing their sister, Dinah (Gen. 34:1–29).

2. A city of refuge on a trade route in the territory of Ephraim (Josh. 20:7). *Sichem:* Gen. 12:6. *Sychem:* Acts 7:16. See also *Cities of Refuge.*

SHECHINAH. See *Shekinah.*

SHEEP. A domesticated animal prized for the food and fleece which it provided, and also used as a sacrificial offering (Lev. 9:2–4; 12:6). Large flocks of sheep were a sign of wealth (Job 1:3). Jesus spoke of straying sheep as a symbol of lost or sinful persons (Luke 15:4–6). See also *Fleece; Lamb; Wool.*

SHEEP GATE. A gate in the wall of Jerusalem repaired under Nehemiah's leadership (Neh. 3:1, 32).

SHEEPFOLD. A strong enclosure which provided protection for sheep. Jesus is the Good Shepherd who protects His sheep (John 10:1–11).

SHEKEL. A Jewish coin or unit of measure. The silver shekel was worth about sixty cents; the gold shekel about eight dollars (Gen. 23:15; Neh. 10:32; Jer. 32:9).

SHEKELS OF SILVER. See *Silverlings.*

SHEKINAH. A visible manifestation of God's glory, usually as a bright light, fire, or cloud (Exod. 13:21; Matt. 17:5).

SHELTER. See *Pavilion.*

SHEM/SEM. The oldest son of Noah who was preserved in the ark (Gen. 5:32). Shem was the father of Elam, Asshur, Arphaxad, Lud, and Aram—ancestors of the Semitic nations known as the Jews, Arameans, Persians, Assyrians, and Arabians (Gen. 10:22). *Sem:* Greek form (Luke 3:36).

SHEMA, THE. The noted confession of faith quoted by faithful Jews each day: "Hear, O Israel: The Lord our God is one Lord" (Deut. 6:4–9). The complete Shema also includes Num. 15:37–41 and Deut. 11:13–21.

SHEMAIAH. Prophet of Judah who warned King Rehoboam not to attack Israel (1 Kings 12:22–24). He revealed that Pharaoh Shishak of Egypt was being used by the Lord to punish Judah for her sins (2 Chron. 12:5–9).

SHEMER. The landowner who sold King Omri of the Northern Kingdom a hill on which the capital city of Samaria was built (1 Kings 16:24). His name is reflected in the city's name.

SHEMINITH. A musical term appearing in the titles of Pss. 6 and 12 and 1 Chron. 15: 21. It may designate the manner of singing or the instrument to be used.

SHEMUEL.

1. Another name for Samuel the prophet. See *Samuel*.

2. A leader of the tribe of Simeon, appointed by Moses to help divide the land of Canaan after its occupation by the Israelites (Num. 34:20).

SHENIR. See *Hermon, Mount*.

SHEOL. See *Hell*.

SHEPHATIAH. A son of David, born at Hebron to his wife Abital (2 Sam. 3:4).

SHEPHERD. A person who tends sheep, an honorable but dangerous vocation among the Jews (Gen. 31:38–40). The word is also used of ministers and of Christ, who referred to Himself as the "Good Shepherd" (John 10:11, 14). See also *Minister; Pastor*.

SHESHACH. See *Babylon*.

SHESHAI. A descendant of Anak driven out of Hebron by Caleb and killed in battle (Judg. 1:10).

SHESH-BAZZAR. See *Zerubbabel*.

SHETH. See *Seth*.

SHEVA. See *Seraiah*, No. 1.

SHEWBREAD (BREAD OF THE PRESENCE). Unleavened bread kept in the temple or tabernacle for ceremonial purposes. Its name indicated it was exhibited in the presence of the Lord (Num. 4:7). *Bread of the Presence:* NRSV.

SHIBBOLETH. A password used to distinguish Ephraimites from Gileadites in battle. Unable to pronounce the first "h" in shibboleth, 42,000 Ephraimites were killed by the Gileadites (Judg. 12:5–6).

SHIELD. A piece of armor, made of wood and covered with hide or metal, and carried in battle for protection (1 Chron. 18:7). See also *Buckler.*

SHIGGAION. A musical term in the title of Ps. 7, possibly referring to an increased tempo for singing.

SHIHOR-LIBNATH. A brook that served as the southwestern boundary of the territory of Asher (Josh. 19:26).

SHILOAH. See *Siloam.*

SHILOH.

1. A town in the territory of Ephraim where the Philistines defeated the Israelites and captured the ark of the covenant (1 Sam. 4:3–11).

2. A title of the coming Messiah which identified Him as a descendant of Judah (Gen. 49:10).

SHIMEA/SHAMMUAH (SHAMMUA). A son of David and Bath-sheba, born at Jerusalem (1 Chron. 3:5). *Shammua:* NIV. *Shammuah:* 2 Sam. 5:14.

SHIMEI. A Benjamite who insulted David when he was fleeing from Absalom (2 Sam. 16:5–13). Pardoned by David, he was later executed by Solomon (1 Kings 2:36–46).

SHIMRON-MERON/SHIMRON. A town in upper Galilee conquered by Joshua (Josh. 12:20). *Shimron:* Josh. 11:1; 19:15.

SHINAR. See *Babylonia.*

SHIP. A seagoing vessel propelled by oars or sails (Jon. 1:4–5). The Jews were not mariners, since most of the Mediterranean coast was controlled by the Phoenicians and Philistines. Solomon's fleet was manned by Phoenicians (1 Kings 9:26–28). See also *Mariner.*

SHISHA. See *Seraiah.*

SHISHAK. See *Pharaoh.*

SHITTAH (ACACIA). A tree which produced lumber used in building the ark of the covenant and furnishing the tabernacle (Exod. 25:10–16; 30:1; Isa. 41:19). *Acacia:* NIV, NRSV.

SHITTIM.

1. The last campsite of the Israelites before they entered the land of Canaan. It was located across from Jericho in Moab on the eastern side of the Jordan River (Num. 25:1).

2. The wood or lumber produced from the shittah tree. See *Shittah*.

SHOA. A tribal enemy of the Jews. The prophet Ezekiel predicted these people would invade Judah (Ezek. 23:23–25).

SHOBAB. A son of David and Bath-sheba, born in Jerusalem after David became king (1 Chron. 3:5).

SHOBACH/SHOPHACH. A commander of Syrian army who was killed in a battle with David's forces (2 Sam. 10:16–18). *Shophach:* 1 Chron. 19:16.

SHOBI. An Ammonite who brought provisions to David at Mahanaim when he fled from Absalom (2 Sam. 17:27–29).

SHOE. See *Sandal*.

SHOOT. See *Rod*.

SHOPHACH. See *Shobach*.

SHOSHANNIM. A musical term, meaning "lilies," in the titles of Pss. 45, 69, and 80, possibly indicating the pitch or tune to which these psalms were to be sung.

SHOULDER. To drop the shoulder signified servitude (Gen. 49:15); to withdraw it denoted rebellion (Neh. 9:29); to put a responsibility upon a person's shoulder was to entrust it to his keeping (Isa. 9:6).

SHOVEL. A tool used by priests to remove ashes from the altar (Exod. 27:3). The word sometimes refers to a winnowing fork or fan (Isa. 30:24). See also *Fan*.

SHRINE. A miniature replica of the temple where the pagan goddess Diana was worshiped, placed in homes as objects of devotion. The silversmiths of Ephesus earned their livelihood by making and selling these trinkets (Acts 19:24). See also *Demetrius,* No. 1.

SHUAH. A son of Abraham by Keturah (Gen. 25:1–2).

SHUHITE. A member of an Arabic tribe which descended from Shuah, son of Abraham and Keturah. Job's friend Bildad was a Shuhite (Job 2:11).

SHULAMITE (SHULAMMITE). A native of Shulam; the beloved or cherished one in Solomon's song (Song of Sol. 6:13). *Shulammite:* NIV, NRSV.

SHUNAMMITE. A woman from Shunem who provided food and lodging for Elisha. The prophet restored her son to life (2 Kings 4:8–37).

SHUR. A wilderness in southern Palestine (Gen. 16:7) where the Hebrew people wandered for three days after passing through the Red Sea (Exod. 15:22).

SHUSHAN/SUSA. A wealthy and powerful city where Persian kings lived and where Esther interceded for her people (Esther 1:2). *Susa:* NIV, NRSV.

SHUTTLE. A weaving device that shoots the thread rapidly from one side of the cloth to the other between threads of the warp. The word is used as a symbol of fleeting time (Job 7:6). See also *Warp; Weaver*.

SIBBOLETH. See *Shibboleth*.

SICHEM. See *Shechem*.

SICKLE. A tool for cutting or harvesting grain (Deut. 16:9). The word is also used as a symbol of God's coming judgment (Rev. 14:14–19).

SIDON/ZIDON. A Canaanite city about twenty miles north of Tyre, founded by Sidon, the oldest son of Canaan (Gen. 10:15). Noted for its shipbuilding (Ezek. 27:8), silverware, and dyed fabrics, Sidon was often rebuked by the prophets for its idolatry (Isa. 23:4; Ezek. 28:21). Jesus ministered in this city (Matt. 15:21, 28). *Zidon:* Josh. 11:8.

SIEGE. An extended military assault and blockade against a walled city. King Sennacherib of Assyria besieged Jerusalem and other fortified cities of Judah (Isa. 36:1). See also *City; Fenced City*.

SIEVE. Cooking utensil for sifting flour or meal. Early sieves were made of bulrushes, horsehair, or papyrus (Amos 9:9).

SIGN. An event foretelling future happenings or a miracle confirming a person's faith (John 4:48). Jesus warned the wicked to heed the sign of Jonah's deliverance from the whale (Matt. 16:1–4). Jesus foretold signs of His return

(Matt. 24:3, 29–31). See also *Miracle; Token.*

SIGNET. An official or royal seal, used like a signature to legalize documents (Jer. 22:24).

SIHON. An Amorite king who refused to allow the Israelites to pass through his territory on their way to Canaan, only to be defeated by Moses (Num. 21:21–30).

SILAS/SILVANUS. A leader in the Jerusalem church who accompanied Paul on the second missionary journey and who was imprisoned with him at Philippi (Acts 15:40–41; 16:19, 23). He was also with Paul at Corinth and Thessalonica (2 Cor. 1:19). *Silvanus:* 2 Thess. 1:1.

SILK. A cloth derived from the silkworm (Rev. 18:12).

SILOAM/SHILOAH/SILOAH. A reservoir in Jerusalem supplied with water through King Hezekiah's underground tunnel from a spring outside the city (2 Kings 20:20). Jesus commanded a blind man to wash in the Pool of Siloam for healing (John 9:6–7). *Shiloah:* Isa. 8:6; *Siloah:* Neh. 3:15. See also *Hezekiah; Pool.*

SILVER. A precious metal used in utensils and jewelry (Gen. 44:2). First mentioned in the days of Abraham (Gen. 13:2), silver was used as a medium of exchange and was valued by weight (Ezek. 27:12).

SILVERLINGS (SILVER SHEKELS, SHEKELS OF SILVER). Bits of silver used like money as a medium of exchange (Isa. 7:23). *Silver shekels:* NIV; *Shekels of silver:* NRSV.

SILVERSMITH. A craftsman who formed silver into valuable objects. The Ephesian silversmiths made models of the temple of Diana (Acts 19:24–29). See also *Finer.*

SIMEON.

1. A son of Jacob by Leah (Gen. 29:33) and ancestor of one of the twelve tribes of Israel (Gen. 46:10). He was held hostage by Joseph to assure Benjamin's safe arrival in Egypt (Gen. 42:24, 36). See also *Tribes of Israel.*

2. A righteous man who blessed the child Jesus in the temple at Jerusalem (Luke 2:25–35).

3. A Christian prophet at Antioch associated with Paul and Barnabas (Acts 13:1). He was also called *Niger.*

SIMON.

1. Simon Peter, one of the twelve apostles or disciples of Christ and the leader of the church in Jerusalem after the resurrection and ascension of Jesus. A fisherman from Galilee, Peter followed Jesus after he was encouraged to do so by his brother Andrew (John 1:40–41). He was called *Cephas* by Jesus, a name meaning "stone" (John 1:42), perhaps indicating the promise which Jesus saw in him in spite of his reckless temperament and impetuous personality. Peter swore he would never forsake Christ, but he denied Him three times on the night before His crucifixion (Matt. 26:69–75). He went on to become a bold spokesman for Christ in the early years of the Christian movement (Acts 2:14–40). Peter's surname was *Bar-jona* (Matt. 16:17). *Son of Jonah:* NIV, NRSV. See also *Twelve, The*.

2. Another of the twelve apostles or disciples of Jesus, called Simon Zelotes (Luke 6:15) or Simon the Canaanite (Matt. 10:4) to distinguish him from Simon Peter. He may have been a zealot, a Jew fanatically opposed to Roman rule. See also *Canaanites,* No. 2; *Twelve, The; Zelotes*.

3. A magician or sorcerer condemned by the apostle Peter because he tried to buy the power of the Holy Spirit (Acts 8:18–21).

4. A tanner at Joppa and apparently a friend with whom the apostle Peter lodged (Acts 9:43; 10:6, 17, 32).

SIN. Rebellion against God. Adam and Eve's disobedience in the Garden of Eden resulted in the introduction of sin into the human race (Rom. 5:12–14). Sin is committed against three parties: ourselves (Prov. 8:36), others (Rom. 5:12), and God (Ps. 51:4; 1 Cor. 8:12). Sin is described as transgression (Matt. 15:3), perversion of the right (1 John 5:17), disobedience (Rom. 5:19), rebellion (Isa. 1:2), and lawlessness (1 John 3:4). The consequence of unforgiven sin is spiritual death, but God's gift to the believer is eternal life through Jesus Christ (Rom. 6:23). See also *Evil; Iniquity*.

SIN OFFERING. An offering of a sacrificial animal presented to God to gain forgiveness for sins, particularly those committed unintentionally or in ignorance (Lev. 4:2–3). A sin offering for all the people was made once a year by the high priest on the Day of Atonement (Lev. 16:6, 15). See also *Atonement, Day of; Sacrifice*.

SIN, WILDERNESS OF. A wilderness region between the Red Sea and Sinai where manna and quail were miraculously provided for the Israelites by the Lord (Exod. 16:1–8).

SINAI/SINA/HOREB. Mountain peak more than one mile high in the wilderness of Sinai where Moses tended sheep and saw the burning bush with God's call to deliver His people (Exod. 3:1–6). *Horeb:* KJV, NIV, NRSV. Later it was the site where Moses received the Ten Commandments and other parts of the law from God (Exod. 19–23). *Sina:* Greek form (Acts 7:30).

SINEW. A muscle along the thigh by which muscles are attached to bones (Job 10:11). Because of Jacob's thigh injury, Israelites avoided eating the sinew of the thigh (Gen. 32:25–32). See also *Thigh*.

SINIM (ASWAN, SYENE). An unidentified country or region—perhaps China, Egypt, or the wilderness of Sin—from which Jewish exiles would return (Isa. 49:12). *Aswan:* NIV; *Syene:* NRSV.

SINITES. Members of a tribe descended from Canaan who settled in northern Phoenicia (Gen. 10:17; 1 Chron. 1:15). They were perhaps inhabitants of Sin, a city near Mt. Lebanon.

SION. See *Zion*.

SIPHMOTH. A place in southern Judah where David hid from King Saul during his days as a fugitive (1 Sam. 30:26–28).

SIRION. See *Hermon, Mount*.

SISERA. A Canaanite commander killed by Jael, who drove a tent peg through his head while he slept (Judg. 4:2–22). See also *Deborah; Jael*.

SISTER. A general term for any near female relative, including a stepsister or half sister (2 Sam. 13:2; Matt. 13:56). The word is also used to denote members of the same spiritual family (Rom. 16:1).

SITNAH. The second well dug by Isaac near the Philistine city of Gerar after a dispute with herdsmen over water rights (Gen. 26:21).

SIVAN. The third month of the Hebrew year (Esther 8:9), corresponding closely to our June.

SKULL, THE. See *Calvary*.

SLANDER. A deceitful and destructive statement against another (Ps. 52:2). Such statements are uttered by the wicked against the righteous (Job 1:9–11) and believers (1 Pet. 2:12).

SLANDERER. See *Reviler*.

SLAVE. A person who had been bought as a piece of property and pressed into service by his or her owners. Slavery was common in Bible times, but Christian teachings brought some moderation of the practice (Eph. 6:5–9). Paul appealed to Philemon to receive his runaway slave Onesimus as a brother in the faith (Philem. 15–18).

SLAVEMASTERS. See *Taskmasters*.

SLAYER. See *Manslayer*.

SLIME (TAR, BITUMEN). A tarlike substance, possibly bitumen or mortar, used in building the tower of Babel (Gen. 11:3). It was used as mortar for bricks and waterproofing (Exod. 2:3). *Tar:* NIV; *Bitumen:* NRSV. See also *Pitch*.

SLING. Weapon made of leather thongs and used to throw stones (Judg. 20:16). David killed Goliath with a sling (1 Sam. 17:50).

SLUG. See *Snail*.

SLUGGARD. A lazy, inactive person. This habitual idleness will lead to poverty (Prov. 13:4; 20:4). Paul declared that those who won't work shouldn't eat (2 Thess. 3:10). See also *Idleness*.

SMITH. A metal worker who fabricate tools, weapons, and ornamental objects. Tubal-cain is the first smith mentioned in the Bible (Gen. 4:22). See also *Finer*.

SMYRNA. A city of Ionia about sixty miles north of Ephesus where one of the seven churches of Asia Minor was located (Rev. 1:11). The Lord encouraged this church, which was being persecuted by the "synagogue of Satan" (Rev. 2:8–11).

SNAIL (SLUG). A creature with a spiral shell which leaves a trail of slime. The psalmist expressed hope that his enemies would "melt away" even as a snail shrinks after depositing its slime (Ps. 58:7–8). *Slug:* NIV.

SNARE (NOOSE). A trap or net for catching animals. The word is used figuratively for the pitfalls of the wicked (Job 18:10) *Noose:* NIV. It also represents calamity or death (2 Sam. 22:6).

SNOW. Frozen precipitation. One snowfall is recorded in the Bible (2 Sam. 23:20). The word is used figuratively of winter (Prov. 31:21) and moral purity (Matt. 28:3).

SNUFFER, SNUFFDISH. Two separate tools for ceremonial use, one for trimming the wicks of lamps in the tabernacle and the other for carrying away the trimmings (Exod. 25:38). See also *Tongs*.

SO. See *Pharaoh,* No. 2.

SOAP. See *Sope*.

SOBER (SENSIBLE, TEMPERATE, SELF-CONTROLLED). Moderation or seriousness, a quality desired in church leaders (1 Tim. 3:2). *Sensible:* NRSV (1 Tim. 3:11). *Temperate:* NIV, NRSV. This is an appropriate attitude for believers as we await the Lord's return (1 Thess. 5: 5–6). *Self-controlled:* NIV.

SODA. See *Nitre*.

SODOM/SODOMA. One of five cities destroyed by God because of its wickedness (Gen. 19:1–28). It is often mentioned in the Bible as a symbol of evil and as a warning to sinners (Isa. 1:9; Rev. 11:8). *Sodoma:* Greek form (Rom. 9:29). See also *Cities of the Plain; Gomorrah*.

SODOMITE (TEMPLE PROSTITUTE). A man who engaged in sexual activities with other men—a perversion condemned by God (Deut. 23:17–18). *Temple prostitute:* NRSV.

SOJOURNER. A person who lived temporarily in a foreign country (Heb. 11:9). Abraham sojourned in Egypt (Gen. 12:10) as did the Jews in captivity and exile (Ezra 1:4). The word is also used symbolically of Christians in the world (1 Pet. 1:17). See also *Alien; Foreigner*.

SOLDIER. A person engaged in military service (Num. 1:3). The concept is also used figuratively of Christian workers (Eph. 6:11–18).

SOLEMN ASSEMBLY. A religious gathering, usually occurring during a major Jewish festival, which was devoted to repentance, confession, and prayer (Lev. 23:36; Deut. 16:8).

SOLOMON. David's son and successor as king of Israel (reigned about 970–930 B.C.). Solomon got off to a good start by praying for divine wisdom and insight (1 Kings 3), and he developed fame as a wise and efficient king of great wealth (1 Kings 4:1–28). At God's command, he completed the building of the temple in Jerusalem (1 Kings 5–8). But he drifted away from commitment to the one true God through his marriages with pagan wives (1 Kings 11:1–8). He also oppressed his people with burdensome taxes to support his ambitious kingdom-building projects (1 Kings 12:4). After Solomon's death, the ten northern tribes rebelled under Jeroboam and formed their own nation known as Israel, or the Northern Kingdom (1 Kings 12:1–19).

SOLOMON, POOLS OF. Water reservoirs built by King Solomon near Bethlehem to supply water for Jerusalem through a system of underground passages (Eccles. 2:6).

SOLOMON'S PORCH (SOLOMON'S COLONNADE, SOLOMON'S PORTICO). A porch on the eastern side of the temple in Jerusalem which featured a double row of elaborate columns about forty feet high (Acts 3:11). *Solomon's Colonnade:* NIV; *Solomon's Portico:* NRSV. Jesus entered the temple by Solomon's porch (John 10:23).

SOLOMON'S SERVANTS. Canaanites enslaved by Solomon and forced to work on the temple and other building projects (1 Kings 5:17–18).

SON. A male descendant. The birth of a son brought joy and celebration, since a family's heritage and traditions were passed on through its sons (Gen. 21:2).

SON OF GOD. A title of Christ which emphasizes His deity. An angel revealed to Mary that she would give birth to the "Son of God" (Luke 1:35). After Jesus was baptized, a voice from heaven declared, "This is my beloved Son" (Matt. 3:17). John's Gospel was written specifically to encourage belief in the Son of God (John 20:31). See also *Emmanuel; Jesus Christ; Messiah.*

SON OF MAN. A title of Christ, used often by Jesus Himself, which emphasized His humanity and Messiahship. This title was probably inspired by Daniel's prophecy of God's messenger who would come on a mission of redemption (Dan. 7:13–14). See also *Messiah.*

SONG OF SOLOMON. A short book of the O.T. filled with expressions of affection between two lovers (see 1:13; 4:1–11; 7:2–10). These words have been interpreted both symbolically and literally. Some insist the song symbolizes God's love for His people Israel, while others believe the book is a healthy affirmation of the joys of physical love between husband and wife. Most scholars believe Solomon wrote the book, since he is mentioned several times in the poems (1:1, 5; 3:7, 9, 11; 8:11–12). See also *Solomon.*

SOOTHSAYER (DIVINER). A fortune-teller who claimed to have the power to foretell future events (Josh. 13:22), reveal secrets (Dan. 2:27) and interpret dreams (Dan. 4:7). *Diviner:* NIV, NRSV. Paul and Silas healed a soothsayer in Philippi who was being exploited. See also *Enchanter; Medium.*

SOP. A small portion of food or bread, held in the hand in accordance with Palestinian dining customs, and used to soak up liquid foods, such as soup (John 13:26–30).

SOPATER. A Christian who accompanied Paul on the third missionary journey (Acts 20:4). This may be the same person as Sosipater (Rom. 16:21). See *Sosipater.*

SOPE (SOAP). An alkaline substance used for bathing and for purifying metals. Jeremiah indicated sope would clean externally but could not remove sin or iniquity (Jer. 2:22). *Soap:* NIV, NRSV.

SORCERY (MAGIC). The exercise of power received from evil or departed spirits to gain hidden knowledge (Exod. 7:11; Acts 8:9–24). *Magic:* NRSV. The practice of sorcery and witchcraft was specifically prohibited by God (Lev. 19:31). See also *Magic; Witchcraft.*

SOREK. A valley between Jerusalem and Ashdod; the home of Delilah, who betrayed Samson (Judg. 16:4).

SORROW. Grief or sadness, which may be caused by sin (Gen. 3:16–17), the death of a loved one (John 11:33–35), or persecution (Esther 9:22). The Christian's eternal hope is a source of comfort in times of sorrow (1 Thess. 4:13, 18). See also *Mourn.*

SOSIPATER. A kinsman of Paul whose greetings were sent to the church at Rome (Rom. 16:21). This may be the same person as Sopater (Acts 20:4). See *Sopater*.

SOSTHENES. A ruler of the synagogue at Corinth who was beaten by a mob when Paul was arrested for preaching there (Acts 18:17). This may be the same person as the believer greeted by Paul in 1 Cor. 1:1.

SOUL. The part of man's inner nature which is the seat of our appetites, passions, and sensations. Sometimes the word *soul* means "person" (Rom. 13:1). See also *Spirit*.

SOUR WINE. See *Vinegar*.

SOUTH COUNTRY (NEGEV, NEGEB). A hilly, wilderness region in southern Palestine around the Dead Sea. This region is also called "the South" and "the land of the South" (Judg. 1:16). *Negev:* NIV; *Negeb:* NRSV.

SOUTH RAMOTH. A place bordering the desert in southern Judah where David hid when fleeing from King Saul (1 Sam. 30:26–27).

SOVEREIGN. See *Potentate*.

SOVEREIGNTY OF GOD. A theological phrase which expresses the truth that God is in control of the universe. God's creation of man and the world implies His continuing rule and sovereignty (Gen. 1:1; Ps. 8:1–5). His supreme authority is also expressed by His title, "Almighty" (Rev. 1:8). In His holy character, the Sovereign must punish sin, but He has graciously provided salvation for all who trust Christ (Rom. 9:22–24). See also *Almighty; Omnipotence*.

SOWER. One who plants seeds, as in Jesus' parable of the sower (Matt. 13:3–23). Sowing was done mostly by hand.

SPAIN. A country in southwestern Europe which Paul expressed a desire to visit (Rom. 15:24, 28). It was known to ancient Greeks as Iberia and to Romans as Hispania. Jonah's ship was headed for Tarshish, Spain, when he was thrown overboard by the superstitious sailors (Jon. 1:3, 15).

SPAN. A measure of length equal to about nine inches (Exod. 28:16). The word was also used to indicate a small amount of space or time (1 Sam. 17:4; Isa. 40:12).

SPARROW. A small bird, common in Palestine, which was sold as food for the poor (Matt. 10:29, 31).

SPEAR. A weapon of war (2 Sam. 2:23), consisting of a metal point on the end of a long shaft (1 Sam. 13:22). It was similar to but bigger than a dart or javelin. See also *Dart; Javelin.*

SPEARMEN. Soldiers with light arms, such as spears (Acts 23:23).

SPECK. See *Mote.*

SPECKLED BIRD (BIRD OF PREY). A phrase of uncertain meaning. Jeremiah compared the nation of Israel to a speckled bird (Jer. 12:9). *Bird of prey:* NRSV.

SPELT. See *Fitch; Rie.*

SPICE. An aromatic vegetable compound used in perfumes and ointments (Exod. 30:23–36) and also used to prepare bodies for burial (Mark 16:1).

SPIDER. An insect whose frail web provided a lesson on the fleeting schemes of the wicked (Job 8:14; Isa. 59:5).

SPIES. The twelve scouts, one from each of the twelve tribes of Israel, sent to investigate Canaan and report on their findings (Num.13:1–3, 30–33).

SPIKENARD (NARD). An expensive and highly prized perfume or ointment (Song of Sol. 4:13–14) which was used to anoint Jesus' hands and feet (John 12:3). *Nard:* NIV, NRSV.

SPINNING. The process of making yarn into cloth by hand on a rotating loom or wheel (Prov. 31:19). See also *Warp; Weaver.*

SPIRIT. A word which denotes man's reason, conscience, and nobler affections (2 Cor. 7:1; Eph. 4:23)—in contrast to the soul—our appetites, passions, and sensations. The root meaning of the word is "wind" (John 3:8). See also *Ghost; Soul.*

SPIRITIST. See *Wizard.*

SPIRITS IN PRISON. A much-debated phrase from 1 Pet. 3:18–20 which seems to indicate that Christ, in His spiritual existence, preached to the "spirits in prison" who disobeyed God during the days of Noah. Some scholars claim that Christ did not descend into hell but that His eternal spirit (which later was made alive in His resurrection) preached to the spirits at the time of their disobedience.

SPIRITUAL GIFTS. Gifts bestowed freely by the Holy Spirit upon believers (Jas. 1:17) for the edification of fellow believers and the church (Rom. 1:11; 1 Cor. 12:28). Gifts listed in Romans are preaching, serving, teaching, encouraging, giving, leading, and helping others (Rom. 12:6–8). Gifts listed in 1 Corinthians are wisdom, knowledge, faith, healing, miracles, prophecy, discernment of spirits, tongues, and interpretation of tongues (1 Cor. 12:8–11). Love is the supreme spiritual gift (1 Cor. 12:31; 13:13).

SPIT. To spit was a gesture of extreme contempt (Num. 12:14), but Jesus used saliva to cure a man's blindness (Mark 8:23).

SPOIL (PLUNDER, BOOTY). Plunder taken in war or seized by bandits (Num. 31:9). *Plunder:* NIV; *Booty:* NRSV. David established strict regulations for division of the spoils of war among his soldiers (1 Sam. 30:20–25). See also *Booty*.

SPOON (PITCHER, FLAGON). A shallow dish or pan used as a censer for burning incense in the tabernacle and temple (Exod. 25:29). *Pitcher:* NIV; *Flagon:* NRSV. See also *Pitcher; Flagon*, No. 2.

STABLE. A shelter for animals. Ezekiel denounced the Ammonites by prophesying the city of Rabbah would become a stable for livestock (Ezek. 25:2, 5).

STACHYS. A fellow believer at Rome greeted and commended by Paul (Rom. 16:9).

STACTE (GUM RESIN). An ingredient used in the sacred incense burned in temple ceremonies, possibly a gum or spice from the styrax tree (Exod. 30:34). *Gum resin:* NIV.

STAFF. A long stick or rod used to goad animals, to remove fruit from trees (Isa. 28:27), and as support or defense for the old and infirm (Exod. 21:19).

STALL. A stable and storage area. King Solomon had at least 4,000 stalls "for horses and chariots" (2 Chron. 9:25).

STANDARD (ENSIGN). Banner, flag, or streamer to identify groups of troops or warriors. In the wilderness, each tribe of Israel marched under its own unique banner

(Num. 2:2, 34). *Ensign:* NRSV. See also *Ensign*.

STANDARD BEARER. A person who carried the flag or standard of his army or his people, a highly regarded position (Isa. 10:18).

STAR. A luminous body visible in the sky at night. The Hebrews regarded all heavenly bodies as stars, except the sun and moon (Gen. 1:16). The stars were considered a noble mark of God's creative power (Ps. 19:1). Stars were used symbolically for rulers, princes, angels, and ministers (Job 38:7; Dan. 8:10; Rev. 1:16–20). Christ was called "the bright and morning star" (Rev. 22:16).

STARGAZERS. Astrologers; persons who predicted the future by the movement of the stars. The Babylonians were noted for their reliance on astrology (Isa. 47:1, 13). See also *Astrologer; Wise Men*.

STATUTE (DECREE). A law, commandment, or official pronouncement which regulates behavior and conduct (Exod. 18:16). *Decree:* NIV. See also *Commandment; Decree*.

STEADFASTNESS. Persistence and patience in one's faith and activities (Heb. 3:6, 14). Believers are encouraged to endure chastening (Heb. 12:7) and persecution (Rom. 8:35–37). See also *Patience; Perseverance*.

STEEL. KJV word for copper or brass (Jer. 15:12). See also *Brass*.

STEP. See *Pace*.

STEPHANAS. A Christian from the city of Corinth who visited Paul (1 Cor. 1:16).

STEPHEN. A zealous believer who became the first martyr of the Christian cause. A Jewish believer of Greek background, Stephen was among the seven "deacons" selected by the early church to provide relief for other Greek-speaking Christians (Acts 6:5–8). His criticism of O.T. laws and traditions brought him into conflict with Jewish leaders, and he was stoned to death on a charge of blasphemy (Acts 7:55–58).

STEW. See *Pottage*.

STEWARD. A person employed as a custodian, manager, or administrator, usually of a large household (Gen.

43:19). Christians are urged to be faithful stewards of God's gifts (1 Cor. 4:1–2). See also *Treasurer*.

STEWARDSHIP. Wise and responsible use of one's God-given resources. Christian stewardship is based on God's ownership of all things (Gen. 1:1; Ps. 24:1–2) and man's assigned dominion of God's creation (Gen. 1:26; 2:15). Good stewardship involves faithfulness in use of one's time (Eph. 5:16), talents (2 Tim. 1:6; 2:15), and money (Mal. 3:10). See also *Tithe*.

STIFFNECKED. See *Neck*.

STOCKS (SHACKLES). A wooden frame for public punishment of offenders, containing holes for confining hands, feet, and sometimes the neck (Job 33:11). *Shackles:* NIV (Jer. 20:2–3). See also *Fetters*.

STOICKS (STOICS). A group of philosophers encountered by Paul in his visit to Athens (Acts 17:18). *Stoics:* NIV, NRSV. Highly independent moralists, the Stoics were fatalistic in their outlook on life. See also *Epicureans*.

STOMACH. See *Maw*.

STOMACHER (RICH ROBE). An expensive, festive robe worn by women (Isa. 3:24). *Rich robe:* NRSV.

STONE. See *Rock*.

STONECUTTER. See *Hewer*.

STONING. The Jewish mode of capital punishment, specified in the law for these offenses: Sacrificing children to idols (Lev. 20:2–5), breaking the Sabbath (Num. 15:32–36), idolatry (Deut. 17:2–7), rebellion of children against parents (Deut. 21:18–21), and adultery (Deut. 22:23–24). Godly men who were stoned for their faith included the prophets (Heb. 11:37), Stephen (Acts 7:59), and Paul, who was presumed dead (Acts 14:19–20).

STORE CITY (STORAGE TOWN). A city or a supply depot in a city for the storage of food, equipment, and weapons of war (2 Chron. 8:4). *Storage town:* NRSV. See also *Treasure City*.

STOREHOUSE. A building for storing food. Joseph built grain storehouses in Egypt to get ready for the years of famine (Gen. 41:48–49).

STORK. A long-necked migratory bird similar to the crane (Ps. 104:17); an unclean animal to the Jews (Lev. 11:19).

STORM. See *Tempest; Whirlwind.*

STRANGER. See *Foreigner.*

STRAW. A food for livestock. Also used as a strengthening and binding ingredient in bricks (Exod. 5:7, 16).

STREET. A traffic lane in a city. Streets were mostly crude, crooked, and narrow, much like a dirty alley (Jer. 37:21). The street in Damascus called Straight was exceptionally wide (Acts 9:11).

STRIFE. Bitter conflict caused by self-seeking (Luke 22:24) or a worldly spirit (1 Cor. 3:3). Strife may be avoided by unselfishness and a brotherly spirit (Gen. 13:7–8; Phil. 2:3). See also *Contention.*

STRONG DRINK. See *Wine.*

STRONGHOLD. See *Misgab; Tower.*

STRUTTING ROOSTER. See *Greyhound.*

STUBBLE. The short stumps of grain stalks left in the ground after harvesting (Exod. 5:12). Regarded as worthless, stubble symbolized instability and impermanence (Isa. 33:11).

STUMBLINGBLOCK. A hindrance to belief or understanding. Israel's iniquity and idolatry were a stumblingblock (Jer. 18:15). Paul urged Christians not to offend or serve as a hindrance to a weak brother (Rom. 14:13). The preaching of "Christ crucified" was a stumblingblock to the Jews (1 Cor. 1:23).

SUBURBS (PASTURE LANDS). The open country around a city used for grazing livestock or other purposes (Josh. 21:11). *Pasture lands:* NIV, NRSV.

SUCCOTH. The Hebrews' first camping site in the wilderness after leaving Rameses in Egypt (Exod. 12:37).

SUCCOTH-BENOTH. An idol set up in Samaria by the pagan peoples who colonized the area after Israel fell to the Assyrians (2 Kings 17:29–30).

SUCKLING. An infant or young animal not yet weaned from its mother's milk. As judge, Samuel offered a suckling lamb as a burnt offering to the Lord (1 Sam. 7:9).

SUFFERING. Pain or distress. Suffering for Jesus' sake may be regarded as fellowship with Christ (Phil. 3:10) and as a stewardship (Phil. 1:29). See also *Affliction; Anguish.*

SUICIDE. To take one's own life. Suicide may be brought on by hopelessness (Judg. 16: 28–30), sin (1 Kings 16:18–19), disappointment (2 Sam. 17:23), and betrayal (Matt. 27:3–5). This act violates the principles of life's sacredness (Gen. 9:5–6; 1 Cor. 6:19) and God's sovereign rule (Rom. 9:20–21).

SUKKIIM (SUKKITES). An African or Ethiopian tribe allied with Pharaoh Shishak of Egypt when he invaded Judah (2 Chron. 12:3). *Sukkites:* NIV.

SULFUR. See *Brimstone.*

SUMER. The southern division of ancient Babylonia (now southern Iraq), consisting largely of the fertile plain between the Tigris and Euphrates rivers. In the O.T., it was called Shinar (Gen. 10:10) or Chaldea (Jer. 50:10). See also *Babylonia.*

SUN. The luminous solar body that provides light and heat to Earth. Some of the ancient civilizations surrounding Israel worshiped the sun, and even the Israelites burned incense to the sun on occasion (2 Kings 23:5). God is spoken of figuratively as a sun and shield (Ps. 84:11).

SUPERSCRIPTION (INSCRIPTION). Words engraved on coins or other surfaces. The superscription "King of the Jews" was placed above Jesus on the cross (Mark 15: 26). *Inscription:* NRSV.

SUPERSTITION. Ideas or impressions based on ignorance or fear. Many superstitions grow out of ignorance of the one true God (Rom. 1:25, 32).

SUPPER. The main daily meal of ancient times, usually the evening meal (Luke 14:16) as observed by Jews, Greeks, and Romans. In the N.T. the word is used of the Passover (John 13:1–2) and the Lord's Supper (1 Cor. 11:20).

SUPPLICATION (PETITION). An earnest prayer or request. Paul urged supplication with thanksgiving as an antidote to anxiety (Phil. 4:6). *Petition:* NIV. See also *Petition.*

SUPPLY CITY. See *Store City; Treasure City.*

SUPREME COMMANDER. See *Tartan.*

SUR. A gate of Solomon's temple in Jerusalem (2 Kings 11:6), also called "gate of the foundation" (2 Chron. 23:5).

SURETY (GUARANTEE). One who guarantees payment of another person's debt or obligation. Jesus' perfect priesthood was a surety or guarantee of a better covenant (Heb. 7:22). *Guarantee:* NIV, NRSV.

SURVIVORS. See *Remnant.*

SUSA. See *Shushan.*

SUSANNA. A female follower of Jesus who apparently provided food and lodging for Him and perhaps His disciples (Luke 8:2–3).

SWADDLING CLOTHES, SWADDLINGBANDS. Square cloth like a quilt or a blanket which was wrapped around a newborn baby (Luke 2:7–12). This cloth was held in place by swaddlingbands—narrow strips of cloth (Job 38:9).

SWALLOW. Swift bird which nests in buildings and makes a mournful sound (Ps. 84:3; Prov. 26:2).

SWAN (WHITE OWL, WATER HEN). An unclean water bird, perhaps the ibis or water hen (Lev. 11:18). *White owl:* NIV; *Water hen:* NRSV.

SWEARING. See *Oath.*

SWINE (PIGS). Pigs or hogs. The flesh of swine was forbidden as food (Lev. 11:7). *Pigs:* NIV, NRSV. Swine were regarded as offensive to the Lord (Isa. 65:2–4).

SWORD. A sharp blade carried by soldiers as a weapon of war. Simeon and Levi used swords in the massacre at Shechem (Gen. 34:25).

SYCAMINE (MULBERRY). A tree or shrub which bore a fruit similar to blackberries (Luke 17:6). *Mulberry:* NIV, NRSV. See also *Mulberry.*

SYCHAR. A city of Samaria where Jesus talked to the woman at Jacob's well (John 4:5–40).

SYCHEM. See *Shechem,* No. 2.

Excavated ruins of a synagogue at Capernaum, a city associated with Jesus' ministry in Galilee.

Courtesy Israel Ministry of Tourism

SYCOMORE (SYCAMORE). A fig-bearing tree valued for its fruit and soft, durable wood (Luke 19:4). *Sycamore:* NIV, NRSV.

SYENE. See *Sinim*.

SYMBOL. A word, action, or object which stands for truths or spiritual realities. Circumcision was a symbol of God's covenant with Israel (Rom. 4:11). The rainbow signified God's promise not to destroy the world by water again (Gen. 9:12–13). The tearing of the temple curtain at Christ's death represented the believer's direct access to God through Jesus (Matt. 27:50–51).

SYNAGOGUE. A house of worship for the Jews which developed during their period of exile in Babylonia and Persia. Synagogues shifted the emphasis of the Jews from animal sacrifices to worship and teaching of the law. Paul regularly proclaimed the message of Christ in Jewish synagogues on his missionary journeys outside Palestine (Acts 18:4).

SYNOPTIC GOSPELS. A phrase used for the Gospels of Matthew, Mark, and Luke, to set them apart from the Gospel of John. The synoptic Gospels are similar in their straightforward and factual treatment of the life of Jesus, while John gives the theological meaning of these facts and events.

SYNTYCHE. A female believer in the church at Philippi whom Paul exhorted, along with Euodias, to make peace with each other (Phil. 4:2).

SYRACUSE. A prosperous city on the eastern coast of Sicily visited by Paul (Acts 28:12).

SYRIA/ARAM. A nation north east of Israel which was a persistent enemy of the Jews across several centuries (1 Kings 15: 18–20), particularly from David's administration until Syria fell to the Assyrians about 700 B.C. This nation was allied with Babylonia and Assyria at one point in its history; thus its name *Syria*. When Jesus was born, Syria was a province under Roman control (Luke 2: 2). This nation was also known as *Aram* (Num. 23:7). See also *Damascus*.

SYRIA-DAMASCUS. See *Damascus*.

SYRO-PHOENICIAN. An inhabitant of Phoenicia during the time when Phoenicia was part of the Roman province of Syria. Jesus ministered in this area (Mark 7:25–31).

SYRTIS. See *Quicksands*.

-T-

TAANACH/TANACH. A Canaanite city west of the Jordan River conquered by Joshua and assigned to the Levites (Josh. 12:21). *Tanach:* Josh. 21:25.

TABERAH. A camping site in the wilderness where many Israelites were killed by fire because of their complaining (Num. 11:1–3).

TABERNACLE/TENT OF MEETING. A tent or portable sanctuary built in the wilderness at God's command as a place of worship for the Israelites (Exod. 40:2–8). It was also called the *Tent of Meeting* because it was considered a place of encounter between God and His people. The tabernacle foreshadowed Christ's incarnation when "the Word was made flesh and dwelt among us" (John 1:14). See also *Holy Place; Holy of Holies*.

Mount Tabor on the plains of Jezreel near Nazareth in Galilee.
Courtesy Israel Ministry of Tourism

TABERNACLES, FEAST OF/ FEAST OF BOOTHS. A festival, also known as the Feast of Booths and the Feast of Ingathering (Exod. 23:16; Num. 29:12), observed annually during the harvest season to commemorate Israel's wilderness wandering experience. The people lived in tents or booths in remembrance of their days as tent dwellers while waiting to enter Canaan (Lev. 23:39–43).

TABITHA/DORCAS. A Christian widow at Joppa whom Peter restored to life (Acts 9:36–40). Her Greek name was *Dorcas*.

TABLET. A flat piece of stone on which the Ten Commandments were engraved by the finger of God (Exod. 24:12).

TABOR, MOUNT. A mountain on the border of the territories of Zebulun and Issachar about six miles from Nazareth in Galilee. From this mountain the judge Deborah sent Barak to defeat Sisera and the Canaanites (Judg. 4:6–14).

TABRET (TAMBOURINE). A musical instrument which was probably similar to the tambourine (Gen. 31:27). *Tambourine:* NIV, NRSV.

TADMOR (TAMAR). A trading center between the city of Damascus in Syria and the Euphrates River which was rebuilt by King Solomon about 1000 B.C. (1 Kings 9:17–18). *Tamar:* NRSV.

TAHPANHES/TAHAPANES/TEHAPHNEHES. An Egyptian city on the Nile River to which citizens of Judah fled after the fall of Jerusalem to the Babylonians (Jer. 43:7–10). *Tahapanes:* Jer. 2:16; *Tehaphnehes:* Ezek. 30:18.

TAHPENES. Queen of Egyptian pharaoh in King Solomon's time (1 Kings 11:18–22).

TALEBEARER (GOSSIP). A person who gossips about or slanders another with destructive words (Prov. 18:8). *Gossip:* NIV. See also *Busybody; Gossip*.

TALENT. A common unit of weight or measure of monetary value used by the Hebrews, Greeks, and Romans (Matt. 25:14–30).

TAMAR.

1. The widow of Er and Onan, sons of Judah, who eventually bore Judah's twin sons, Perez and Zerah (Gen. 38:6–30). *Thamar:* Jesus' ancestry (Matt. 1:3).

2. Absalom's sister who was sexually assaulted by her half brother Amnon. Absalom avenged the crime by killing Amnon (2 Sam. 13:1–32).

3. NRSV word for Tadmor (1 Kings 9:17–18). See *Tadmor*.

TAMARISK. A small tree or shrub. King Saul and his sons were buried under a tamarisk (1 Sam. 22:6).

TAMBOURINE. See *Tabret; Timbrel*.

TANNER. A person who cured animal skins. This probably was not a reputable vocation among the Jews because of the problem of defilement by touching unclean animals. Peter lodged with a tanner at Joppa (Acts 10:5–6). See also *Leather*.

TAPESTRY. An expensive curtain or cloth embroidered with artwork and owned generally by the wealthy (Prov. 7:16; 31:22).

TAR. See *Slime*.

TARE. A weed, now known as the darnel plant, which resembles wheat. In Jesus' parable, tares represent wicked seed sown by Satan that will ultimately be separated and destroyed (Matt. 13:25–40).

TARPELITES. A tribe which colonized Samaria after the citizens of the Northern Kingdom were carried to Assyria as captives about 722 B.C. (Ezra 4:9). See also *Samaritan*.

TARSHISH/THARSHISH. A coastal city, probably in Spain, which was the destination of the ship boarded by the prophet Jonah (Jon. 1:3). *Tharshish:* 1 Kings 10:22.

TARSUS. Capital city of the Roman province of Silicia and the place where Paul was born (Acts 9:11). Once an important center of learning, Tarsus was on the Cydnus River about ten miles north of the Mediterranean Sea.

TARTAK. A false god worshiped by the Avites, a people who colonized Samaria after the Northern Kingdom fell to the Assyrians (2 Kings 17:31).

TARTAN (SUPREME COMMANDER). The title of the commander of the Assyrian army who demanded the surrender of Jerusalem from King Hezekiah (2 Kings 18:17). *Supreme commander:* NIV.

TASKMASTERS (SLAVEMASTERS). Egyptian overseers or supervisors who forced the Hebrew slaves to do hard labor at the command of the pharaoh (Exod. 1:11–14). *Slavemasters:* NIV.

TASSEL. See *Fringe*.

TATNAI (TATTENAI). A Persian official who appealed to King Darius of Persia to stop the Jews from rebuilding the temple in Jerusalem (Ezra 5:3–9). *Tattenai:* NIV, NRSV.

TAU. The twenty-second and last letter of the Hebrew alphabet, used as a heading over Ps. 119:169–176.

TAVERNS, THE THREE. A station on the Roman road known as the Appian Way about thirty miles south of Rome where believers met the apostle Paul (Acts 28:15).

TAX COLLECTOR. See *Publican*.

TAXES. Money, goods, or labor paid by citizens to a government. The Hebrews originally paid taxes known as tithes or firstfruits to support priests and Levites. The tax burden grew heavier under kings, particularly Solomon, and rebellion against his son and successor Rehoboam eventually split the kingdom (1 Kings 12:4, 8). The Romans sold the privilege of collecting taxes to independent contractors, resulting in great extortion (Luke 19:2, 8). See also *Toll*.

TEACHER. A person who communicates knowledge or religious truth to others. Teachers are mentioned along with pastors as persons whose skill and ministry are needed in the church (Eph. 4:11–12). See also *Master*.

TEACHER OF THE LAW. See *Scribe*.

TEAR. See *Rend*.

TEARS. Visible signs of sorrow. Jesus shed tears over the unbelief of Jerusalem (Luke 13:34) and wept at the grave of his friend Lazarus (John 11:35).

TEBETH. The tenth month of the Hebrew year (Esther 2:16).

TEETH. See *Tooth*.

TEHAPHNEHES. See *Tahpanhes*.

TEIL (TEREBINTH). A common tree in Palestine which resembled the elm or oak (Isa. 6:13). *Terebinth:* NIV, NRSV.

TEKOA/TEKOAH. A fortress city of Judah near Bethlehem; home of Amos the prophet (Amos 1:1). *Tekoah:* 2 Sam. 14:4.

TEL, TELL. An Arabic word for "mound," or a hill marking the site of an ancient city which has been built up over centuries of occupation. See also *Archaeology of the Bible*.

TEL-ABIB. A Babylonian city on the Chebar River where Ezekiel lived with the other Jewish captives (Ezek. 3:15).

TEMPERANCE (SELF-CONTROL). Moderation, restraint, or self-discipline—behavior that should characterize believers (2 Pet. 1:6). *Self-control:* NIV, NRSV. See also *Moderation; Sober*.

TEMPEST (STORM). A furious storm. Jesus calmed a tempest on the Sea of Galilee to save His disciples (Matt. 8:24–26). *Storm:* NIV.

TEMPLE. The central place of worship for the Jewish people. Three separate temples were built on the same site in Jerusalem.

The first was Solomon's temple, built about 961–954 B.C. A partition divided the holy place from the holy of holies (1 Kings 6:2; 20, 31). Ten golden candlesticks, the table of shewbread, and the ark of the covenant were housed in this temple.

Zerubbabel's temple was completed in 515 B.C. by Jews who returned to Jerusalem after a period of exile among the Babylonians and Persians. The partition was replaced by a veil or curtain. The ark, which had been destroyed by the Babylonians, was not replaced.

About 10 B.C. Herod the Great began reconstruction of Zerubbabel's temple. The third temple was more ornate and larger than its predecessors, with outer courts added. The infant Jesus was brought to this temple for dedication, and here Jesus taught and drove out the moneychangers (Mark 11: 15; John 2:14–15). This temple was destroyed by the Romans in A.D. 70. A Moslem mosque stands on the site today. See also *Herod,* No. 1; *Zerubbabel*.

TEMPLE PROSTITUTE. See *Sodomite*.

TEMPLE SERVANTS. See *Nethinim*.

TEMPORARY RESIDENT. See *Foreigner*.

TEMPTATION. Testing, or enticement to sin (Matt. 4:1–10). Jesus' temptation experiences provide a guide to help believers resist Satan the tempter (Matt. 4:10; Heb. 2: 18). God promises a means of escape for every temptation (1 Cor. 10:13).

TEN COMMANDMENTS. The ethical commands given by God to Moses on Mt. Sinai. Also called the *Decalogue,* the Ten Commandments summarize the basic moral laws of the O.T. Four of these commandments enjoin duties to God (Exod. 20: 1–11), while six deal with obligations to other people (Exod. 20:12–17). Jesus summed up these commandments in two great principles—supreme love for God and loving our neighbors as ourselves (Matt. 22: 37–40).

TENT. The house or dwelling-place of nomadic peoples (Gen. 12:8). Tents were made of goat hair and supported by poles and ropes tied to stakes. See also *House*.

TENT OF MEETING. See *Tabernacle*.

TENTH DEAL. A dry measure equaling one-tenth of an

ephah (Exod. 29:40). See also *Ephah*.

TENTMAKER. A skilled workman who made tents, a lucrative trade in Bible times. Paul supported himself as a tentmaker. (Acts 18:3).

TERAH/THARA. The father of Abraham and a native of Ur in Chaldea or ancient Babylonia. Through his sons Abraham, Nahor, and Haran, he was an ancestor of the Israelites, Ishmaelites, Midianites, Moabites, and Ammonites (Gen. 11:26–31). *Thara:* Jesus' ancestry (Luke 3:34).

TERAPHIM. Small images representing human figures which were venerated in households as guardians of good fortune (Judg. 17:5). Rachel stole her father's teraphim when Jacob left for Canaan (Gen. 31: 19, 35). See also *Household Idols*.

TEREBINTH. See *Teil*.

TERTIUS. Paul's scribe who took dictation for the epistle to the Romans (Rom. 16:22).

TERTULLUS. A lawyer who accused Paul of desecrating the temple in a hearing before Felix at Caesarea (Acts 24:1–8).

TESTAMENT. A covenant or agreement with legal standing. The Old and New Testaments are covenants ratified first by the blood of sacrificial animals and then by the blood of Christ (Exod. 24:8; Matt. 26:28). See also *Covenant*.

TESTIMONY. A declaration of truth, based on personal experience (Acts 4:20). The testimony of Paul and Barnabas at Iconium was confirmed by their performance of miracles (Acts 14:3). See also *Record; Witness*.

TETH. The ninth letter of the Hebrew alphabet, used as a heading over Ps. 119:65–72.

TETRARCH. The governor or ruler of a Roman province (Luke 3:1). See also *Governor*.

THADDAEUS. See *Judas, Brother of James*.

THAMAR. *See Tamar, No. 1*

THANK OFFERING. A sacrificial animal presented to God as an expression of thanks for an unexpected special blessing (2 Chron. 29:31). See also *Sacrifice*.

THANKSGIVING. The act of expressing one's gratitude. The psalmist praised the Lord for

Excavated ruins of an ancient Roman theater at Beth-shan.
Courtesy Israel Ministry of Tourism

His goodness and blessings (Ps. 116:12–19). Our Christian inheritance of salvation and eternal life should inspire our thanksgiving to God (Col. 1:12). See also *Praise*.

THARA. See *Terah*.

THARSHISH. See *Tarshish*.

THEATER. An outdoor meeting place, similar to a stadium, where dramatic performances and sporting events were held. The theater at Ephesus was an impressive Roman structure made of stone and marble which seated thousands (Acts 19:29–31).

THEBES. See *No*.

THEBEZ. A fortified city near Shechem where Abimelech died when a stone was dropped on his head from a defense tower (Judg. 9:50–55).

THEOCRACY. A government in which God is the ruler. Israel was an imperfect example of this form of rule, beginning with their deliverance from Egypt (Exod. 15:13) and the giving of the law at Mt. Sinai (Exod. 19:5–8), until Samuel agreed to the people's demand for a king (1 Sam. 8:5).

THEOPHANY. Visible appearance of God. Examples are the burning bush (Exod. 3:1–6), the pillar of cloud and fire (Exod. 13:21–22), and the cloud and fire at Mt. Sinai (Exod. 24: 16–18). Some scholars believe theophanies before the incarnation of Jesus were visible manifestations of the pre-incarnate Son of God (John 1:1, 18).

THEOPHILUS. A friend of Luke to whom he addressed his writings—the Gospel of Luke and the Book of Acts (Luke 1:3; Acts 1:1). See also *Luke*.

THESSALONIANS, EPISTLES TO THE. Two N.T. epistles written by the apostle Paul to the believers in the church at Thessalonica. The theme of both letters is the second coming of Christ, although Paul also included instructions on sexual morality (1 Thess. 4:1–8) and the need for diligent labor rather than idle speculation (1 Thess. 4:9–12; 2 Thess. 3:6–15). Paul declared that the believer's assurance in Christ's return should motivate them to righteous living (1 Thess. 3:13; 5:23) but that uncertainty about the exact time of His return should make them watchful and alert (1 Thess. 5:1–11).

THESSALONICA. A city on the Macedonian coast where Paul preached and founded a church. It was also the scene of a riot incited by Jews who opposed the preaching of Paul and Silas (Acts 17:1–9).

THEUDAS. The leader of an unsuccessful revolt mentioned by Gamaliel before the Sanhedrin. Gamaliel probably named this person to discourage premature action that might result in bloodshed (Acts 5:35–36).

THIEF. A robber. Double restitution for theft was required under Mosaic Law. Those who did not conform to this requirement could be sold as slaves (Exod. 22:3–7).

THIGH. The part of the leg between the hip and the knee. Placing the hand under the thigh signified obedience or subjection. Abraham's servant swore by this method that a Canaanite wife would not be chosen for Abraham's son Isaac (Gen. 24:2–9). See also *Sinew*.

THIRTY PIECES OF SILVER. The blood money given to Judas to betray Christ—the usual price for a slave. A remorseful Judas threw his silver on the temple floor and hanged himself (Matt. 27:3–8).

THISTLE. A briar or thorn, which was used for hedges and burned for fuel (Isa. 33:12; Hos. 2:6). The word was also used figuratively of neglect and desolation (Prov. 24:30–31).

THOMAS. One of the twelve apostles or disciples of Jesus, also called *Didymus* or "twin" (Luke 6:15), who refused to believe that Christ was alive until he could actually see and feel the wounds on Christ's resurrected body. Upon touching His hands and side, Thomas cried, "My Lord and my God" (John 20:25–28). See also *Twelve, The*.

THONG. A strip of leather. Paul was bound with thongs at Jerusalem (Acts 22:25–29). See also *Latchet*.

THORN. A plant with heavy briars or thistles. A crown of thorns was placed on Jesus' head in mockery as He hung on the cross (Matt. 27:29).

THORN IN THE FLESH. An unknown affliction from which the apostle Paul prayed to be delivered (2 Cor. 12:7–8). Some scholars believe it was an eye ailment, since he normally dictated his epistles and apologized for his own large handwriting (Gal. 6:11).

THORNBUSH. See *Bramble*.

THRESHINGFLOOR. A place where grain was threshed, or separated from the stalk and husk after harvesting (2 Sam. 6:6). See also *Fan; Winnowing*.

THROAT. The throat was compared to an "open sepulchre" because of the deadly falsehoods which it could utter through the mouth (Ps. 5:9; Rom. 3:13). See also *Lips; Mouth; Tongue*.

THRONE. An ornate chair occupied by kings (1 Kings 2:19), and sometimes priests and judges (1 Sam. 1:9; Jer. 1:15) as a symbol of their power and authority. The word is also used to designate the Lord's supreme authority (Isa. 6:1).

THUMB. The thumb was involved in the ceremony consecrating Aaron and his sons to the priesthood. The blood of rams was smeared on their thumbs as well as their ears and feet (Exod. 29:19–20).

THUMMIN. See *Urim and Thummin*.

THUNDER. Since thunder was rare in Palestine, it was considered a form of speaking by the Lord (Job 40:9) and often regarded as a sign of His displeasure (Exod. 9:23; 1 Sam. 12:7).

THYATIRA. A city in the Roman province of Asia and home of Lydia, a convert under Paul's ministry (Acts 16:14). Noted for its dye industry, Thyatira was also the site of one of the seven churches of Asia Minor addressed by the apostle John. This church was commended for its faith and good works but condemned for its tolerance toward the false prophetess Jezebel and her heretical teachings (Rev. 2:18–24).

THYINE WOOD (CITRON WOOD, SCENTED WOOD). A valuable wood resembling cedar used for fine cabinet work (Rev. 18:12). *Citron wood:* NIV. *Scented wood:* NRSV. It was also burned as incense because of its fragrance.

TIBERIAS. A city on the western shore of the Sea of Galilee (John 6:1, 23) built by Herod Antipas and named for the Roman emperor Tiberius. It was shunned by many Jews because it was built on a cemetery site. Tiberias became a center of learning after the fall of Jerusalem in A.D. 70.

TIBERIUS. See *Caesar,* No. 2.

TIBNI. A king of Israel (reigned about 885–880 B.C.) who ruled at the same time as Omri. Upon Tibni's death, Omri became the sole claimant to the throne (1 Kings 16:21–22).

TIGLATH-PILESER III/ TILGATH-PILNESER III/ PUL. A powerful Assyrian king (reigned about 745–727 B.C.) who defeated the Northern Kingdom and carried Jewish captives to Assyria (2 Kings 15:29; 16:1–10). *Tilgath-pilneser:* 2 Chron. 28:20. *Pul:* 1 Chron. 5:26.

TIGRIS. A major river of southwest Asia which is possibly the same as the *Hiddekel* of the Garden of Eden (Gen. 2:14). Beginning in the Armenian mountains, the Tigris flows southeastward for more than 1,100 miles until it joins the Euphrates River. Mesopotamia, or "the land between the rivers," lies between these two streams. See also *Euphrates.*

TILE (CLAY TABLET, BRICK). A slab of baked clay used as roofing on houses (Ezek. 4:1). *Clay tablet:* NIV; *Brick:* NRSV. The tiles were removed from a roof to give a paralyzed man access to Jesus for healing (Luke 5:18–19). See also *Brick.*

TILGATH-PILNESER. See *Tiglath-pileser*.

TIMBREL (TAMBOURINE). A small hand drum or percussion instrument believed to resemble the tambourine (Exod. 15:20). *Tambourine:* NIV, NRSV. See also *Tabret*.

TIMNATH-SERAH/ TIMNATH-HERES. A town in the territory of Ephraim given to Joshua as an inheritance and the place where he was buried (Josh. 24:29–30). *Timnath-heres:* Judg. 2:9.

TIMON. One of the seven men chosen as "deacons" in the church at Jerusalem (Acts 6:1–5).

TIMOTHY/TIMOTHEUS. A young missionary friend of Paul, also called *Timotheus* (see Rom. 16:21), who accompanied the apostle on some of his travels and briefly shared his imprisonment at Rome (Heb. 13:23). Born to a Greek father and a Jewish mother (Acts 16:1), Timothy was reared by his mother Eunice and grandmother Lois in a godly home (2 Tim. 1:5). He was converted during Paul's first visit to Lystra (Acts 16:1) and served for a time as leader of the church at Ephesus (1 Tim. 1:3; 4:12). Paul addressed two of his pastoral epistles to Timothy. See also *Eunice*.

TIMOTHY, EPISTLES TO. Two short epistles of the apostle Paul to his young friend and fellow missionary, Timothy. The first epistle is practical in scope, instructing Timothy to teach sound doctrine (1:1–20), organize the church appropriately (2:1–3:16), beware of false teachers (4:1–16), administer church discipline (5:1–25), and exercise his pastoral gifts with love and restraint (6:1–21).

Second Timothy is perhaps Paul's most personal epistle, in which he expresses tender affection for the young minister (1:1–2:20) and speaks of approaching days of persecution for the church (3:1–4:5) as well as the possibility of his own execution (4:6–22). See also *Pastoral Epistles; Timothy*.

TIN. A well-known and malleable metal (Num. 31:22) brought by ship from Tarshish and used in making bronze (Ezek. 27:12).

TINDER. See *Tow*.

TIPHSAH. A place which designated the eastern boundary of Solomon's kingdom (1 Kings

4:24), identified today as Thapsacus on the Euphrates River.

TIRE. A headdress, such as a turban, or an ornament worn in the hair by a high priest, a bridegroom, or women (2 Kings 9:30; Isa. 3:18).

TIRHAKAH. See *Pharaoh.*

TIRSHATHA (GOVERNOR). The title of the governor of Judea under Persian rule. Both Zerubbabel and Nehemiah were appointed by Persian kings to this position (Ezra 2:63; Neh. 7:65). *Governor:* NIV, NRSV. See also *Governor; Lieutenant.*

TIRZAH. A Canaanite town captured by Joshua (Josh. 12:24). In later years it served as a capital of the Northern Kingdom until Samaria was built (1 Kings 14:17).

TISHBITE. An inhabitant of Tishbeh, a city of Gilead. The prophet Elijah was called a Tishbite (1 Kings 17:1).

TITHE. One-tenth of a person's income presented as an offering to God. Abraham paid tithes to Melchizedek (Gen. 14:18–20), and Jacob vowed to give tithes in accordance with God's blessings (Gen. 28:20–22). In N.T. times, the Pharisees were scrupulous tithers (Matt. 23:23). Jesus encouraged generosity and promised to bless sacrificial giving (Luke 6:38). Paul endorsed the principle of proportionate giving (1 Cor. 16:2). See also *Stewardship.*

TITTLE. A dot or other small mark which distinguished similar letters of the alphabet. Jesus used the word to emphasize the enduring quality of the law's most minute requirement (Matt. 5:18).

TITUS. A Greek Christian and traveling companion of Paul who was sent by the apostle to correct problems in the church at Corinth (2 Cor. 7:6; 8:6, 23). Titus also served as a church leader in Crete (Titus 1:5–3:11). See also *Crete.*

TITUS, EPISTLE TO. A short epistle written by the apostle Paul to his helper and companion Titus, who apparently was serving as a leader of the church on the island of Crete (1:5). Paul dealt with several practical church matters, including the qualifications of elders (1:5–9), dealing with false teachers (1:10–16), and the behavior of Christians in an immoral world (3:1–11). See also *Pastoral Epistles*.

TOB/ISH-TOB. A place in Syria east of the Jordan River where the judge Jephthah took refuge (Judg. 11:3, 5). The soldiers of Tob sided with the Ammonites against David (2 Sam. 10:6, 8). *Ish-tob:* 2 Sam. 10:8.

TOBIAH. An Ammonite servant of Sanballat who ridiculed the Jews and opposed Nehemiah's reconstruction of Jerusalem's wall (Neh. 2:10, 19; 4:3, 7). See also *Sanballat*.

TOI/TOU. King of Hamath who sent his son with presents to congratulate King David on his victory over King Hadadezer of Zobah in Syria (2 Sam. 8:9–12). *Tou:* 1 Chron. 18:9.

TOKEN (SIGN). A sign or signal. Circumcision was a token of God's covenant with Abraham (Gen. 17:11). The blood on the Israelites' doorposts was a sign for the death angel to "pass over" these houses (Exod. 12:13). *Sign:* NIV, NRSV. See also *Miracle; Sign*.

TOLA. A minor judge of Israel who succeeded Abimelech and ruled for twenty-three years (Judg. 10:1–2). See also *Judges of Israel*.

TOLERANCE. See *Forbearance*.

TOLL (TAX). A tax or fee levied against the citizens of a conquered nation (Ezra 4:13). *Tax:* NIV. See also *Taxes; Tribute*.

TOMB. See *Sepulchre*.

TONGS. A tool for handling hot coals or trimming burning lamps (Exod. 25:38; Num. 4:9); probably the same as *snuffer*. See also *Snuffer*.

TONGUE. The organ of the body associated with speech. The tongue may be used as an instrument of punishment (Gen. 11:1–9) or blessing (Acts 2:1–13) and for good or evil (Jas. 3:5–10). See also *Lips; Mouth; Throat*.

TONGUES, SPEAKING IN. Glossolalia or ecstatic utterances; a spiritual gift exercised by some believers in the N.T. church. This gift apparently first occurred on the day of Pentecost with the outpouring of God's spirit on believers (Acts 2:1–13). Paul also mentioned this gift in 1 Cor. 14:2–28, although it is unclear whether this is the same as the phenomenon described in Acts.

TOOTH. The gnashing or grinding of one's teeth symbolized frustration or despair (Matt. 8:12).

TOPAZ (CHRYSOLITE). A precious stone, thought to resemble modern chrysolite, used in the high priest's breastplate (Exod. 28:17). *Chrysolite:* NRSV. It is also used in the foundation of New Jerusalem (Rev. 21:20). See also *Chrysolyte*.

TOPHET (TOPHETH). A place of human sacrifice in the Valley of Hinnom near Jerusalem (Jer. 7:31–32). *Topheth:* NIV, NRSV. See also *Hell; Hinnom, Valley of*.

TORAH. A Hebrew word, meaning "teaching" or "instruction," and used for the Pentateuch or the law, the first five books of the O.T. See also *Law, Law of Moses; Pentateuch*.

TORCH. A burning brand made of resinous wood or twisted flax and used to light one's path at night (John 18:3). See also *Lantern*.

TORTOISE (GREAT LIZARD). A reptile regarded as unclean by the Jews (Lev. 11:29). *Great lizard:* NIV, NRSV.

TOU. See *Toi*.

TOW (TINDER). The waste or refuse produced from flax when spinning thread. Isaiah used the word figuratively of the weakness of sinful people when facing God's punishment (Isa. 1:31). *Tinder:* NIV, NRSV.

TOWER (STRONGHOLD). A defensive turret in a city wall or a tall structure used as a watchtower. The word is also used figuratively of God's protection (2 Sam. 22:3). *Stronghold:* NIV, NRSV.

TOWNCLERK (CITY CLERK). An official of the city of Ephesus who restored order after a riot against Paul (Acts 19:29–41). *City clerk:* NIV.

TRADITION. An unwritten code or interpretation of the law which the Pharisees considered as binding as the written law itself (Matt. 15:2).

TRANCE. A state of semiconsciousness, often accompanied by visions. Peter's trance at Joppa prepared him for a ministry to Cornelius the Gentile. See also *Dreams and Visions*.

TRANSFIGURATION OF JESUS. A radical transformation in the Savior's appearance through which God was glorified. Accompanied by His disciples Peter, James, and John, Jesus went to a mountain at night to pray. Moses and Elijah appeared and discussed Jesus' death, emphasizing Jesus as the fulfillment of the law and the prophets. Shining with God's glory from within, Christ was overshadowed by a cloud and a voice declaring, "This is my beloved Son. . .hear ye him" (Matt. 17:1–8). These experiences attested Christ's divinity and mission and helped prepare Jesus and His disciples for the events leading to His death.

TRANSGRESSION. A violation of God's law, which may be personal (1 Tim. 2:14), public (Rom. 5:14), or premeditated (Josh. 7:19–25). Transgression produces death (1 Chron. 10: 13) and destruction (Ps. 37:38), but it may be forgiven by confession (Ps. 32:1, 5) through the atoning death of Christ (Isa. 53:5–6).

TRANSJORDAN. A large mountainous plateau or tableland east of the Jordan River, generally referred to in the KJV as the land "beyond Jordan" (Gen. 50:10; Matt. 4:15). This is the area from which Moses viewed the Promised Land (Deut. 34:1–4). After the conquest of Canaan, it was occupied by the tribes of Reuben, Gad, and East Manasseh.

TRAVAIL. The labor pains associated with childbirth (Gen. 38:27). The word is also used figuratively of the birth of God's new creation (Rom. 8:22–23).

TREASURE CITY (STORE CITY, SUPPLY CITY). A fortified city in which a king stored his valuables. The Hebrew slaves built treasure cities at Pithom and Raamses for the Egyptian pharaoh (Exod. 1:11). *Store city:* NIV; *Supply city:* NRSV. See also *Store City*.

TREASURE OF ALL NATIONS. See *Desire of All Nations*.

TREASURER (STEWARD). An important financial officer in a king's court, charged with accounting for receipts and disbursements (Isa. 22:15–23). *Steward:* NIV, NRSV. See also *Steward*.

TREASURY. The place in the temple where offerings were received (Mark 12:41– 44). Thirteen trumpet-shaped receptacles for offerings were placed in the outer court.

TREATY. See *League*.

TREE OF KNOWLEDGE OF GOOD AND EVIL. A specific tree placed in the Garden of Eden to test the obedience of Adam and Eve. Eating of the fruit of this tree was specifically prohibited by the Lord (Gen. 2:9–17). After they ate the forbidden fruit, Adam and Eve were banished from the garden and became subject to toil and death (Gen. 3:3–24).

TREE OF LIFE. A tree in the Garden of Eden with fruit which would bring eternal life if eaten (Gen. 3:22). In the heavenly Jerusalem there will also be a tree of life, with leaves for the healing of the nations (Rev. 22:2).

TRESPASS OFFERING. A sacrificial animal offering presented for lesser sins or offenses after full restitution to persons wronged had been made (Lev. 5:6–7, 15–19). See also *Sacrifice*.

TRIALS OF JESUS. A series of trials or appearances of Jesus before Jewish and Roman authorities which ended with His death. Jesus appeared before Annas, the former high priest (John 18:12–23); Caiphas, the current high priest, and the full Jewish Sanhedrin (Matt. 26:57–68); Pilate, the Roman governor (John 18:28–38); and Herod Antipas, ruler of Galilee (Luke 23:6–12); before finally being sentenced to death by Pilate (Mark 15:6–15).

TRIBES OF ISRAEL. The tribes which descended from the sons of Jacob—Asher, Benjamin, Dan, Gad, Issachar, Judah, Levi, Naphtali, Reuben, Simeon, and Zebulon (Gen. 49:1–28)—plus the two sons of Joseph, Ephraim and Manasseh (Gen. 48:5). After the conquest of Canaan, these tribes were assigned specific territories in the land, with the exception of Levi, the priestly tribe. The Levites were assigned to forty-eight different towns and scattered among all the other tribal territories to perform ceremonial duties. See also *Levites*.

TRIBULATION. Affliction and trouble caused by persecution (1 Thess. 3:4) and severe testing (Rev. 2:10, 22). The tribulation of believers may be overcome by patience (Rom. 8:35–37, 12:12) and a joyful spirit (2 Cor. 7:4). See also *Affliction; Persecution*.

TRIBULATION, GREAT. A time of great suffering and affliction in the end-time, sent upon the earth by the Lord to accomplish His purposes (Dan. 12:1; Rev. 7:14). Students of the Bible disagree on whether this event will precede or follow Christ's millennial reign or come before the ushering in of the new heavens and new earth. See also *Millennium; Persecution*.

TRIBUTE. A toll or tax imposed on citizens by a government. Every Hebrew male over age twenty paid an annual tribute of a half-shekel to support temple services (Exod. 30:13; Matt.17:24–27). See also *Half-Shekel Tax; Taxes; Toll*.

TRIGON. See *Sackbut*.

TRINITY, THE. God as expressed through the Father, the Son, and the Holy Spirit. The word *trinity* does not appear in the Bible, but the reality of the triune God was revealed in the O.T. at the creation of the world (Gen. 1:1–3, 26). In the N.T., the trinity was revealed at Christ's baptism (Matt. 3:16–17) and in His teachings (John 14:26; 15:26) as well as His Great Commission (Matt. 28:19). The Holy Spirit, whom Christ sent, convicts of sin, inspires believers, and empowers them for service (John 16:8, 13). The Father gives converts to Christ, and they hear His voice and follow Him (John 10:27, 29).

TRIUMPHAL ENTRY OF JESUS. Jesus' entry into Jerusalem on the Sunday before His crucifixion the following Friday. He was greeted by shouts of joy from the crowds, who were looking for an earthly king. With His entry, Jesus acknowledged He was the promised Messiah—but a spiritual deliverer rather than a conquering military hero (Matt. 21:2–11).

TROAS. An important city on the coast of Mysia where Paul received a vision. A man across from Troas in Macedonia pleaded, "Come. . .and help us" (Acts 16:8–10).

TROGYLLIUM. A city near Ephesus where Paul stopped after his third missionary journey (Acts 20:15).

TROPHIMUS. A Christian who accompanied Paul on the third missionary journey (Acts 20:4).

TROUSERS. See *Hosen*.

TRUMPET. A wind musical instrument made of animal horn or metal. Trumpets were used in temple ceremonies (1 Chron. 16:6–9). See also *Ram's Horn*.

TRUMPETS, FEAST OF. A Jewish religious festival, also called the *Seventh Month Festival* (Lev. 16:29). It was ushered in by the blowing of trumpets and observed by reading the law and presenting burnt offerings (Lev. 23:24–25; Neh. 8:2–3, 8–12). The exact reason for its observance is not clear.

TRUST. To put one's confidence in a person or thing. God's name and His Word are worthy of our trust (Ps. 33:21; 119:42). Christ warned that humans may deceive and be unworthy of trust (Matt. 10:17–21), but we may place ultimate trust and confidence in Him (John 6:35–37). See also *Faith*.

TRUTH. That which is reliable and consistent with God's revelation. Truth is established by God's law (Ps. 119:142– 144) and personified by Jesus Christ (John 14:6). Believers are purified by obedience to the truth (1 Pet. 1:22) and worshiping God in spirit and truth (John 4:23–24).

TRYPHENA. A fellow believer at Rome greeted and commended by Paul (Rom. 16:12).

TRYPHOSA. A fellow believer at Rome greeted and commended by Paul (Rom. 16:12).

TUBAL. The fifth son of Japheth (Gen. 10:2) and ancestor of a tribe descended from Tubal and Japheth. Isaiah mentioned Tubal as a people who would declare God's glory among the Gentiles (Isa. 66:19).

TUMORS. See *Emerods*.

TURBAN. See *Mitre*.

TURTLEDOVE (DOVE). A migratory bird noted for its plaintive cooing and affection for its mate (Song of Sol. 2:12). A turtledove was an acceptable sacrificial offering for the poor (Lev. 12:6–8). *Dove:* NIV. See also *Pigeon*.

TWELVE, THE. The twelve apostles or disciples chosen by Jesus. They were Andrew; Bartholomew (Nathanael); James, son of Alphaeus; James, son of Zebedee; John; Judas; Lebbaeus (Thaddaeus); Matthew; Philip; Simon the Canaanite; Simon Peter; and Thomas (Matt. 10:1–4; Mark 3:13–19; Luke 6:12–16).

TWIN BROTHERS. See *Castor and Pollux.*

TYCHICUS. A Christian who accompanied Paul on his third missionary journey (Acts 20:4).

TYPE. A person or thing which foreshadows something else. For example, the brass serpent placed upon a pole by Moses in the wilderness (Num. 21:4–9) pointed to the atoning death of Jesus on the cross (John 3:14–15).

TYRANNUS. A man of Ephesus who allowed Paul to use his lecture hall. Paul taught here for two years after he was banned from the local synagogue (Acts 19:8–10).

TYRE/TYRUS. An ancient coastal city of Phoenicia north of Palestine. Hiram, Tyre's ruler, helped David and Solomon with their building projects (1 Kings 5:1–10). In the prophet Ezekiel's day, the city was a thriving trade center. He predicted Tyre's destruction because of its sin and idolatry (Ezek. 28:6–10). Jesus visited the city (Mark 7:24), and Paul landed here (Acts 21:3, 7). *Tyrus:* Amos 1:10.

TZADDI. The eighteenth letter of the Hebrew alphabet, used as a heading over Ps. 119:137–144.

-U-

UCAL. An unknown person to whom proverbs in the book of Proverbs are addressed (Prov. 30:1).

ULAI. A river of Persia beside which Daniel was standing when he saw the vision of the ram and goat (Dan. 8:2–16).

ULCERS. See *Emerods.*

UMPIRE. See *Daysman.*

UNBELIEF. Refusal to believe in God and to acknowledge His works (John 16:9). Unbelief is caused by Satan's power (John 8:43–47), an evil heart (Heb. 3:12), and self-glorification and pride (John 5:44). Those who refuse to believe and reject the gospel are in turn rejected by God (John 3:18–20; 8:24). See also *Atheism; Infidel.*

UNBELIEVER. See *Infidel.*

UNCIRCUMCISED. A Jewish term for impurity or wickedness of any kind (Jer. 6:10) as well as a general reference to

Gentiles (Rom. 2:25–29). See also *Circumcision.*

UNCLEAN. A term for physical, spiritual, or ritual impurity—a condition for which rituals of purification were prescribed (Lev. 11–15). See also *Clean.*

UNCLEAN ANIMALS. Under Mosaic Law, only animals that chewed the cud and were cloven-footed were considered "clean" and suitable for eating (Lev. 11:2–3). Even touching the flesh of an "unclean" animal made a person unclean (Lev. 11:8).

UNDERGARMENT. See *Breeches.*

UNDERSTANDING. See *Knowledge; Wisdom.*

UNICORN (WILD OX). A large animal of great strength, probably the wild ox (Num. 23:22). Yoking it and harnessing its power was considered impossible (Job 39:9–11). *Wild ox:* NIV, NRSV.

UNLEAVENED BREAD, FEAST OF. See *Passover and Feast of Unleavened Bread.*

UNPARDONABLE SIN. Blasphemy against the Holy Spirit, or attributing the work of Christ to Satan, as the critics of Jesus did: "By the prince of the devils casteth he out devils" (Mark 3:22–30). Many interpreters believe this sin consists of decisively and finally rejecting the testimony of the Holy Spirit regarding Christ's person and work.

UNPLOWED GROUND. See *Fallow Ground.*

UNTEMPERED MORTAR (WHITEWASH). A thin layer of clay used as a protective coating on the exterior walls of buildings. The term is used figuratively of the futile promises of false prophets (Ezek. 13:10–15); 22:28). *Whitewash:* NIV, NRSV.

UPHAZ. A place in Arabia where gold was obtained, perhaps the same place as Ophir (Jer. 10:9).

UPPER EGYPT. See *Pathros.*

UPPER ROOM. A chamber or room usually built on the roof of a house and used in the summer because it was cooler than the regular living quarters (Mark 14:15). Such a room was the site of Jesus' last meal with His disciples (Luke 22:12). See also *Loft.*

UR OF THE CHALDEES (UR OF THE CHALDEANS). A city in Mesopotamia where Abraham spent his early life with his father Terah and his wife Sarah before he was called by the Lord to go to Canaan (Gen. 11:28, 31). *Ur of the Chaldeans:* NIV, NRSV. Excavation has revealed that Ur was a thriving city and center of moon worship. See also *Mesopotamia.*

URBANE (URBANUS). A fellow believer greeted and commended by Paul (Rom. 16:9). *Urbanus:* NIV, NRSV.

URIAH

1. A Hittite warrior in David's army whose wife Bathsheba was taken by David after the king plotted to have Uriah killed in battle (2 Sam. 11:15, 24–27). *Urias:* Greek form (Matt. 1:6).

2. NIV, NRSV name for the prophet Urijah. See *Urijah.*

URIJAH (URIAH). A faithful prophet in Jeremiah's time who was killed by King Jehoiakim for predicting God's judgment on Judah (Jer. 26:20). *Uriah:* NIV, NRSV.

URIM AND THUMMIN. Two objects in the breastplate of the high priest (Exod. 28:30), possibly colored stones cast as lots to help determine God's will (Num. 27:21). See also *Lots, Casting of.*

USURY (INTEREST). Interest on money loaned. Under the Mosaic Law, Jews could exact interest only from non-Jews, not from their own countrymen (Lev. 25:36–37). *Interest:* NIV, NRSV. Nehemiah denounced those who were breaking this law (Neh. 5:7, 10). See also *Debt; Loan.*

UZ. A place in southern Edom west of the Arabian desert where Job lived (Job 1:1; Jer. 25:20).

UZZA (UZZAH). An Israelite who was struck dead for touching the ark of the covenant while carting it to Jerusalem (1 Chron. 13:7–11). *Uzzah:* NIV, NRSV.

UZZIAH/AZARIAH/OZIAS. The son and successor of Amaziah as king of Judah (reigned about 767–740 B.C.). A godly king, excellent general, and noted city builder (2 Chron. 26:1–15), he contracted leprosy as a divine punishment for assuming duties that belonged to the priesthood (2 Chron. 26:16–21). *Azariah:* 2 Kings 14:21; *Ozias:* Jesus' ancestry (Matt. 1:8).

-V-

VAGABOND (WANDERER). A wanderer or fugitive. Life as a fugitive was part of the curse against Cain for murdering his brother Abel (Gen. 4:12). *Wanderer:* NIV, NRSV. The "vagabond Jews" of Acts 19:13 were professional exorcists.

VALE OF SIDDIM. A valley of tar pits near the Dead Sea where Sodom and Gomorrah were located (Gen. 14:2–10).

VALLEY OF DRY BONES. A vision of the prophet Ezekiel. When Ezekiel addressed the bones, representing Israel's exile in a foreign land, they came to life by God's Spirit. This served as God's assurance that His people would return one day to their native land (Ezek. 37:1–14). See also *Ezekiel, Book of.*

VANITY. Emptiness and futility. Life is vain and empty unless it is lived in obedience to God and His will (Ecc. 12:13).

VASHTI. The queen of Ahasuerus of Persia who refused the king's command to appear with the royal court and was replaced by Esther (Esther 1:10–12; 2:2, 15–17).

VAU. The sixth letter of the Hebrew alphabet, used as a heading over Ps. 119:41–48.

VEGETABLES. See *Pulse*.

VEIL (CURTAIN).

1. A screen or curtain which separated the holy place and the holy of holies in the tabernacle and temple. This veil was torn at Christ's death to symbolize direct access of all people to God's salvation through Jesus Christ (Matt. 27:51) *Curtain:* NIV, NRSV (Heb. 4:14–16). See also *Court of the Gentiles; Middle Wall of Partition*.

2. NIV word for *muffler*. See *Muffler*.

VENGEANCE. See *Revenge*.

VENISON (GAME). The flesh of any wild animal used for food. Isaac loved his son Esau because he was a "cunning hunter" who cooked venison (Gen. 25:27–28). *Game:* NIV, NRSV. See also *Hunter*.

VENOM (POISON). A poisonous fluid secreted by animals such as snakes and scorpions. The word is used figuratively of the destructive power of wine (Deut. 32:33). *Poison:* NRSV. See also *Poison*.

The Via Dolorosa, Jesus' crucifixion route through the old city of Jerusalem. *Courtesy Israel Ministry of Tourism*

VENOMOUS SNAKES. See *Fiery Serpents.*

VERMILION. A bright red substance used for ornamentation and painting of houses and images (Ezek. 23:14).

VESTIBULE. See *Porch.*

VIA DOLOROSA. The name, meaning "way of sorrow," for the traditional route which Jesus took from Pilate's judgment hall to Calvary for His crucifixion. It is impossible to determine the precise route, since Jerusalem was destroyed by the Romans in A.D. 70 and then rebuilt. This name does not appear in the Bible.

VIAL (FLASK). A bottle or flask which held oil or other liquids (1 Sam. 10:1). *Flask:* NIV.

VILLAGE. A collection of houses or a small town not protected by a defensive wall (Ezek. 38:11).

VINE. A plant which bore grapes. The word is also used figuratively of Israel (Hos. 10:1). Jesus referred to Himself as the "true vine" (John 15:1).

VINE OF SODOM. A plant which grew near the Dead Sea and produced a beautiful fruit which was unfit to eat—a fitting description of Israel's idolatry (Deut. 32:32).

VINEGAR (SOUR WINE). A beverage consisting of wine or strong drink that was excessively fermented until it turned sour. This drink was offered to Jesus on the cross (Matt. 27:34, 48) *Sour wine:* NRSV.

VINEYARD. A field or orchard of grapevines. The word is used symbolically for Israel (Ps. 80:8, 15–16).

VINTAGE. The time of year for making wine. Grapes were gathered with shouts of joy (Jer. 25:30), then put in baskets and carried to the winepress (Jer. 6:9). See also *Wine.*

VIOL (LYRE). A stringed musical instrument probably similar to the psaltery (Isa. 5:12). *Lyre:* NIV. See also *Harp; Psaltery.*

VIPER. See *Asp.*

VIRGIN. A general term for a young unmarried woman (Gen. 24:16).

VIRGIN BIRTH. The miraculous conception of Jesus by the Holy Spirit and His birth to the Virgin Mary. This event was

A model of ancient Jerusalem, showing its massive outer wall with built-in defense towers. *Courtesy Israel Ministry of Tourism*

foretold by the prophet Isaiah (Isa. 7:14) and revealed to Mary by an angel (Luke 1:26–33). The Messiah's supernatural conception in a human mother corresponds to His unique role as God-man. See also *Advent of Christ, The First; Incarnation of Christ*.

VIRTUE. Moral excellence in association with power and ability—a characteristic of Jesus (Luke 6:19).

VISION. See *Dreams and Visions*.

VOCATION (CALLING). A calling based on God's purpose and grace (2 Tim. 1:9). Paul urged believers to "walk worthy" of their Christian vocation (Eph. 4:1). *Calling:* NIV, NRSV. See also *Calling*.

VOID (EMPTY). Containing nothing; empty. The earth was formless and void before God shaped it and filled it with life through His creative power (Gen. 1:2). *Empty:* NIV.

VOW. A pledge or agreement to perform a service for God in return for some expected benefit (Gen. 28:20–22).

VOW OFFERING. A gift or freewill offering which accompanied a vow to the Lord (Deut. 23:23).

VULTURE (RED KITE, BUZZARD). A large bird which fed mostly on dead animals or other wastes and was thus considered unclean (Lev. 11:14). *Red kite:* NIV; *Buzzard:* NRSV. See also *Ossifrage*.

-W-

WADI. A riverbed which is dry except during the rainy season (Gen. 26:19). This word does not occur in the Bible, but Palestine has hundreds of these wadis.

WADI OF EGYPT. See *River of Egypt*.

WAFER. A thin cake made of fine, unleavened flour and anointed with oil for meal offerings (Exod. 29:2). Wafers were sometimes sweetened with honey (Exod. 16:31).

WAGES. Payment for work rendered by field hands or common laborers. Wages were paid daily, at the end of the workday (Lev. 19:13).

WAGON. A crude wooden cart pulled by oxen (Gen. 45:19). See also *Cart*.

WALL. A massive fence of stone or brick around a city for protection against enemy attack (2 Sam. 18:24). Defense towers and even houses were often built on these walls (Isa. 2:15). See also *Fenced City; Siege*.

WALL OF PARTITION. See *Middle Wall of Partition*.

WANDERER. See *Vagabond*.

WAR. Armed conflict between nations or tribes. The Hebrews considered their conflicts with enemy nations as the Lord's battles (Num. 10:9). Early skirmishes were fought by spearmen, archers, and slingers; horses and chariots were a later development in Israel's history. The prophets envisioned an age without war (Mic. 4:3).

WARD. A prison cell or lockup room. This word is also used for a detachment of soldiers on guard duty (Acts 12:10). See also *Prison*.

WARDROBE. A place where royal robes or priestly vestments were kept (2 Kings 22:14).

WARP. The long threads in hand-spun cloth. These threads are extended lengthwise in the loom and crossed by the *woof,* or threads running in the opposite direction. See also *Weaver*.

WARRIORS. See *Mighty Men.*

WASH. To cleanse (Matt. 27:24). The Hebrews emphasized cleanliness and ceremonial purity. Washing the hands before meals or the feet after a journey were considered religious duties (Matt. 15:2). See also *Clean; Purification.*

WASHERMAN'S FIELD. See *Fuller's Field.*

WATCHMAN (SENTINEL). A guard or sentry stationed at city gates. These watchmen also patrolled the streets and called out the hours of the night (2 Sam. 18:24–27). *Sentinel:* NRSV.

WATCHTOWER. A tall guard station or lookout post which provided early warning of approaching dangers (Isa. 21:5–11).

WATER. In Palestine's arid climate, water was a precious commodity. People were dependent on wells or cisterns during the dry summer and fall. Public wells or reservoirs were provided for travelers (Gen. 26:19). Jesus promised the "water of life" to a sinful Samaritan woman (John 4:10–14). See also *Well.*

WATER CARRIER. See *Drawer of Water.*

WATER HEN. See *Swan.*

WATER OF JEALOUSY. A mixture of water with dust prescribed as a test for a woman accused of adultery by her husband (Num. 5:11–31).

WATER OF SEPARATION (WATER OF CLEANSING). Water mixed with ashes to purify a person after defilement through contact with the dead (Num. 19:13–22). *Water of cleansing:* NIV. See also *Bitter Water.*

WATERING TROUGH. See *Gutter.*

WATERPOT. A large clay vessel in which water for the household was stored (John 2:6–7).

WATERS OF MEROM. A lake ten miles north of the Sea of Galilee through which the Jordan River flows on its southward passage (Josh. 11:5–7).

WAVE OFFERING (ELEVATION OFFERING). A sacrificial animal presented to God to celebrate restoration of a right relationship with God. The sacrifice was "waved" before the Lord to gain acceptance (Exod.

29:24). *Elevation offering:* NRSV. See also *Sacrifice.*

WAX. A substance formed by bees while making honey. The word is also used figuratively for the punishment of the wicked in God's presence (Ps. 68:2).

WAY OF THE SEA. A road which ran from Sidon in Phoenicia to Egypt, passing through Palestine (Isa. 9:1). See also *Highway; Road.*

WAY, THE. A term of contempt for the Christian faith used by the enemies of the early church (Acts 9:2; 24:14, 22).

WEALTH. See *Mammon; Money.*

WEASEL. An unclean animal, possibly the mole or polecat (Lev. 11:29).

WEAVER. A craftsman who made cloth from several different raw materials, including wool and camel hair (Exod. 35:35; Lev. 13:47). The Hebrews may have learned the art of weaving in Egypt.

WEDDING. A marriage ceremony. A Jewish wedding was a festive occasion with the entire community participating. The bride wore jewels and an ornamented white robe with a veil. The bridegroom, accompanied by friends and musicians, proceeded to the bride's home to conduct her to the wedding hall. Festivities continued for seven days (Matt. 25:6–10; Luke 12:36; 14:8). See also *Betrothal; Dowry; Marriage.*

WEED. See *Cockle.*

WEEKS, FEAST OF. See *Pentecost.*

WELL. A large pit dug in the ground to reach groundwater. Wells were usually covered with stone slabs or surrounded by low stone walls (John 4:6). The word is also used figuratively of salvation (Isa. 12:3) and wisdom (Prov. 16:22). The phrase "wells without water" shows the futility of wickedness (2 Pet. 2:17). See also *Water.*

WHALE. A large sea-dwelling mammal (Gen. 1:21). The "great fish" that swallowed Jonah is thought to be an enormous white shark, common in the Mediterranean Sea (Jon. 1:17).

WHEAT. A grain which was ground and baked into bread (1 Kings 5:11). The wheat harvest was observed as a festival and time of celebration (Exod. 34:22). See also *Corn*.

WHIRLWIND (GALE, STORM). A great storm or tempest (Job 37:9). Elijah was transported to heaven by a whirlwind (2 Kings 2:1, 11). The word was also used figuratively for swift and sudden destruction (Isa. 17:13). *Gale:* NIV; *Storm:* NRSV. See also *Tempest*.

WHITE OWL. See *Swan*.

WHITED SEPULCHRE. See *Sepulchre*.

WHITEWASH. See *Untempered Mortar*.

WICKEDNESS. Evil, malice, and wrongdoing. See *Evil; Iniquity; Sin*.

WIDOW. A woman whose husband had died. Fair and just treatment of widows was enjoined under Mosaic Law (Exod. 22:22). In the N.T., visiting the fatherless and widows was cited as evidence of true religion (Jas. 1:27). See also *Levirate Marriage*.

WIFE. A married woman. Wives are urged to love and respect their husbands and to be faithful to them (Eph. 5:33; Prov. 31:11–12). Husbands and wives are to be mutually committed to each other and fulfill each other's needs (1 Cor. 7:2–5). See also *Family; Husband*.

WILD OX. See *Unicorn*.

WILDERNESS. A dry, desolate, uncultivated region where little vegetation grew. John the Baptist preached in the Judean wilderness (Matt. 3:1). See also *Desert*.

WILDERNESS WANDERINGS. The aimless course taken by the Hebrew people in the Sinai Peninsula for forty years after they left Egypt—God's punishment for their sin of disobedience (Deut. 1:1; Josh. 5:6). God provided food and guidance through Moses until they arrived in Canaan (Exod. 16:35; Neh. 9:24).

WILL OF GOD. God's desire and wish for His people. The Father's will is that those who believe on the Son will have eternal life and that none will be lost (John 6:39–40). The disciples of Jesus were taught to pray for God's will to be done on earth as it is in heaven (Matt. 6:10). Paul urged the Christians at Rome to allow God to transform their minds to know the perfect will of God (Rom. 12:2).

WILLOW (POPLAR). A tree which grew by streams; perhaps the weeping willow (Ps. 137:1–2). Its branches were used for booths at the Feast of Tabernacles (Lev. 23:40). *Poplar:* NIV. See also *Poplar*.

WIMPLE (CLOAK). A mantle, scarf, or shawl worn around the neck by women (Isa. 3:22).*Cloak:* NIV, NRSV.

WIND. The movement of the air. The Bible speaks of the "four winds" (Jer. 49:36): The north wind (Job 37:22), the warm south wind (Luke 12:55), the cool west wind bringing rain (Luke 12:54), and the scorching east wind from the desert (Job 27:21). Jesus illustrated the freedom of the Holy Spirit with the mysteries of the wind (John 3:8).

WINDOW. A small opening in a house or public building which let in light and cool breezes (1 Chron. 15:29). These openings were probably covered with shutters or latticework.

WINE/STRONG DRINK. The juice of grapes, fermented to produce a strong beverage which was very popular among the Jews (Gen. 40:11). Commonly referred to as *strong drink* (Prov. 31:6), wine was prohibited to Nazarites (Num. 6:3) as well as to priests before they officiated at the altar (Lev. 10:9). Excessive consumption of wine was denounced (Prov. 20:1; Eph. 5:18). See also *Grape*.

WINEBIBBER (DRUNKARD). A person addicted to wine (Prov. 23:20–21). Jesus was accused of being a winebibber because He befriended sinners (Matt. 11:19). *Drunkard:* NIV, NRSV.

WINEPRESS. A vat or tank where juice was squeezed from grapes in the wine-making process. Usually hewn out of rock, the winepress had an upper vat where the grapes were crushed and a lower vat that received the juice (Judg. 6:11; Isa. 63:2–3). See also *Grape*.

WINESKIN. See *Bottle*.

WING. A symbolic expression for God's protection. He delivers His people on the wings of eagles (Exod. 19:4).

WINNOWING. The process of separating chaff or straw from the grains of wheat by beating the stalks and throwing them into the air; symbolically, to rid oneself of sin or worldly desire (Matt. 3:12). See also *Fan; Threshingfloor*.

WINTERHOUSE (WINTER APARTMENT). A dwelling used by kings in the winter months (Jer. 36:22). *Winter apartment:* NIV, NRSV.

WISDOM. Knowledge guided by insight and understanding. Reverence for God is the source of wisdom (Prov. 9:10). Wisdom is more valuable than riches (Prov. 8:11) and produces good fruit (Jas. 3:17). Christ is the key that opens the hidden treasures of God's wisdom (Col. 2:3).

WISDOM LITERATURE. A distinct category of literature in the Bible, including Job, Proverbs, Ecclesiastes, and some of the psalms, so named because they deal with some of the most important ethical and philosophical issues of life—the meaning of suffering, the nature and purpose of God, human relationships, etc.

WISE MEN. Astrologers from Mesopotamia or Persia, often referred to as the *magi,* who brought gifts to the infant Jesus in Bethlehem (Matt. 2:10–11). See also *Astrologer*.

WITCHCRAFT. The practice of sorcery or black magic by witches and wizards—an activity denounced by God (Deut. 18:10; Mic. 5:12). King Saul displeased God by asking the witch of En-dor to summon the spirit of Samuel from the dead (1 Sam. 28:3–25). See also *Magic; Sorcery*.

WITNESS. One who gives testimony regarding an event or another person's character. Under Mosaic Law, the testimony of at least two persons was required to convict a person of a capital offense (Deut. 17:6). False witnesses were punished severely (Deut. 19:18–19). Believers are empowered to serve as witnesses for Christ (Acts 1:8). See also *Record; Testimony*.

WIZARD (SPIRITIST). A male witch, or practitioner of black magic, who claimed to have secret knowledge given by a spirit from the dead (2 Kings 21:6). *Spiritist:* NIV. Under Mosaic Law, wizards were to be put to death by stoning (Lev. 20:27). See also *Familiar Spirit*.

WOE. An expression of extreme grief or distress (Matt. 24:19). The word also expressed the threat of future punishment (Jer. 48:46).

WOLF. A fierce wild animal of the dog family which posed a threat to sheep (Isa. 11:6). Jesus also used the word figuratively of false prophets (Matt. 7:15).

WOMB. Barren women regarded themselves as cursed by the Lord (1 Sam. 1:5–10). Children were described as "fruit of the womb" and a blessing from God (Ps. 127:3–5). See also *Barren; Children*.

WOODCUTTER. See *Hewer*.

WOOF. See *Warp*.

WOOL. The furlike coat of sheep which was highly prized by the Jews for making clothes (Prov. 31:13). Its vulnerability to moths was a problem (Matt. 6:19). See also *Fleece; Sheep*.

WORD OF GOD. God's revelation of Himself to man, especially through Jesus and the Bible (Heb. 4:12). The written Scriptures, which Christians accept as the Word of God, testifies to Jesus as the eternal and living Word of God (John 1:1; 5:39). See also *Bible; Logos*.

WORK. Labor in a worthwhile cause; fruitful activity. A Christian's work should be performed as service to the Lord (Eph. 6:6–8).

WORKS. Good deeds performed as an expression of a believer's commitment to Christ. Works cannot save or justify (Eph. 2:9), but they do fulfill God's purpose for His people. We are created in Jesus Christ in order to perform good works for the building of God's kingdom (Eph. 2:10).

WORLDLY. See *Carnal*.

WORM. An insect which destroyed plants and consumed dead flesh (Job 7:5). The word is also used symbolically of human helplessness or insignificance (Isa. 41:14) and frailty (Ps. 22:6).

WORMWOOD. A plant noted for its bitter taste (Jer. 9:15). The phrase "gall and wormwood" describes something offensive or sorrowful (Deut. 29:18). See also *Hemlock*.

WORSHIP. The praise and adoration of God expressed both publicly and privately (Deut. 6; 1 Chron. 16:29). The Jews worshiped in the tabernacle until the temple became their worship center. After their period of exile among the Babylonians and Persians, they worshiped in neighborhood synagogues. The book known as Psalms contains many spiritual songs and hymns chanted or sung in public worship. See also *Hymn; Praise; Psalms, Book of.*

WORTHY. Of value or merit. The Lamb of God is worthy of praise because He redeemed us, made us kings and priests, and will share His reign with us (Rev. 5:9–14).

WRATH. Strong anger or indignation. Human wrath may be kindled by false accusation (Gen. 31:36) or disobedience (Num. 31:14–18), but God's wrath is exercised against ungodliness (Rom. 1:18), idolatry (Ps. 78:58–59), and unbelief (John 3:36). See also *Judgment; Punishment.*

WREATH. See *Garland.*

WRITING. The Hebrews probably learned writing from the Egyptians. Earliest writing was done on stone, clay tablets, papyrus, and animal skins. See also *Ink; Paper.*

-X-

XERXES. See *Ahasuerus.*

-Y-

YAHWEH. The Hebrew spelling of the major name for God in the O.T., translated in most English Bibles as "Lord" or "Jehovah." See *Jehovah.*

YARN. Thread used in weaving cloth. Yarn was produced from linen and wool fiber as well as the hair of camels and goats (Exod. 35:25–26). See also *Warp; Weaver.*

YEAR OF JUBILEE. See *Jubile.*

YEAST. See *Leaven.*

YIRON. See *Iron,* No. 1.

YOKE. A wooden collar or harness placed on the neck of draft animals and attached to plows and other agricultural tools (Jer. 31:18). The word was also used to denote servitude or oppression (1 Kings 12:4–14). Jesus declared His yoke is not burdensome (Matt. 11:29–30).

YOKEFELLOW (COMPANION). A fellow worker or comrade in a common cause. Paul appealed to an unnamed "yokefellow" in Philippi to help two women resolve their differences (Phil. 4:3). *Companion:* NRSV.

-Z-

ZABULON. See *Zebulun.*

ZACCHAEUS. A wealthy tax collector who, after a conversation with Jesus at Jericho, vowed to give half of his wealth to the poor and make fourfold restitution to those whom he had cheated. Jesus declared that salvation had come to Zacchaeus (Luke 19:1–10). See also *Publican.*

ZACHARIAH. The son and successor of Jeroboam II as king of Israel. Zachariah ruled only about three months (about 753–752 B.C.). before being assassinated by Shallum (2 Kings 14:29; 15:8–12).

ZACHARIAS (ZECHARIAH). A godly priest and the father of John the Baptist. Zacharias was stricken speechless for his reluctance to believe a son would be born to him in his old age (Luke 1:18–22). *Zechariah:* NIV, NRSV.

ZADOK. The priest who anointed Solomon king. He served as high priest for a time under both David and Solomon (2 Sam. 8:17; 1 Kings 1:39; 2:35).

ZAIN. The seventh letter of the Hebrew alphabet, used as a heading over Ps. 119:49–56.

ZALMONAH. A place in the wilderness where the Israelites camped (Num. 33:41–42).

ZALMUNNA. A Midianite king killed by Gideon's army (Judg. 8:4–21). See also *Zebah.*

ZAMZUMMIMS (ZANZUMMITES, ZAMZUMMIM). A race of giants who lived in the region later occupied by the Ammonites (Deut. 2:20, 21). *Zanzummites:* NIV; *Zamzummim:* NRSV. See also *Zuzim.*

ZAPHNATH-PAANEAH. See *Joseph,* No. 1.

ZAREAH. See *Zorah.*

ZARED (ZERED). A brook and valley near the Dead Sea crossed by the Israelites during their wilderness wandering (Num. 21:12). *Zered:* NIV, NRSV.

ZAREPHATH/SAREPTA. A coastal town of Phoenicia where Elijah restored a widow's son to life. Elijah lodged with her during a drought (1 Kings 17:10–24). *Sarepta:* Luke 4:26.

The tomb of the prophet Zechariah, in the Kidron Valley outside the old city wall of Jerusalem.

Courtesy Israel Ministry of Tourism

ZEAL. Ardent desire and determination (Phil. 3:6). Isaiah predicted the "zeal of the Lord" would establish the Messiah's kingdom (Isa. 9:7).

ZEALOTS. See *Zelotes*.

ZEBADIAH. A commander in David's army who directed 24,000 warriors (1 Chron. 27:7).

ZEBAH. A Midianite king killed by Gideon's army (Judg. 8:21). See also *Zalmunna*.

ZEBEDEE. A Galilean fisherman and father of two of Jesus' disciples, James and John (Matt. 4:21–22).

ZEBOIM/ZEBOIIM. One of the five cities near the Dead Sea destroyed along with Sodom and Gomorrah because of its sin (Deut. 29:23). *Zeboiim:* Gen. 14:8. See also *Cities of the Plain*.

ZEBULUN/ZABULON. The sixth son of Jacob and Leah (Gen. 30:19–20) and the tribe descended from Zebulun's three sons (Num. 26:26). This tribe settled in the fertile hill country of Galilee (Josh. 19:10–16). *Zabulon:* Greek form (Matt. 4:13). See also *Tribes of Israel*.

ZECHARIAH.

1. A prophet after the Babylonian conquest of Judah who probably helped rebuild the temple in Jerusalem (Ezra 5:1), and author of the O.T. book which bears his name.

2. NIV, NRSV name for *Zacharias*. See *Zacharias*.

ZECHARIAH, BOOK OF. A prophetic book of the O.T. written to encourage the Jewish people during the difficult years back in their homeland following their period of exile among the Babylonians and Persians. Zechariah, through a series of eight visions (1:7–6:8) and four specific messages from God (7:4–8:23), encouraged the people to complete the task of rebuilding the temple in Jerusalem. The prophet also presented God's promises for the future, including the coming of the Messiah (9:9–10:12), the restoration of the nation of Israel (10:1–12), and the universal reign of God (14:1–14). See also *Messiah*.

ZEDEKIAH/MATTANIAH. The last king of Judah (reigned about 597–587 B.C.), who was renamed and placed on the throne as a puppet ruler by King Nebuchadnezzar of Babylonia (2 Kings 24:15, 17). Ignoring Jeremiah's advice, he rebelled against the Babylonians, only to be blinded and taken to Babylon in chains after seeing his sons put to death (2 Kings 25:6–7). His original name was *Mattaniah* (2 Kings 24:17).

ZEEB. A Midianite prince killed by Gideon's army (Judg. 7:25).

ZELAH (ZELA). The place where King Saul and his son Jonathan were buried in the territory of Benjamin (2 Sam. 21:14). *Zela:* NIV, NRSV.

ZELOPHEHAD. A member of the tribe of Manasseh whose five daughters petitioned for the right to inherit his property because he had no sons. Their request was granted on the condition that they not marry outside the tribe (Num. 26:33; 27:1–8).

ZELOTES (ZEALOT). A member of a political-religious party of zealous Jews in N.T. times whose aim was to overthrow Roman rule and establish a Jewish theocracy. Jesus' disciple known as Simon the Canaanite may have been a member of this party or sympathetic with its views (Luke 6:15). *Zealot:* NIV, NRSV. See also *Canaanites,* No. 2.

ZENAS. A Christian lawyer whom Paul asked Titus to bring while the apostle was spending the winter at Nicopolis (Titus 3:12–13).

ZEPHANIAH. A priest and friend of Jeremiah and author of the O.T. book which bears his name. Zephaniah often served as a messenger between Jeremiah and King Zedekiah of Judah (Jer. 21:1–2). After Jerusalem fell, he was killed by the Babylonians (Jer. 52:24–27).

ZEPHANIAH, BOOK OF. A short prophetic book of the O.T. known for its vivid portrayal of the certainty of God's judgment against the nation of Judah (1:1–2:15). The prophet also declared that God would spare a faithful remnant (3:13), through which His promise of a future Messiah would be accomplished.

ZEPHATH/HORMAH. A Canaanite town near Kadesh destroyed by the tribes of Simeon and Judah. It was occupied by the tribe of Simeon and renamed *Hormah* (Num. 21:3; Judg. 1:17).

ZERED. See *Zared*.

ZERUBBABEL/ZOROBABEL/SHESH-BAZZAR. A leader of the second group of Jews who returned to Jerusalem about 520 B.C. after their period of exile in Babylonia and Persia (Ezra 2:2). He supervised the rebuilding of the temple and helped restore religious practices among his people (Zech. 4:1–14; Ezra 6:14–22). He apparently was appointed governor of Judah by King Cyrus of Persia (Hag. 2:21). *Zorobabel:* Jesus' ancestry (Matt. 1:12). *Shesh-bazzar:* Ezra 5:14.

ZEUS. See *Jupiter*.

ZIBA. A former servant of King Saul who helped David locate Jonathan's son Mephibosheth. He became Mephibosheth's servant on the land restored by the king (2 Sam. 9:2–11).

ZIDON. See *Sidon*.

ZIF (ZIV). The second month of the Hebrew year, corresponding to *Iyyar* in the later Jewish calendar (1 Kings 6:1, 37). *Ziv:* NIV, NRSV.

ZIGGURAT. A tall Mesopotamian temple tower, built like a pyramid with staircases outside and a shrine for pagan worship on top. The tower of Babel was a ziggurat (Gen. 11:1–9). See also *Babel, Tower of*.

ZIKLAG. A city on the border of Judah assigned to David by King Achish of Gath as a place of refuge from King Saul (1 Sam. 27:5–6).

ZILPAH. Leah's maid who became a concubine of Jacob and bore two of his twelve sons, Gad and Asher (Gen. 30:9–13). See also *Jacob; Leah.*

ZIMRAN. A son of Abraham by his concubine Keturah (Gen. 25:1–2).

ZIMRI. A chariot commander under King Elah of Israel who killed the king and assumed the throne (about 885 B.C.), only to commit suicide seven days later to escape the wrath of Omri's army (1 Kings 16:8–18).

ZIN. A desert wilderness near the Dead Sea through which the Hebrews passed. Moses' sister Miriam died and was buried here (Num. 20:1).

ZION/SION. One of the hills on which Jerusalem was built and the site of an ancient Jebusite fortress before the city was captured by David. In Solomon's time this section of Jerusalem was extended to include the temple area. Sometimes all of Jerusalem is referred to as "Zion" (1 Kings 8:1). *Sion:* Rev. 14:1. See also *Jerusalem.*

ZIPH. A city in the hill country of Judah where David hid from King Saul (1 Sam. 23:14–18).

ZIPPORAH. A daughter of Jethro the Midianite priest, the wife of Moses, and mother of Moses' sons Gershom and Eliezer (Exod. 2:21–22).

ZIV. See *Zif.*

ZOAR/BELA. An ancient city of Canaan destroyed, along with Sodom and Gomorrah, because of its sin (Gen. 19:20–25). This city was also known as *Bela* (Gen. 14:2). See also *Cities of the Plain.*

ZOBAH/ZOBA/HAMATH-ZOBAH. A Syrian kingdom which warred bitterly against King Saul (1 Sam. 14:47). *Zoba:* 2 Sam. 10:6, 8. *Hamath-zobah:* 2 Chron. 8:3.

ZOPHAR. One of Job's friends or "comforters" (Job 2:11).

ZORAH/ZAREAH/ZOREAH. The place where the judge Samson was born near Dan in the lowlands of Judah (Judg. 13:24–25). *Zareah:* Neh. 11:29. *Zoreah:* Josh. 15:33.

ZOROBABEL. See *Zerubbabel*.

ZUPH. The land where Saul first met the prophet Samuel while searching for his father's lost donkeys (1 Sam. 9:5–14).

ZUR. The Midianite king killed by Israelites during the wilderness wandering years (Num. 31:8).

ZUZIM (ZUZITES). A race of giants in the land east of the Jordan River (Gen. 14:5). *Zuzites:* NIV. Probably the same tribe as the *Zamzummims*. See also *Zamzummims*.